THE PROPHETESS AND THE PATRIARCH

The Other Voice in Early Modern Europe:
The Toronto Series, 96

FOUNDING EDITORS
Margaret L. King
Albert Rabil, Jr.

SENIOR EDITOR
Margaret L. King

SERIES EDITORS
Vanda Anastácio
Julie D. Campbell
Jaime Goodrich
Elizabeth H. Hageman
Sarah E. Owens
Deanna Shemek
Colette H. Winn

EDITORIAL BOARD
Anne Cruz
Margaret Ezell
Anne Larsen
Elissa Weaver

ELIZABETH POOLE

The Prophetess and the Patriarch: The Visions of an Anti-Regicide in Seventeenth-Century England

Edited by

KATHARINE GILLESPIE

Iter Press
NEW YORK | TORONTO
2024

© Iter Inc. 2024
New York and Toronto
IterPress.org
All rights reserved
Printed in the United States of America

978-1-64959-072-5 (paper)
978-1-64959-073-2 (pdf)
978-1-64959-074-9 (epub)

Library of Congress Cataloging-in-Publication Data

Names: Poole, Elizabeth, author. | Gillespie, Katharine, editor.

Title: The prophetess and the patriarch : the visions of an anti-regicide in seventeenth-century England / Elizabeth Poole ; edited by Katharine Gillespie.

Other titles: Visions of an anti-regicide in seventeenth-century England

Description: New York : Iter Press, 2024. | Series: The other voice in early modern Europe : the Toronto series ; 96 | Includes bibliographical references and index. | Summary: "In 1649, Elizabeth Poole appeared at the Whitehall debates in London to prophesy in front of Parliament's army shortly after it had defeated the crown in the English civil wars. Invited to help deliberate the fate of Charles I, Poole advised the army to spare the king's life but to put him on trial for tyranny and to enter into a new compact with the people. After her visions proved controversial, she was defamed. She retaliated by printing her prophecies and two new defenses of her original revelations. This volume publishes Poole's pamphlets in full for the first time"-- Provided by publisher.

Identifiers: LCCN 2023028046 (print) | LCCN 2023028047 (ebook) | ISBN 9781649590725 (paper) | ISBN 9781649590732 (pdf) | ISBN 9781649590749 (epub)

Subjects: LCSH: Great Britain--History--Charles I, 1625-1649. | Great Britain--History--Civil War, 1642-1649.

Classification: LCC DA422 1649 .P66 2024 (print) | LCC DA422 1649 (ebook) | DDC 941.06/2--dc23/eng/20230729

LC record available at https://lccn.loc.gov/2023028046

LC ebook record available at https://lccn.loc.gov/2023028047

Cover Illustration

Detail from Peter Paul Rubens, "The Meeting of David and Abigail" (c. 1630). National Gallery of Art. Reproduced with permission.

Cover Design

Maureen Morin, Library Communications, University of Toronto Libraries.

Contents

Acknowledgments	vii
Illustrations	ix
Abbreviations	xi

INTRODUCTION	1

PAMPHLETS BY ELIZABETH POOLE

A Vision: Wherein Is Manifested the Disease and Cure of the Kingdom	59
An Alarm of War	69
An[other] Alarm of War	82

APPENDIX 1: Contexts for Elizabeth Poole	105
William Kiffin et al., *The Confession of Faith*	105
William Kiffin, *A Brief Remonstrance*	124
Anonymous, *A Discovery of Six Women Preachers*	136

APPENDIX 2: Transcript of Elizabeth Poole's Appearances in Whitehall	143
William Clarke, *General Council at Whitehall, 29 December 1648*	144
William Clarke, *General Council 5 Jan. 1648 at Whitehall*	149

APPENDIX 3: Two Pamphlets Cited by Elizabeth Poole	155
Excerpt from Henry Ireton, *A Remonstrance of His Excellency Thomas Lord Fairfax*	155
John Lilburne, *Foundations of Freedom; or, An Agreement of the People*	160

APPENDIX 4: Pamphlets about Elizabeth Poole	175
Anonymous, *The Manner of the Deposition of Charles Stewart, King of England*	175
Excerpt from Anonymous, *To Xeiphos Ton Martyron*	182
Anonymous, *The English Devil; or, Cromwell and His Monstrous Witch Discover'd at White-Hall*	192

APPENDIX 5: Other Pamphlets Relevant to Elizabeth Poole	203
Henry Ireton and John Lambert, *The Heads of Proposals*	203
Francis White, *The Copies of Several Letters Contrary to the Opinion of the Present Powers*	213

Bibliography	235
Index	247

Acknowledgments

Thank you first and foremost to Elizabeth H. Hageman, both for including me as an author in the Other Voice series and working tirelessly with me to produce the best volume possible. I have dedicated my scholarship to making a space in which the voices of forgotten women can speak; contributing this volume to this series helps to advance that work.

Many thanks also to a generous grant provided by the National Endowment for the Humanities. The late Professor Albert Rabil, a founding editor of the Other Voice series, expended a great deal of time and energy in obtaining this funding for the series, thereby ensuring it receives the attention and resources it deserves.

I would like to also extend my gratitude to Mark Bainbridge, Special Collections librarian at Worcester College, Oxford, for providing me with copies of the relevant sections on Elizabeth Poole from the Clarke Papers and for providing permission to reprint one of its pages in this volume. I would like to thank the British Library for providing permission to reprint the title pages of Elizabeth Poole's first three pamphlets as well as the title page to *The English Devil*, and the University of Minnesota for permission to reprint the title page of her last publication, *A Prophecy Touching the Death of King Charles*.

I am very grateful to Miami University for supporting me with the time and finances I needed to work on this volume. Three different chairs of the English Department—Kerry Powell, Keith Tuma, and LuMing Mao—deserve special acknowledgment for their recognition of the merits of this work. I would also like to thank my colleagues at Miami who offered moral support and/or advice: James Bromley, Kaara Peterson, Carla Pestana, the late Drew Caton, Wietse DeBoer, and Rene Baernstein. I am grateful to Bart Wilson at Chapman University for encouraging me during the final stages of production.

I am indebted to an anonymous external reader who provided useful and timely advice as I completed work on the volume. This input represented a much-needed boost at a late stage in a long game.

Sonia Parrish deserves enormous credit for transcribing Elizabeth Poole's writings. Maureen Bell was enormously helpful in her willingness to develop a theory about the identity of Poole's printer. Marcus Nevitt also generously weighed in with his own expertise on the subject. My husband, Michael Valdez Moses, contributed his impressive editorial skills at a crucial juncture. He also helped out with warm words of encouragement when they were needed the most.

My sons, Jack and Neal, can always be counted on for affection, adventure, and comic relief.

viii *Acknowledgments*

And last but not least, thank you to Theo the cat for keeping me company by snoozing next to my computer while I worked.

Illustrations

Cover.   Detail from Peter Paul Rubens, "The Meeting of David and Abigail" (c. 1630). National Gallery of Art. Reproduced with permission.

Figure 1.   Title page, Anonymous, *A Prophecy Touching the Death of King Charles* (1649). Andersen Library Rare Books, University of Minnesota Libraries. Reproduced with permission.   55

Figure 2.   Title page, Elizabeth Poole, *A Vision: Wherein Is Manifested the Disease and Cure of the Kingdom* (1649). British Library. Reproduced with permission.   59

Figure 3.   Title page, Elizabeth Poole, *An Alarm of War* (1649). British Library. Reproduced with permission.   69

Figure 4.   Title page, Elizabeth Poole, *An[other] Alarm of War* (1649). British Library. Reproduced with permission.   82

Figure 5.   Internal title page, Elizabeth Poole, *An[other] Alarm of War* (1649). British Library. Reproduced with permission.   88

Figure 6.   William Clarke, "General Council at Whitehall, 29 December 1648." *The Clarke Papers*, Clarke MSS, vol. 67, page 128. Worcester College, Oxford. Reproduced with permission.   145

Figure 7.   William Clarke, "General Council at Whitehall, 29 December 1648." *The Clarke Papers*, Clarke MSS, vol. 67, page 129. Worcester College, Oxford. Reproduced with permission.   147

Figure 8.   Title page, Anonymous, *The English Devil; or, Cromwell and His Monstrous Witch Discover'd at White-Hall* (1660). British Library. Reproduced with permission.   192

Abbreviations

EEBO	*Early English Books Online*
GV	The Geneva Bible
KJV	The King James Version of the Bible
ODNB	*Oxford Dictionary of National Biography*
OED	*Oxford English Dictionary*
Wing	*Short Title Catalogue of Books Printed in England . . . 1641–1700.* Edited by Donald Wing et al. 2nd ed. 3 vols. New York: Modern Language of America, 1972–1988.

Introduction

The Other Voice

The voice of Elizabeth Poole (1622–1668?) is truly "other." The daughter of a householder, she was not formally educated for a life of letters. A girl who ran away from home to join an Independent Baptist congregation, she was a dissenter from both her family and the established church. A seamstress, she earned her own living. A student of radical ministers and mystics, she imbibed teachings derived from alchemy and theosophy. A prophet, she both enjoyed respect for her wisdom and experienced denigration as a seductress and a witch. The author of prophecies and commentaries, she vexed conventional distinctions among literary, religious, and political writing. But she is worthy of being recognized as a significant "other voice" today because she wrote about the unexpected role she played as a prophet in one of the most dramatic moments in history: the unprecedented beheading of an English monarch, Charles I, by his own Parliament in the winter of 1649.[1]

The daughter of Robert Poole, Elizabeth Poole was baptized in the London parish of St Gregory by St Paul's on December 20, 1622.[2] She became a seamstress by trade. While sewing for a living may have gained her a degree of self-sufficiency, it was not known to be easy or lucrative. As was said of "the Distressed Seamstress" in an old ballad of the same name: She abides in "a sad wretched state, / Laboriously toiling, both night, noon, and morning, / For a wretched subsistence."[3] If this in any way characterizes Poole's life as a young woman, it is even less surprising that she, like a number of men and women who worked in trades, was attracted to the radical religious groups springing up all over England in the mid-seventeenth century.

These groups were known for their "enthusiasm," that is, for seeking a transcendent experience of ecstatic union with one another and with God.[4] Their

---

1. For an outline of Elizabeth Poole's life, see Manfred Brod, "Poole, Elizabeth (bap. 1622?, d. in or after 1668), prophetess," *ODNB*, ed. Lawrence Goldman (Oxford: Oxford University Press, 2004–).

2. Parish records, St Gregory by St Paul's, London, Guildhall Library, MS 10231. In Manfred Brod, "Politics and Prophecy in Seventeenth-Century England: The Case of Elizabeth Poole," *Albion: A Quarterly Journal Concerned with British Studies* 31, no. 3 (Autumn, 1999): 395–412, Brod also cites the International Genealogical Index. As he additionally notes, a Robert Poole was "reported in 1638 living at the West End of St. Paul's, where he paid £20 per year in rent, about average for the district." Brod's source for the information regarding Robert Poole is T. C. Dale, *The Inhabitants of London in 1638*, 2 vols. (London: Society of Genealogists, 1645), 1:65.

3. Roy Palmer, *A Ballad History of England: From 1588 to the Present Day* (London: B.T. Batsford Ltd., 1979).

4. For vivid accounts of radical sectarian activity, see J. F. McGregor and Barry Reay, eds., *Radical Religion in the English Revolution* (Oxford: Oxford University Press, 1984); and Andrew Bradstock,

2 *Introduction*

preachers were often self-styled and unschooled, electing to depart from ecclesiastical scripts and to preach extemporaneously and passionately as the spirit moved them. They believed in visions and other signs that the age of miracles was not over. They allowed women to speak in church and at times to prophesy. Some even allowed women to preach, at least to other women.[5] Because their meetings were illegal, they met in barns, fields, taverns, and homes. Baptists, the denomination to which Poole gravitated, also baptized one another in rivers and streams and healed themselves through ceremonies involving the laying on of hands. Fifth Monarchists believed that Christ was due to return and establish the New Jerusalem in England. Ranters believed that in the age of the new spirit, life was governed by spiritual and physical love and sin was no more. Adamites were said to practice nakedness as a return to Edenic purity. Muggletonians followed the example of the two witnesses from Revelation in believing in the power of prophecy and the inevitability of witnessing the end-times and the onset of a new dispensation. Ranters denied the authority of institutions and upheld the divinity of the spirit within each individual. They ranted or cursed in their preachings, holding all speech to be divine when uttered in a state of grace. Diggers founded agrarian communes and hoped to establish communism in England. These groups' experiments with alternative practices and belief systems scandalized polite society to the point that its adherents believed "the world had been 'turned upside down.'"[6] In reaction, they had dissenters arrested, fined, and/or subjected to various forms of corporal punishment. Some groups, such as the Diggers, died out; others, such as the Baptists, persevered.

Like Poole, many members of alternative congregations moved from religious dissent to political activism when they participated in the English Civil War of the 1640s.[7] The Civil Wars were a struggle for power waged by Royalist Cavaliers, on the one side, and Parliamentarian Roundheads, on the other.[8] Their military confrontations were only one dimension, albeit a violent and costly one, of their all-encompassing conflicts with one another, conflicts that dominated English culture and debates about religious and political ideas for decades. Royalist Cavaliers were the king's men, dressing in lace and velvet, wearing their hair long and curled, celebrating the leisured life of wine, women, and song, attending

---

Radical Religion in Cromwell's England: A Concise History from the English Civil War to the End of the Commonwealth (London: I. B. Taurus, 2011).

5. For a report on women preaching to other women, see Anonymous, *A Discovery of Six Women Preachers* (London: 1641), pp. 136–141, in appendix 1.

6. Christopher Hill, *The World Turned Upside Down: Radical Ideas During the English Revolution* (London: Penguin, 1984).

7. Blair Worden, *The English Civil Wars: 1640–1660* (London: Phoenix, 2010).

8. Christopher Hibbert, *Cavaliers and Roundheads: The English Civil War, 1642–1649* (New York: Scribner, 1993).

mandatory church services, honoring the seasonal festivities and rituals established by their lords and clergy, and touting the virtues of "court and country."[9] Their supporters were a combination of peasants and aristocrats who generally came from the shires and other rural areas in the agrarian north and west of England. The Parliamentarian Roundheads came from cities, including London, port towns, commercial and industrial centers, and other developed areas in the south and east. They were known as Roundheads because they cut their hair short to signify their commitment to God above all others, including the king. They promulgated godliness, righteousness, and industry and believed they were upholding the ancient English customs of liberty and a balance of power between sovereign and Parliament. They rejected Charles I's growing absolutism, and it was their constant challenges to his authority that led him to declare war on Parliament and its supporters in 1641. After eight years of bloody warfare, his Royalist troops admitted defeat and he was held prisoner while awaiting trial.

The debates over what to do with the defeated king and how to settle a new government in his stead were tense and prolonged.[10] They took place most intensively during the years 1648–1649 at the royal palace of Whitehall and involved members of Parliament, officers of Parliament's New Model Army, rank-and-file soldiers, religious radicals, and political activists. The story of how a young runaway Baptist seamstress came on two different days to deliver visions to the General Council of the Army—styling herself their "servant in the Church and Kingdom of Christ"[11]—during their deliberations of England's future forms one of the most fascinating chapters in the history of "other voices" in English literature and history. Poole's visions were delivered in a combination of spoken and written form. They consisted of advice "concerning the KING in reference to his being brought to Trial, what they are therein to do, and what not, both concerning his Office and Person," as Poole puts it.[12] She had these visions printed a short time thereafter, and then, when her divinely inspired advice was, as she states, "disobeyed," she felt compelled by subsequent attacks on her character to follow that publication up with two other pamphlets, *An Alarm of War* and a second *Alarm of War*, both affirming her commitment to her original messages and defending her reputation as a godly spokeswoman.[13] Her pamphlets are complicated

---

9. Perez Zagorin, *Court and the Country: Beginning of the English Revolution* (Sydney, Australia: Law Book Company of Australasia, 1969).

10. Austin Woolrych, *Soldiers and Statesmen: The General Council of the Army and Its Debates, 1647–1648* (New York: Clarendon, 1987); Charles Spenser, *Killers of the King: The Men Who Dared to Execute Charles I* (London: Bloomsbury, 2015).

11. Elizabeth Poole, *A Vision: Wherein Is Manifested the Disease and Cure of the Kingdom* (London: 1649), p. 68. Page number refers to the present edition.

12. Poole, *A Vision*, p. 60.

13. Elizabeth Poole, *An Alarm of War* (London: 1649), pp. 69–81, and *An[other] Alarm of War* (London: 1649), pp. 82–103. Page numbers refer to the present edition.

4   *Introduction*

combinations of prophecies, political and religious commentary, letters, complaints, self-vindication, self-promotion, and lament. They challenge us to expand our definition of literature to the furthest extreme in order to accommodate their eccentricities and to accept that political theory can come in the most unlikely of forms from the most unlikely of actors on the historical stage, especially political theory that is critical of the royal creed of patriarchalism and interested in promoting a more democratic alternative. Poole's "other voice," then, speaks at not only an intriguing moment in history when a king is executed but also at a pivotal juncture in history when ancient forms of paternalistic government begin to give way to modern forms of popular rule.[14] As Poole writes, "the Conquest was not without divine pleasure, whereby Kings came to reign, though through lust they tyrannized, which God excuses not, but judges, and his judgements are fallen heavy, as you see, upon *Charles* your Lord."[15]

The "Fiercest Furies": Elizabeth Poole's Historical Context

When King James VI of Scotland assumed the English throne in 1605 and became James I of England, he was following in the wake of decades of Elizabeth I's self-representation as a "virgin queen." Thus he was eager to establish his persona through the traditional figures of fatherhood, marriage, and headship.[16] To do so, he crafted a number of documents laying out his "patriarchalist" political philosophy.[17] His 1609 speech to Parliament provides a particularly stark articulation of rule by the father-king. "The state of monarchy is the supremest thing upon earth," James declared, for "kings are not only God's lieutenants upon earth, and sit upon God's throne, but even by God himself they are called gods."[18] As a god, "a king is truly *parens patriae*, the politic father of his people."[19] Thus, he, like God, enjoys the right over his "children" to "create, or destroy, make, or unmake at his

14. For a useful overview of the revolution, see the introduction in Michael J. Braddick, ed., *The Oxford Handbook of the English Revolution* (Oxford: Oxford University Press, 2015).

15. Poole, *An Alarm of War*, p. 67.

16. For an excellent account of the life of King James, see Alan Stewart, *The Cradle King: The Life of James VI and I, the First Monarch of a United Great Britain* (London: St. Martin's, 2003). See also J. Wormald, "James VI and I (1566–1625), king of Scotland, England, and Ireland," *ODNB*.

17. Along with speeches to Parliament, James wrote two major treatises on kingship: *The True Law of Free Monarchies* (Edinburgh: 1597; rpt. London: 1642) and *Basilikon Doron* (Edinburgh: 1599). See also Gordon J. Schochet, *Patriarchalism in Political Thought* (London: Basic, 1975); and Gordon J. Schochet, "Patriarchalism, Politics and Mass Attitudes in Stuart England," *Historical Journal* 12, no. 3 (1969): 413–41.

18. James VI and I, *The King's Majesty's Speech to the Lords and Commons of this Present Parliament at Whitehall* (London: 1609), 6.

19. James VI and I, *The King's Majesty's Speech to the Lords and Commons of this Present Parliament at Whitehall*, 6.

Introduction 5

pleasure, to give life, or send death, to judge all, and to be judged nor accountable to none."[20] Subjects owe both their souls and bodies to their king because he also functions as "the head of this microcosm of the body of man," thereby possessing the power of "directing all the members of the body to that use which the judgement in the head thinks most convenient."[21] As the head, the king is also the body's "physician," responsible for resolving its "ailments" by "applying sharp cures," cutting off "corrupt members," and/or letting "blood in what proportion it thinks fit, and as the body may spare."[22] As James elaborates in *The True Law of Free Monarchies* (1597), all kings, starting with the first king of the Old Testament, Saul, are endowed with these powers. This means all the land is "wholly theirs" and by them "distributed" and that, "of necessity," they are "the authors and makers of the laws" rather than subjects to them.[23] Even tyrants must be endured because kingship is a "yoke" that is "laid upon" the people by God and can never be removed regardless of "how hard that ever it seem to be."[24] Thus when "malefactors or rebellious subjects" endanger the "health of the commonwealth," the king "must care and provide for their remedy, in case it be curable; and if otherwise, cut them off for fear of infecting the rest."[25]

This language of curing and protecting sounds benevolent. However, when James makes such claims, he is referring to the fact that he—like monarchs before him—is licensed to literally torture and kill people deemed threatening to his welfare or that of the kingdom at large. This policy of *peine forte et dure* (pain strong and long) was not officially legal in England but was rationalized as an "instrument of state" and used by the Common Law Courts and the king's extra-legal Privy Council (the so-called court of the Star Chamber).[26] During the sixteenth century, torture had been deployed by the Catholic Queen Mary against Protestants and by the Protestant monarchs Henry VIII, Edward VI, and Elizabeth I, respectively, against Catholics and radical Protestants. In the last years of Elizabeth's reign, "the rack seldom stood idle in the Tower."[27] When James was in power, he used his 1610 speech to reassure Parliament that the king's power over matters of

20. James VI and I, *The King's Majesty's Speech to the Lords and Commons of this Present Parliament at Whitehall*, 7.

21. James VI and I, *The King's Majesty's Speech to the Lords and Commons of this Present Parliament at Whitehall*, 6, 10.

22. James VI and I, *The King's Majesty's Speech to the Lords and Commons of this Present Parliament at Whitehall*, 10.

23. James VI and I, *The True Law of Free Monarchies*, 41.

24. James VI and I, *The True Law of Free Monarchies*, 6.

25. James VI and I, *The True Law of Free Monarchies*, 10–11.

26. E. G. Black, "Torture Under English Law" (1927). https://scholarship.law.upenn.edu/cgi/viewcontent.cgi?referer=https://www.google.com/&httpsredir=1&article=8145&context=penn_law_review/.

27. Black, "Torture Under English Law."

6   *Introduction*

life and death was limited, since it was "ordained by God *ad aedificationem, non ad destructionem*," meaning, for constructive rather than destructive purposes. But James continued to "cure" the problems he believed plagued his kingdom by making liberal use of the power of *peine forte et dure*. And as he made clear, the decisions regarding who or what constituted a disease were his alone: after all, no entity would remove its own head; much less would a head cut itself off. Even if a king is so "monstrously vicious" that "his inordinate lusts and passions carry him away," it must be understood that it is the king's subjects who are at fault, because "a wicked king is sent by God for a curse to his people, and a plague for their sins."[28] The "only lawful means" of dealing with a tyrant is for his subjects to "move God to relieve them of their heavy curse" through "patience," "earnest prayers," and "amendment of their [own] lives."[29]

We can only imagine how, less than four decades later, in 1648, James's pronouncements would have resonated in the mind of his son and heir, Charles I, as he languished in prison, waiting to learn if he would face trial and even possibly execution for tyranny after declaring war on Parliament in 1641.[30] Something had occurred in history that made it possible for his subjects to lay claim to the royal power of *peine dure et forte* and to diagnose their head as the corrupt member of the body politic that needed to be cured, possibly cut off, if the body politic was to survive. What had Charles I done? As was charged against him by the January 6th *Act of the Commons of England Assembled in Parliament for Erecting of a High Court of Justice for the Trying and Judging of Charles Stuart, King of England* (1649):

> Whereas it is notorious that Charles Stuart, the now King of England, not content with those many encroachments which his predecessors had made upon the people in their rights and freedoms, hath had a wicked design totally to subvert the ancient and fundamental laws and liberties of this nation, and in their place to introduce an arbitrary and tyrannical government, and that besides all other evil ways and means to bring this design to pass, he hath prosecuted it with fire and sword, levied and maintained a civil war in the land, against the Parliament and kingdom; whereby the country hath been miserably wasted, the public treasure exhausted, trade decayed, thousands of people murdered, and infinite other mischiefs committed; for all which high and treasonable offenses the said Charles

---

28. James VI and I, *The True Law of Free Monarchies*, 13, 14.

29. James VI and I, *The True Law of Free Monarchies*, 14.

30. To learn more about the fraught life of Charles I, see Christopher Hibbert, *Charles I: A Life of Religion, War, and Treason* (London: St. Martin's Griffin, 2015). See also Mark Kishlansky and John Morrill, "Charles I (1600–1649), King of England, Scotland, and Ireland," *ODNB*.

Stuart might long since justly have been brought to exemplary and condign punishment.[31]

Because Charles had been defeated after his attempt to deploy the power of life and death by declaring war on his subjects, he was now "subject" to his conqueror's will and submissive to their declaration that he was the sick member in need of removal by way of execution.

Charles was bitter and dismayed: in his eyes, he had followed his father's dictates in believing it was he, as the king and patriarch, who possessed the power of life and death over his subjects, rather than the other way around. For even as James had also declared that kings who transgressed their "limits" would be dealt with as tyrants, he insisted they would not be punished by Parliament or the people, for these entities possessed no right to pass judgement upon their sovereign. Rather "wicked kings" would be "remitted" to God for he is "their only ordinary judge."[32] Those who believe they have the right to call their king to account and possibly even to behead him are Satanic usurpers of divine power—hardly freedom fighters. As Charles I insisted right up to the moment of his beheading, it is "sedition in subjects to dispute what a king may do in the height of his power."[33] If the people possess any "liberty and freedom," it "consists in having the government of those laws, by which their life and their goods may be most their own."[34] It is "not for having share in government," for a "subject and a sovereign are clean different things."[35] Because Charles's execution took place in 1648/9, he did not live long enough to read the treatise supporting his assertion that a subject and a sovereign were "clean different things," written by Robert Filmer in 1680 and titled *Patriarcha*.[36] In this tract, Filmer grounds subjection to the patriarch in the "original grant of government" that God bestowed upon Adam after Eve ate the forbidden fruit. In this first act of submitting one person to another's rule, God commanded Eve to obey her husband. From that point forward, the fates of women and all social subordinates resided with their heads as those heads consisted of fathers, brothers, husbands, masters, lords, and kings. Those subjects who mistook themselves for sovereigns were, as Charles I put it some thirty years

---

31. Parliament of England, *Act of the Commons of England Assembled in Parliament, for Erecting of a High Court of Justice, for the Trying and Judging of Charles Stuart, King of England* (London: 1648/9).

32. James VI and I, *The True Law of Free Monarchies*, 16.

33. Charles I, "Speech at His Trial" (https://constitution.org/1-History/primarysources/charles.html).

34. Charles I, "Speech at His Trial."

35. Charles I, "Speech at His Trial."

36. Sir Robert Filmer, *Patriarcha; or, the Natural Power of Kings* (London: 1680), chapter 1, section 4. See G. Burgess, "Filmer, Sir Robert (1588?–1653), political writer," *ODNB*.

8   Introduction

earlier in a poem he allegedly wrote while still a prisoner in Carisbrooke Castle, "the fiercest furies."[37]

So who were these "furies" who refused to recognize the power of the patriarch? On what terms did they accrue to themselves the power of life and death over their father? In no small part, they were the architects of democracy—men *and women* from a wide range of backgrounds who voiced a chorus of shared precepts that rejected patriarchalism and asserted instead that all were rights-bearing "sovereign individuals" or heads unto themselves.[38] To earn this claim, they drew upon a strain of "resistance theory" that originated with such ancient philosophers as Cicero and was adapted by such Renaissance thinkers as John Major, who representatively stated, "A people may deprive their king and his posterity of all authority, when the king's worthlessness calls for such a course, just as it first had power to appoint him king."[39] Renaissance-era resistance theorists frequently cited the Christian precept that the one true king was Christ. Human kings ruled by the consent of the people and so were not simply the makers of laws but were also subject to God's higher law. If they transgressed that higher law, then their subjects were free, indeed obligated, to define them as the true Satanic rebels and remove them. The myriad of individuals who articulated these ideas in a wide variety of modes and situations paved the way for the writings of John Locke, who in *Two Treatises of Government* (1698) declared that because humans were "all the workmanship of one omnipotent, and infinitely wise maker," then "they are his property, whose workmanship they are, made to last during his, not one another's pleasure."[40] And "unless it be to do justice on an offender," no one can "take away, or impair the life, or what tends to the preservation of the life, the liberty, health, limb, or goods of another."[41]

The individuals who anticipated Locke by drawing upon earlier resistance theories and developing them in the circumstances surrounding the trial of Charles I included Elizabeth Poole. The two meetings at which Poole appeared

---

37. Charles I, "Majesty in Misery; or, An Imploration to the King of Kings," in *The Memoirs of the Lives and Actions of James and William, Dukes of Hamilton and Castle-Herald*, ed. Gilbert Burnet, 379 (Oxford: Oxford University Press, 1852). On *EEBO*, this work is attributed to the poet George Wither. See George Wither, "Majesty in Misery; or, An Imploration to the King of Kings" (London: 1648).

38. Gary S. De Krey, *Following the Levellers*, Vol. 1: *Political and Religious Radicals in the English Civil War and Revolution, 1645–1649* (London: Palgrave Macmillan, 2017).

39. John Major, *John Major's Greater Britain* (Edinburgh: T. and A. Constable, 1892), 213–14. See also A. Broadie, "Mair [Major], John (c. 1467–1550), historian, philosopher, and theologian," *ODNB*.

40. John Locke, *Two Treatises of Government* (1698, Online Library of Liberty: https://oll.libertyfund.org/titles/locke-the-two-treatises-of-civil-government-hollis-ed/), treatise 2, chapter 2. See J. Milton, "Locke, John (1632–1704), philosopher," *ODNB*. See also Julian Franklin, *John Locke and the Theory of Sovereignty: Mixed Monarchy and the Right of Resistance in the Political Thought of the English Revolution* (Cambridge: Cambridge University Press, 1981).

41. Locke, *Two Treatises of Government*, treatise 2, chapter 2.

(under the auspices of her known role as a prophetess) before the officers of Parliament's army as they occupied Whitehall Palace took place after their victory over the king in the Civil Wars. At these meetings, the officers exercised what they believed was their right to decide whether or not the king should live or die for warring against his own people. Poole certainly felt empowered to participate in this mission, and to do so while believing her message was given to her by God. Far from seeing herself as a fury or a guilty and powerless subject such as Eve, Poole, like her army brethren, believed she possesses the sovereign right to "cure" the nation by advising the officers to try the king "in his conscience," for in her estimation, and that of many others, he had surely exceeded his limits as their husband and father. Unlike a number of her fellows, however, Poole urged the council to refrain from killing him. Instead, she offered the novel solution of "divorcing" the king rather than executing him. As we shall explore in greater detail, this unique encounter between the patriarch and the prophetess represents no less than an encounter between a divine right theory of kingship that was increasingly under siege and an emergent philosophy of popular sovereignty in which individuals claimed the right to resist, depose, and separate themselves from a ruler who did not acknowledge or respect their liberties. Wives, too, it would seem—insofar as they represented not only women but all subordinates—had rights.

Many Americans associate the idea of a principled revolt against monarchy with the American Revolution of 1776. But England's Parliament waged its own cultural and martial wars against Charles I in the 1640s and, after defeating his troops and beheading him for treason, experimented with republican government in the 1650s, over a century before colonists overthrew King George III and founded the American republic.[42] Elizabeth Poole's appearance on the historical stage in the late 1640s as an "other voice" thus places her at one of the most dramatic junctures in not only English history but also world history as it has evolved to define liberty as freedom from unelected forms of government. As Michael Kirby explains,

> The trial and execution of a king is a remarkable event in the history of any nation. The trial and execution of a King of England is so extraordinary a happening, in one of the world's oldest and most successful monarchies, that it ought not to be forgotten. The vivid events of the trial and execution which followed, meant that no absolute monarch could again successfully claim the autocratic powers which King Charles I had enjoyed. These facts resound even today throughout the world. They underlie the rights of the people which

42. Kevin Phillips, *The Cousins' Wars: Religion, Politics, Civil Warfare, and the Triumph of Anglo-America* (London: Basic, 1999).

10 *Introduction*

give ultimate legitimacy to the constitutional arrangements in countries still unknown when the King faced his end.[43]

To be sure, not all historians have agreed that the English Civil Wars—or what
Poole referred to as the "distresses of this land"—represented an authentically
republican revolution against monarchy. The idea that it did was established by
the "Whig" historians of the late nineteenth and early twentieth centuries who
argued that the wars were the culmination of centuries worth of desire on the part
of Parliament's House of Commons to limit the increasingly absolutist ambitions
of the Crown in order to protect the "ancient" rights of *freeborn* Englishmen.[44]

Marxist scholars of the 1960s and 1970s concurred that the wars represented a revolution, but they attributed the revolt to a class struggle between the
aristocracy and tradesmen, emergent industrialists, yeomen farmers, and liberal-
ized members of the gentry who participated in the religious and political dissent
movements that played a part in a larger battle for the ultimate goal of communist
emancipation.[45] Both Whig and Marxist views were challenged in the 1970s by
"revisionist" historians who countered that the wars had less to do with long-term
conflicts among readily articulated sets of ideas—whether those ideas comprised
liberal aspirations for liberty and rights or Marxist endeavors to achieve absolute
class equality within a propertyless social order—than they did with internecine
disputes and power grabs within the court itself. These disputes stemmed from
historically specific circumstances and the vicissitudes of particular personalities
and practices rather than the long historic unfolding of a political or economic
"logic."[46]

43. Michael Kirby, "The Trial of King Charles I: Defining Moment for Our Constitutional Liberties"
(London: Anglo-Australian Lawyers' Association, January 22, 1999): http://www.hcourt.gov.au/as-
sets/publications/speeches/former-justices/kirbyj/kirbyj_charle88.htm/.

44. The classic texts of Whig history include Samuel Gardiner, *The Fall of the Monarchy of Charles I,
1637–1649*, volumes 1–2 (London: Longmans, Green, 1882); Samuel Gardiner, *The History of England
from the Accession of James I to the Outbreak of the Civil War, 1603–1642*, volumes 1–10 (London:
Longmans, Green, 1883); Samuel Gardiner, *History of the Great Civil War, 1642–1649*, volumes
1–4 (London: Longmans, Green, 1901); and Samuel Gardiner, *Oliver Cromwell* (London: London:
Longmans, Green, 1901). See also Charles H. Firth, *Oliver Cromwell and the Rule of the Puritans
in England* (New York: Putnam, 1900); Charles H. Firth, *Cromwell's Army: A History of the English
Soldier during the Civil Wars, the Commonwealth, and the Protectorate* (London: Methuen, 1902); and
Charles H. Firth, *The Last Years of the Protectorate* (London: Longmans, Green, 1909).

45. See, for example, A. L. Morton, *The Story of the English Revolution* (London: Communist Party
of Great Britain, 1948); Christopher Hill, *The Century of Revolution: 1603–1714* (New York: W. W.
Norton, 1992); and Christopher Hill, *Liberty Against the Law* (New York: Viking, 1996).

46. For examples of revisionist history, see Conrad Russell, ed., *The Origins of the English Civil War*
(London: Palgrave, 1973); and Conrad Russell, ed., *Unrevolutionary England, 1603–1642* (London:
Hambledon, 1990).

Introduction 11

David Norbrook has taken issue with this approach, stating that "a cultural theory ought not to lead to the logical decision that the English Revolution cannot have happened."[47] Indeed, Norbrook argues that students of American history need to be more aware of the American revolution's roots in and indebtedness to its English counterpart of a hundred years earlier. What is more, in his statement regarding cultural theory, Norbrook criticizes not only revisionists but also 1980s "new historicist" and "cultural materialist" scholars who asserted that any revolution, waged in any context, including Renaissance England, did not represent true dissent or "subversion" but was rather a "scare tactic" generated by institutional authorities so that they could "contain" their own manufactured threats in ways that allowed them to rationalize their authority. In keeping with this perspective, new historicists and cultural materialists, like revisionists, tend to focus less upon the literatures of the Civil Wars and more on literatures produced by and for the court—a corpus constituted through patronage that, in their analyses, illustrated how dissent was generated by authorities who could then heroically resolve it. In this "closed economy" of deference and subjection, real historical change was difficult.[48]

Like Norbrook, James Holstun has challenged this analysis, reasserting the value of both Whig and Marxist interpretations by drawing attention to the numerous voices of dissent that populated the newly emergent public sphere of print and debate of the mid-seventeenth century, whether those voices represent proto-liberal, proto-communist, or other genuinely heterodox views. As Holstun argues, if we ignore the concerns of these disputatious voices and focus instead upon the court's internal struggles and/or its wishful fantasies of complete control over increasingly discontented subjects, then we fail to craft a complex model of the ideational dimensions of the remarkable events that comprised this truly revolutionary period: "the two Civil Wars, the rise of [Parliament's] New Model Army and the Putney Debates, the regicide and its aftermath, the formation of a Royalist counter-culture in exile, the Leveller Rising of 1649, the appearance of female prophets, the proliferation of political theory (patriarchalist, Hobbist, casuist, democratic, socialist, republican) and religious sects (Independents, Separatists, Baptists, Ranters, Quakers, Muggletonians, and millenarians of various stripes)."[49] And as Gaby Mahlberg and Dirk Wiemann add, while the ideas that drove these events and groups varied, there is an identifiable "core logic" of "revolutionary

---

47. David Norbrook, "The Life and Death of Renaissance Man," *Raritan* 8 (1999): 89–110 (108).

48. See, for example, Stephen Orgel, *The Illusion of Power* (Berkeley: University of California Press, 1975); Jonathan Dollimore, *Radical Tragedy: Religion, Ideology, and Power in the Drama of Shakespeare and His Contemporaries*, 3rd ed. (London: Red Globe, 2010); and Stephen Greenblatt, *Shakespearean Negotiations: The Circulation of Social Energy in Renaissance England* (Berkeley: University of California Press, 1989).

49. James Holstun, ed., *Pamphlet Wars: Prose in the English Revolution* (London: Frank Cass, 1992), 4.

12 *Introduction*

republicanism" that links them, "namely[,] that absolute monarchy—whatever its adherents might claim to the contrary—was inherently arbitrary, and thus enslaved its subjects."[50]

Elizabeth Poole's remarkable life intersects with an astonishing number of the factors that constitute this more dynamic model of anti-patriarchalist contestation that Holstun describes, and her writings help constitute the opposition to absolutely monarchy that unites the otherwise diverse and at times fragmented opposition to the king. The fact that she was a woman has made her especially interesting to scholars. Indeed, debates over the causes and effects of the wars produced corresponding debates over the power that women may have had to participate in and affect the Civil Wars. There is no explanation for Poole's presence at the Whitehall debates over the king's fate. This omission has led scholars such as David Underdown and Brian Patton to surmise that she was a mere pawn of major male power brokers.[51] Because these power brokers brought her to Whitehall to exploit her reputation as a prophetess for their own political ends, they contend, Poole herself had little effect on the proceedings. But as scholars such as Diane Purkiss and Sue Wiseman have argued, women were not just victims of the wars but helped to make them and Poole was no exception.[52] Even though she was a woman and an obscure seamstress from a small village, Poole's "other voice" could not be contained and is with us today because, as an early adapter of print capitalism, a religious dissenter, a recognized prophet, a partial ally of the Levellers, and a critic of patriarchalist monarchy, she became an unlikely but noteworthy spokesperson for republican precepts as they were frequently advanced through a synthesis of political, philosophical, and religious discourses. If we follow Holstun and others in moving from a "great man" theory of history to an understanding of history as a phenomenon forged by broader-based movements, forces, and subcultures, then we can identify Elizabeth Poole as part of an influential culture of opposition that affected such early liberal republican English thinkers as John Locke and the American revolutionaries.

---

50. Gaby Mahlberg and Dirk Wiemann, eds., *Perspectives on English Revolutionary Republicanism* (New York: Routledge, 2016).

51. David Underdown, *Pride's Purge: Politics in the English Revolution* (New York: Oxford University Press, 1971), 183.

52. Diane Purkiss, *The English Civil War: Papists, Gentlewomen, Soldiers, and Witchfinders in the Birth of Modern Britain* (London: Harper Perennial, 2007); Susan Wiseman, *Conspiracy and Virtue: Women, Writing, and Politics in Seventeenth-Century England* (Oxford: Oxford University Press, 2006).

"The Lord Has a Controversy with the Great and Mighty Men of Earth": The Historical Context of the English Civil Wars

The Civil War battles of the 1640s were brutal.[53] As Elizabeth Poole would later characterize these exceptional years in her messages to Parliament's officers, it was a time when "the Lord has a controversy with the great and mighty men of earth."[54] There were three rounds of such "controversies"; each conveys the degree to which the desire to limit or abolish patriarchalism informs the actions of those who fomented them. The first began in 1641 when, after a decade and a half of heated confrontations with Parliament, King Charles I declared war on his own people. The war lasted until 1646. Supporters of the king believed he had the right to exercise the power of life and death over his rebellious subjects, while his opponents upheld the idea, dating back to the Magna Carta, that as Parliament stated in its *Petition of Right* (1628), the people possessed their own "rights and liberties, according to the laws and statutes of this realm."[55] While England's Parliament had not yet become the sort of democratic or representative body it is today, it did act as a balance of power that held the sovereign to some semblance of a higher rule of law. Even more to the point regarding Charles I, Parliament tried to hold him to some semblance of fiscal restraint. The *Petition of Right* was issued in no small part because from the time Charles took power in 1628, he issued such extreme demands as insisting that Parliament give him the ample funding he needed to continue his father's involvement of England in Europe's Thirty Years' War (1618–1648).[56] Parliament's resistance to funding this long and costly dynastic conflict was so staunch that Charles was emboldened to dissolve Parliament and declare martial law over large parts of the kingdom. When he recalled Parliament in 1628 to again demand funding, Parliament used the *Petition of Right* to ask Charles to concede to their new law that "from thenceforth no person should be compelled to make any Loans to the King against his will because such Loans were against

---

53. Michael Braddick, *God's Fury, England's Fire: A New History of the English Civil Wars* (London: Penguin, 2009).

54. Poole, *A Vision*, p. 62.

55. Parliament of England, *Petition of Right* (1682, Constitution Society: https://constitution.org/1-History/eng/petright.htm), clause XI.

56. The war was waged by Charles's brother-in-law, Frederick V, Elector Palatine (married to Charles's sister, Elizabeth of Bohemia), and Christian IV of Denmark to try to retake their hereditary lands and titles from the Habsburg Monarchy. Charles's intervention consisted of warring with Spain in hopes that he could coerce its Catholic king, Philip IV, to persuade the Holy Roman Emperor, Ferdinand II, to return the disputed territories to Frederick in conjunction with his title as "the Electorate of the Palatinate." See R. Asch, "Elizabeth, Princess [Elizabeth Stuart] (1596–1662), queen of Bohemia and electress palatine, consort of Frederick V," *ODNB*.

14 *Introduction*

reason and the franchise of the Land."[57] Charles was enraged to the point where he felt justified in not only dissolving Parliament yet again but in governing alone under a policy of "Personal Rule" until 1640. While Charles asserted his right to do so on the basis of ancient custom, his detractors saw it as further proof of his growing absolutism, referring to it as his "Eleven Years' Tyranny" and launching special objections to the fact that, deprived of Parliament funding, he continued to raise monies through such "extralegal" means as imposing naval taxes—or "ship money"—on inland counties.

Despite the anger such measures provoked, Charles insisted that he alone possessed the power to head his "body politic." While he reconvened Parliament in 1640, he did so not to ameliorate his subjects' concerns but to pass legislation that would finance yet another war. This war would involve a campaign against Scotland for deviating from the mandatory practices of the Church of England. But this new Parliament also stuck to the commitment made by its predecessors to honor monarchy only insofar as its scope was limited and Parliament's power as a guarantor of that limitation was respected. Because of its unwillingness to fulfill Charles's demands for war monies, the newly convened Parliament was dissolved by the bitter king within a mere three weeks of its convening in 1641, thereby earning it the name of "the Short Parliament." Fortunately for Parliament, the Short Parliament had used its three weeks to pass the Triennial Act, a piece of legislation requiring Parliament to be called at least once every three years and stipulating that, if the king failed to issue the summons himself, members could assemble on their own. This act did indeed allow the members of the former "Short Parliament" to reconvene on their own authority and rule until 1660, thereby earning it the more distinguished title of the "Long Parliament." This Long Parliament also took advantage of its time by passing more laws limiting Crown power, including ending the king's ability to levy taxes without Parliament's consent and abolishing the controversial royal courts of the Star Chamber and the High Commission. It also refused to finance the campaign against the Scots for which it had been reconvened. This Scottish campaign, a series of confrontations that came to be known as the Bishops' Wars, was a sign not only that the wars resulted from disputes over the extent of royal power but that these disputes extended beyond England and into the other realms of the Crown, inspiring some modern historians to rename the English Civil Wars as the "Wars of the Three Kingdoms."[58] The Bishops' Wars also signified the degree to which the disputes traversed both the political and the religious spheres.[59] Indeed, given that the monarchs of post–Reformation England

---

57. Parliament of England, *Petition of Right*, clause I.

58. John Kenyon and Jane Ohlmeyer, eds., *The Civil Wars: A Military History of England, Scotland, and Ireland, 1638–1660* (Oxford: Oxford University Press, 1998).

59. Mark Charles Fissell, *The Bishops' Wars: Charles I's Campaigns against Scotland, 1638–1640* (Cambridge: Cambridge University Press, 1994).

were also heads of Anglicanism, challenges to the Crown's power threatened the institutional status of the established church and vice versa. Charles, like the Archbishop of Canterbury, William Laud, believed in "High Anglicanism" based upon the creed of Arminianism, the idea that grace was available to anyone who expressed their desire for it by following the Church of England's rules of worship.[60] Laud's strict enforcement of Anglican rules, including his insistence upon the use of the *Book of Common Prayer* in all services, alienated many, but none more so than those radical Protestants or "Puritans" who were increasingly fined, arrested, and even at times tortured by Laud's agents for abstaining from attending mandatory services because, they insisted, Arminian Anglicanism differed little from the Catholicism against which it protested. The outrage among some Puritans was so great that in 1640 around fifteen thousand citizens presented the Root and Branch Petition to Parliament calling for the complete dissolution of the Church of England down to its "root and branches."[61]

The Bishops' Wars of 1639–1640 were an important aspect of this larger religious conflict. They began with the expensive and controversial military attacks that Charles launched against the Presbyterian Church in Scotland after its leaders resisted his imposition of the *Book of Common Prayer*[62] upon their own liturgical practices.[63] In 1638, the General Assembly of the Church of Scotland voted to reject the *Book of Common Prayer* and to declare bishops unlawful. Charles demanded that they rescind these claims, and when the Scots refused, he launched his two unsuccessful attacks, the first in 1639 and the second a year later. His defeat resulted in a series of humiliations. In turn, these humiliations were

---

60. Charles Carlton, *Archbishop William Laud* (London: Routledge, 1998).

61. Anonymous, "Root and Branch Petition" (1640) in Henry Gee and William John Hardy, eds., *Documents Illustrative of English Church History* (New York: Macmillan, 1896), 537–55.

62. The *Book of Common Prayer* was originally published under King Edward IV in 1549 to further cement the Church of England's break with Roman Catholicism. It codified the prayers that were to serve as official liturgy on all important occasions, as well as the "propers," the prescribed words for daily church services. The book was eliminated by the Catholic Queen Mary I in 1553. It was reintroduced in a slightly amended form by Queen Elizabeth I in 1559. In 1604, King James I/VI ordered further amendments, but the book proved controversial, not only for Scottish Presbyterians who were punished for refusing to adopt it during the Bishops' Wars, but also for more radical Protestant groups who did not believe that liturgy should be dictated by an established church. See Church of England, *The Book of the Common Prayer* (London: 1549).

63. Like many of the conflicts that Charles faced, the struggle with the Scots was inherited from his father. As James had warned the Scots after they demanded the right to retain their own presbytery structure rather than submitting to the power of the bishops in the English church, if they were saying that there should be "no bishop," then they were also saying that there should be "no king." But as the Scottish Presbyterian, Andrew Melville, replied, King James must remember that the true kingdom belongs to Christ, "whose subject King James the Sixth is, and of whose kingdom not a king, nor a lord, nor a head, but a member." See Andrew Melville, "Two Kings, Two Kingdoms," in *The Life of Andrew Melville*, ed. Thomas McCrie, 391–92 (Edinburgh: William Blackwood, 1824).

16 *Introduction*

among the many factors that led Charles to recall Parliament in 1641 in hopes that it would supply him with the funds necessary to subdue the Scots.[64] And yet, as noted, Charles's own Parliament, led by John Pym, refused to side with him, thereby committing yet another lèse-majesté, or "offense against the ruler," as Charles viewed it, and signifying once again the degree to which the struggles between Parliament and Crown stemmed from disagreements over the nature and extent of patriarchal power.

Another sign that the wars involved all of the Crown's realms and represented a widespread revolt against patriarchal overreach was the fact that many Catholic Irish men and women became involved due to their desire for Catholicism to be "tolerated" by the Crown.[65] After Charles failed to gain Parliament's support for his plan to force the rebellious Scots to submit to the English church, he turned to Irish Catholic landholders, promising them freedom of worship if they would provide the aid that Parliament denied him. The resulting outrage in England and Scotland was further inflamed when a group of Irish Catholics from Ulster massacred thousands of members of the "New English" (Anglo-Irish Protestant) population. The New English had owned plantations in that part of Ireland for only thirty years, but in the eyes of the native Irish, they were thieves who had stolen "land [that] was theirs and lost by their fathers."[66] Charles failed to respond to the "Ulster Uprising" against the Anglo-Irish Protestants. This failure, along with the fact that he had actually conspired with the Irish Catholics against the Protestant Scots (not to mention that his wife, Queen Henrietta Maria, was a French Catholic), contributed to the sense that, even before the first shot of the Civil Wars was fired on English soil, the king was at war with his own Parliament and the English people. Even after Charles finally acted to quell the rebellion in 1642 by sending a large army to Dublin, his Parliament was not appeased. They feared that these twenty thousand troops would soon be used against them. These fears were not groundless, as Parliament's John Pym soon suspected that one of Charles's most highly ranked courtiers, Thomas Wentworth, Earl of Strafford, was urging the king to use the army he had raised in Ireland to force the entire kingdom, including England, to bend to his will. For this and other offenses, Strafford was beheaded in 1641.[67] The execution of such a prominent courtier fueled

64. Scotland invaded England, occupying much of its northern territories. Charles was forced to pay the Scots £850 a day and to reimburse them for the costs they incurred during his invasions in order to prevent them from taking even more English lands and looting and burning its cities.

65. Michael O'Siochru, *Confederate Ireland, 1642–49* (Dublin: Four Courts, 1999).

66. David Edwards and Padraig Lenihan, eds., *Age of Atrocity: Violence and Political Conflict in Early Modern Ireland* (Dublin: Four Courts, 2007), 154.

67. Strafford had served as the king's lord deputy in Ireland and was granted the title of earl in exchange for persuading Irish Catholic landowners to buy their religious freedom by paying higher taxes that were directed, in defiance of Parliament's opposition, toward the Scottish campaign. When the Ulster Uprising ensued, Strafford's standing was further compromised in the eyes of many Parliamentarians,

further tensions between Parliament and the Crown. In 1642, Charles marched 499 soldiers into the House of Commons to arrest five of its members for conspiracy. Having been tipped off, the five members escaped, but the Long Parliament still recognized the danger it was courting through its resistance to Charles's ambitions. Since the kingdom did not retain a "standing" army in the modern sense, Parliament, to protect itself, passed the Militia Ordinance to provide itself with the right to appoint lord lieutenants to form the already-existing county militias into an army. At this point, Charles too recognized that the conflicts had escalated to the point of civil war. Departing from London, he drew upon the ancient law of the Commission of Array to gather his own troops. In 1642, these Royalist forces, with the king at their head, raised the royal standard at Nottingham and declared war on Parliament and anyone who supported it.

While some communities remained neutral, a number chose sides. The Royalist Cavaliers proclaimed allegiance to the king in the name of preserving the ancient tradition of "court and country." The Roundheads supported Parliament—in some cases to defend the customary balance of powers in government and in others to abolish monarchy. Parliament was joined in 1643 by the Scots, who wished to fight not only the king but also those Irish Catholic troops who agreed to help the Crown wage war upon them in exchange for their own religious freedom. They composed *A Solemn League and Covenant for Reformation and Defense of Religion, the Honor and Happiness of the King, and the Peace and Safety of the Three Kingdoms of Scotland, England, and Ireland* (1643), a document declaring their military solidarity but also stipulating a set of specific terms upon which that solidarity was predicated.[68] Once the stipulations were granted, the Scottish aid that was forthcoming enabled Parliament to win control of northern England at the Battle of Marston Moor in 1644.

---

and it was then that he was arrested and executed. See R. Asch, "Wentworth, Thomas, first earl of Strafford (1593–1641), lord lieutenant of Ireland," *ODNB.*

68. Anonymous, *A Solemn League and Covenant for Reformation and Defense of Religion, the Honor and Happiness of the King, and the Peace and Safety of the Three Kingdoms of Scotland, England, and Ireland* (London: 1643). For a discussion of this vital document, see Stuart Reid, *Crown, Covenant, and Cromwell: The Civil Wars in Scotland 1639–1651* (Havertown, PA: Frontline, 2013). One stipulation laid out by these "Covenanters" was that, if Parliament was defeated, the Scots would refuse to join them in bowing to the king's authority. Another was that, if Parliament triumphed, it would impose Scottish Presbyterianism as the new state religion on England. Later on, this commitment to Presbyterianism in England was further advanced by the *Westminster Confession of Faith*, a document released in 1646 by the "Westminster Assembly," a group of ministers convened by Parliament in 1643 to craft new doctrines for modes of worship and structures of government for a new church in England. Because these new doctrines laid out by the *Confession* were crafted largely by Presbyterians, the more radically Protestant "Congregationalist" groups who believed in a more decentralized system of churches "gathered" through voluntary association refused to adopt them until they were modified to conform more with their vision. This revised document was termed the *Savoy Declaration* and was finally adopted in 1658.

18 *Introduction*

Another important development for Parliament occurred in 1645 with the passage of the Self-denying Ordinance. This ordinance, driven by the more radically Protestant members of Parliament, disallowed its members from holding military office, thereby diffusing the growing Scottish Presbyterian influence in Parliament's forces (a harbinger, as will be discussed in detail, of numerous internal conflicts that plagued the Parliamentarian coalition, despite their shared commitment to limiting royal power). The ordinance also professionalized the army by coalescing its local troops into a single large "New Model Army."[69] As its name suggests, this army, led by Generals Thomas Fairfax and Oliver Cromwell, was designed to be a new, more democratic order that would "model" both an unprecedented type of military organization as well as the decentralized political order for which many of its members were fighting.[70] In the summer of 1645, this New Model Army routed Charles's troops in the Battles of Naseby and Langport and further cemented Parliament's victory at such contests as the siege of Wallingford Castle in the summer of 1646. Ironically, in May, Charles had already sought protection from the Presbyterian Scottish army by surrendering to them in Nottinghamshire, but the Scots ultimately granted custody of their royal captive to the English Parliament. In October, Parliament signified its commitment to further reducing the power of church and crown by passing the *Ordinance for the Abolishing of Archbishops and Bishops in England and Wales and for Settling Their Lands and Possessions upon Trustees for the Use of the Commonwealth.*[71] In March, the Royalists suffered their final defeat at Harlech Castle in Wales, thereby marking what many hoped would be the end of the Wars of the Three Kingdoms. As it turns out, it was only the first round.

Despite (or perhaps because of) his defeat and captivity in 1647 in Carisbrooke Castle, Charles escalated the behaviors that first earned him the ignominious monikers of traitor and tyrant. The king's ability to persist was aided by the fact that those who fought against him also fought among themselves. While the leaders of the New Model Army were negotiating a new settlement with Charles, he secretly approached the Scots and promised them that, in exchange for helping him escape and regain his throne, he would reform the English church along Presbyterian lines. The Scots agreed, crafting a document called *The Engagement between the King and the Scots* in which they contracted with the king to invade

---

69. See Firth, *Cromwell's Army.*

70. Officers were chosen on the basis of rank rather than title, and soldiers were encouraged to fight for ideals rather than plunder. Drawing upon several places in scripture where believers are exhorted to serve as models for others, the soldiers had been "called," as they quoted Paul as saying in the First Epistle general of Peter, to lead as "an example" by following in "the footsteps" of Christ's suffering "for us" (1 Peter 2:21, GV).

71. Parliament of England, *Ordinance for the Abolishing of Archbishops and Bishops in England and Wales and for Settling Their lands and Possessions upon Trustees for the Use of the Commonwealth* (London: 1646).

England on his behalf.[72] This betrayal of Parliament precipitated a second round of civil warfare, which raged from 1647 to 1649, when Cromwell's men finally scored a decisive victory against a troop of Scots in the north of England. However, the third round of warfare began almost immediately thereafter and revolved around the other of the three kingdoms, Ireland.

The Irish had continued to believe that siding with Charles against Parliament would gain toleration for Catholicism and, as the wars evolved, Charles's "Irish Confederates" also began to hope that their allegiance would earn them political independence. But outraged Parliament troops spared them no mercy. Scottish Covenanters seeking revenge for the Ulster Uprising committed their own atrocities against the Irish people during their defeat of the Confederates in 1642. Aided by support from the Pope's ambassador, the Irish Confederates fought back in 1646, but their eventual loss to the New Model Army and the arrest of Charles in 1648 forced them back into an alliance with English Royalists. When the terms of this alliance proved unacceptable, the Irish approached George Monck, the northern commander of the New Model Army, and offered to help him fight the king. But with no deal forthcoming, the Irish Confederates returned to their original strategy of fighting against Parliament. The battle dragged on until 1653, when the Irish Confederate and Royalist troops officially surrendered their arms.[73] In the meanwhile, throughout the mid-to-late 1640s, the Scots had also never given up their efforts to side with whomever would enable them to convert the English church to Presbyterianism. As they continued to invade England from the north, the New Model Army continued to fight back, staging its own invasion of Scotland in 1650 and officially bringing an end to this third and final phase of the wars at the Battle of Worcester on September 3, 1651.

But while the wars ended in Parliamentarian triumph, the various factions that constituted the victors were forced to even more fully confront the differences among themselves. As stated earlier, while many joined Parliament's cause to defend the English tradition of balancing powers, which they believed Charles had subverted, others had done so to attain more radical ends, including ending monarchy altogether and replacing it with some variation upon a republic as well as implementing religious toleration or, in some cases, the complete separation of church and state. Such competing ends had become especially apparent during the years that comprised the second round of warfare and its culmination in

---

72. Covenanters, *The Engagement between the King and the Scots* (London:1647).

73. The brutality visited upon the Irish by Cromwell's troops during these struggles has never been forgotten. In Drogheda, nearly 3,500 people were massacred after the town was captured. By some estimates, almost 30 percent of Ireland's population was either killed or exiled, while most Irish Catholic lands were confiscated and redistributed to either Parliamentary soldiers who fought in Ireland or to Englishmen and women who had settled in Ireland before the wars began. Scottish Presbyterians took over Northern Ireland and formed a majority there, which further fomented the "troubles" that continued well into the twentieth century.

20 *Introduction*

the arrest of Charles I. While Parliament and its army were generally united in their conviction that the captive king was a treasonous "man of blood," they were divided over the question as to what should be done to punish him and possibly to replace him with another form of government. In keeping with the army's commitment to a more democratic process of decision-making, the officers agreed to hold debates on this question. These Whitehall debates were generally civil but tense.[74] As Elizabeth Poole warned when she appeared in Whitehall, the army had to be careful to "betray not" the "trust" of the people for whom it had fought.[75] Indeed, the story of how the men into whose hands this trust had fallen struggled to prevent their disagreements with one another from derailing the revolution against the king forms an important chapter in the history of the wars. In turn, this chapter provides an essential context for understanding the function that Elizabeth Poole fulfilled in the one and only execution of an English monarch by its Parliament.

Oliver Cromwell of course played a major part in this chapter.[76] The man who would eventually replace Charles as head of state, Cromwell had been a yeoman farmer and brewer from Huntingdon who converted to Puritanism sometime around 1638. A member of Parliament in the 1620s, he helped when the wars broke out to capture a ship carrying valuable silver plate intended to finance Royalist troops. Cromwell then raised his own cavalry troop in Cambridgeshire, which became a full regiment in 1643. He was next appointed governor of Ely and lieutenant general of horse in Manchester's army. He performed a critical service in Parliament's pivotal victory at Marston Moor in 1644. These are just a few examples of the military and political leadership abilities that would eventually lead to his becoming the first leader of the first post-monarchical political order in English history. As one of two lieutenant governors, he was among the most influential participants in the Army's postwar discussions as to what was to be done with the defeated king and the new order of government. However, the soldiers of the New Model Army also played a significant role in the debates that led to Elizabeth Poole's appearance before the army's General Council as it considered the king's fate. Even as the soldiers had joined their officers in waging warfare against the king's Cavalier troops, a number of regiments were driven to compose petitions lodging a series of grave complaints against their own superiors. One example was *Four Petitions to His Excellency Sir Thomas Fairfax* (1647), a request for General Thomas Fairfax to demand that Parliament pay its soldiers

---

74. Carolyn Polizzotto, "Speaking Truth to Power: The Problem of Authority in the Whitehall Debates of 1648–9," *English Historical Review* 131 (February 1, 2016): 31–63.

75. Poole, *A Vision*, p. 64.

76. Ian Gentles, *Oliver Cromwell: God's Warrior and the English Revolution* (London: Palgrave, 2011). See also John Morrill, "Cromwell, Oliver (1599–1658), lord protector of England, Scotland, and Ireland," *ODNB*.

arrears they were still owed for their service and to refute rumors that Parliament planned to disband the New Model Army and form a new army designed to invade Ireland.[77] Fairfax was unable to deliver on either demand. This failure was all the more troubling for the soldiers given that, after the surrender of the Royalists following the Second Civil War, Parliament did indeed issue a declaration calling for the disbandment of the New Model Army. While such a move might seem logical given that the wars appeared to be concluded and England had no tradition of a standing army, it was also the case that the Declaration labeled the Army petitioners who had criticized Parliament as enemies of the state and collaborators with the king. The disbandment was thus further resisted by many soldiers even after it had begun, not only because of the aspersions cast upon them but also because they did not trust Parliament to implement the sort of government for which so many of them had gone to war.

A group of "agitators," including Francis White, a captain in Sir Thomas Fairfax's regiment of foot, were elected by the rank-and-file soldiers to arbitrate their rights with the General Council of Officers and, thereafter, the House of Commons. In May, they composed *A Solemn Engagement of the Army, under the Command of His Excellency Sir Thomas Fairfax* (1647) to signify their trust in Fairfax and to demand the following: that, instead of being disbanded, the soldiers receive their long-overdue pay; that they be given immunity against acts carried out during time of war; that there be made provision for maimed soldiers, war widows, and orphans; and that Parliament more speedily expedite its attempts to settle affairs with the king.[78] In June, at a gathering on Kentford Heath near Newmarket, Fairfax and the other members of the General Council of the Army agreed to adopt the *Solemn Engagement*, but the House condemned it. In response, eight cavalry regiments elected two Agitators each to reiterate the soldiers' views to the senior officers, but in June of 1647, a group of Presbyterian members of Parliament organized the London militia—the only military unit not under the control of the New Model Army—to try to force the Army to disband. In an attempt to further protect the interests of the soldiers, a junior officer under Fairfax's command, Cornet George Joyce, commandeered a cavalry unit to kidnap the king from his Parliamentary guards at Holdenby House and declared that he was now under protective custody of the New Model Army. While unhappy with this act of insubordination, Fairfax understood Joyce's motive, as the House's

---

77. Anonymous, *Four Petitions to His Excellency Sir Thomas Fairfax* (London: 1647). Thomas Fairfax was chosen to represent the army's demands because he had earned the soldiers' trust as a lieutenant general in the wars. For an engaging profile of Fairfax, see Andrew Hopper, *Black Tom: Sir Thomas Fairfax and the English Revolution* (Manchester: Manchester University Press, 2007). See also Ian Gentles, "Fairfax, Thomas, third Lord Fairfax of Cameron (1612–1671), parliamentarian army officer," *ODNB*.

78. Anonymous, *A Solemn Engagement of the Army, under the Command of His Excellency Sir Thomas Fairfax* (London: 1647).

22 Introduction

willingness to pit the London militia against its own army represented a significant power grab. On June 8, Fairfax took his own action by rescinding the *Solemn Engagement* and informing Parliament that the king was now the army's prisoner and all further negotiations would take place through its representatives.

A year later, Francis White published *The Copies of Several Letters Contrary to the Opinion of the Present Powers* (see appendix 5) to once again protest Parliament's objectionable treatment of the army, which led to the army's takeover of the king.[79] Like White, soldiers who supported the army's actions did so not only to protest the lack of pay and other issues but also because they believed that, by handing control of the military over to Parliament, they would open the door to Charles I's return to the throne or, alternatively, to rule by a military junto composed of Presbyterians and their Scottish allies in the military. Some soldiers were so committed to the belief that the New Model Army was the institution most dedicated to safeguarding the English people's liberties that they purged their own ranks of officers who favored the disbandment. They then marched into London (in defiance of Fairfax's order to remain twenty-five miles outside of the city as disagreements over their dissolution continued to be adjudicated with Parliament) and took control of the city, thereby remaining intact.[80]

In the meanwhile, negotiations for a permanent settlement of the government continued. On August 1, the army's General Council, led by Commissioner-General Henry Ireton, Cromwell's son-in-law, and Major-General John Lambert offered *The Heads of Proposals* (see appendix 5) as the basis for a new constitutional arrangement with Charles I.[81] But Parliament refused its terms and instead offered a revised version of a document it had earlier crafted called the *Newcastle*

---

79. Francis White, *The Copies of Several Letters Contrary to the Opinion of the Present Powers, Presented to the Lord General Fairfax, and Lieutenant General Cromwell* (London: 1649). White, like Poole, was a vocal opponent of executing the king. See appendix 5, pp. 213–233.

80. Their ability to take control of London depended on an ironic turn. Some members of Parliament who favored the army's disbandment were forced to seek protection from that very army when, in July 1647, Parliament was invaded by protesters demonstrating their support of Presbyterian calls for the army's dissolution. These protestors forced fifty-eight members, as well as the two Speakers, to flee. This meant that the army's defiance of Parliament's orders to disband, along with its occupation of London, did, in the end, ironically serve to protect Parliament against disruptive forces. For the time being, Parliament was thus motivated to preserve the army.

81. Henry Ireton, *The Heads of Proposals, Agreed on by His Excellency Sir Thomas Fairfax, and the Council of the Army* (London: 1647). See appendix 5, pp. 203–212. Its terms included guaranteeing that Parliaments would be called every two years; forcing Royalists to wait five years before seeking office; retaining the Church of England but reducing the power of bishops; allowing the *Book of Common Prayer* to be read in church but not to be mandated; and protecting people from punishment for refusing to attend church services. For more on Henry Ireton, see David Farr, *Henry Ireton and the English Revolution* (Suffolk: Boydell, 2006). See also Ian Gentles, "Ireton, Henry (bap. 1611, d. 1651), parliamentarian army officer and regicide," *ODNB*. For information about John Lambert, see David Farr, "Lambert [Lambart], John (bap. 1619, d. 1684), parliamentary soldier and politician," *ODNB*.

Propositions.[82] In September, the king expressed a preference for *The Heads of Proposals*, but Parliament resisted and negotiations continued even as some of the more radical members of the opposition to monarchy, such as Henry Marten, tried to pass a vote that would end negotiations with the Crown altogether. In October, five of the more radical regiments elected "New Agents," led by the Leveller, John Wildman, and put forth *The Case of the Army Truly Stated*, a document that called for such reforms as a written constitution, biennial elections, and manhood suffrage.[83]

Cromwell and Ireton, among others, rejected the radical proposal contained in *The Case of the Army Truly Stated* and reoffered the king a more moderate settlement. This brought about further discontent from those members of the army who were also involved in the group that had come to be known as the Levellers, because of their opposition to the kind of institutionalized hierarchies dictated by feudal aristocracy and their commitment to the "leveling" principles of democracy. Nurtured in the cradles of religious dissent, men such as John Lilburne and Richard Overton were leading members of this group of men and women from relatively humble backgrounds who sought to apply the more democratic ways in which many of their churches were formed to the nation at large.[84] They came together in the early 1640s as part of the growing religious and political radicalism among the soldiers in the New Model Army and helped pave the way for turning the Army into a more democratic institution through its election of "agitators."[85] They also helped craft the aforementioned *The Case of the Army Truly Stated*, a document that also instantiated the Levellers' commitment to the rule of law by insisting that all future Parliaments be regulated by a constitution. In the fall of 1647, the Army officers demanded that the Levellers meet and explain their reasoning. Two debates at the Church of St. Mary the Virgin in the town of Putney, now a part of southwest London, resulted, the first on October 28, 1647, and the second on November 11. At these "Putney debates," the Army officers continued

---

82. Anonymous, *The Propositions of the Houses Sent to the King at Newcastle* (Edinburgh: 1646). This document resembled *The Heads of the Proposals* in some ways but differed insofar as it allowed for only a limited toleration of religious separatism and forbade all use of the *Book of Common Prayer*.

83. Thomas Fairfax, *The Case of the Army Truly Stated* (London: 1647).

84. For more on John Lilburne, see Michael Braddick, *The Common Freedom of the People: John Lilburne and the English Revolution* (Oxford: Oxford University Press, 2018). See also A. Sharp, "Lilburne, John (1615?–1657), Leveller," *ODNB*. For information about Richard Overton, see B. Gibbons, "Overton, Richard (fl. 1640–1663), Leveller and pamphleteer," *ODNB*.

85. Specifically, the movement first formed around protests against the imprisonments of Lilburne and Overton. Lilburne was first incarcerated in 1645 for criticizing members of Parliament for living in luxury while the common men fought and died in the wars. He was imprisoned again in 1646 for accusing a Parliamentarian officer of conspiring with Royalists. Overton was arrested for publishing a pamphlet calling for the disbandment of the House of Lords. While in prison, he penned *An Arrow Against All Tyrants and Tyranny* (London: 1646), this fiery tract came to serve as a Leveller manifesto.

24 *Introduction*

to promote Ireton's *The Heads of Proposals* while the Levellers reiterated *The Case of the Army Truly Stated*.[86] In addition, the Levellers circulated a new document, *An Agreement of the People*, that they hoped would be adopted as the constitution for a true commonwealth in England.[87] Unlike *The Heads of Proposals*, *An Agreement of the People* eschewed involving the king in negotiations, insisting instead that democratic institutions needed to be brought into existence by democratic means and proposing that a representative government be formed in which most men would enjoy the right to vote. This demand was polarizing and the debates ended in a deadlock.[88]

Such conflicts among the factions that comprised the Parliamentarian alliance were also evident in the negotiations that took place with the king while he was Parliament's prisoner. The king's machinations during the wars had led the Army to refuse any further negotiations with him. However, at the behest of Presbyterians in Parliament, this resolution was lifted so that, from September through November 1648, the king was temporarily freed from Carisbrooke Castle and enabled to travel to Newport, Isle of Wight, to negotiate a treaty. This treaty became known as the Treaty of Newport.[89] Even as the king appeared to negotiate, however, he also insisted that any terms he agreed to would ultimately be declared null and void given that he was the king and could not rightfully be forced to do anything. Matters were further complicated by the fact that Parliament's negotiating commissioners were divided into two factions: one that served the ongoing Presbyterian interest of negotiating a deal with the king that would enable him to return to the throne in exchange for implementing Presbyterianism, and another that favored a more ambitious agreement that would guarantee religious freedom for all and other rights. When Parliament expressed interest in allowing the king to travel to London to continue talks, some of the more radical elements in the army signaled their objections by returning him to captivity, this time in Hurst Castle on the English mainland. They then demanded he be tried for treason.

---

86. Michael Mendle, ed., *The Putney Debates of 1647: The Army, the Levellers, and the English State* (Cambridge: Cambridge University Press, 2010).

87. John Lilburne, *An Agreement of the People for a Firm and Present Peace upon Grounds of Common Right* (London: 1647). For the revised version of this document, *Foundations of Freedom; or, An Agreement of the People* (London: 1648), see appendix 3, pp. 160–174.

88. On the one hand, Ireton protested that men who were not residents or did not own property should not be able to vote on affairs that impacted citizens and property holders who held a "permanent interest" in England. On the other hand, prominent Levellers such as Thomas Rainsborough and John Wildman retorted that, as Rainsborough put it, even the "poorest he" should be acknowledged as possessing this right, one of the many rights that the Levellers held to be inalienable. See Ian Gentles, "Rainborowe [Rainborow], Thomas (d. 1648), parliamentarian army officer and Leveller," *ODNB*.

89. House of Commons, *Treaty of Newport* (1648), James Marshall and Marie-Louise Osborn Collection, Beinecke Rare Book and Manuscript Library, Yale University. See also Graham Edwards, *The Last Days of Charles I* (Stroud, Gloucestershire, UK: Sutton, 1999).

Ireton requested that Fairfax purge Commons of any members who opposed this decision. When Fairfax balked, Ireton composed *A Remonstrance*, arguing that, under *salus populi suprema lex* (the safety of the people is the supreme law), the king could be tried when he endangered the people he had sworn to defend. This document was presented to Fairfax, who was especially eager to approve it after Commons voted to allow the king to return to London and resume control over all his lands and incomes. *A Remonstrance* was then signed and adopted by the army's General Council under the full title *A Remonstrance of His Excellency Thomas Lord Fairfax, Lord General of the Parliaments Forces* (see appendix 3).[90]

Even as *A Remonstrance* represented a new level of agreement among the army's General Council of Officers, its rank-and-file members, and the Levellers, it was rejected by Parliament because it was said to constitute an undesirable alternative to the continuation of the Newport negotiations. While the king's answers to the Treaty of Newport were deemed barely adequate, the House of Commons nonetheless voted on December 5, 1648, to accept them. Fearing a return of monarchy, the officers on December 6 sent Colonel Pride's Regiment of Foot to purge Parliament of all members who had voted to reject the *Remonstrance* in favor of negotiating with the king. After the purge, the reduced Parliament became known as the "Rump Parliament"; it was hoped that this body, populated by those who favored religious independency, would dispense with negotiations with the king, end the wars, and establish a true republic. The Rump did annul the Treaty of Newport and prepared for the king's trial. But it balked when the Levellers restated their demand for the adoption of *An Agreement of the People* as the constitutional basis for the new order. The Rump ordered a number of Levellers to be arrested and one of their leaders, Richard Arnold, executed. On September 11, 1648, the Levellers protested with a petition, *To the Right Honorable the Commons of England*. Because it was signed by roughly one-third of all Londoners, this petition signified that support for democracy was not confined to the army.[91]

The rising influence of the Levellers also led to more conflict with the army officers.[92] Even as the Levellers agreed to a number of the officers' positions as they had put them forth in the *Remonstrance*, including the idea that the king could and should be tried, they resisted the idea that the army had the legitimacy to convene a jury that would put the king to death. Cromwell was a leading

90. Henry Ireton, *A Remonstrance of His Excellency Thomas Lord Fairfax, Lord General of the Parliament's Forces* (London: 1648). See appendix 3, pp. 155–160.

91. Anonymous, *To the Right Honorable the Commons of England* (London: 1648).

92. The tensions grew so heated that, on October 30, when the Leveller leader Thomas Rainsborough was killed under murky circumstances at the siege of Pontefract Castle, his funeral became the occasion for a large Leveller demonstration in London. Thousands of mourners paid tribute by wearing the group's trademark sea green ribbons, designed to invoke scriptural comparisons of the people to the great waters of the sea. This momentum carried over into yet another attempt to have *An Agreement of the People* adopted.

26 *Introduction*

voice in favor of regicide, citing as his rationale the scripture, "The land cannot be cleansed of the blood that is shed therein, but by the blood of him that shed it."[93] This stance also placed him at odds with men such as Thomas Fairfax. Even though Fairfax was appointed to the army's High Court of Justice commissioned to try the king, he was opposed to killing him. He boycotted preliminary sessions and staged several attempts to prevent the regicide. For Elizabeth Poole's part, she was considered significant enough by the council to have "access to the officers singly or in groups, and a seat in the plenary session when she wanted it" while these complex negotiations unfolded.[94] It's simply not clear why or how this was the case. It's possible that she appeared upon her own volition. A more widely accepted scenario is that the close relationship between her minister, William Kiffin, and Cromwell prompted the latter (and/or Ireton) to exploit Poole's status as a prophet in order to persuade the army's rank-and-file and to support his political goals. A new picture is also beginning to form, one that identifies Poole as something of a liaison between prominent religious radicals and Levellers, on the one hand, and the army officers, on the other.[95] Regardless of who helped gain Poole's admission to the proceedings or why, it does appear safe to say that her other voice as a prophetess was already considered powerful enough to sway the opinions of highly influential men, especially as her messages spoke to the vital

93. Numbers 35:33, GV.

94. Manfred Brod, "A Radical Network in the English Revolution: John Pordage and His Circle, 1646–54," *English Historical Review* 119, no. 484 (November 2004): 1230–53 (1234).

95. Manfred Brod surmises that Poole may have been brought before the council by Frances Allen, a Leveller soldier who, like Poole, spent time living in the town of Abingdon. As Brod notes, Poole would have had ample opportunity in Abingdon to form connections with not only Allen but also numerous Leveller soldiers given that they numbered highly among the ranks of a London garrison that was quartered in the town through the end of 1645. Allen was a particularly favorable candidate for such an alliance insofar as he served as one of the agitators for the army's complaints in 1647 and, at the Putney debates that same year, claimed that God inspired him to speak out in favor of the Leveller agenda. He served on the General Council of Officers and was a known supporter of the minister and mystic John Pordage, who, as we shall read, wielded a great deal of influence over Poole's thinking. Another candidate is Thomas Rainsborough, the prominent Leveller leader who, starting in 1646, became the commander of the Abingdon garrison. Like Allen, Rainsborough was a member of the General Council of Officers and had a religious tie to Poole: his army chaplain, John Pendarves, was another of Poole's Baptist ministers. It's also possible that Poole's visit was arranged by her religious compatriot, Nathaniel Rich, a colonel of a regiment of horse in the New Model Army, a spokesman on behalf of the soldiers' grievances against their officers, a committed republican and opponent of monarchy, and a supporter of the idea that the king should be tried but not put to death. Finally, there was William Erbery, an army clergymen who was a widely known preacher and likewise a member of John Pordage's circle; indeed, his membership extended back to the time the group was formed in Reading. Erbery played a significant role in the development of Pordage's ideas and, not long after Poole's appearance before the General Council of Officers, he delivered a message that echoed Rich in supporting her most basic plea for the council to try the king but spare his life. Brod, "A Radical Network in the English Revolution," 1237.

question they faced as to whether or not the king could or should pay with his life for waging war against his own people.

"I Speak unto You as Men, Fathers, and Brethren": The Life and Work of Elizabeth Poole

In spite of her participation in the landmark events described above, we don't have much information about Elizabeth Poole's life. As mentioned, it is believed she was baptized on December 20, 1622, at the St Gregory by St. Paul's parish in London. It is also believed that she was the daughter of Robert Poole, a householder who is said to have enjoyed a solid professional reputation in West St. Paul's. At roughly sixteen, Poole defied her father's wishes by leaving home to join an Independent Baptist church headed by the charismatic young preacher William Kiffin.[96] Kiffin was a Welshman who abandoned his apprenticeship to a glover and, in 1631, became a Puritan. After formally rejecting the Church of England in 1638, he joined an Independent congregation in London, soon becoming its pastor and helping to articulate the Particular Baptist creed that attracted such adherents as Poole.[97] Poole's voluntary affiliation with the Baptist church makes her a constituent part of the long-unfolding Protestant Reformation of the Roman Catholic Church. Initially designed to purge Roman Catholicism of certain "pagan" rituals, this movement splintered over time into a number of diverse offshoots, including Puritans, the more extreme of whom became increasingly convinced that state churches could never be "purified" and so should be dissolved altogether or at least forced to coexist with alternative modes of worship. Although lay groups such as the Lollards had existed for centuries, seventeenth-century England was home to an increasing number of "congregationalists," people who believed that a church should be modeled upon the independent, self-governing congregations featured in the New Testament. While some congregationalists maintained that members could participate in a church of their own choice while continuing to attend compulsory Sunday services at their assigned parish, others went so far as to separate completely from the established church and adhere solely to their own private and voluntarily "gathered" congregations.

By joining a Baptist church, Poole aligned herself with a denomination that took the idea of voluntarism and self-government to extremes, arguing that even baptism should be consensual.[98] The roots of the Baptist church reach back to Zurich, where, in 1525, the Protestant city council outlawed a group that believed

96. For more on Kiffin, see Benjamin Ramsbottom, *Stranger Than Fiction: The Life of William Kiffin* (Harpenden, UK: Gospel Standard Trust, 2017). See also M. Haykin, "Kiffin, William (1616–1701), Particular Baptist minister and author," *ODNB*.

97. This congregation later became known as the Devonshire Square Baptist Church.

98. William R. Estep, *The Anabaptist Story: An Introduction to Sixteenth-Century Anabaptism* (Grand Rapids, MI: Eerdmans, 1995).

that children should not be baptized—a practice for which Baptists argued there was no scriptural basis—because they were incapable of consent. Rather, they should be baptized as adults, when they could fulfill their obligation to conscientiously make a "confession of faith" in Christ. Those who had already been baptized as children could undergo a second voluntary baptism administered by other congregants. In advocating "believer's baptism," Baptists—or "Anabaptists" as they were derisively known for their practice of "re-baptizing"—were following the example of John the Baptist, who baptized willing adults, including of course Jesus, without any formal degree in theology or license from the state. According to their doctrine of "general atonement," God authorized anyone in a state of grace to baptize others as long as they were consenting adults. After Anabaptists implemented adult baptism as well as a communist-style government in Münster, Germany, in the early 1530s, they were attacked and their leaders imprisoned, tortured, and executed, their bodies hung in cages from the steeple of St. Lambert's Church as a warning to others.[99]

Such warnings were effective only to a degree; even as individual Baptist congregations were persecuted, the creed of Baptism itself spread. In 1609, two groups of English Baptist separatists fled to the Netherlands to escape punishment for holding secret meetings.[100] One group returned in 1611 to London, where it drew people like Poole who were dissatisfied with the official state religion due to its residual "papism," including its practice of infant baptism. But even as these Baptists joined their European predecessors in believing that the doctrine of general atonement licensed anyone in a state of grace to baptize others, they rejected their continued adherence to the idea that baptism was a "sacrament"—a sacred ritual guaranteeing salvation. Instead, they were "Particular Baptists," who maintained that the ultimate decision regarding a soul's state rested with God, not man. Christ did not die for everyone but for an "elect" few.[101]

Whether General or Particular, the entire scenario of lay baptism represented a threat to patriarchy, from the father's prerogative of insuring that the daily life of his household conformed to the church's precepts, through to the ordained priest's role in securing an individual's salvation in the afterlife, to the king's headship of the state church. Baptists denied the charge that unbaptized infants could not enter heaven, but their critics continued to assert that "Anabaptists" damned infants. Baptist ceremonies also generated controversy for not being held in churches but, because they were illegal, in secret and at night, thereby even

---

99. Claus-Peter Clasen, *Anabaptism, a Social History, 1525–1618: Switzerland, Austria, Moravia, South and Central Germany* (Ithaca, NY: Cornell University Press, 1972).

100. Matthew C. Bingham, *Orthodox Radicals: Baptist Identity in the English Revolution* (Oxford: Oxford University Press, 2019).

101. Samuel D. Renihan, *From Shadow to Substance: The Federal Theology of the English Particular Baptists (1642–1704)* (Oxford: Centre for Baptist History and Heritage, 2018).

Introduction 29

further, and quite literally, dislocating the patriarchal institutions of church and home. Critics painted these ceremonies in salacious terms. The illicitness of night and the fact that the secret locations involved bodies of water and hence degrees of nakedness—reportedly, converts wore sheets while being "dipped"—enabled rumors that the gatherings were not religious affairs but pretenses for free love. Popular male ministers were accused of preying upon the young women who comprised a high percentage of the membership in these private churches.

Elizabeth Poole was one such young woman, and her minister, William Kiffin, was one of the magnetic male preachers suspected of using their charisma to attract young women and gullible servants. Like other unlicensed men and women who took on the role of preacher, Kiffin derived his rationale from such scripture as 1 Corinthians, in which the ability to preach, like the ability to baptize, is represented as a "gift" given by God rather than a social privilege. But his success also made him a target. The Presbyterian Thomas Edwards accused him of being a "pretended" preacher who "by his enticing words, seduced and gathered a schismatical rabble of deluded children, servants and people, without either parents' or masters' consent."[102] Taking advantage of this growing public sphere of print and discussion that enabled such formulations to be widely circulated, Kiffin, who by this time had also become a prosperous leather merchant wealthy enough by 1642 to donate horses and riders to Parliament's army, was also known for his willingness to debate his opponents. For example, in 1644, he debated the Dutch Calvinist minister, Cesar Calandrini, because Calandrini feared that members of his congregation were defecting to the Baptists.[103] As Kiffin countered, all individuals, including women, were drawn to the church out of love not for man but for God, their "first husband."[104]

In 1645, Kiffin published *A Brief Remonstrance of the Reasons and Grounds of those People Commonly Called Anabaptists*, in which he debates Robert Poole, the man believed to have been Poole's father, after the latter objected to his

---

102. Thomas Edwards, *The First and Second Part of Gangraena; or, A Catalogue and Discovery of Many of the Errors, Heresies, Blasphemies, and Pernicious Practices of the Sectaries of This Time* (London: 1646), 6. See P. Baker, "Edwards, Thomas (c. 1599–1648), Church of England clergyman and religious controversialist," *ODNB*.

103. In 1676, Kiffin joined four other London Baptist leaders to debate Baptist evangelist Thomas Collier, a member of Kiffin's first church in London, over Collier's denial of original sin in his tract *A Body of Divinity* (London: 1676). In 1681, Kiffin published *A Sober Discourse of Right to Church-Communion* to debate John Bunyan, whose tracts *A Confession of My Faith* (London: 1672) and *Differences in Judgment about Water-Baptism* (London: 1681) criticized the Particular Baptists for demanding that new members be (re)baptized before participating in other ceremonies.

104. William Kiffin, *Certain Observations Upon Hosea The Second the 7. & 8. Verses* (London: 1642), (1).

30 *Introduction*

daughter's membership in Kiffin's church.[105] The queries by Robert Poole that Kiffin answers revolve around infant baptism. But they also highlight the general challenge this issue posed to the father's authority over his home and the spiritual estate of his subordinates. When Poole objects that the defection of his children and servants to Kiffin's congregation amounts to a lack of fealty to him, Kiffin responds that they were in fact showing proper loyalty to their true household, the holy household of the independent church as it was headed by God the father. Adult baptism signified one's desire to belong to this "community of believers," which conferred egalitarian membership into the body spiritual, "being by one spirit baptized into one body." Grounds for membership within this alternative community reinforce the degree to which Baptists challenged not only domestic but also political forms of authority that rested upon patriarchal precepts. The idea of the "priesthood of all believers" as put forth in Revelation 1:5–6—"And from Jesus Christ which is that faithful witness . . . And made us Kings and Priests unto God"—inspired Baptists to not only open access to the offices of preaching and baptizing but also to practice a more decentralized and egalitarian style of organization for their own churches.[106] In place of appointing a hierarchy of archbishops, bishops, and priests, some independent churches or "houses of God" nominated elders or even elected deacons as laid out in 1 Timothy 3.[107] These nurseries of democracy helped prove that individuals and voluntary associations were capable of self-government.

The New Model Army was one of the earliest organizations to adapt these principles to its own division of men into regiments that adjudicated their collective needs and communicated them to officers by way of elected representatives. As stated earlier, this in turn was to form the basis for a new-modeled England in which the hierarchical structure of the patriarchal body politic ruled by the head of the father-king would be replaced by a more horizontal structure of equality and unity. This vision of "spiritual equality" also became the basis for claims to individual rights and limited government by such thinkers as John Locke. In his well-known *A Letter Concerning Toleration* (1692), Locke is credited with

105. William Kiffin, *A Brief Remonstrance of the Reasons and Grounds of Those People Commonly Called Anabaptists* (London: 1645). See appendix 1, pp. 124–136. The debate may have taken place face-to-face at Robert Poole's request. When Kiffin arrived, he discovered that Robert Poole was accompanied by a number of well-known Anglican polemicists. Even an experienced debater like Kiffin was intimidated and so retreated. A year later, he published *A Brief Remonstrance* in order to finally respond to the queries with which he was to have been presented at the original meeting. See Brod, "Politics and Prophecy in Seventeenth-Century England," 397.

106. Revelation 1:5–6, GV. See also Peter 2:9, GV: "But you are a chosen generation, a royal Priesthood, a holy nation, a people set at liberty, that you should show forth the virtues of him that has called you out of darkness into his marvelous light."

107. 1 Timothy 3:7–9, GV: "He sets out Bishops and Christian deacons with their wives, children, and family; he calls the Church the house of God."

providing a theoretical defense for the right of religious dissenters to guard their consciences against the illegitimate encroachment of the magistrate.[108] But the separatists and semi-separatists of the mid-seventeenth-century both enacted and articulated their right to religious freedom and their belief in religious toleration.[109] Locke not only followed religious dissenters in welcoming this vision, but he took it even further by drawing upon its logic to eschew monarchy in favor of an order that acknowledged an even broader spectrum of individual rights.

The more extreme end of this spectrum was composed of higher law theory, the idea that all individuals, including kings, were subject to obey God's laws and so, in the event that the laws of rulers were deemed to be out of sync with those of God, individuals were entitled to resist. The English Baptists' detractors feared these implications for monarchy early on, citing the incidents involving the Baptists of Münster, Germany, as precedent. To assure the public that their purpose was "not at all to intermeddle with the ordering or altering civil government" but "solely for the advancement of the Gospel," Kiffin and his fellows published *The Confession of Faith* in 1644.[110] But the *Confession* heightened as many fears as it allayed by implying that laws made by civil governments were to be obeyed only if they comported with God's laws. As the authors signed the document, "we do therefore here subscribe it, some of each body in the name and by the appointment of seven congregations . . . holding Jesus Christ to be our head and Lord; *under whose government we desire alone to walk*" (emphasis added).[111] Given that the king was head of both church and state, this radical investiture of the body politic with a "right of exit" enabling people to reject forms of authority they deemed illegitimate could not be limited to the religious sphere.

Women played an important role in this "transposition" of religious into political liberty. Elizabeth Poole derived her own license to prophesy from the tenets put forth in *The Confession of Faith*, both presuming upon and demonstrating the relevancy of the individual's right to express their own religious convictions and apply them to other political contexts, including the family and the polity. The participation of other women, as was the case with men, likewise began with the basic desire to preach and prophesy to those who voluntarily gathered around them, as they believed scripture enabled them to do. Indeed, women were among the many "mechanic" or working-class "tub preachers" who became

108. John Locke, *A Letter Concerning Toleration* (Indianapolis: Liberty Fund, Online Library of Liberty), https://oll.libertyfund.org/titles/locke-a-letter-concerning-toleration-and-other-writings/.

109. W. K. Jordan, *The Development of Religious Toleration in England* (Gloucester, MA: P. Smith; Reprint, 1965).

110. William Kiffin et al., *The Confession of Faith* (London: 1644). See appendix 1, pp. 105–124. Page numbers refer to the present edition. Quotation from Murray Tolmie, *The Triumph of the Saints: The Separate Churches of London 1616–1649* (Cambridge: Cambridge University Press, 1977), 182.

111. Kiffin et al., *The Confession of Faith*, p. 108.

32 Introduction

ministers by quite literally building pulpits for themselves out of such everyday materials as washtubs. Historian Phyllis Mack estimates that somewhere around three hundred women were active as preachers and/or prophets at one time or another between 1640 and 1660.[112] A few left behind writings. In 1644, Sarah Jones published *To Sion's Lovers* defending independent churches in which "brethren and sisters [are] united together."[113] Katherine Chidley's *The Justification of the Independent Churches of Christ* (1641) calls for the privatization of religion.[114] Lady Eleanor Davies published a series of prophecies from the 1620s through the 1650s; these included *A Warning to the Dragon and All His Angels* (1625), an early harbinger of trouble for Charles.[115] A 1650s group known as the Fifth Monarchists produced two important women writers: Mary Cary and Anna Trapnel.[116] Trapnel's practice of delivering her prophecies while lying in bed in a state of a fast-induced trance was inspired by Sarah Wight, whose own twelve-day's worth of fasting and delivering prophecies was recorded by her minister, Henry Jessey

112. Phyllis Mack, *Visionary Women: Ecstatic Prophecy in Seventeenth-Century England* (Berkeley: University of California Press, 1992), 165.

113. Sarah Jones, *To Sion's Lovers* (London: 1644), B2. She followed up with a broadside titled *This Is Light's Appearance in the Truth* (London: 1650).

114. Katherine Chidley, *The Justification of the Independent Churches of Christ* (London: 1641). See also Ian Gentles, "Chidley, Katherine (fl. 1616–1653), religious controversialist and Leveller," *ODNB*.

115. Lady Eleanor Davies, *A Warning to the Dragon and All His Angels* (1625). For a modern edition of Davies's writings, see Lady Eleanor Davies, *Prophetic Writings of Lady Eleanor Davies*, ed. Esther S. Cope (Oxford: Oxford University Press, 1995) See also Lady Eleanor Davies, *Eleanor Davies: Printed Writings 1500–1640*, ed. Teresa Feroli (London: Routledge, 2016); Lady Eleanor Davies, *Eleanor Davies: Writings 1641–1646; Printed Writings, 1641–1700*, ed. Teresa Feroli (London: Routledge, 2011); and Lady Eleanor Davies, *Eleanor Davies: Writings 1647–1652; Printed Writings 1641–1700*, ed. Teresa Feroli (London: Routledge, 2018). For information on Davies's life, see Esther S. Cope, *Handmaid of the Holy Spirit: Dame Eleanor Davies, Never Soe Mad a Ladie* (Ann Arbor: University of Michigan Press, 1993); and D. Watt, "Davies [née Touchet; other married name Douglas], Lady Eleanor (1590–1652), prophetess," *ODNB*.

116. For accounts of the Fifth Monarchists, see Bernard S. Capp, *The Fifth Monarchy Men: A Study in Seventeenth-Century English Millenarianism* (London: Faber and Faber, 2011); and Louise Fargo Brown, *The Political Activities of the Baptists and Fifth Monarchy Men in England During the Interregnum* (London: Forgotten, 2012). For information on Mary Cary, see Anonymous, "Cary, Mary (b. 1620/21), millenarian," *ODNB*. Cary published four tracts prophesying the imminent return of Christ and his establishment of the Fifth Monarchy: *The Little Horn's Doom & Downfall* (London: 1651); *The Resurrection of the Witnesses* (London: 1648); *The Resurrection of the Witnesses, and England's Fall from (the Mystical Babylon) Rome Clearly Demonstrated to be Accomplished* (London: 1653); and *A Word in Season to the Kingdom of England; or, A Precious Cordial for a Distempered Kingdom* (London: 1647). Anna Trapnel published *The Cry of a Stone* (London: 1654); *A Legacy for Saints* (London: 1654); *Strange and Wonderful News from Whitehall* (London: 1654); and *Anna Trapnel's Report and Plea* (London: 1654). See S. Davies, "Trapnel, Anna (fl. 1642–1660), self-styled prophet," *ODNB*. See also Hilary Hinds, ed., *Anna Trapnel's Report and Plea; or, A Narrative of Her Journey from London into Cornwall* (Toronto: Iter Press; Tempe: Arizona Center for Medieval and Renaissance Studies, 2016).

Introduction 33

and published as *The Exceeding Riches of Grace Advanced by the Spirit of Grace, in an Empty Nothing Creature (viz.)*[117] *Mistress Sarah Wight* (1658).[118] In 1657, Mary Howgill published *A Remarkable Letter of Mary Howgill to Oliver Cromwell, Called Protector* and, in 1662, she issued *The Vision of the Lord of Hosts*, a hindsight explanation of Cromwell's defeat and the restoration of Charles II in 1660.[119]

Not all women affiliated with religious independency published tracts communicating satisfaction with the men who led their churches. Trapnel believed she was persecuted by independent male preachers because she threatened their newly acquired monopoly over the ministerial franchise. A Baptist named Anne Wentworth asserted that she was treated cruelly by her Baptist fellows because she complained of near-lethal spousal abuse by her husband.[120] Susanna Parr's *Susanna's Apology Against the Elders* (1659) conveys resentment over being *forced* to speak in church.[121] These cases illustrate the degree to which the democratic practices that defined independent churches were enabling for women seeking greater freedom but also, like democracy itself, slower to grant them full autonomy.

As we shall see, Poole herself experienced this dichotomy. Even as her reputation as a prophet led her to Whitehall, her status as a woman rendered her vulnerable in matters of controversy. By the time she delivered her messages, she had already left Kiffin's London congregation and moved to Abingdon to join another congregation with Baptist leanings, this one headed by the vicar of St Helen's in Abingdon, John Pendarves. Pendarves's wife, Thomasine, and Poole became friends and, as will become apparent, Thomasine will have her own role to play in Poole's story.

But after she delivered her messages, she was accused by her former London congregation, led by Kiffin, of having years earlier committed some sort of sexual transgression. She did not deny the charge but did deny that the incident merited the public shaming she was given by Kiffin and his allies. Indeed, the fact that the accusation came right on the heels of her appearances in Whitehall suggest that

---

117. Latin abbreviation for *videlicet*, a contraction of the Latin word *videre licet* meaning "it is permitted to see." Commonly used as a synonym for "namely" or "that is."

118. Henry Jessey, *The Exceeding Riches of Grace Advanced by the Spirit of Grace, in An Empty Creature (viz.) Mrs. Sarah Wight* (London: 1658). In 1656, Wight had also published words of divine thanksgiving under her own name in *A Wonderful Pleasant and Profitable Letter* (London: 1656). See K. Bullock, "Wight, Sarah (b. 1631), mystic," *ODNB*.

119. Mary Howgill, *A Remarkable Letter of Mary Howgill to Oliver Cromwell, called Protector* (London: 1657) and *The Vision of the Lord of Hosts* (London: 1662).

120. Anne Wentworth, *A True Account of Anne Wentworth's Being Cruelly, Unjustly, and Unchristianly Dealt with by Some of Those People Called Anabaptists* (London: 1676); Anne Wentworth, *A Vindication of Anne Wentworth* (London: 1677); and Anne Wentworth, *The Revelation of Jesus Christ* (London?: 1679). See Catie Gill, "Wentworth, Anne (1629/30–1693?), religious writer," *ODNB*.

121. Susanna Parr, *Susanna's Apology Against the Elders* (London: 1659). See K. Bullock, "Parr, Susanna (fl. 1650–1659), religious writer," *ODNB*.

34 *Introduction*

the incident was resurrected by those who didn't like her prophecies in order to discredit her.

While she was enraged, she was not deterred. She simply continued her membership in the Abingdon congregation as well as the "little society" that had formed around the minister John Pordage toward the end of the First Civil War, first in Reading and then near Abingdon.[122] This association would prove as pivotal as Poole's Baptism in the formation of her resistance theory. Pordage was a Cambridge graduate who developed an interest in the mystical idea that humans are "engaged in a difficult spiritual pilgrimage leading, after many checks and setbacks, to a mystical union with the deity."[123] Derived from alchemy, this union was represented by "the chemical wedding, where male and female principles come together after due purification by fire" to form "one androgynous body."[124] The male part of the union is represented by a prelapsarian Adam, while the female is represented by both Eve and Sophia, the feminized virtue of wisdom.[125] This celebration of a female figure as the symbol for the "head" as the source of knowledge literalized the idea of spiritual (and hence general) equality that the Baptists promulgated through scripture and their own institutional practices. Indeed, through Pordage's writings, these alchemical ideas filtered into his growing Bradfield society, which included a number of Baptists like Poole.[126] For example, Pordage's *Mundorum Explicatio* (1663) provides a detailed description of the process by which the "pilgrim" achieves unity with the divine. After the fragmentation of nature that humans experienced in the wake of the fall, God still allows individuals to redeem themselves through love; but the way is difficult, for the postlapsarian world is now a "fighting stage" between the "two powers" of Satanic corruption and the elevating Spirit.[127] The "Immortal Spark Divine," which still resides in every soul, however, will prevail if its possessor exercises their very own "Kingly Freedom" and "eschews the bad, [and] turns to the good his will."[128] The pilgrim's success in doing so is signified by the fact that the figure, "blessed

122. Brod, "A Radical Network in the English Revolution," 1230. See A. Hessayon, "Pordage, John (bap. 1607, d. 1681), religious leader and physician," *ODNB*.

123. Brod, "A Radical Network in the English Revolution," 1231. While at Cambridge, Pordage avidly read Paracelsus, whose teachings formed the basis of the Cambridge curriculum. While working toward his doctorate at Leyden University in the Netherlands, Pordage studied the writings of the German mystic, Jacob Boehme.

124. Brod, "A Radical Network in the English Revolution," 1232.

125. Sophia is used to represent wisdom in Hellenistic philosophy and religion, Platonism, Gnosticism, and Christian theology. Her name forms one of the roots for the word "philosophy": "Philo" as in "love" and "Sophia" as in "wisdom" equals "philosophy as the love of wisdom."

126. See, for example, John Pordage, *Innocency Appearing, Through the Dark Mists of Pretended Guilt* (London: 1655); *Mundorum Explicatio* (London: 1663); and *Theologia Mystica* (London: 1683).

127. Pordage, *Mundorum Explicatio*, 48.

128. Pordage, *Mundorum Explicatio*, 83, 87, 89.

CHASTITY," calls Cupid to shoot his "silver bow" into the pilgrim's heart so that "He is in Love but with SOPHIA."[129]

This focus upon Sophia as a feminized and virtuous figure of wisdom might explain why a number of women were attracted to the Bradfield group. These included not only Poole, but also women from Pordage's own family, the female mystic, Mary Pocock, and Thomasine Pendarves.[130] In 1649, Pendarves was involved in a pamphlet written by a fellow member, Abiezzer Coppe, the leader of the so-called Ranters group, which was famous for promoting sexual and spiritual equality for women.[131] This publication, *Some Sweet Sips, of Some Spiritual Wine*, contains a number of letters exchanged between Coppe and Pendarves, to whom Coppe was teaching the art of prophesy.[132] The letters draw from the erotic imagery in the Old Testament's "Song of Songs," in which the Holy Spirit destroys all hierarchies, including those that divide genders.[133] Within the group, Pordage dramatizes this unity of male and female by encouraging his male and female associates to join one another in performing such "mystical rites" as wearing all white, dancing on the lawn, speaking in mystical tones, singing songs, and adopting sacred names that enabled them to act out biblical and/or alchemical narratives.

Also similar to the Baptists was the Bradfield group's belief that anyone was eligible to prophecy and baptize, assuming they had been given the gifts to do so by God. Pordage's *Theologia Mystica* (published posthumously) recounts how he received his "grand Mysteries and high Arcanums" through "Vision."[134] His *Mundorum Explicatio* identifies baptism as the primary cure by which an errant soul finds its way back to God and wisdom. After narrating Satan's victory over man, Pordage describes John the Baptist standing by the "brook" of Jordan and inviting "man" to be baptized so that he can win "Heaven's high Race."[135] Once the race is won, the soul joins the equality of sovereign "peers" in the "new kingdom."[136]

These rich and radical ideas infuse Poole's messages to the army's General Council of officers as she takes on the role of wise woman reminiscent of Sophia.

129. Pordage, *Mundorum Explicatio*, 185.

130. Manfred Brod, "Pendarves, John (1622/3–1656), Particular Baptist minister," *ODNB*.

131. A. Hessayon, "Coppe, Abiezer (1619–1672?), Baptist preacher and Ranter," *ODNB*.

132. Abiezzer Coppe, *Some Sweet Sips, of Some Spiritual Wine Sweetly and Freely Dropping from One Cluster of Grapes* (London: 1649).

133. In one letter, Pendarves addresses Coppe as "My true love in the spirt of oneness" (39) and proclaims, "my having so free a commerce with all sorts of appearances, was my spiritual liberty" and "a perfect Law too" (42). Coppe responds, "I know that Male and Female are all one in Christ, and they are all one to me" (46).

134. Pordage, *Theologia Mystica* (London: 1683), 65.

135. Pordage, *Mundorum Explicatio*, 132.

136. Pordage, *Mundorum Explicatio*, 100.

36 *Introduction*

As she will proclaim to the officers, the Holy Spirit infused her with a vision that will help them find the cure that will regenerate the war-torn state of England into a unified kingdom of peers. Her first appearance took place on December 29, 1648, and her second on January 5, 1649. In the minutes taken for these sessions, the army secretary, William Clarke, introduced her as "Elizabeth Poole of Abington" and thereafter referred to her as the "Woman" (see figures 6 and 7).[137] In *The Manner of the Deposition of Charles Stewart*, she was described as a "woman of great wisdom and gravity" who came "of Hertfordshire" with a "message" from God.[138] Her own account of what transpired during those two visits survives in a six-page pamphlet titled *A Vision: Wherein Is Manifested the Disease and Cure of the Kingdom*.[139] In the opening, Poole states that the pretext for her message was her reading of Ireton's *A Remonstrance of His Excellency Thomas Lord Fairfax, Lord General of the Parliament's Forces*. She addresses his claim that, because the king had violated his oath to maintain the bond of trust with his people, he should no longer be considered the disperser of the cure but the cause of the disease and so subject to execution. As Ireton's document argues, "we may then justly lay England's liberties for defunct, when that which should be the conservative [the cure], shall be turned indeed the bane [the poison]."[140] If necessary, the army must prepare itself to perform "Capital Punishment upon the principal Author . . . of our late wars" through the exercise of "Exemplary Justice."[141] In her vision, Poole similarly adopts the language of curing to argue that the removal of the king is essential if the body politic is to survive. Unlike Ireton, she does not believe that removal should take place through the "exemplary justice" of capital punishment. Instead, she offers the rather unusual alternative of "divorce." She unfolds the logic for this alternative recommendation over the course of not only her first vision but also her second. She lays the groundwork in the first vision by arguing that the reading of Ireton's *Remonstrance* placed her in a state of sympathetic suffering for the ill body of the kingdom:

---

137. William Clarke, "General Council at Whitehall, 29 December 1648" and "General Council 5 Jan. 1648 at Whitehall," in *The Clarke Papers*, Clarke MSS, volume 67 (Worcester College, Oxford): 128–33. See appendix 2, pp. 143–153; page numbers refer to the present edition. For information on Clarke, consult F. Henderson, "Clarke, Sir William (1623/4–1666), military administrator," *ODNB*.

138. Anonymous, *The Manner of the Deposition of Charles Stewart, King of England, by the Parliament, and General Council of the Army* (London: 1649). See appendix 4, pp. 175–182. Page numbers refer to the present edition.

139. Elizabeth Poole, *A Vision: Wherein Is Manifested the Disease and Cure of the Kingdom* (London: 1649).

140. Ireton, *A Remonstrance of His Excellency Thomas Lord Fairfax, Lord General of the Parliament's Forces*. See appendix 3, p. 160. Page number refers to the present edition.

141. Ireton, *A Remonstrance of His Excellency Thomas Lord Fairfax, Lord General of the Parliament's Forces*, p. 64. Page number refers to the original.

I have been (by the pleasure of the most High) made sensible of the distresses of this land, and also a sympathizer with you in your labors: for having sometimes read your *Remonstrance*, I was for many days a sad mourner for her, the pangs of a travailing woman were upon me and the pangs of death often times panging me, being a member in her body of whose dying state I was made purely sensible.[142]

Whereas the Royalist paradigm ascribed the body politic's problems to subjects' defiance of their king as God's divine emissary, Poole argues that the body is ill because it or "she" is laboring to give birth to a new political order. The army is part of that body as it struggles to produce the new dispensation, but the body is in danger of dying because labor has stalled as the internal conflicts over what to do with the king drag on. Thus Poole intervenes to offer a cure. As a "sympathizer" with the army in their labors, Poole now takes on the role of the physician who will cure the body's ills. But this cure will not happen in the "old way," meaning by way of the king; rather it will happen in the "new way" that licensed Baptists to baptize one another so that they could join the alternative body of the spiritual community. In this scenario, Poole will act as a midwife who helps facilitate the delivery of the child. But her sympathy is so great that it reminds us that Poole is also a member of the body and so shares in the labors by delivering this very vision as the curative she is licensed to minister because she enjoys the "gift of faith."[143]

Poole's prescription is that the army must play the role of a "strong man" who helps the "crooked, sick, weak and imperfect in body" of "this Nation" to improve its state. This prescription harkens back to the Pordage circle's belief in man's service to Sophia. However, while in the past, some members of the army had so "bewailed her state" that they offered to "gladly be a sacrifice for her," Poole argues that rather than dissolve itself, the army should renew its "faithfulness" by staying intact and remaining "diligent" on behalf of "the cure of this woman."[144] She does retain the "kingly power" of heading the body politic by ascribing it to the army. However, this kingly function would comport with the higher law of "divine will," not because it enabled the army to wield absolute power but because it forced the officers to "stand in the presence of the Lord" and become "dead" to their own "interests, lives, liberties, freedoms" or "whatsoever" they might call their "own."[145]

After delivering her first vision, Poole is asked to rephrase it in less mystical terms so her listeners can be clear about her intentions. Specifically, she is asked, "Whether she conceived they were called to deliver up the trust to them

142. Poole, *A Vision*, p. 61.

143. Poole, *A Vision*, p. 61.

144. Poole, *A Vision*, p. 61.

145. Poole, *A Vision*, p. 62.

38 *Introduction*

committed either to Parliament or People."[146] By stating that the army was to serve the people's interests rather than its own, Poole had implied that the army should hand over its power. This was Ireton's aim in the *Remonstrance*; as he argued, once the army has dealt with the matter of the king's power and "person" (his life), it must set some "reasonable and certain period to [its] own power, by which time that great and supreme Trust reposed in [it], shall be returned into the hands of the people from, and for whom" the army had "received it."[147] But Poole does not agree, answering instead, "No, for this reason, it being committed to their [the army's] care and trust."[148] Once again, however, Poole states that by "care" she means working on behalf of the people's interests. Moreover, Poole adds that the army should see itself not in the role of father so much as of an older brother who "takes the people along" with it as "younger brethren who may be helpful to you."[149] The officers should act as "watchmen" whose "account" of their "Stewardship" would be "required" at "their hands," presumably by God but also by the people.[150] And finally, when asked whether the army could "remain free of the aspersions of the people" were it to remain intact, Poole replies that they could do so as long as they would be as "content" to lose their own lands, houses, wives, and children, in the pursuit of their postwar obligations as they had been to "lay down their lives" on the battlefield during the wars.

Poole's first vision was largely well received, perhaps because it walked a fine line between insisting that the army retain control for the time being, on the one hand, and alluding to a universal political enfranchisement along Leveller lines, on the other.[151] In terms of the former, William Clarke's notes revealed that the army council approved her message by granting that, as Ireton is reported to have said, they "could see nothing in her but those [things] that are the fruits of the Spirit of God."[152] But her message also influenced the Levellers: immediately after its delivery, John Lilburne issued *A Plea for Common-Right and Freedom* proposing to elevate the Council of Officers to the status of an executive governing body. This proposal was never fulfilled but its source of inspiration in Poole's

146. Poole, *A Vision*, p. 65.

147. Ireton, *A Remonstrance of His Excellency Thomas Lord Fairfax, Lord General of the Parliament's Forces*, p. 65. Page number refers to the original.

148. Poole, *A Vision*, p. 63.

149. Poole, *A Vision*, p. 63.

150. Poole, *A Vision*, p. 63.

151. As the Royalist weekly newsbook, *Mercurius Pragmaticus*, reported in its Tuesday, December 26, 1648—Tuesday, January 9, 1649 edition: "She told the Grandees of their sins, and the Levellers of their transgressions; after which the Brethren ordered her thanks, and were it not too large, I would have printed her Sermon. It might have served handsomely to have shown the private quarrels and deadly feuds which run in their Divisions, and petty sub-Divisions of Faction." See Blair Worden, *Literature and Politics in Cromwellian England* (Oxford: Oxford University Press, 2007), 18.

152. Clarke, "General Council at Whitehall," p. 148.

Introduction 39

appearance reveals the degree to which she affected the negotiations that took place around the king's trial and execution.

The success of her first visit is also underscored by the fact that she appeared again on January 5th. On this occasion, she circulated her message on paper. She cites her pretext for returning to the council as her reading of a revised version of the Levellers' *Agreement of the People*.[153] Less equivocally than before, she reiterates her request that the army not follow this Leveller agenda of handing power over to the people. However, she then states that the "free admission" with which she was met on her first visit has emboldened her to return with a message pertaining to the king's life: The council should "try the king in his conscience," she states, but "touch not his person."[154] This advice contradicted Ireton's and Cromwell's desire to see the king executed and reinforced Leveller demands that the king, like every Englishman, deserved a trial. But as mentioned earlier, Poole's prescription for the cure involved "divorcing" the king rather than executing him.

She advances this argument by reaffirming to the officers that the king is their "Father and husband" whom they are obliged to honor and obey as his wife and child. But they must also recognize that he has become a threat to their body and so must be removed. As she states in a phrase reminiscent of the language used in the Baptists' *The Confession*, the king is to be obeyed "in the Lord" and "no other way," for if the king's law contravenes God's law, then God's law must triumph.[155] By way of example, Poole advises her "brethren" to "play the part of Abigail" from 1 Samuel, wherein Abigail successfully discourages David from killing her loathsome husband, Nabal, for denying David and his men succor as they fled from the tyrant Saul.[156] While conceding her husband's cruelty, Abigail insists that revenge belonged to God, and so David should not despoil his own imminent government with a founding act of usurping violence. Likewise, the council should spare Charles's life by simultaneously honoring him as their husband and protecting themselves from the brutality of human revenge. But while Poole defends the king's life, she agrees that his "conscience" should be placed on trial for forgetting his "Subordination to divine Father-hood and head-ship."[157] By doing

---

153. John Lilburne, *Foundations of Freedom; or, An Agreement of the People: Proposed as a Rule for Future Government* (London: 1648). See appendix 3, pp. 160–174.

154. Poole, *A Vision*, p. 68.

155. Poole, *A Vision*, p. 65.

156. Poole, *A Vision*, p. 66. For a discussion of Poole's use of Abigail, see Katharine Gillespie, *Domesticity and Dissent in the Seventeenth Century: English Women Writers and the Public Sphere* (Cambridge: Cambridge University Press, 2004), 148–49, and Susan Wiseman, "'Public,' 'Private,' 'Politics': Elizabeth Poole, the Duke of Monmouth, 'Political Thought' and 'Literary Evidence,'" *Women's Writing* 14 (2007): 338–62.

157. Poole, *A Vision*, p. 65.

40 *Introduction*

so, Poole is offering a version of resistance theory reminiscent of the writings of Poole's associate in the Pordage group, Mary Pocock.

In 1649, Pocock wrote *The Mystery of the Deity in the Humanity*, in which she applies the concept of marriage between Sophia and Adam to the relationship between Parliament and King Charles.[158] As Pocock writes, "This is the representative, King and Parliament, whose happy condition is bound up in the enjoyment of each other, in the union of the manhood, in the power of the Godhead: And this is the glory of the King, in his paradisiacal kingdom."[159] However, Pocock observes, this "happy condition" has been disturbed by Charles's betrayal; thus his union with his wife is dissolved: "Oh King, you have broken wedlock with God and your wife, Therefore O King, you have lost your kingly glory, and the true glory of a King, and your power is now dead in you."[160] As Brod argues, for Pocock, "the crisis could only be resolved by reuniting the King with his various female compliments."[161] This was not the case for Poole. She does adopt Pocock's transformation of Sophia from what Phyllis Mack describes as a conventionally "passive" entity who is only "activated by divine masculine revelation" into an active entity capable of, as Pocock writes, divesting herself of "the sin of the king, or Adam, who loves only himself and self-seeing reason, rather than dwelling peacefully with Eve, or divine reason."[162] As Poole writes, "And if [the king] will usurp over her, she appeals to the Fatherhood for her offense, which is the spirit of Justice, and is in you. For I know no power in England to whom it is committed, save yourselves (and the present Parliament) which are to act in the Church of Christ, as she by the gift of faith upon her, shall be your guide for the cure of her body."[163] However, rather than reforming the king, Poole instructs the council to "commit" this "unsound member to Satan (though the head) as it is flesh, that the spirit might be saved in the day of the Lord."[164] This phrase "commit an unsound member to Satan" invokes the sectarian rhetoric of divorce whereby both male and female believers were permitted to end a marriage with an "unregenerate" spouse by renouncing them with the recognition that only God can redeem them, and thus they must be committed to his care. The idea of divorcing the unregenerate is also invoked by Coppe in *Some Sweet Sips, of Some Spiritual Wine* when

---

158. Mary Pocock, *The Mystery of the Deity in the Humanity* (London: 1649).

159. Pocock, *The Mystery of the Deity in the Humanity*, quoted in Nigel Smith, *Perfection Proclaimed: Language and Literature in English Radical Religion 1640–1660* (Oxford: Oxford University Press, 1989), 211.

160. Pocock, *The Mystery of the Deity in the Humanity*, quoted in Brod, "A Radical Network in the English Revolution," 1238.

161. Brod, "A Radical Network in the English Revolution," 1238.

162. Pocock, *The Mystery of the Deity in the Humanity*, quoted in Mack, *Visionary Women*, 100.

163. Poole, *A Vision*, p. 67.

164. Poole, *A Vision*, p. 67.

he argues that the soul's betrothal with God is achieved only by serving "a bill of divorce to all carnal fleshly fellowships."[165] Poole goes even further, arguing that the king is so carnal that he must be committed to Satan, rather than to God.

Poole also appropriates and transforms the Royalist language of marriage as a "yoke" in order to make her case for divorce. When the king came to mistakenly believe he had "begotten" his wife as a "generation to his own pleasure" and "lust," then "is the yoke taken from your necks (I mean the neck of the spirit and law, which is the bond of your union, that the holy life in it might not be profaned, it being free and can not be bound)."[166] This divorce is to be undertaken by the army as it acts "in relation to the people."[167] The idea that a wife is "begotten" for the purposes of lust reminds us that many early modern texts—as well as laws—defended a husband's right to beat his wife. Poole, however, ends this passage by insisting that the wife has a legitimate right to defend herself against abuse; so too, then, do the people. As she advises, the body must "accordingly . . . hold the hands of your husband, that he pierce not your bowels with a knife or sword to take your life. Neither may you take his."[168] Poole's insistence upon reciprocity is meant to protect the lives of both the husband and the wife. Just as the king does not have the right to harm or kill his wife, so too must the wife refrain from physically harming or killing her husband. Poole further emphasizes this point by identifying herself as an equal to the army council members and quoting the golden rule: "I speak unto you as Men, Fathers, and Brethren in the Lord (who are to walk by this rule). Whatsoever you would that men should do unto you, do you the same unto them."[169]

Historically, the development of "contract theory" has been associated with male political philosophers such as John Locke and Thomas Hobbes. But Poole's messages tell us that non-elite peoples also sought to hold their governors accountable by developing means to remove those who exploited their power. These popular political theories were often articulated through genres that we do not recognize today as political theory: prophecies, letters, and poetry. But by revising our understanding of how political ideas were articulated, we again can see how broad the spectrum of opinion was and how many people, formally educated or not, participated in some of the most electrifying conversations in English history. These debates did not take place in the universities, the halls of Parliament, or the courts; instead they took place in the "court of public opinion" made possible by the unprecedented availability of print.

165. Coppe, *Some Sweet Sips, of Some Spiritual Wine*, p. 13.

166. Poole, *A Vision*, p. 65.

167. Poole, *A Vision*, p. 152.

168. Clarke, *General Council 5 Jan. 1648 at Whitehall*, p. 68.

169. Poole, *A Vision*, p. 68.

42 *Introduction*

The pro-regicides won the debate; in fact, as Brod notes, by January 5, "the ordinance to establish the High Court of Justice for the purpose of trying the King had already passed through the House of Commons and would be activated (over the protest of the House of Lords) the day after Poole's appearance."[170] While this ordinance was rejected by the House of Lords, the House of Commons passed an "Act" condemning the king to die for high treason, as a "tyrant, traitor, murderer and public enemy."[171] As a result, Charles I was beheaded on a stage erected in front of the Banqueting House of the Palace of Whitehall on January 30, 1649. As he had during his imprisonment and trial, he maintained a demeanor of detachment, believing himself to be unimpeachable by a Parliament that, in his eyes, had no legal authority to question, much less try and execute, him. His performance was as divisive as had been his reign. Many believed he had been martyred by a demonic crew of rebels. For others, his death represented the welcome demise of a faded feudal order and the onset of a more democratic future. Thus, within a month after the king was beheaded, both the House of Lords and monarchy itself were abolished.

The new democratic future was, however, not cemented by these abolitions. After Cromwell and Ireton obtained the king's execution, they worked to neutralize the Levellers' more egalitarian vision for a new England by prohibiting soldiers from petitioning. That March, eight soldiers approached Fairfax to request that the ban be rescinded, but instead five of the eight were discharged. Three hundred more soldiers were dismissed after announcing they would not serve in Ireland until the ban was lifted and *An Agreement of the People* adopted. One Leveller agitator, Robert Lockyer, was hanged amid the growing tensions.[172] Like the funeral of Thomas Rainsborough, Lockyer's service drew thousands of mourners who marched behind his casket wearing sea green ribbons. The Leveller movement grew so large that, in April 1649, Cromwell and Ireton ordered that John Lilburne, Richard Overton, William Walwyn, and Thomas Prince be imprisoned.[173] The Levellers refused to bend and so Cromwell struck back, ordering an attack at Banbury that culminated in the shooting death of three leaders on May 17. Even though William Walwyn and Richard Overton gained release from the Tower, the movement could not survive the loss of so many prominent members. Cromwell had succeeded in eliminating the Levellers as a political threat and consolidating his own power as the leader of a new order, the exact nature of which remained undetermined.

---

170. Brod, "Politics and Prophecy in Seventeenth-Century England," 399.

171. Brod, "Politics and Prophecy in Seventeenth-Century England," 399.

172. Ian Gentles, "Lockyer, Robert (1625/6–1649), Leveller and parliamentarian soldier," *ODNB*.

173. B. Taft, "Walwyn, William (bap. 1600, d. 1681), Leveller and medical practitioner," *ODNB*; P. Baker, "Prince, Thomas (fl. 1630–1657), Leveller," *ODNB*.

Apparently, Elizabeth Poole was also to be eliminated as a political threat to the new order: it was shortly after she delivered her second message that William Kiffin had her ousted from his London congregation for sexual impropriety. Poole herself was the first to conclude that the charges were a cover for a political motivation. Immediately upon returning to Abington to join John Pendarves' Particular Baptist congregation, Poole returned to print to once again defend her messages as divine emanations from God.

On May 17, 1649, just four months after the king's execution, Poole published a second tract titled *An Alarm of War*.[174] This tract is a compilation of documents, including a reprint of the visions contained in her first tract, an address by Poole to her readers introducing them to a lengthy letter written to her congregation by a friend defending her reputation, and then a copy of the letter itself.[175] The document also features new material. The title page cites Isaiah 30:15–18, an assertion that wrongs will be righted by God, not man, for "blessed are all they that wait for him," and Psalm 68:12, a provocative statement that reads, "Kings of armies did flee apace: and she that tarried at home divided the spoil. Wherefore separate the precious from the vile, and return yet."[176] *An Alarm* also contains a new section titled "A Friend to truth and of the Author to the Reader"; this section consists of Poole's accusation that the ministers of her congregation slandered her for delivering a message to the council that was not to its leaders' liking, specifically its warning against "taking away the life of the king."[177] As she argues, the ministers, including "W. K." or William Kiffin, were "endeavoring to weaken the Message by scandalizing and reproaching the Messenger."[178] Poole admits that she had engaged in "some follies" but dismisses them as having been "committed many years ago, and long since repented of."[179] She then restates her commitment to her original vision and adds a new comparison of herself to the Woman in the Wilderness from Revelations, a Virgin Mary–like figure who, in the end-times, travails to birth the "man child" destined to conquer the beast. Slandering her may be effective in the short term, but it is ultimately doomed to failure, as her detractors will be exposed as hindrances to the installation of Christ's reign rather its deliverers.

This section also introduces the letter written by a supportive friend. The letter is signed as "T. P.," likely the initials for Thomasine Pendarves, the fellow Abington congregation member and wife of John Pendarves who was introduced

174. Poole, *An Alarm of War*, pp. 70–81.

175. Perhaps Poole included a reprint of *A Vision* because the print in the original pamphlet was so blurry as to be nearly indecipherable.

176. Psalm 68:12, GV; Isaiah 30:15–18, GV.

177. Poole, *An Alarm of War*, p. 70.

178. Poole, *An Alarm of War*, p. 72.

179. Poole, *An Alarm of War*, p. 72.

44 *Introduction*

earlier. T. P.'s six-page letter is addressed to "The Congregation of Saints, walking in fellowship with *Mr.* William Kiffin," and dated March 6 (roughly two months after Poole's final appearance before the army's General Council). While Pendarves was unwilling for whatever reason to identify herself by her full name, she did expressly characterize herself as a *"friend of Mrs.* Elizabeth Poole" and, as promised in Poole's introduction to the letter, defended Poole's character. As T. P. writes, "Be careful how you meddle with the spirit that breaths in her, for surely brethren . . . I have found a most divine spirit in her."[180] T. P. also admonishes Poole's enemies for compromising her ability to earn money as a seamstress: "You cannot be ignorant that she hath no livelihood amongst men, but what she earns by her hands; and your defaming her in this manner cannot in an ordinary way but deprive her of that."[181] Evidence of the historical significance of this incident in Poole's life lies in the fact that T. P.'s letter was republished in a collection of private epistles compiled by Giles Calvert titled *News from the New Jerusalem* (1649).[182] This compilation sought to cement ties among those who, like Poole, had opposed the execution but still believed the founding of a new godly order was imminent.

The last pamphlet Poole is known to have published was also titled *An Alarm of War* (London: 1649).[183] This second *Alarm* begins with Poole's "Preface to the Reader," a remarkable statement that acknowledges that some might wonder how, after experiencing "so reproachful a pursuit by them that are called Saints," she could "hold up [her] head anymore to speak to them."[184] She can do so, she insists, because it was God's desire to "stain the pride and glory of all flesh" in her and "to blind the eyes of the wise, that they seeing might not perceive."[185] In other words, Poole accepts that God wishes to humble her but still insists she is there to enlighten those who fail to understand: "The eyes of the wise must be blind, that the blind may receive sight."[186] She again asserts that the army leadership must rule on behalf of the people rather than simply safeguarding or even enriching their own "privileges, interests, lives, liberties, freedoms."[187] In the next section, titled "To the Pretended Church," she also once again lambastes the Baptist congregation that

180. Poole, *An Alarm of War*, p. 75.

181. Poole, *An Alarm of War*, p. 74.

182. Thomasine Pendarves, "25. Letter: The Copy of a Letter, as it was sent from Mrs. T. P., in behalf of Mrs. E. P. To a Congregation of Saints in London, under the form of Baptism," in *News from the New Jerusalem*, ed. Giles Calvert, 121–36 (London: 1649). See A. Hessayon, "Calvert, Giles (bap. 1615, d. 1663), bookseller," *ODNB*.

183. Elizabeth Poole, second *An Alarm of War* (London: 1649), pp. 83–103. Page numbers refer to the present edition.

184. Poole, second *Alarm*, p. 84.

185. Poole, second *Alarm*, p. 84.

186. Poole, second *Alarm*, p. 84.

187. Poole, second *Alarm*, p. 84.

excommunicated her. Her bitterness is evident in her striking characterization of the congregation as "the pretended Church and Fellowship of Saints in London, who pursued me with their weapons of war to shoot me to death at the General Council of the Army, not regarding the Baby Jesus in my Greeting." To prove Christ was at work in her message, she "divorces" the congregation, just as she had encouraged the army to do with the king, telling her former congregants that she now "commits" them "to God the only wise and infinite Father" and wishes them "farewell."[188] The final section is the main one. It is demarcated as such by its own title page. This internal title page features the same title as the main title page, *An Alarm of War* (see figure 5).[189] But whereas the front cover of this *Alarm* (as well as the first one) featured verses from Isaiah 30 and Psalm 68, this internal title page in the second *Alarm* features verses 17–21 from Ezekiel 39. And whereas the main content item of the first *Alarm* was the letter from T. P., the main section of the second *Alarm* contains a lengthy piece of writing by Poole herself in which she angrily "launch[es] deep into the sides" of her "Brethren" by insisting, "I must forsake your evil and adulterate party," for "nothing would satisfy you, but the blood of the King; a man with whom you were in Covenant, and had sworn to defend his Person."[190] She also reiterates and defends her original message to the council, stating, "It is true indeed, a just woman must deliver up her Husband to the just claim of the law, though she might not accuse him to the law, or yet rejoice over him to see his fall."[191]

The final publication attributed to Poole is a reissue of her three pamphlets under a new title: *A Prophecy Touching the Death of King Charles*[192] (see figure 1). While this "collected works" preserves the original content of all three pamphlets, its title page is new, featuring verses 18–21 from Isaiah 14. As the title page tells us, these verses are identical to those used by the congregationalist minister Hugh Peter to "preach before the King, a little before he was beheaded." Peter was a signatory to Charles's death order; these verses provide a religious rationale for why the army did not follow the advice of those who, like Poole, opposed regicide.[193] As the verses state, kings who destroy their own realms "are slain, *and thrust through with a sword*."[194] What is more, their children must be slaughtered, "for the iniquities of their father let them not rise up, nor possess the Land, nor fill the face of the world with Enemies." It is interesting to speculate why these verses were cited in Poole's last tract. Perhaps they signify the degree to which

188. Poole, second *Alarm*, p. 87.

189. Poole, second *Alarm*, p. 88.

190. Poole, second *Alarm*, p. 90.

191. Poole, second *Alarm*, p. 94.

192. Elizabeth Poole, *A Prophecy Touching the Death of King Charles* (London: 1649).

193. Carla Gardina Pestana, "Peter, Hugh (bap. 1598, d. 1660)," *ODNB*.

194. Isaiah 14:18–21, GV.

46 *Introduction*

Poole had already anticipated and debunked the logic used by the regicides to rationalize their enactment of God's revenge. The citations from Isaiah 30:15–18 that Poole herself had featured on the title page of her first and second *Alarm* had warned her readers that it was the Lord who was "the God of Judgement," not man; indeed, "blessed are they that wait for him." And, as she put it even more pointedly in a quotation from Romans 12:19 in her *A Vision*, "For vengeance is mine, I will repay it, says the Lord."[195] Alternatively, the reference to the children who will be slain along with their father might be an allusion to the people writ large rather than the king's literal children, suggesting that those who executed their father-king will also be destroyed.

In any event, the republication of Poole's works in the face of the condemnations she experienced for her opposition to Cromwell and his allies repudiates centuries worth of attempts to undermine women's authority by demonizing them as witches and whores. In fact, as Dorothy Ludlow claimed in 1978, Poole's visions and alarms establish her as one of the "first women political polemicists" in English letters.[196] Given the work scholars have done on Poole's writings in the wake of Ludlow's groundbreaking thesis, we can add that Poole was also one of the first women to challenge the political polemics of kingship and envision a more democratic alternative.

"A Monstrous Witch": The Afterlives of Elizabeth Poole's Texts

While Poole published nothing else, it is known that she was active as a preacher during the 1650s. She also defended John Lilburne when he was on trial in London for returning to England illegally in 1653, after being exiled to Amsterdam for conspiring to overthrow Cromwell. While allies of Lilburne staged a diversion, she took over the pulpit at the army chapel at Somerset House and preached for roughly two hours in defense of Lilburne before being taken away. In her sermon, Poole explicated Isaiah 8, a set of instructions by God telling the prophet not only to speak to the people of the coming disaster he will visit upon them for having "refused the waters of a Shiloh that run softly" but also to write his prophecies down on a scroll "with a man's pen."[197] To cement his obedience to this command, the prophet couples with a "Prophetess, who conceived and bore a son."[198] This child is to serve as one of the "signs and wonders in Israel" that the "Lord of hosts,

---

195. Poole, *A Vision*, p. 67.

196. Dorothy Ludlow, "'Arise and Be Doing': English Preaching Women 1640–1660," unpublished dissertation, Indiana University, 1978.

197. Isaiah 8:1, GV.

198. Isaiah 8:3, GV.

which dwells in mount Zion" sends as harbingers of his intentions for mankind.[199] Later, in 1668, Poole, along with Elizabeth Calvert, was arrested for operating an illegal printing press in her house at the Mint, a run-down part of Southwark.[200] After being imprisoned at the Gatehouse Prison in Westminster, she disappeared from the historical record.

She does not, however, disappear from the "pamphlet wars." New insights into the workings of the council meetings are provided by Secretary William Clarke's official transcripts of the meetings. In particular, they provide additional support for the idea that Poole's messages comported with those of the Levellers. First, her interlocutors interpreted her message to mean that the army should "go forward and stand up for the liberty of the people as it was their liberty and God had opened the way to them."[201] Second, Clarke records the Leveller colonel Rich as saying, "What she has said" is "correspondent with what I have made [known] as [manifested] to me before" (brackets in the original).[202] Finally, after Ireton is assured of the "humility and self denial" with which Poole delivered her visions, he asks that the council "come to the business that is before you," which was a consideration of *An Agreement of the People*.[203] At this time, the committee moved to approve several provisions in the document, including preventing future representatives from benefitting financially by doubly serving as treasurer or any other financial officer in the government; prohibiting the government from infringing upon individual rights and expropriating or destroying citizens' property; and insisting that all members of the military subordinate their power to the legislative branch upon pain of death.[204] To be sure, the positive conclusion to Poole's first appearance did not prevent some council members from testing her authenticity as a messenger during her second appearance. However, the nature of the exchanges suggests that the officers took her seriously as a rational discussant.

We also have pamphlets that tell us something about the larger public's reception of her prophecies. The aforementioned pamphlet, *The Manner of the Deposition of Charles Stuart*, published just after the king was captured, sentenced, and tried, contains a subtitle promising that the pamphlet will include "Also the

---

199. Isaiah 8:18, GV. Such public forms of support for Lilburne appear to have helped the celebrated cause of "Freeborn John." When he was acquitted, the soldiers assigned to guard him cheered along with the sizable crowds gathered outside his jailhouse.

200. Maureen Bell, "Seditious Sisterhood: Women Publishers of Opposition Literature at the Restoration," in *Voicing Women: Gender and Sexuality in Early Modern Writing*, ed. Kate Chedgzoy, Elizabeth Hansen, and Suzanne Trill, 185–95 (Edinburgh: Edinburgh University Press, 1998).

201. Clarke, "General Council at Whitehall," p. 144.

202. Clarke, "General Council at Whitehall," p. 146.

203. Clarke, "General Council at Whitehall," p. 149.

204. Whether Poole herself would have agreed with any one or all of these provisions, particularly the last one, is not clear.

48   *Introduction*

words of a woman, who pretends to have seen a vision, to the General Council of the Army."[205] The word "pretends" might give modern readers the impression that the author holds a negative view of Poole. But the contents suggest otherwise. It is true that, unlike Poole, the author opposed both the trial and the beheading, and the army is denigrated not only for taking it upon itself to try the king but also for trying to pass a law stipulating "that no King be hereafter admitted but upon the Election, and upon trust from the people."[206] But the pamphlet also affirms Poole's opposition to the regicide by confirming fears that executing the king would backfire. When Charles was asked what he would do if sentenced to death, he answered that he would "die patiently like a Martyr."[207] While Poole never explicitly argued that killing the king would enable him to play this deeply bathetic role, she did predict it would go against the grain of the people's or "wife's" sense of honor for him as their father and husband. Finally, *The Manner of the Deposition* contains an almost reverential account of the way in which her vision predicts the army's triumph over monarchy:

> Out of Hartfordshire unto the General Council of the Army, is come a woman of great wisdom and gravity who told them she had a message to them from God and desired they should hear her, which they accordingly did with much acceptance. She says they shall surely be prosperous, and attain their desires for a speedy settlement of the Kingdom, and that all powers shall be subdued under their feet.[208]

The title of a pamphlet published two years later, in 1651, informs us that other members of the general public were far less acquiescent to the seeming fait accompli of Parliament's victory. Titled *To Xeiphos Ton Martyron* (1651), this pamphlet accuses Poole of being part of a centuries-long conspiracy by Catholics, Jews, merchants, religious independents, and others to cast the throne onto the "dung-hill of Democracie."[209] As the author explains, to destroy Protestantism, the magistracy, and the ministry, Cromwell and his coconspirators had to overcome all opposition to the execution of the king, especially the powerful Presbyterian faction within Parliament. To achieve this goal, Cromwell pretended to cooperate with the Levellers and, more importantly, to placate those religious "soft heads" who "had a good meaning to do no evil, but to promote the Kingdom of Christ, and throw down Anti-Christ, and then according to their duty [as they

205. Anonymous, *The Manner of the Deposition*, p. 176.

206. Anonymous, *The Manner of the Deposition*, p. 179.

207. Anonymous, *The Manner of the Deposition*, p. 180.

208. Anonymous, *The Manner of the Deposition*, pp. 181–182.

209. Anonymous, *To Xeiphos Ton Martyron* (London: 1651), p. A1. Page number refers to the original. See appendix 4, pp. 182–191. Page numbers refer to the present edition.

were taught], to take possession of, and (as Saints) reign over the kingdom."[210] Cromwell persuaded them to join his cause—or "provided fit food to feed such fantasies" as the author put it—by "providing a monstrous witch full of all deceitful craft, who being put into brave clothes, pretended she was a lady that was come from a far country, being sent by God to the army with a revelation, which she must make known to the army, for necessity was laid upon her."[211] This witch was of course no other than Elizabeth Poole.

Given what we've learned about the fates of assertive women in early modern times, the author's casting of Poole into the role of a witch is unfortunate but not surprising. The author does indeed seem to believe that Poole was a witch who, at the invitation of Cromwell and Ireton, disguised herself as a virtuous and even noble prophetess in order to carry out their "deceit" upon the hapless soldiers who fought the wars in hopes of establishing a more godly order. In this scenario, Poole was not just a well-meaning albeit naive tool of Cromwell's but a willing co-dissembler. She was brought to Whitehall and "had her lesson taught her" by Cromwell and Ireton before she appeared before the council.[212] And to "beget the more attention and belief" in their agenda as it was to be endorsed by a visionary women, Cromwell and Ireton "extolled the excellency of revelation, and conceived that this prophetess being a precious saint, and having much of God in her, ought to be heard."[213] "In such glorious days as these," Cromwell reportedly enthused, "God did manifest himself extraordinarily."[214]

In the last seventeenth-century tract to mention Poole's participation in the trials, she is also cast as a witch who carries out Cromwell's diabolical design. Boldly titled *The English Devil; or, Cromwell and His Monstrous Witch Discover'd at White-Hall* (1660) (see figure 8), this pamphlet is also written anonymously but, unlike the previous one, focuses solely on Poole's and Cromwell's actions and characters.[215] In keeping with its publication in the year of the restoration of the monarchy under Charles II, the pamphlet's author has a decidedly jaded opinion of both. Poole is not only a "monstrous witch" but a "hellish monster," while Cromwell is an "audacious rebel" who rose Satanically from a brewer to a would-be king and then became a tyrant who trampled over the very rights the people fought for under his leadership.[216] Despite this more narrow focus, however, the overall thrust of the argument is remarkably similar to that of *To*

210. Anonymous, *To Xeiphos Ton Martyron*, p. 188.

211. Anonymous, *To Xeiphos Ton Martyron*, pp. 188–189.

212. Anonymous, *To Xeiphos Ton Martyron*, p. 189.

213. Anonymous, *To Xeiphos Ton Martyron*, p. 189.

214. Anonymous, *To Xeiphos Ton Martyron*, p. 189.

215. Anonymous, *The English Devil; or, Cromwell and His Monstrous Witch Discover'd at White-Hall* (London: 1660). See appendix 4, pp. 192–201. Page numbers refer to the present edition.

216. Anonymous, *The English Devil*, p. 194.

50 Introduction

Xeiphos Ton Martyron. In fact, *The English Devil* simply reprints *To Xeiphos*'s section on Poole verbatim. Once again, there is no mention of her own pamphlets, or of the fact that her messages against killing the king contradicted Cromwell's will. There is only a sense that she played a demonic role in overthrowing the monarchy and paving the way for a democratic alternative. Despite the complaint about Cromwell's trampling upon his people's rights, there is no evidence that the author supported Cromwell's Protectorate; instead, it's implied that it was blessedly nipped in the bud when Cromwell died and his son, Richard, briefly ruled until Charles II claimed the Crown.

Even as Poole's contemporaries paint competing pictures of her character and her role in the king's trial and execution, most modern critics (albeit not all, as discussed earlier) do not adopt the perspective that she was either a mere puppet whose strings were being pulled by Cromwell and Ireton or a malevolent conspirator. And while they disagree over whether her visions were conservative or radical in nature, and whether they had any real impact on long-term history, they take her messages seriously as exercises in political theory, however unorthodox a form that theory takes. Historians were among the first to value prophecy as a medium for women writers such as Poole to contribute to the religious and political debates that defined mid-seventeenth-century England.[217] Their studies include Ludlow's unpublished but influential dissertation "'Arise and Be Doing': English Preaching Women 1640–1660" (1978); Phyllis Mack's *Visionary Women: Ecstatic Prophecy in Seventeenth-Century England* (1992); and Stevie Davies's *Unbridled Spirits: Women of the English Revolution: 1640–1660* (1998).[218] Literary critical treatments such as Rachel Trubowitz's "Female Preachers and Male Wives: Gender and Authority in Civil War England," Suzanne Trill's "Religion and the Construction of Femininity" (1996), and Anne Hughes's *Women, Men and Politics in the English Civil War* (1999) offer pathbreaking assessments of how the female prophet's authority illustrates the "fluidity of gender boundaries during

---

217. Female prophets were not a singularly English phenomenon. For studies of other traditions, see Ottavia Niccoli, *Prophecy and People in Renaissance Italy* (Princeton, NJ: Princeton University Press, 1990); Richard L. Kagan, *Lucrecia's Dreams: Politics and Prophecy in Sixteenth-Century Spain* (Berkeley: University of California Press, 1990); Elizabeth Petrol, *Medieval Women's Visionary Literature* (New York: Oxford University Press, 1986); Sabina Flanagan, *Hildegard of Bingen, 1098–1179: A Visionary Life* (London: Routledge, 1989); Suzanne Noffke, *Catherine of Siena: Vision through a Distant Eye* (Collegeville, MN: Liturgical, 1996); Armando Maggi, *Uttering the Word: The Mystical Performances of Maria Maddalena De' Pazzi, a Renaissance Visionary* (Albany, NY: State University of New York Press, 1998); Tamar Herzig, *Savonarola's Women: Visions and Reform in Renaissance Italy* (Chicago: University of Chicago Press, 2008); Ronald E. Surtz, *The Guitar of God: Gender, Power, and Authority in the Visionary World of Mother Juana De La Cruz (1481–1534)* (Philadelphia: University of Pennsylvania Press, 1990); Amy Schrader Lang, *Prophetic Woman: Anne Hutchinson and the Problem of Dissent in the Literature of New England* (Berkeley: University of California Press, 1987).

218. Ludlow, "'Arise and Be Doing"; Mack, *Visionary Women*; Stevie Davies, *Unbridled Spirits: Women of the English Revolution: 1640–1660* (London: Women's Press, 1998).

these revolutionary decades."[219] Hilary Hinds's *God's Englishwomen* places Poole and other radical religious women writers of the time at the forefront of modern feminism.[220] And in *Romantic Women Writers, Revolution, and Prophecy: Rebellious Daughters, 1786–1826* (2013), Oriane Smith pays homage to the precedent set by Poole and other female prophets active in the English Civil Wars for women in later revolutions.[221]

Other scholars investigate Poole's influence on the history of political ideas. Brian Patton offers Poole's use of divorce as a solution to the problematic relationship with the king as an example of how a conservative trope such as marriage could contain "potentially radical social implications."[222] Manfred Brod writes a detailed account of the complex politics surrounding Poole's appearances before the council.[223] He also published a reexamination of Poole's legacy in the context of the larger "radical network" of the Pordage circle, thereby demonstrating how ideas emerge from a "primeval ideological soup" with "some ideas being incorporated" by history and "others rejected."[224] In *Political Speaking Justified: Women Prophets and the English Revolution*, Teresa Feroli argues that Poole's "desire to preserve the person of Charles reveals her lingering attachment to the ideal of divine right monarchy."[225] My own study, *Domesticity and Dissent in the Seventeenth Century: England Women Writers and the Public Sphere*, asserts that Poole's use of divorce as a figure for removing the king from power should be recognized as an early articulation of contract theory, in which a woman's right to exit oppressive political relations was recognized.[226] Marcus Nevitt's *Women and the Pamphlet Culture of Revolutionary England, 1640–1660* argues that Poole's "anti-regicidal

---

219. Rachel Trubowitz, "Female Preachers and Male Wives: Gender and Authority in Civil War England," in *Pamphlet Wars: Prose in the English Revolution*, ed. James Holstun, 112–33 (London: Frank Cass, 1992); Suzanne Trill, "Religion and the Construction of Femininity," in *Women and Literature in Britain, 1500–1700*, ed. Helen Wilcox, 30–55 (Cambridge: Cambridge University Press, 1996); Anne Hughes, *Women, Men and Politics in the English Civil War* (Keele, UK: Keele University Press, 1999). Quotation from Trubowitz, "Female Preachers and Male Wives," 113.

220. Hilary Hinds, *God's Englishwomen: Seventeenth-Century Radical Sectarian Writing and Feminist Criticism* (Manchester: Manchester University Press, 1996).

221. Oriane Smith, *Romantic Women Writers, Revolution, and Prophecy: Rebellious Daughters, 1786–1826* (Cambridge: Cambridge University Press, 2013).

222. Brian Patton, "Revolution, Regicide, and Divorce: Elizabeth Poole's Advice to the Army," in *Place and Displacement in the Renaissance*, ed. Alvin Vos, 133–45 (Binghamton, NY: Medieval & Renaissance Texts & Studies, 1995).

223. Brod, "Politics and Prophecy in Seventeenth-Century England," 399.

224. Brod, "Doctrinal Deviance in Abingdon: Thomasine Pendarves and her Circle." *Baptist Quarterly* 41, no. 2 (2005): 92–102 (92).

225. Teresa Feroli, *Political Speaking Justified: Women Prophets and the English Revolution* (Newark: University of Delaware Press, 2006), 69.

226. Gillespie, *Domesticity and Dissent*, 115–65.

complaint" was a vehicle through which "the woman writer could re-negotiate the restrictions and oppressions of her condition and claim public-sphere space to comment on the state of the political nation."[227] Susan Wiseman's *Conspiracy and Virtue* calls for us to keep in mind that, just because radical religious women writers "have no place in the [current] canon of political theory or the literary canon does not mean that their texts had no impact at the moment of publication or subsequently."[228] We need to consider "what our own languages and expectations bring to the evidence"—an important project for future generations.[229]

Shannon Miller's book-length study *Engendering the Fall* demonstrates Poole's subsequent influence by examining the impact that unrecognized women writers had upon John Milton, as she argues, female prophecy "become a model" that Milton drew upon to "speak to politically resonant issues" during the Restoration, when, as a member of the failed revolutionary government, he was marginalized as a "Diabolical Rebel" who had spread "impious doctrines."[230] In "Tyranny and Tyrannicide in Mid-Seventeenth-Century England: A Woman's Perspective?," Claire Gheeraert-Graffeuille discusses not just Poole's but also other women's participation in the debates over Charles I's fate and notes how, in spite of the overwhelming prohibitions against female participation in political affairs, ideology trumped gender when it came to the ethics of regicide.[231] Poole has even inspired a novelist to write a fictionalized treatment of her life. In Katherine Clements's *The Crimson Ribbon* (2014), Poole is depicted sympathetically as a victim of witch hunts.[232]

The scholarly and popular discussions incited by Poole's texts are young but already rich and diverse. As publications such as this one make her writings available to more and more readers, those discussions will mature into an even greater complexity and lead to further integration of "other" voices into mainstream histories.

Editorial Principles and Practices

Elizabeth Poole's visions appear in four distinct pamphlets, even as, at times, some elements overlap. Poole's first pamphlet is fully titled *A Vision: Wherein Is Manifested the Disease and Cure of the Kingdom. Being the Sum of What Was*

---

227. Marcus Nevitt, *Women and the Pamphlet Culture of Revolutionary England, 1640–1660* (London: Ashgate, 2006), 84.

228. Wiseman, *Conspiracy and Virtue*, 174.

229. Wiseman, *Conspiracy and Virtue*, 174.

230. Shannon Miller, *Engendering the Fall: John Milton and Seventeenth-Century Women Writers* (Philadelphia: University of Pennsylvania Press, 2008), 81.

231. Claire Gheeraert-Graffeuille, "Tyranny and Tyrannicide in Mid-Seventeenth-Century England: A Woman's Perspective?" *Études Épistémè* 15 (June 2009): 139–52.

232. Katherine Clements, *The Crimson Ribbon* (London: Headline, 2014).

Delivered to the General Council of the Army, December 29, 1648. Together with a True Copy of What Was Delivered in Writing (the Fifth of This Present January) to the Said General Council, of Divine Pleasure concerning the King in Reference to His Being Brought to Trial, What They Are Therein to Do, and What Not, Both concerning His Office and Person. By E. Poole, Herein a Servant to the Most High God. London, Printed in the Year, 1648 (see figure 2). It contains three messages: the first two were delivered orally during her initial visit to the army's General Council on December 29, 1648/9, and the third was delivered in paper form during her return visit on January 5. The copy transcribed into modern form here is housed among George Thomason's tracts in the British Library [E.537(24)] and is available on *EEBO*.[233] The title page of this copy features a handwritten notation by Thomason marking the date on which he obtained the pamphlet: "*Jan: 9th.*" That handwritten note is not reproduced here, because it is not part of the original publication. The pagination of *A Vision* has one error: What should be marked as page 4 is marked as page 6. That error is corrected in this volume. Page 5 is correctly marked as such, as is the actual page 6 (the final page in the publication).

Poole's second publication appeared later in 1649 under the title *An Alarm of War Given to the Army and to Their High Court of Justice (so called) Revealed by the Will of God in a Vision to E. Poole (Sometime a Messenger of the Lord to the General Council, Concerning the Cure of the Land and the Manner Thereof) Foretelling the Judgements of God Ready to Fall upon Them for Disobeying the Word of the Lord in Taking Away the Life of the King: Also a Letter to the Congregation, in Fellowship with Mr. Kiffin, in Vindication of E. P.* (see figure 3). It contains a defiant reprint of the visions published in her first tract; an address to Poole's readers describing a letter of support for Poole sent to her congregation by "T. P."; and a copy of the letter itself. Numbered Thomason E.555(23) in the Thomason Tracts housed in the British Library, the copy transcribed here is available on *EEBO*. The copy contains a handwritten note by Thomason of "May 17," indicating that he obtained the pamphlet on that day. He has also handwritten the number "23" on the title page to indicate the pamphlet's place in his collection. These notations do not appear in the original and so are not reproduced here. The first six pages of the pamphlet that consist of a reprint of Poole's *A Vision: Wherein Is Manifested the Disease and Cure of the Kingdom* are not reproduced because that document is already included in this edition. Thus, the transcription of *An Alarm* that is included here begins with "A Friend to Truth and of the Authors to the Readers," the second section of the pamphlet, which begins on page 7 in the original and consists of Poole's introduction to the letter written by "T. P." to Poole's Baptist congregation in defense of Poole after her excommunication from William Kiffin's

---

233. George Thomason was a noted printer and collector of pamphlets who typically penned the date upon which he acquired his purchases on their title pages. He also assigned each pamphlet a number. His vast collection of pamphlets survived to comprise the archive now known as the "Thomason Tracts." See David Stoker, "Thomason, George (c. 1602–1666)," *ODNB*.

54 *Introduction*

church. As noted earlier (p. 43), T. P. is presumed to be Thomasine Pendarves, the wife of John Pendarves, the minister of the Baptist congregation that Poole joined after being excommunicated from Kiffin's.

Poole's third tract, published later in 1649, is also titled *An Alarm of War*. Numbered Thomason E.555(24) in the British Library, this copy is also available on *EEBO*. In the paratextual materials, this volume refers to this tract as either the "second *Alarm*" or "An[other] *Alarm*." In doing so, it follows the lead of George Thomason, who distinguished between the two *Alarms* by handwriting the word "other" into the printed title of his copy (see figure 4) of the second *Alarm* in order to render the word "An" into "Another." He has also written "with precedg" (with proceeding) at the top of the title page, apparently to insure that, while the second *Alarm* is to be distinguished from the first, it is also to be understood as a continuation of it. The title page additionally features a handwritten note by Thomason of "May 17th," informing us that he obtained it on the same day as he did the first *Alarm*. Finally, he has written the number "24" on the title page to indicate the pamphlet's place within his collection. These handwritten notations are not reproduced in this volume, as they are not part of the original pamphlet. The title page of the second *Alarm* does feature minor changes from the first that enable Poole to foreground an all-caps version of her full name, "ELIZABETH POOLE," as the conduit for God's revelations. The title pages of both *Alarms* feature the same verses from Isaiah 30 and Psalm 68. The title page embedded in the second *Alarm* features verses from Ezekiel 39 (see figure 5).[234]

This volume does not reproduce the "Errata" section of the first *Alarm*. "Errata" denotes corrections made by authors and/or printers to typographical errors within the main text. They are typically added to the ends of texts so that readers may cross-reference the corrections with the original (erroneous) usages. However, to make matters of titling, dating, format, and so on even more complicated than they already are in the case of Poole's pamphlets, the corrections listed in the first *Alarm* are not for that text but for the second *Alarm* that is yet to come. Officially, the second *Alarm* succeeded the first chronologically and in terms of content. But including errata (perhaps mistakenly) for the second *Alarm* in the first confirms that the two texts were written closely together and published simultaneously. In this edition's reprint of the second *Alarm*, the corrections listed in the "Errata" are already implemented for the reader's convenience.

In 1649, there appeared a republication of *A Vision, An Alarm of War*, and the second *Alarm of War* under a new title, *A Prophecy Touching the Death of King Charles* (see figure 1). That work is not included here as it replicates the contents of the three originals. That said, it is worth noting that the reissue does contain some minor changes to the originals. The title pages of the three pamphlets are not included, even as the content of the pamphlets is virtually identical to the originals.

---

234. Poole, *An[other] Alarm*, p. 88.

The type in *A Vision* has been reset so that some words are spelled differently (e.g., "walke" vs. "walk") and some phrases that were italicized in the original are not italicized in the reprint. The first *Alarm* does not, as does the original, reprint the contents of *A Vision*, but does reprint all other sections in their original order.

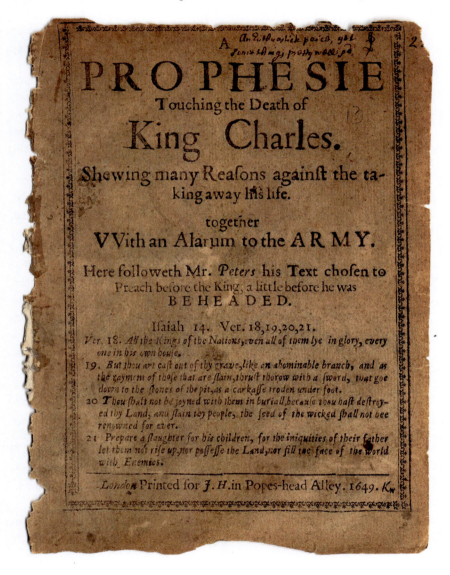

Figure 1. Title page, Anonymous, *A Prophecy Touching the Death of King Charles* (1649). Andersen Library Rare Books, University of Minnesota Libraries. Reproduced with permission.

56 *Introduction*

In appendix 3, *An Agreement of the People* is reprinted in full with the exception of a two-column chart containing the names of eighty-two counties, cities, universities, boroughs, and/or towns that the Levellers believed should be included in future election cycles so that the country could achieve a more just distribution of representatives. That list is omitted for the sake of space.

In appendix 5, *The Heads of Proposals* includes corrections of the original tract's error-ridden enumeration system of its proposals. These corrections are described in footnotes.

The printer of at least two of Poole's tracts may have been Matthew Simmons, a well-known publisher of radical texts, including a number by John Milton.[235] Unlike many pamphlets, the covers of Poole's do not name a printer. Thus, the supposition that it could be Simmons is based on other tell-tale signs. One clue lies in the fact that the title pages of the first *Alarm* and *A Prophecy Touching the Death of King Charles* state that these pamphlets were "to be sold in Popeshead Ally" (with the second *Alarm* adding that it was also to be sold in Corn-hill). The Popes-head Ally address places the printer on the same street as Hannah Allen and other booksellers who dealt in prophetic, radical, or sectarian books. Matthew Simmons was known to have printed several pamphlets for Hannah Allen.

Another clue lies in the printer's ornaments featured on the title page of *A Vision* and the page marked "Preface to the Reader" in the second *Alarm*. These ornaments are distinctive to Simmons. More circumstantial evidence favoring Simmons lies in the fact that pamphlets by other female prophets such as Anna Trapnel (*Cry of a Stone* and *A Legacy for Saints*) were also sold by Hannah Allen and feature the same ornaments. (Poole's first *Alarm* features no such ornaments; its much plainer appearance suggests it may have been printed by someone other than Simmons.)[236]

This volume contains five appendices. The first contains works that contextualize Poole's rise as a religious authority. *The Confession of Faith* puts forth the principles of the Baptist faith that influenced Poole's messages. William Kiffin's *A Brief Remonstrance* recounts the tense question-and-answer session that Kiffin, Poole's minister, had with her father, Robert Poole, after the latter complained when his daughter and servants joined Kiffin's controversial congregation. The pamphlet, *A Discovery of Six Women Preachers,* provides insight into the public

---

235. I am grateful to Maureen Bell for offering this hypothesis in an email correspondence on February 28, 2019, after closely scrutinizing Poole's pamphlets. For Simmons, see I. Gadd, "Simmons, Matthew (b. in or before 1608, d. 1654), bookseller and printer," *ODNB*.

236. As Maureen Bell noted in an email correspondence dated March 3, 2019, identifying a printer by his or her ornaments can be tricky. Printers could lend their ornaments to one another or use similar ornaments. However, in the case of the second *Alarm*, the unique ornaments featured at the top of the "Preface to the Reader" page offers especially good evidence that the printer was Simmons. This evidence is supported by the fact that he printed a number of other radical tracts during these years.

response to the new forms of female religious authority that Poole was able to access through her affiliation with the Baptist faith.

The second appendix includes works that are wholly about Elizabeth Poole. William Clarke's "General Council at Whitehall, 29 December 1648" and "General Council 5 Jan. 1648 at Whitehall" consists of the meeting minutes taken during Poole's appearances before the New Model Army's General Council of Officers as it decided whether or not to execute Charles I.

The third appendix contains works that Poole cited in her pamphlets. The excerpt from Henry Ireton's *A Remonstrance of His Excellency Thomas Lord Fairfax* (1648) contains support for regicide; the document was directly cited by Poole during her first visit to the council as the provocation for her grief over England's future. During her second appearance, Poole cites *Foundations of Freedom; or, An Agreement of the People* (1648)—the second version of the constitution that the Leveller John Lilburne wrote as an alternative to Ireton's *Heads of Proposals*—as the grounds for her opposition to the army's dissolution. The headnotes to these works in the appendices contain further explanations of their relevance to the volume along with the locations of the originals.

The fourth appendix is comprised of three anonymously written tracts containing substantial sections dedicated to Elizabeth Poole: *The Manner of the Deposition of Charles Stewart, King of England*; *To Xeiphos Ton Martyron*; and *The English Devil; or, Cromwell and His Monstrous Witch Discover'd at White-Hall.* Together they reveal the array of perspectives on Poole's character elicited by her controversial participation in the debates. While the first portrays her as a woman of wisdom, the second and third depict her as a malevolent conspirator against the kingdom and as a witch.

The fifth appendix provides two other works of interest to students of Poole. *The Heads of Proposals* is Henry Ireton's constitution for the new nation; it was circulated among the army as an alternative to the Levellers' more radical constitution. In the visions that Poole delivered during her two visits to the General Council of Officers, Poole endorsed its position that the army not immediately hand power over to the people as the Levellers wished. Francis White's *The Copies of Several Letters Contrary to the Opinion of the Present Powers* exposes us to another individual actor in the Civil Wars who, like Poole, supported the trial of the king for treason but opposed his execution.

To make this edition more accessible to modern readers, the following alterations to the texts have been implemented. Spelling and punctuation have been modernized to conform to contemporary American usage. The various spellings and/or abbreviations of Poole's name have been standardized to a single usage: Elizabeth Poole. Archaic usages such as "appealeth" and "spake" have been converted into their modern equivalents. Pronouns printed as, for example, "your selves" (yourselves) have been contracted. The original texts' use of italics for emphasis or to mark (some) Bible verses has been retained, as have capital letters for

58   *Introduction*

some proper nouns except where it proves distracting. Whereas Poole sometimes used semi-colons or colons to mark subordinate clauses or divide sentences, this edition substitutes commas or periods in places where it promotes clarity. Alternatively, while Poole sometimes uses commas in ways that make it difficult to discern her meaning, this edition omits those commas.

The dates in this volume have been modernized. This is because the calendar we use today is of relatively recent invention. In Roman times, the Julian calendar was used. In this calendar, as in today's, the new year began on January 1. This calendar was used in England until the twelfth century, when a different calendar was introduced. In this calendar, the new year was changed to begin on March 25, also known as "Lady Day" because it marks the celebration of the Annunciation of Christ's birth to the Virgin Mary. For a time, both the Julian calendar and this other calendar, now known as the "Old Style calendar," were used. But in 1582, the Gregorian or New Style calendar was adopted. In this calendar, the start of the new year was reset to January 1, as under the Julian calendar. However, in England, Wales, Ireland, and the British colonies, the changeover from the Old Style to the New Style calendar did not occur until 1750 (in Scotland not until 1752). For the sake of consistency and clarity, this volume translates Old Style dates, where they are used, into New Style dates. So, for example, when texts using the Old Style calendar mark the execution of Charles I as having taken place on January 30, 1648, this volume uses the New Style calendar to change it to January 30, 1649. An exception is made for the cover pages of the primary texts. On these reproductions, the original dates are retained and footnotes are used to provide the New Style date.

In the absence of information about which version of the Bible Poole used, the Geneva Bible has been chosen as the source for her numerous biblical quotations and allusions. The Geneva Bible was produced in the late sixteenth century by English dissenters who had taken up residence in Geneva, Switzerland. I use it here both because it was known to have become the Bible of choice for many religious dissenters such as Poole and because the wording of Poole's citations or paraphrases frequently approximates the Geneva Bible as or more closely than any other version, including the King James version.[237] Exceptions to this general rule are noted in footnotes. The spelling in scriptures quoted from both the Geneva Bible and the King James Bible has also been standardized to reflect contemporary American usage.

Changes have been made to the formatting of scriptural citations in *The Confession of Faith*, contained in appendix 1. In the original, scriptural citations are assigned a letter within the main text (e.g., "a," "b," "c," etc.)—almost like a footnote—with the citation itself appearing in the right- or left-hand margin of the main text. Because of the difficulty of reproducing that format here, this volume moves all marginal citations into the footnotes.

---

237. David Daniell, *The Bible in English: History and Influence* (New Haven, CT: Yale University Press, 2003).

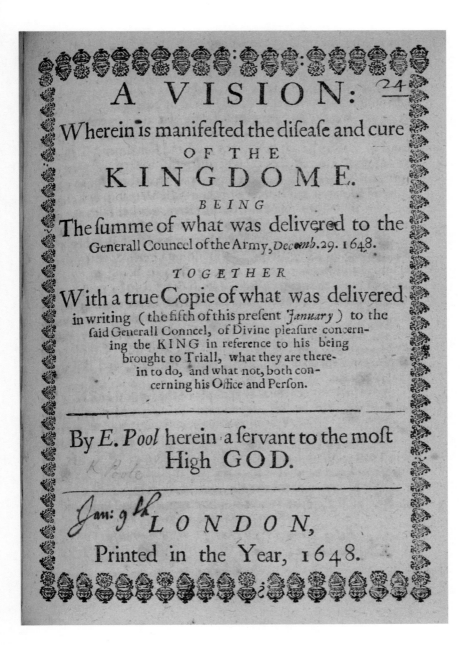

Figure 2. Title page, Elizabeth Poole, *A Vision: Wherein Is Manifested the Disease and Cure of the Kingdom* (1649). British Library. Reproduced with permission.

A VISION:
Wherein is manifested the disease and cure
of the
KINGDOM.
BEING
The sum of what was delivered to the
General Council of the Army, *December 29, 1648*.[1]

TOGETHER
With a true Copy of what was delivered
in writing (the fifth of this present January) *to the*
said General Council, of Divine pleasure concern-
ing the KING in reference to his being
brought to Trial, what they are there-
in to do, and what not, both con-
cerning his Office and Person.

By E. Poole, herein a servant to the most
High GOD.

LONDON,
Printed in the Year, 1648.
The Sum of What was Delivered to the
Council of War, December 29, 1648.[2]

---

1. The year printed on the cover reflects the Old Style calendar. The New Style year is 1649.

2. The date of the first of Poole's two visits to the army's General Council at which the council discussed the fate of the king and the future government of England. The year reflects the Old Style calendar. The New Style year is 1649.

A Vision: Wherein Is Manifested the Disease and Cure of the Kingdom 61

Sirs,

I have been (by the pleasure of the most High) made sensible of the distresses of this land[3] and also a sympathizer with you in your labors: for having sometimes read your *Remonstrance*,[4] I was for many days made a sad mourner for her; the pangs of a travailing woman[5] were upon me, and the pangs of death oft-times panging me, being a member of her body of whose dying state I was made purely sensible.[6] And after many days mourning, a vision was set before me, to show her cure, and the manner of it by this similitude:[7] a man who is a member of the army, having sometimes much bewailed her state, saying, *he could gladly be a sacrifice for her*, was set before me, presenting[8] the body of the army, and on the other hand, a woman crooked, sick, weak, and imperfect in body, to present unto me the weak and imperfect state of the kingdom. I, having the gift of faith upon me for her cure, was thus to appeal to the person on the other hand, that he should improve his faithfulness to the kingdom by using diligence for the cure of this woman, as I by the gift of faith upon me should direct him.[9] Nevertheless, it is not the gift of faith in me, say I, nor the act of diligence in you, but a dependence on the divine will which calls me to believe and you to act. Wherefore I being called

---

3. The Civil Wars and ideological conflicts over crown and church.

4. *A Remonstrance of His Excellency Thomas Lord Fairfax, Lord General of the Parliament's Forces, and of the General Council of Officers* (London: 1648), the document written by army officer Henry Ireton, which argues that the people have the right to try the king and sentence him to death for waging war on his own subjects. See appendix 3, pp. 155–160.

5. A woman in "travail" or labor. A possible reference to Revelation 12:1–2, GV: "And there appeared a great wonder in heaven: a woman clothed with the sun, & the moon was under her feet, and upon her head a crown of twelve stars. And she was with child and cried travailing in birth, and was pained ready to be delivered." This "woman in the wilderness" was often interpreted as a figure for the true church, whose delivery of the chosen man-child had to be accomplished in the midst of battle with the great Satanic dragon.

6. Made aware of the body's dying state, to the point of sharing that state, because as a member of the body politic herself, Poole too experiences its "senses."

7. A comparison or metaphor.

8. Representing or standing for.

9. A reference to 1 Corinthians 12:4–11: "Now there are diversities of gifts but the same spirit. And there are diversities of administrations, but the same Lord. And there are diversities of operations but God is the same which works all in all. But the manifestation of the Spirit is given to every man to profit withal. For to one is given by the Spirit the word of wisdom and to another of knowledge, by the same Spirit. And to another is given faith, by the same Spirit and to another the gifts of healing by the same Spirit. And to another the operations of repeat works and to another prophecy and to another the discerning of spirits and to another diversities of tongues and to another the interpretation of tongues. And to all these things works even the selfsame Spirit, distributing to every man severally as he will. For as the body is one and has many members and all the members of the body, which is one, though they be many, yet are but one body, even so is Christ" (GV).

62 ELIZABETH POOLE

to believe ought not to stagger,[10] neither you being called to act should be slack; for look how far you come short of acting (as before the Lord for her cure), not according to the former rule by men prescribed for cure but according to the direction of the gift of faith in me, so far shall you come short of her consolation and look how far you shall act, as before the Lord, with diligence for her cure, you shall be made partakers of her consolation.

She being after demanded,[11] *Whether she had any direction to give the Council?* She answered, *no, for the present, for she was in this case presented to herself as the church which spirit is in you and shall guide you.*

I am therefore to signify unto you that there is but one step between you and restoration, the which whosoever take not warily shall stumble and fall and be taken,[12] and that is this, you are to stand as in the presence of the Lord, to be dead unto all your own interests, lives, liberties, freedoms[13] or whatsoever you might call yours, yet pleading for them still with men, speaking to everyone in his own language, for they are your due with them; but except you are as ready to resign them up to the will of the eternal pleasure, as to plead them with men, you shall surely lose them,[14] *For he that will save his life shall lose it, and he that will lose it shall save it.*[15]

The Lord has a controversy with the great and mighty men of earth, with the captains, and rulers, and governors.[16] You may be great and mighty upon the

---

10. The term "stagger" is used several times in the King James Bible to denote the idea that those without faith stagger like drunken men because they are unable to act with straightforward conviction. As Job 12:25, KJV, reads: "They grope in the dark without light, and he makes them to stagger like a drunken man." Alternatively, those who possess faith are able to move firmly forward and act with strength. As Romans 4:20, KJV, reads: "He staggered not at the promise of God through unbelief; but was strong in faith, giving glory to God."

11. Asked.

12. Psalm 27:2, GV: "When the wicked, even my own enemies and my foes come upon me to eat up my flesh, they stumbled and fell."

13. An echo of advice delivered by Paul to the Philippians in chapter 2, verse 3, GV: "That nothing be done through contention or vain glory, but that in meekness of mind every man esteem other better than himself."

14. The pronoun "them" refers to the aforementioned "lives, liberties, freedoms, or whatsoever" that the army must sacrifice in order to perform its proper duty of protecting the people.

15. A citation of Mark 8:35, GV, Luke 9:24 and 17:33, GV, Matthew 16:25, GV, and John 12:25, GV. In each of these gospels, Jesus is reported to have delivered this declaration to his disciples so as to emphasize to them that if they wish to take up the cross on his behalf, they must be prepared to lose their lives. Doing so, however, will guarantee them eternal salvation.

16. Revelation 6:14–17, GV: "And heaven departed away as a scroll when it is rolled and every mountain and isle were over out of their paces. And the Kings of the earth and the great men and the rich men and the chief captains and the mighty men and every bond man and every free man hid themselves in dens and among the rocks of the mountains and said to the mountains and rocks, 'Fall on us

A Vision: Wherein Is Manifested the Disease and Cure of the Kingdom 63

earth, and maintain his controversy, but against the mighty men of the earth is his controversy held; for as you are the potsherd of the earth, he will surely break you to pieces until there be not a sherd left to carry coals on.[17] The kingly power is undoubtedly fallen into your hands, therefore my advice is that you take heed to improve it for the Lord. You have justly blamed those who have gone before you for betraying their trust therein.[18] I speak not this as you are soldiers but as the spirit of judgment and justice is most lively appearing in you; this is therefore the great work which lies upon you, to become dead to every pleasant picture which might present itself for your delight, that perfectly dying in the will of the Lord you may find your resurrection in him.

She being afterwards asked by some of the chief officers, *Whether she conceived they were called to deliver up the trust to them committed either to Parliament or people?* She answered, *No, for this reason, it being committed to their care and trust, it should certainly be required at their hands, but take them with you as younger brethren who may be helpful to you. Nevertheless know that you are in the place of watchmen, wherefore slack not your watch over them, for the account of the stewardship shall be required at your hand.*[19]

It was further said unto her, "*How then shall we be free from the aspersions of the people, who will be ready to judge that we improve this interest for our own ends?*" She answered, *Set yourselves as before the Lord to discharge the trust committed to you and trust him with your reward. I speak not this that you should be exalted above your brethren, but that you might stand in faithfulness to discharge your duty, For he that will save his life shall lose it, and he that will lose it shall save it.*[20] You have been noblemen, behaving your selves with much valor and courage (as among men), now therefore lose not your reward for this will be the greatest piece of courage that ever you were made the examples of if you shall be as well contented to lose house, land, wife and children, or whatever you might call yours in divine will, as ever you were to lay down your lives in the field.[21]

---

and hide us from the presence of him that sits on the throne and from the wrath of the Lamb. For the great deal of his wrath is come and who can stand?'"

17. Isaiah 45:9, GV: "Woe be unto him that strives with his maker, the potsherd with the potsherds of the earth: shall the clay say to him that fashions it, 'What makes you? or thy work, it hath no hands?'"

18. A reference to the king and his court who preceded the army in power but betrayed the trust they had been given by God to put the people's lives and interests before their own. The army must not make the same mistake.

19. 1 Corinthians 4, KJV: "Let a man so account of us, as of the ministers of Christ, and stewards of the mysteries of God."

20. Mark 8:35, Luke 9:24 and 17:33, Matthew 16:25, and John 12:25.

21. In warfare, on the battlefield.

64 ELIZABETH POOLE

Sirs,[22]

I have considered *An Agreement of the People*[23] that is before you, and I am very jealous[24] lest you should betray your trust in it (in as much as the kingly power is fallen into your hands) in giving it up to the people; for thereby you give up the trust committed to you and in so doing you will prove yourselves more treacherous than they that went before you, they being in no way able to improve it without you. You justly blame the king for betraying his trust and the Parliament for betraying theirs. This is the greatest thing I have to say to you: betray not you your trust.

I have yet another message to show you. I know not what acceptance it may find with you, yet I am content, here it is, let it find what acceptance it may. I leave it with you.[25]

The message is as follows.

Dear Sirs,

Having already found so free admission into your presence, it has given me the greater encouragement (though, more peculiarly, the truth persuading me thereunto) to present you with my thoughts in these following lines. I am in divine pleasure made sensible of the might of the affairs that lie upon you and the spirit of sympathy abiding in me constrains me to groan with you in your pains.[26] You may remember I told you the kingly power is undoubtedly fallen into your hands, which power is to punish evildoers and to praise them that do well.[27] Now therefore my humble advice to you is that you stand as in the awful presence of the most high Father, acting your parts before God and man. You stand in the place of interpreters, for many hard sayings present themselves to you, and will do, look for it; wherefore see that you give unto men the things that are theirs and

---

22. Poole's salutation marks the beginning of her second visit to the council on January 5.

23. *Foundations of Freedom; Or, An Agreement of the People*, crafted by the Levellers and intended to serve as a constitution and bill of rights for a new English republic. See appendix 3, pp. 160–174.

24. The term "jealous" is being used in relation to its cognate "zealous," or passionately desirous, as it is derived from the word "yeast" and its attendant verb, "to boil, ferment" (*OED*).

25. Poole's second message appears to have been written upon a piece of paper that she first read aloud to the council and then handed out to one or more of the members before departing.

26. A continuation of the comparison of the army to a woman in painful labor, struggling to give birth to a new political order in England, and to herself as both a sympathizer in that endeavor—a midwife or "gossip"—as well as a fellow laborer whose visions are intended to help shape the future.

27. A reference to 1 Peter 2:13–14, GV, in which Peter commands Christ's followers, "Submit yourselves unto all manner or ordinance of man for the Lord's sake, whether it be unto the king, as unto the superior, Or unto governors, as unto them you are sent of him for the punishment of evildoers, and for the praise of them that do well."

A Vision: Wherein Is Manifested the Disease and Cure of the Kingdom   65

unto God the things that are his.[28] It is true indeed, as unto men (I know that I appeal by the gift of God upon me) the king is your father and husband who you were to and are to obey in the Lord and no other way.[29] For when he forgot his subordination to divine faith-hood and headship, thinking he had begotten you a generation to his own pleasure and taking you as a wife for his own lusts,[30] thereby is the yoke taken from your necks.[31] I mean the neck of the spirit and law which is the bond of your union, that the holy light in it might not be profaned, it being free and unable to be bound: *For the law of the spirit of life in Christ Jesus has freed us from the law of sin and of death,* for the letter of the law which speaks to the flesh that kills, therefore you must suffer of men in the flesh, for the Lord's sake, that so dying to your own bodies (that is to all self interest in divine will) you might also receive your resurrection, for you must die before you rise.[32] You must lose your lives, interests, liberties, and all (before you can save them), casting your crown at the feet of the Lamb who only is worthy,[33] yet still pleading for them with men, for they are your due with them, a share they may not deny you. *Blessed are*

28. Matthew 12:21, GV: "Then said he unto them, 'Give therefore to Caesar, the things which are Caesar's, and give unto God, those which are God's.'"

29. The qualifying phrase, "in the Lord and no other way," is a direct echo of the Baptists' *The Confession of Faith* (appendix 1, p. 123).

30. The king violated God's law by serving his own lust for power and pleasure rather than honoring the people in the way that, according to Paul, Christ was to honor the church as his bride. See Ephesians 5:25–28, GV: "Husbands, love your wives, even as Christ loved the church and gave himself for it. That he might sanctify it and cleanse it by the washing of water through the word. That he might make it unto himself a glorious Church, not having a spot or wrinkle, or any such thing: but that it should be holy and without blame. So ought men to love their wives, as their own bodies: he that loves his wife, loves himself."

31. The term "yoke" refers to the implement that binds two oxen together into a team, not unlike the contracts that bind husband and wife and king and subject into a single unit. It may also be a reference to the "Norman Yoke," a derogatory term used by a number of English radicals, including the Levellers, to refer to what they viewed as the state of bondage forced upon the English by the 1066 Norman invasion of Anglo-Saxon England, when an ostensibly more French and hence absolutist style of monarchy was introduced.

32. Romans 8:2–8, GV: "For the Law of the Spirit of life *which is* in Christ Jesus, has freed me from the law of sin and death. For (that was impossible to the Law, inasmuch as it was weak, because of the flesh) God sending his own Son, in the similitude of sinful flesh, and for sin, condemned in the flesh. That the righteousness of the Law might be fulfilled in us, which walks not after the flesh, but after the Spirit. For they that are after the flesh, savor the things of the flesh: but they that are after the Spirit, the things of the spirit. For the wisdom of the flesh *is* death: but the wisdom of the Spirit *is* life and peace. Because one wisdom of the flesh is enmity against God: for it is not subject to the Law of God, neither indeed can be. So then they that are in the flesh, can not please God."

33. Revelation 4:10–11, GV: "The four and twenty elders fall down before him that sat on the throne, and worship him, that lives for ever more, and cast their crowns before the throne, saying, 'You are worthy, O Lord, to receive glory and honor and power: for you have created all things, and for your will's sake they are and have been created.'" These verses are part of the more extensive prophecy in

the dead which die in the Lord, for they rest from their labors, and their works do follow them.[34]

From your own labors, I wish you rest in the Lord, that the fruit of your labors which is the life of your faith may follow you to prison and to death; know this, that true liberty either is not bound to anything, nor from anything, for it is subject to this or that (neither this nor that in divine will). Nevertheless as from the Lord you have all that you have and are, so to the Lord you owe all that you have and are for his own namesake. So from the king in subordination.

You have all that you have and are, and also in subordination you owe him all that you have and are, and although he would not be your father and husband, subordinate but absolute, yet know that you are for the Lord's sake to honor his person. For he is the father and husband of your bodies, as unto men, and therefore your right cannot be without him, as unto men. I know and am very sensible that no small straight lies upon you in respect of securing his person (for the manifold conceived inconveniences following and the necessities of evil event) in respect of raising more wars, and also other things well known to you that will present themselves impossible for you to avoid; nevertheless this is my humble and hearty prayer to the everlasting Father (which I present to you in words that you may be edified thereby). Remember I said everlasting Father, for so we shall know him for our consolation[35] that it might please him of his infinite, eternal life and goodness to grant you a sure and certain knowledge of this, that all things which are impossible with men (at the utmost extent of impossibility) are possible with him who only says it and it comes to pass, the Lord of hosts, the God of the whole earth who commands all hosts of men, angels and devils, whose eyes run to and fro throughout the face of the whole earth, to show himself strong in the behalf of all those that trust in him.[36] Wherefore put your swords into his hands for your defense and fear not to act the part of Abigail, seeing Nabal had refused it (by appropriating his goods to himself) in relieving David and his men in their

---

Revelation 4, which predicts that, in the end-times, the beasts will be defeated when the council of ruling elders cedes its power to God.

34. Revelation 14:13, GV: "Then I heard a voice from heaven, saying unto me, Write, Blessed *are* the dead which hereafter die in the Lord. Even so says the Spirit, for they rest from their labors, and their works follow them."

35. 2 Thessalonians 2:16–17, GV: "Now the same Jesus Christ our Lord and our God, even the Father which has loved us, and has given us everlasting consolation and good hope through grace, Comfort your hearts and establish you in every word and good works."

36. 2 Chronicles 16:9, GV: "For the eyes of the LORD behold all the earth to show himself strong with them that are of perfect heart toward him: though have then done foolishly in this: and therefore from henceforth you shall have wars." This verse is extracted from the history of Asa, the king of Judah, who formed an alliance with the Syrian king, Benhadad, in order to fend off encroachments from his Jewish rival, Baasha, the king of Israel. Because Asa turned to a Syrian king to guarantee the safety and expansion of his kingdom rather than to God, he was punished. As he is told, "Herein thou hast done foolishly: therefore from henceforth thou shalt have wars."

A Vision: Wherein Is Manifested the Disease and Cure of the Kingdom 67

distress. It was to her praise, it shall be to yours, fear it not; only consider, that as she lifted not her hand against her husband to take his life, no more do you against yours.[37]

For as the Lord revenged his own cause on him, he shall do on yours; *For vengeance is mine, I will repay it, says the Lord*,[38] who made him the Savior of your body, though he has profaned his Savior-ship. Stretch not forth the hand against him,[39] for know this, the Conquest was not without divine pleasure whereby kings came to reign, though through lust they tyrannized, which God excuses not but judges and his judgments are fallen heavy, as you see, upon *Charles* your Lord.[40] Forget not your pity toward him for you were given him a helper in the body of the people, which people are they that agreed with him to subject unto the punishment of evildoers and the praise of them that do well, which law is the spirit of your union, and although this bond be broken on his part.

You never heard that a wife might put away her husband as he is the head of her body, but for the Lord's sake suffers his terror to her flesh though she be free in the spirit of the Lord. And he being incapable to act as her husband, she acts in his stead, and having the spirit of union abiding in her, she considers him in his temptations, as tempted with him. And if he will usurp over her, she appeals to the fatherhood for her offense, which is the spirit of justice and is in you. For I know no power in England to whom it is committed, save yourselves (and the present Parliament), which are to act in the church of Christ, as she by the gift of faith upon her, shall be your guide for the cure of her body, that you might therefore commit an unsound member to Satan (though the head) as it is flesh, that the spirit might be saved in the day of the Lord (I believe).[41] And accordingly

37. A reference to incidents recorded in 1 Samuel 25 that, as noted in the introduction (pp. 39–40), involved Abigail, David, and Nabal.

38. Romans 12:19, GV: "Vengeance is mine: I will repay, says the Lord."

39. 1 Samuel 26:9–11, GV: "And David said to Abishai, 'Destroy him not: for who can lay his hand on the Lord's anointed, and be guiltless?' Moreover David said, 'As the Lord lives, either the Lord shall smite him, or his day shall come to die, or he shall defend into battle and perish. The Lord keep me from laying my hand upon the Lord's anointed: but, I pray thee, take now the spear that is at his head, and the pot of water, and let us go hence.'"

40. An allusion to the moment in 1 Samuel 8 when, after Samuel's corrupt sons failed to live up to their father's high standards as a judge, the Jews requested that Samuel provide them with a king. Samuel was displeased, as was God, who believed that in casting Samuel away, the Jews had also, as he said, "cast me away, that I should not reign over them" (8:7, GV). God's worst fears were confirmed when Saul, the man who was finally appointed as king, turned out to be a tyrant. The term "Conquest" is another possible reference to the "Norman Conquest."

41. As discussed in the introduction (pp. 40–41), the idea of committing an unsound member of the body to Satan, even if it is the head itself, echoes the Baptists' model of divorce. The implication is not that the king's head should be literally cut off but rather that it (he) should be consigned by God to eternal damnation.

you may hold the hands of your husband that he pierce not your bowels with a knife or sword to take your life. Neither may you take his. I speak unto you as men, fathers, and brethren in the Lord (who are to walk by his rule): *Whatsoever you would that men should do unto you, do you the same unto them.*[42] I know it would affright you to be cut off in your iniquity, but O, how fain would you have your iniquity taken away![43] Consider also others in their amazement.[44] I know you have said it and I believe that if you could see suitable sorrow for so great offense you should embrace it. I beseech you in the bowels of love for there it is I plead with you, look upon the patience of God toward you and see if it will not constrain you to forbearance for his sake. I know the spirit of sanctity is in you and I know as well the spirit of bondage holds you oft-times that you cannot but groan for deliverance. Wherefore I beseech you for the Lord's sake, whose I am and whom I serve in the spirit, that you let not go the vision that I showed you concerning the cure of *England*, as it was presented to me. Wherein the party acting, being first required to stand as in the awful presence of God and to act for her cure according to the direction that he should receive from the church, by the gift of faith upon her. Act he must, but not after any former rule by men prescribed for cure but after the rule of the gift of faith, which I humbly beseech the Almighty Lord to establish in you. I rest,

Your servant in the Church and
Kingdom of Christ,

Elizabeth Poole.

After the delivery of this, she was asked *whether she spoke against the bringing of him to trial or against their taking of his life.*

She answered, *bring him to trial, that he may be convicted in his conscience, but touch not his person.*

FINIS.

42. The so-called Golden Rule, attributed in the Christian tradition to Jesus of Nazareth, as he is quoted as reciting it in Matthew 7:12, GV ("Therefore whatsoever you would that men should do to you, even so do you to them, for this is the Law and the Prophets"), Luke 6:31, GV ("And as you would that men should do to you, so do you to the likewise"), and Luke 10:27, GV ("And he answered, and said, You shall love thy Lord God with all your heart, and with all your soul, and with all your strength, and with all your thought, and your neighbor as your self").

43. To be separated from God due to one's sins, a condition that can only be remedied through repentance. This idea is referred to throughout the Bible, but the wording of this warning to the council most directly recalls Isaiah 59:2, GV ("But your iniquities have separated between you and your God, and your sins have hid his face from you, that he will not hear") and Psalm 94:20, GV ("Has the throne of iniquity fellowship with you, which forgoes wrong for a law?").

44. The army's General Council must take into account how amazed or horrified many members of the public would be if the council actually executed the king.

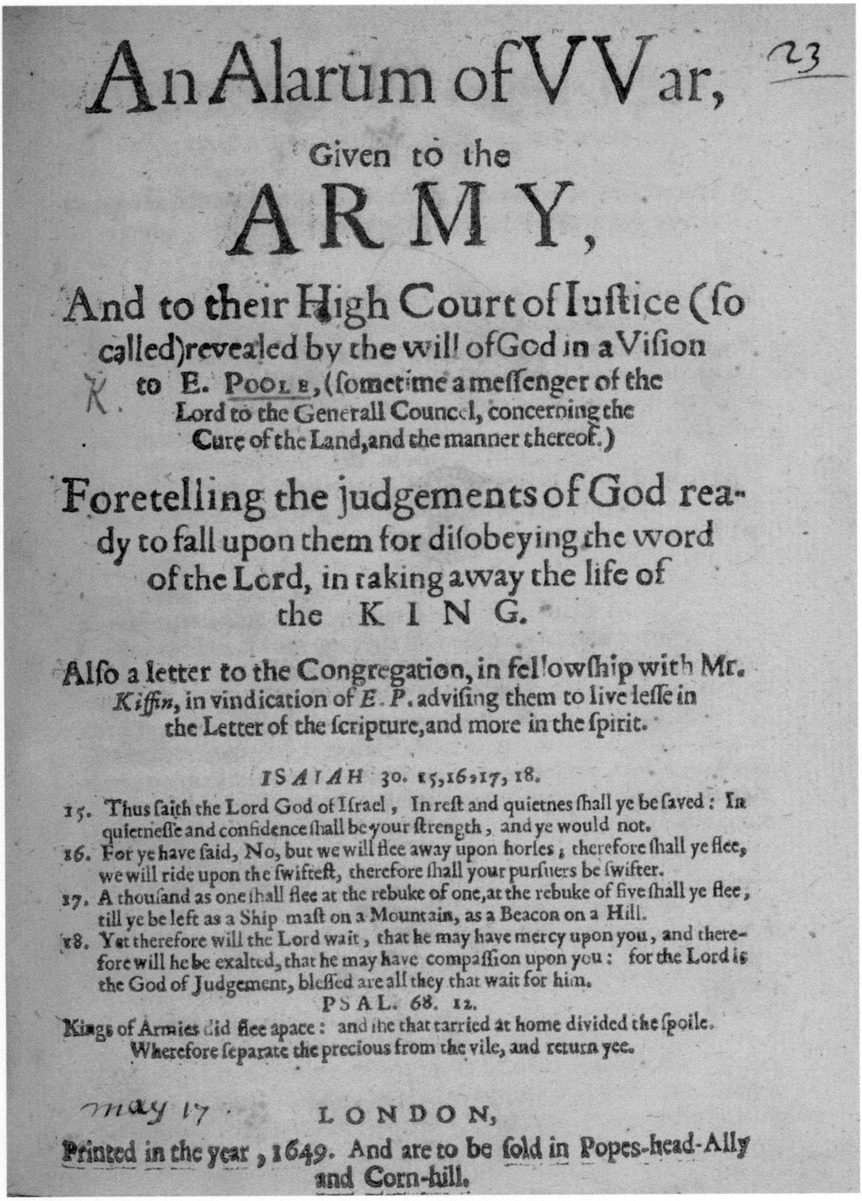

An Alarum of VVar,

Given to the

ARMY,

And to their High Court of Iustice (so
called)revealed by the will of God in a Vision
to E. POOLE, (sometime a messenger of the
Lord to the Generall Councel, concerning the
Cure of the Land, and the manner thereof.)

Foretelling the judgements of God ready to fall upon them for disobeying the word
of the Lord, in taking away the life of
the KING.

Also a letter to the Congregation, in fellowship with Mr.
Kiffin, in vindication of *E.P.* advising them to live lesse in
the Letter of the scripture, and more in the spirit.

ISAIAH 30. 15,16,17, 18.

15. Thus saith the Lord God of Israel, In rest and quietnes shall ye be saved: In
quietnesse and confidence shall be your strength, and ye would not.

16. For ye have said, No, but we will flee away upon horses; therefore shall ye flee,
we will ride upon the swiftest, therefore shall your pursuers be swifter.

17. A thousand as one shall flee at the rebuke of one, at the rebuke of five shall ye flee,
till ye be left as a Ship mast on a Mountain, as a Beacon on a Hill.

18. Yet therefore will the Lord wait, that he may have mercy upon you, and therefore will he be exalted, that he may have compassion upon you: for the Lord is
the God of Judgement, blessed are all they that wait for him.

PSAL. 68. 12.

Kings of Armies did flee apace: and she that tarried at home divided the spoile.
Wherefore separate the precious from the vile, and return yee.

may 17   LONDON,
Printed in the year, 1649. And are to be sold in Popes-head-Ally
and Corn-hill.

Figure 3. Title page, Elizabeth Poole, *An Alarm of War* (1649). British Library.
Reproduced with permission.

An Alarm of War,[45]
Given to the
ARMY,
and to Their High Court of Justice (so
Called) Revealed by the Will of God in a Vision
to E. Poole (sometimes a messenger of the
Lord to the General Council, concerning the
Cure of the Land, and the Manner Thereof.)
Foretelling the judgments of God ready
to fall upon them for disobeying the word
of the Lord, in the taking away the life of
the KING.

Also a letter to the Congregation, in Fellowship with Mr.
Kiffin, in vindication of *E. P.,* advising them to live less in
the Letter of the scripture, and more in the spirit.

ISAIAH 30:15, 16, 17, 18.

15. Thus said the Lord God of Israel, in rest and quietness shall you be saved; In
quietness and confidence shall be your strength, and you would not.

16. For you have said, No, but we will flee away upon horses; therefore shall ye
flee, we will ride upon the swiftest, therefore shall your pursuers be swifter.

17. A thousand as one shall flee at the rebuke of one, at the rebuke of five shall ye
flee, until you be left as a ship mast on a mountain, as a Beacon on a Hill.

18. Yet therefore will the Lord wait, that He may have mercy upon you: for the
Lord is the God of Judgment, blessed are all they that wait for him.[46]

---

45. Poole's title is a reference to Jeremiah 4:19, one of the most important books of prophecy in the Old
Testament. Her wording here is closer to the King James Bible than to the Geneva Bible: "My bowels,
my bowels! I am pained at my very heart; my heart makes a noise in me; I cannot hold my peace,
because you have heard, O my soul, the sound of the trumpet, the alarm of war." Jeremiah delivered
this passage as part of his sustained warning to the Jews that they would suffer severe punishment,
including the destruction of Jerusalem, for their impious acts of idolatry, covetousness, lying, cruelty,
rebellion, and general disdain for God's word. By using the phrase "alarm of war" as her title, Poole
tells her readers that she is serving the army's General Council and the members of its High Court
of Justice her own "jeremiad," that is, a mode of writing named after Jeremiah because it consists of
warnings of the suffering that awaits those who violate God's strictures.

46. Like the book of Jeremiah, Isaiah consists of prophecies that both warn the Israelites of the destruction they will incur for their infidelity to God's laws and promise them redemption. The passages from

PSALM 68:12

Kings of armies did flee apace: and she that tarried at home divided the spoils. Wherefore separate the precious from the vile, and return ye.[47]

LONDON

Printed in the year, 1649. And are to be sold in Popes-head Alley and Corn-hill.

A Friend to Truth and of the Authors to the Reader[48]

The occasion of the next ensuing letter (written by T. P. in vindication of the author) was this: the author, Mrs. E. Poole, having delivered a message of the Lord to the General Council of the Army forewarning them against that great sin, foretold of by the apostle to be the sin of these latter days, viz.[49] self love,[50] the forsaking of which would be a great stop and let to the Independent design, viz. the taking away of the life of the king.[51] There arose diverse false witnesses,[52] viz. W. K.,

---

Isaiah 30 quoted here refer to God's inveighing against the Jews for seeking the Egyptian Pharaoh's protection rather than God's.

47. While the first sentence in this citation is from Psalm 68:12, GV, the second is yet another threat derived from Jeremiah 15:19, GV: "Therefore thus says the LORD, If you return, then will I bring you again, and you shall stand before me: and if you take forth the precious from the vile, you shall be as my mouth: let them return unto you; but return not you unto them."

48. The first six pages of *An Alarm* consist of a reprint of Poole's first pamphlet, *A Vision: Wherein Is Manifested the Disease and Cure of the Kingdom*. As discussed in the introduction (p. 53), because that document has already been included in this edition, the following transcription of *An Alarm* begins with "A Friend to Truth and of the Authors to the Readers," the second section of the pamphlet, which starts on page 7 in the original. As also noted in the introduction (pp. 43–44), T. P. is presumed to be Thomasine Pendarves, the wife of John Pendarves, the minister of the Baptist congregation which Poole joined after being excommunicated from Kiffin's.

49. Latin abbreviation for *videlicet*, a contraction of the Latin phrase *videre licet*, meaning "it is permitted to see." Commonly used as a synonym for "namely" or "that is."

50. 2 Timothy 1–2 predicts that the greatest threat in the final days will be men's self-love: "This know also, that in the last days shall come perilous times. For men shall be lovers of their own selves, covetous, boasters, proud, cursed speakers, disobedient to parents, unthankful, unholy" (GV).

51. A reference to the fact that many leading members of Independent churches favored the execution of the king, a position that placed them at odds with the Levellers. Leading Independents who supported the regicide included members of Poole's own former Baptist congregation, most notably Kiffin, who was one of Cromwell's major allies and the most likely culprit for arranging the excommunication of Poole.

52. An allusion to the idea, put forth in numerous scriptures, that in the end-times there would be many false prophets who would try to mislead believers. As Matthew 24:24, GV, reads, "For there shall arise false Christs, and false prophets, and shall show great signs and wonders, so that if it were possible, they should deceive the very elect." Relatedly, in Revelation, it is said that there will be "two witnesses" whose prophesies would prove true. As Revelation 11:3, GV, states, "But I will give power

72 ELIZABETH POOLE

Mr. P. and Mr. John Fountaine,[53] but none of these stood to the public test but Mr. Fountaine, who endeavoring to weaken the message by scandalizing and reproaching the messenger, charged her with some follies committed years ago and long since repented of, and with other things she knew not.[54] The old serpentine trick now revived, but in a finer dress, for it is not unknown to you (good Reader) how the Lord Christ when in flesh was called a glutton, a wine bibber, a friend of publicans and harlots, and shall Christ in spirit think you fare any better?[55] As also you are not ignorant of that place in Matthew 13:25 where it says *the Kingdom of Heaven is likened unto a man who sowed good seed in his field, but while his men slept his enemy came and sowed tares among the wheat and went his way.*[56] This man is the Lord from heaven who sends his servant to sow right good seed, viz. wheat, the word of God, the Child Jesus, in his field even your hearts, but while you sleep the enemy comes (the Devil, the accuser of the brethren who always comes in a sleeping time in the night and dark understandings of men when they are commanded from him to watch) and stealthily sows tares among the wheat, on purpose to choke the wheat or at least to cause it to be despised. Upon the

---

unto my two witnesses, & they shall prophesy a thousand two hundred, and threescore days, clothed in a sack cloth." It is probably the case that Poole imagines herself as one of Revelation's two witnesses, which means that those who try to paint her as a "false witness" are merely revealing *themselves* to be such.

53. W. K. are the initials for William Kiffin. "Mr. P." is John Pendarves. While the third false witness, John Fountaine, is fully named by Poole, his presence on this list is more difficult to explain. The one "John Fountaine" who appears in the *ODNB* was a judge who, while a Royalist, was critical of the established church and championed a more Presbyterian style of government. If this is the person being referred to here, then it's possible to surmise that his general sympathy for a moderate form of religious Independency explains his appearance in Poole's milieu. But it also appears to be the case that he earned his appearance on Poole's list of false witnesses because he joined forces with those who tried to ruin her reputation as a prophet. In other words, despite his sympathy for Independency, he for some reason opposed Poole. See D. A. Orr, "Fountaine, John (1600–1671)," *ODNB*.

54. While, as mentioned in the previous footnote, Fountaine's inclusion on Poole's list of "false witnesses" is difficult to explain with existing evidence, her wording suggests that he was particularly successful at damaging her reputation, the implication being that he was the one who resurrected some sort of sexual exploit from her past. She does not deny his charge but downplays it by characterizing it as "some follies" she committed in her youth and already repented.

55. Here Poole compares Fountain's tactic of accusing her of sexual slander to the Pharisees' attempt to delegitimate Jesus as a prophet by claiming that, unlike the temperate John the Baptist, Jesus wallowed in the pleasures of the body and the company of degenerates. As Matthew 11:19, GV, reports, "The Son of man came eating and drinking, and they say, Behold a glutton and a drinker of wine, a friend unto Publicans and sinners: but wisdom is justified of her children." See also Luke 7, GV: "The son of man is come, and eats and drinks, and you say, Behold, a man which is a glutton and a drinker of wine, a friend of Publicans and sinners."

56. Matthew 13:25, GV: "But while men slept, there came his enemies, and sowed tares among the wheat, and went his way."

instant of time when Christ was born in the flesh, King Herod, fearing his kingdom and government should be taken away from him, sent forth and slew all the children that were in Bethlehem and in all the coasts thereof.[57] This was a figure of that which was to come, to be done upon the first appearance of Christ in spirit, for as the child of the bond-woman did persecute the child of the free-woman, so they that are born after the flesh do persecute them that are born after the spirit, and the firstborn of the former will persecute them that come in the power of the most high.[58] You know the story in the 12th of the Revelation of the woman clothed with the sun and being with child, cried travailing in birth and pained to be delivered, and a great red dragon having seven heads etc., stood before the woman to devour her child as soon as it was born.[59] The issue of it was the great dragon was cast out, the old serpent called the Devil and Satan the accuser of the brethren, and I make no question but the same effect it shall have upon some. I pray, let these things be considered by you, the Lord himself makes application of this in due time to the hearts of these refined persecutors.[60]

Farewell.

The copy of a letter, as it was sent from T. P., a friend of Mrs. Elizabeth Poole, *to the congregation of saints, walking in fellowship with Mr.* William Kiffin.

Dear brethren in the bowels of love and meekness, I kindly salute you, wishing you an increase of all faithfulness and true knowledge in the mystery of Christ. The cause of my present writing is to acquaint you that providence has lately brought a letter to my hand, directed to my husband, concerning one Mrs. Poole,

57. An allusion to the so-called Slaughter of the Innocents as recounted in Matthew 2:16, when Herod, after hearing the wise men tell of the star that signified the birth of the child who would displace him as the King of the Jews, ordered the death of all males under the age of two: "Then Herod, seeing he was mocked of by Wise men, was exceeding wroth [angry], and sent forth, and slew all the male children that were in Bethlehem, and in all the costs thereof, from two year olds and under, according to the time which he had diligently searched out of the Wise men" (GV).

58. An allusion to Galatians 4:21–31, wherein Paul tells the story of Abraham, Sarah, and Hagar.

59. Just as she did in *A Vision* (p. 61), Poole references the travailing woman in the wilderness, also known as the woman clothed with the sun, as recounted in Revelation 12.

60. John Locke also uses the phrase "refined persecutors" in his *Letters Concerning Toleration*, published for the first time in 1689, some forty years after Poole's "Alarm." The phrase may be a remnant of the Inquisition, when Catholic persecutors went to great lengths to develop new, more "refined" instruments and tactics of interrogation or torture. Alternatively, we might understand the phrase to mean that godly victims of unjust persecution are refined through their sufferings. Such a dynamic is described in Zechariah 13:9, GV: "And I will bring that third part through the fire, and I will refine them as the silver is refined, and will try them as gold is tried: they shall call on my Name, and I will hear them. I will say: It is my people and they shall say, the Lord is my God." In other words, just as gold and silver are refined by fire, so too are God's elect (or "third part") refined by persecutors who ironically advance God's cause by torturing, testing, and ultimately strengthening his saints.

once a member with you, which woman say you for scandalous evils was cast out.[61] Now it being some years since it was done, I humbly desire a little to reason with you about the grounds why this still remains upon your spirits, seeing Christ says *forgive you one another as I forgive you*, and God is said to remember our sins no more. This therefore is a note of forgiveness not to remember, and sure we should show ourselves children of our heavenly father. But further I desire before the Lord that you examine your own hearts in this thing, what your end is in it. If it be you think she is not worthy to have a livelihood among men, then why do you not either by the civil law, if that will take hold of the offense, or by some other way, if nothing will satisfy you but her blood, take some present course that may put an end to this great difference? But if you think this be too gross or more than the offense requires, then I beseech you for the Lord's sake to consider your own actings in this thing, whether you do not as much as in you lies carry on the same design, though more closely from the eyes of the world, but sure before the Lord it can appear no other but the hunting after her life. Nay, is it not more than to take off one single life at once? Or, which is greater cruelty, for a tyrant to take a man's life at once or by degrees? And then yourselves be judges whether your proceedings toward her be not a killing all the day long; for you cannot be ignorant that she has no livelihood among men but what she earns by her hands, and your defaming her in this manner cannot in an ordinary way but deprive her of that and so at last bring her blood upon you. If you say you acquaint none but the saints with it, that is evidence to the contrary for your open publishing it in the Council of War caused the world to take notice of it,[62] and yet your spirits rest not here. Truly, dear friends, as the evil spirit wrought in her one way when with you, so consider whether the same spirit do not highly work in you at this time another way. The Lord give you understanding in all things, but if her life be not that which you aim at, then is it these divine discoveries of life and light which God makes out to the world by her? If it be so, then you are to know that he is too strong you strive with. But about this I would make a little query. First, whether

61. T. P. or Thomasine Pendarves is here detailing how the sexual aspersion cast upon Poole was delivered in letter form and addressed to her husband, John Pendarves, the minister of the two women's congregation. It was written (as we will learn) by two individuals who wished to besmirch Poole's reputation and have her excommunicated from Pendarves's church. William Kiffin and John Fountaine are likely the two authors, although that is not explicitly stipulated here. How Thomasine Pendarves herself came into possession of the letter is deliberately obscured, however T. P. makes it clear that she does not believe that the "scandalous evils" reported in the letter should, at this late a date, be a matter for any concern, much less grounds for casting Poole out of the church and ruining her reputation.

62. The authors of the letter denouncing Poole sent it not only to John Pendarves but also to the members of the army's General Council whom Poole had addressed with her prophecies a short time before. In sending the letter to the Council, the authors imply that their true motivation is political retribution rather than moral outrage.

do you think that, because such evils were manifest in her when with you, therefore it is impossible now that any good should be brought forth by her? Do you not hope to grow better and better? But secondly, is it not God's usual way to manifest himself there highest where in times past he was by the evil spirit kept lowest? Yes, does he not suffer himself for this very end many times, thus to die in appearance and to leave a soul to itself, that so it may see what it is in itself and so learn to die to itself that so he may have the more glorious resurrection in that soul? I beseech you for the Lord's sake to consider these things. As for her outward person, I conceive she cares as little for it as you can, therefore you may take your fill of trampling on it. But I beseech you be careful how you meddle with the spirit that breathes in her, for surely brethren I know not what spirit manifested itself in her while with you, I am sure, and I speak nothing but the truth, that I have found a most divine spirit in her as far as I could discern, and that which comes to the spirit and life of things, and in this methinks you should rejoice, for truly I have heard many professors and professions, but to my knowledge I never heard one come so near the power. I do not speak this as being affected with any person, party, or opinion. I bless my God, I am now in his strength, delivered from that, though some have falsely affirmed my being deluded by her, but I am confident I can say with Paul, and that not only repeating the letter but in truth, that those things which I have received have not been from man, nor woman, nor any other thing, but by the mere revelation of Jesus Christ in me, God manifesting himself in my own flesh.[63] And therefore they much wrong both her and me that affirm it, but especially they wrong or speak a lie of that God that did it for me, and because I hear it so reported amongst you, I thought good to write one word to clear it, that so whether you will hear or whether you will forbear the word of truth might judge you. Give not ear, therefore, to all you hear though from brethren, lest you be brought into a snare.[64] For since the defection of the church's men, yes, good men have been such lovers of themselves and their own opinions that they will speak largely upon little ground to keep up their own glory. God having not yet undone them, for were they once undone men, they would willingly be what God would have them, however the world accounts of them. There is another thing that came to my ear that it should be given into the Council by your two witnesses,[65] that the said Mrs. Poole should say that you cast her out for dif-

---

63. Galatians 1:11–12, GV: "Now I certify you, brethren, that the Gospel which was preached of me, was not after man. For neither received I it of man, neither was I taught it, but by the revelation of Jesus Christ." It is noteworthy that T. P. adds "nor woman" to Paul's disavowal of "man" as the source of his revelation. It is possible she wishes to disabuse her readers of the possibility that Poole pushed her to write her letter of defense, choosing to highlight instead how she was inspired to do so by Christ and the spirit of love.

64. 1 Timothy 3:7, GV: "He must also be well reported of, even of them which are without, lest he fall into rebuke, and the snare of the devil."

65. It is here where we learn that there were apparently two authors of the letter denouncing Poole.

ferences in judgment. And when Colonel Rich[66] and Colonel Harrison[67] asked to whom she spoke it, they said to some of Abington. Now indeed my husband said to you that he thought such a thing, but when he came home and saw so little ground for his thoughts, I think he had but little comfort in telling you so. And then brethren if you upon such slender grounds should act in this strange manner against her, affirming this thing so publicly, I think you have cause to be humbled for it and justly to repent of your evil. I desire you to bear a little with me for truly it appears to me rather to be your rage of spirit than your true love, either to her or truth, for methinks it would favor more of a true Christian spirit if you had first spoken with her and have seen what change the Lord has wrought in her, as knowing that Mary out of whom seven Devils had been formerly cast was made the first messenger of Christ's resurrection, yes and she must bring it to the apostles and not the apostles to her.[68] You say in your letter that you left her to the judgment of the great day and I beseech you brethren, do you not again take her into your own day, for truly I believe that day in a measure has come upon her and the Lord himself is at work with her, therefore do not fear but the work will be well done, only we as well as she must have patience in it, and surely this is the confidence that I have concerning her, that she has seen evil in that estate she walked in with you. And certainly God is good to her in this, showing her what an abominable spirit of wickedness may be hid under the greatest practices and professions of externals, not that these are the cause of it, no, the gold and the silver is mine, said the Lord,[69] but we bestowing it upon our lovers and making ourselves great with

66. The two witnesses told two colonels on the General Council that Poole was excommunicated for speaking against Cromwell, the implication being that they believed the sexual charges were a pretense. The first colonel is Nathaniel Rich, a law student who became a colonel in Parliament's New Model Army in 1645 and a member of Parliament in 1649. Rich supported the regicide but did not serve on the trial commission that handed down the death sentence. As a result, he was spared retribution by Charles II after the restoration of the Crown in 1660. Ian Gentles, "Rich, Nathaniel (d. 1700x02)," *ODNB*.

67. The second colonel referenced is Thomas Harrison, an attorney who rose to the rank of colonel during the wars and to major general at the beginning of the Commonwealth period in 1650. After the regicide, he served as a member of Parliament throughout Cromwell's tenure in office. But he was critical of Cromwell when Cromwell assumed the title of Lord Protector. After the restoration, Harrison was drawn and quartered by Charles II for having signed the death warrant for Charles I. Both Rich and Harrison had affiliations with the Fifth Monarchists. Poole's allusions to herself in *A Vision* as the woman in the wilderness from Revelation suggests that she also shared in the idea that the New Model Army was engaged in the historical fulfillment of scriptural prophecy. Ian Gentles, "Harrison, Thomas (bap. 1616, d. 1660)," *ODNB*.

68. An allusion to Luke 8:1–2. This scripture tells the story of how during his travels with his apostles, Christ cured a number of women of their "evil spirits and infirmities," including Mary Magdalen, "out of whom was cast seven devils" (GV).

69. Haggai 2:9, GV: "The silver is mine, and the gold is mine, says the Lord of hosts." Haggai was a prophet and his short book urged the Jews to fulfill God's mission by rebuilding Solomon's Temple.

his ornaments, he is fain, in love with us, to take us from them or they from us and so find out a more special administration to perfect us in. Oh, the infinite riches of our God! Where does his bounty end? Surely his ways of love are unsearchable and his paths of mercy in which he follows poor fallen man and poor backsliding souls are past finding out. How narrow are our capacities, we judge as men, we may think as some did of David that there is no help for such things in God,[70] but all things in truth will be found possible with him, even where they are altogether past our thoughts and conceptions and become to us impossible. I beseech you, therefore, be persuaded to bow down to him. I know you are conscious that all judgment is not committed unto you and therefore it is possible you may not judge right in this thing, for truly, brethren, we may conceive many things even by the letter of itself and yet, not living in that spirit that wrote the letter, we may err. I pray do not mistake me as if I would in any way speak slightly of the letter, further than it speaks of itself; no, I bless the Father for it, and by sweet experience can say that I was never so confirmed in it now the Lord has drawn me to him out of it, even in that spirit that wrought it. I am for the conscionable use of it, but I would not abuse it. I am sure those men that would set it above the spirit can hardly free themselves from that thing. I hope therefore you will not count it your excellency to walk in the letter, but rather desire the Lord to perfect you in that spirit that writes the letter, for then and never but then shall we be able to walk by right and speak of the letter truly. I have not yet acquainted my husband with your letter.[71] I shall wait upon God what answer to receive from you. For truly dear brethren, upon serious deliberation I know not how to approve myself faithful in the eyes of God to my brethren here, if I should deliver it, for God having put it in my hand, I must also see clearness from him before I part with it. For though blessed be the Father, we have a sweet hopeful people amongst us that wait upon God and have fellowship one with another, yet whether they may digest such things as you write of, I really question, therefore it would be unfaithfulness in me if I, apprehending an evil to them or any other, should not as much as in me lies prevent it. And this I shall do by detaining the letter until further manifestation

70. A reference to King David's famous phase of arrogance, as recounted in 2 Samuel, which began with his prideful desire to build a great house in service to God and culminated in his disastrous affair with Bathsheba. Eventually, as Psalm 32 tells us, David expressed remorse. He was consoled by his son, Nathan, who told him that even though David had committed a mortal sin, God had cleansed and forgiven him.

71. Although addressed to John Pendarves, the letter never reached his hands. And as T. P. insists here, she had no intention of it ever doing so. As stated earlier (p. 74), it is not clear how T. P. was able to intercept the letter before John Pendarves saw it. Nor is it clear how, if the letter was circulated to the army's General Council, Pendarves did not know of it. Finally, we are not told how he knew that Poole had accused her church fellows of excommunicating her for political rather than moral reasons without also knowing of the resurrected sexual charges. What is clear is that T. P. wishes for the congregation to cease from any further use of the slanderous letter to damage Poole's reputation and life.

from God what to do with it. Do not judge me in this thing, I beseech you; I have one judge, even the Lord, and he that put it in my hand will at length clear my integrity in it. I have nothing to do for myself in it, the Lord knows only.

How I may approve myself faithful to men in the Lord and for the Lord's sake; your desire I exceedingly like, that we may be kept form errors and the Lord keep us from all errors, but who must show us what error is but the God of truth himself? We have lived in error and have sucked them in from our cradles and yet who will speak so much against error as we, stating ourselves still in the truth. My sweet friends, the day of truth is but now dawning upon us and how is it opposed? Yes, by those that are children of truth in their measure; yet we have all looked for it and prayed together for it a long time, but truly now we will not own our prayers but turn away our face from our Savior because he comes not in such a garb as we imagined he would, when we know it's his prerogative to clothe himself with what flesh or garments he pleases. Brethren, what would you have? Do you not know a glorious day has been spoken of ever since the prophets and the apostles? Though the day was dawned upon them, yet they bid their hearts not to be terrified as if that day were near, for said he there must be a falling away first and that wicked one revealed, notwithstanding Peter told them he was a partaker of that glory that should be afterward revealed. However, said he, you have a sure word of prophecy to which you do well to take heed, as if he had said, brethren, we have been with the Lord in the mount and have beheld that excellent glory, but yet to you that have not so seen Christ there is a more sure word of prophecy, for visions and revelations do most especially confirm and strengthen those that have them, but here is a word that is spoken to all and is a light shining in a dark place, therefore you do well to take heed to it until the day dawn and the day star arise in your own hearts and you be swallowed up with that glory that now you expect and wait for.[72] Only know this, that no private spirit can understand these scriptures that speak of that day; it must be the spirit of God alone. Let us cease for our own spirits therefore, for they are selfish and private, bound up to this and that, and so it would confine God also, but his Spirit is as large as himself; it's without bonds, it's neither here nor there distinct but is individually everywhere. But that which I desire you to consider from these scriptures is that this day of falling away has been, and all the world has wandered after the beast since the apostles' time, therefore, how near may we expect our glory. We should not be troubling ourselves therefore still with falling away, but now look for a rising, for sure man has had his day and now the Lord will have his day. Now seeing this day of the Lord must have a dawning and some disciples may be taken up into the mount before other some, it should teach us not to judge our brethren that speak

---

72. 2 Peter 19, GV: "We have also a most sure word of the prophets, to which you do well that you take heed, as unto a light that shines in a dark place, until the day dawn, and the day star arise in your hearts."

of higher enjoyments than we have, for we being behind should rather judge ourselves.[73] Seeing we are more in the day of man, and acknowledge ourselves so to be still looking for and hastening to the day of God in which we may act selfishly no longer, but our God may bring forth his own righteousness in us. And truly, brethren, you may be satisfied in this, that we are very industrious to keep ourselves from error, but we know that in his strength we shall be perfected and when he comes and speaks then shall we know that it is he. And truly brethren, I would not have you infidels but believing, this day has taken some unawares, and though many may have it in notion yet I am sure some have it in power. I have one thing more to you concerning your letter, and truly I cannot but wonder at it, that is, how you do so peremptorily to judge the woman that she brought a delusion for a vision of God. I beseech you consider seriously before the Lord whether you are sure it was so or no before you make it so public and send it forth with the authority of a church. Surely friends you will much abuse the authority of your church in affirming mere supposition for truth. The Lord be pleased to open your eyes in this thing; it may be your Father in mercy desires a little to plead with you by a weak instrument[74] and therefore put the letter into my hand that so he might put some stop to your furious driving, and truly I can look upon it no other way. Therefore, willingly meet your God in his merciful acts toward you, for if you do not, the dumb ass next time may reprove you. I confess, souls, I am the weakest of all, a poor undone soul in myself, the Lord alone take all the glory. Yet if I may be useful, as being one of the body, in keeping you from doing greater evils, I shall be willing and rejoice, though I go under never so great an odium myself. For sure friends, account of me how you will, I am one of you and tenderly affect you, and in this thing would have God truly exalted, for this grace is given me to love truth under any appearance, though indeed that may sometimes appear to men to be truth which I cannot close with; but I mean any appearance that my God comes in, and I hope shall be more and more perfect in it, and indeed it is sweet to me that he has given me, through mercy, to know his voice from a stranger. It may be the world may judge me for it because it comes not in their form, but I shall rest in the Lord. Well brethren, if you see mercy to you in that which the Lord has spoken by me, receive it and rejoice in him, it may be I may prove to you as Abigail

73. Possibly a reference to Matthew 26:30–31, GV: "And when they had sung a psalm, they went out into the mount of olives. Then said Jesus unto them: All you shall be offended by me this night, for it is written, I will smite the shepherd, and the sheep of the flock shall be scattered." This scripture implies that, in the end-times, the saints will be separated from the sinners.

74. It may seem that T. P is being self-deprecating by referring to herself as a weak instrument. However, there are numerous instances in the Bible wherein weakness is cast as a strength. As Paul elaborates in 1 Corinthians 1:27–29, GV: "But God has chosen the foolish things of the world to shame the wise, and God has chosen the weak things of the world to shame the things which are strong, and the base things of the world and the despised God has chosen, the things that are not, so that He may nullify the things that are, so that no man may boast before God."

did to David, keep you from shedding blood and from avenging yourselves with your own hand.[75] The Lord show us therefore what the scripture means, *I will have mercy and not sacrifices*: there be many things in the letter of the scripture which we through weakness may think to be sacrifices, as the Pharisees did when God abhors it, and will have none of it in such a time as he calls for mercy; therefore he bids us learn what he means.[76] We may have it and read it and speak it, but to learn the inside of it, learn what it means, will be our comfort and our crown. And truly my dear friends, I am persuaded that this is a time in which mercy is required of us toward our sister and not such sacrifices. If you please to send me a word of an answer, leave it with M. Calvert, at the Black Spread Eagle at the west end of Paul's.[77] I do not think it fit as yet that you acquaint my husband with it, not for unlawfulness sake but convenience; for surely brethren, I am not willingly carried to give you or him or anyone offense, only as the Lord manifests it to His will, and then I must leave father and mother and all and cleave to him.[78] Let me have your answer as soon as you can; but I beseech you, do not answer me but the Lord, and then see how you can justify yourselves. In him therefore shall I wait for it, and dear souls, though I am nothing and can do nothing in myself yet I beseech you do not reject any word of truth, love, and sincerity that God sends by my hand. Job said he did not reject the cause of his maidservant when it came before him,

75. As did Poole in *A Vision* (pp. 66–67), T. P. draws upon the story of Abigail, Nabal, and David from 1 Samuel 25.

76. T. P. references the same scripture that Poole cited earlier, that is Matthew 9, in which the Pharisees called Jesus's legitimacy into question because he kept company with publicans and sinners. T. P. specifically references Matthew 9:13, wherein Jesus responds directly to the Pharisees: "But go and learn what this is, I will have mercy and not sacrifice, for I am not come to call the righteous, but the sinners to repentance" (GV).

77. As part of T. P.'s goal of preventing the charges against Poole from doing further damage, she asks that any contact with her be made through a print shop called the Black Spread Eagle. Like many print shops and bookstalls, the Black Spread Eagle was located in the courtyard of St. Paul's Churchyard. T. P. identifies the owner as M. Calvert, but the Black Spread Eagle belonged to Giles Calvert and his wife, Elizabeth. The couple published numerous non-conformist, anti-monarchical, and republican pamphlets throughout the 1640s and 1650s, including *News from the New Jerusalem*, mentioned in the introduction (p. 44). Giles was arrested for these publications and died in 1663. The Black Spread Eagle was destroyed in the Great Fire in 1666. Elizabeth, however, continued to operate an underground press, which resulted in her arrest in 1668 and trial in 1674. The "M." in T. P.'s instructions may be a typographical error. Possibly, it is a reference to Giles's sister, Martha Calvert, a Quaker. The Calverts published numerous Quaker pamphlets until after Giles's death, when a schism developed between the Quakers and Elizabeth. Maureen Bell, "Calvert, Elizabeth (d. 1675?), bookseller," *ODNB*.

78. A paraphrase of Matthew 19:3–6, in which the Pharisees ask Jesus if it's lawful for a man to divorce his wife if she commits an error. Jesus answers, "'Have you not read, that he which made them at the beginning, made them male and female.' And said 'For this cause, shall a man leave father and mother, and cleave unto his wife, and they two shall be one flesh. Wherefore they are not more two, but one flesh. Let not man therefore put asunder that which God has coupled together'" (GV).

though the word said they contended with him.[79] I can give you more satisfaction, if you please, how I came by the letter. I am sure it was unexpected by me, only the Lord would have it so; and therefore all your care must serve the Lord's designs to bring it to my hand when my husband was not in town. Do not therefore look upon me but look to the Lord, and use me as kindly as Job did his servant, reject not my cause[80] for surely it is not mine. I leave you to the Lord, in whom I desire rightly to guide you in this thing, and am

Your sincere loving sister and servant, from
the greatest to the meanest of you, T. P.

Abington 6.
March 1649[81]

79. T. P. asks her readers to accept her testimony, promising to provide them with information about how she came into possession of the letter, should they require it, and citing Job as an example of a man who was forced to defend himself in spite of Satan's prolonged attempts to torture him into renouncing God. Job conceded that, had he done all the things he was accused of doing, he would indeed deserve punishment. But he was innocent and so did not. Specifically, T. P. invokes Job 31:12–13: "Yea, this is a fire that shall devour to destruction, and which shall root out all my increase, if I did condemn the judgement of servant, and of my maid, when they did contend with me" (GV).

80. Another reference to Job 31:13. Here Job cites his virtues as proof that he is not persecuted because he is a wicked man. Among his virtues are the fact that when his servants, including his maid, argued or "contended" with him, he did not "condemn" their "judgement."

81. As noted in the introduction (p. 54), the "Errata" section of this pamphlet is not reproduced here. The corrections listed in that section have already been implemented in this volume for the reader's convenience.

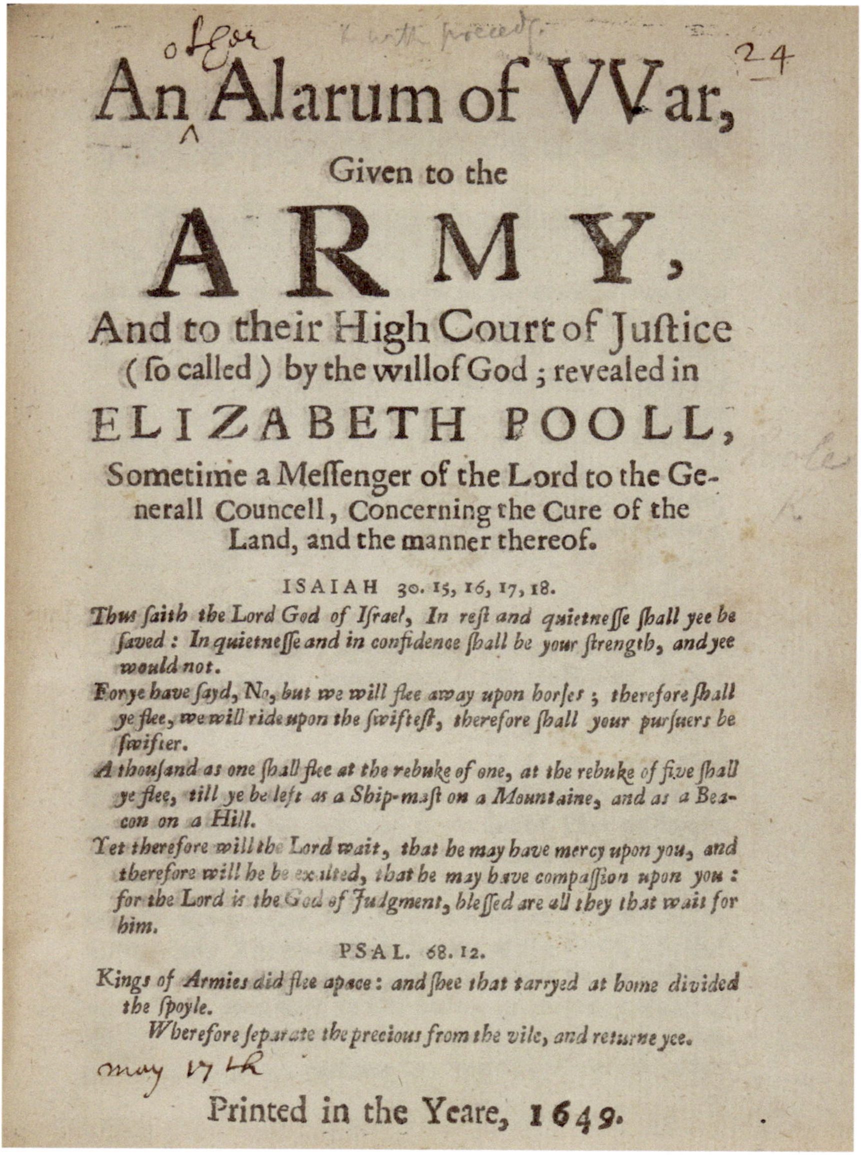

An Alarum of VVar,

Given to the

ARMY,

And to their High Court of Justice
(so called) by the will of God; revealed in

ELIZABETH POOLL,

Sometime a Messenger of the Lord to the Generall Councell, Concerning the Cure of the
Land, and the manner thereof.

ISAIAH 30. 15, 16, 17, 18.

Thus saith the Lord God of Israel, In rest and quietnesse shall yee be saved: In quietnesse and in confidence shall be your strength, and yee would not.

For ye have sayd, No, but we will flee away upon horses; therefore shall ye flee, we will ride upon the swiftest, therefore shall your pursuers be swifter.

A thousand as one shall flee at the rebuke of one, at the rebuke of five shall ye flee, till ye be left as a Ship-mast on a Mountaine, and as a Beacon on a Hill.

Yet therefore will the Lord wait, that he may have mercy upon you, and therefore will he be exalted, that he may have compassion upon you: for the Lord is the God of Judgment, blessed are all they that wait for him.

PSAL. 68. 12.

Kings of Armies did flee apace: and shee that tarryed at home divided the spoyle.

Wherefore separate the precious from the vile, and returne yee.

Printed in the Yeare, 1649.

Figure 4. Title page, Elizabeth Poole, *An[other] Alarm of War* (1649). British Library. Reproduced with permission.

An Alarm of War,[82]
Given to the
ARMY,
and to their High Court of Justice
(so called) by the will of God; Revealed in
ELIZABETH POOLE,
Sometimes a Messenger of the Lord to the General
Council, Concerning the Cure of the
Land, and the manner thereof.

ISAIAH 30:15, 16, 17, 18.
*Thus said the Lord God of Israel, in rest and quietness shall you be
saved: In quietness and in confidence shall be your strength, and you
would not.*
*For you have said, No, but we will flee away upon horses; therefore shall
you flee, we will ride upon the swiftest, therefore shall your pursuers be
swifter.*
*A thousand as one shall flee at the rebuke of one, at the rebuke of five shall
you flee, until you be left as a Ship-mast on a Mountain, and as a Beacon on a Hill.*
Yet, therefore will the Lord wait, that he may have mercy upon you, and
therefore will he be exalted, that he may have compassion upon you:
for the Lord is the God of Judgment, blessed are all they that wait for
him.
PSALM 68:12
*Kings of armies did flee apace: and she that tarried at home divided
the spoil.*
Wherefore separate the precious from the vile, and return you.

Printed in the Year, 1649

---

82. As discussed in the introduction (pp. 53–54), this copy of the pamphlet was owned by the printer and collector George Thomason. Thomason notes that this is a different tract from the first alarm by handwriting the word "other" onto the title page after the word "An," thereby distinguishing this tract as *An*[*other*] *Alarm*. But we also know that the second *Alarm* succeeds the first because Thomason also wrote "With proceedg" (with proceeding) at the top of the page as a reminder that this second *Alarm* is intended as a follow-up to the first, even if the two were written closely together and published at the same time. Once again, the phrase "alarm of war" recalls Jeremiah 4:19, informing us that Poole will deliver a second "jeremiad" to the army and its High Count of Justice, warning them of the dire consequences they will face for executing the king in spite of her vision that he should be tried in his conscience but not put to death.

The Preface to the Reader

Dear reader, you may marvel that I, having had so reproachful a pursuit by them that are called Saints when I was last at the General Council, should hold up my head any more to speak to them; as also having shame cast in the face of my message by many, and others pretending better, notwithstanding, cast it by as not worthy to be regarded, the which the Lord will judge. Wherefore I shall certify to you, dear reader, that those things came to pass according to divine pleasure for two reasons: the first is to stain the pride and glory of all flesh in me; the second is to blind the eyes of the wise that they seeing might not perceive.[83] And if you consider these reasons [as I also assuring you in the strength of the Lord (the which I humbly wait to be established) in that I come to prostrate my neck and all the glory of my flesh to the wrath and malice of men, knowing that that which can be shaken in me and all men must be done away, so that that which cannot be shaken may be established],[84] then you can no more admire, for flesh must be consumed that we might live in the spirit and the eyes of the wise must be blind that the blind may receive sight, for whereas it is said, *You are not my people, there shall you be called the people of the living God.*[85] The manner of the cure of the land, which I received by faith and was often to declare to the army, was that they must set themselves as in the presence of the Lord to act for her cure, according to the rule of the gift of faith as was delivered to them in these words: This is the step that is between you and restoration (the which whosoever take not warily shall stumble and fall and be taken) that you be dead in the will of the Lord to all your privileges, interests, lives, liberties, freedoms, or whatsoever you may call yours, yet pleading them still with men. I did also plead with them about the life of the king, and it

---

83. A paraphrase of several passages in the Bible which insist that God must sometimes obscure the truth in order that it may appear more clearly. In Matthew 13:13, this illuminating act of obscuring takes the form of speaking in parables. As Christ says, "Therefore I speak to them in parables, because they seeing do not see, and hearing, they hear not, neither understand" (GV). Isaiah and Jeremiah identify God's decision to communicate through obscured truth with prophecy. As Isaiah 6:9–10, GV, reads: "And he said, Go and say unto this people, You shall hear in deed, but you shall to understand. You shall plainly see and not perceive. Make the heart of this people fat, make the hearts heavy and shut their eyes, lest they see with their eyes and hear with their ears and understand with their hearts and convert and he heal them." And as Jeremiah 5:21, GV, states, "Hear now this, oh foolish people, and without understanding, which has eyes and see not, which have ears and hear not."

84. Hebrews 12:26–27, GV: "Whose voice then shook the earth, and now hath declared, saying, 'yet once more will I shake, not the earth only, but also heaven.' And this word, Yet, once more signifies the removing of those things, which are shaken, as of things which are made with hands, that the things which are not shaken, may remain."

85. Romans 9:26, GV: "And it shall be in the place where it was said unto you, You are not my people, that there they shall be the children of the living God." This passage is part of Paul's larger message to the Romans regarding the unwillingness of the Jews to accept Jesus as the messiah.

has been said since, if I had spoken indeed in the word of the Lord, they had not had power to have taken his life, though they cannot be ignorant that many have been spoken to in the word of the Lord who have been punished for not obeying. I shall therefore speak to all men in a divided tongue, though it shall be found one in truth, for as all languages were confounded at the building of Babel, so did the Holy Ghost sit on the apostles in cloven tongues of fire and everyone heard another speak in his own language. To signify to us that, as by the building of Babylon all languages were confounded, so by our deliverance from thence shall all be reconciled. And as by the division of tongues all were confounded, so by the knowledge of tongues shall all be reconciled. As it is written, *I will bring thee into Babylon, and thence I will deliver thee* (for Babylon is confusion).[86] When I was with the Council, it was in a vision or revelation, and now I am come with a word of interpretation which I commit to you, dear reader, in the spirit and bowels of love, to judge. Farewell,

Yours in the Kingdom of the Patience of Christ.[87]
ELIZABETH POOLE.

To the pretended Church,
and Fellowship of Saints, in
LONDON,
Who Pursued me with Their weapons of War, to Shoot me to death at the
General Council of the Army, not re-
garding the Babe Jesus in me,
Greetings.

I trust to be made manifest to the discerning reader, to write to you in love, though I cannot (considered as in your then present actions) entitle you otherwise than the pretended Church and Fellowship of Saints. Now, I will speak to the holy seed in you. Dear brethren, the flesh that keeps you in bonds accused me of sin, the which I will gladly own as far as you dare charge me with, who are in bonds as well as I, that you might consider me in temptation, being also tempted, but as your flesh accused me I cannot yield, it never being in my heart to do what you said I confessed. I know it shall be manifest when the thoughts of all hearts shall

86. A sustained adaptation of the story of the Tower of Babel, as recounted in Genesis 11:1–9.

87. The valediction to Poole's address to the reader alludes to and hence identifies her with John, the self-proclaimed primary witness of Christ's suffering and prophet of the end-times. As Revelation 1:9–11, GV, reads, "I John, ever your brother and companion in tribulation in the kingdom and patience of Jesus Christ, was in the isle called Patmos, for the word of God and for the witnessing of Jesus Christ. And I was ravished in spirit on the Lords day and heard behind a great voice, as it had been of a trumpet, saying, 'I am alpha and omega, the first and the last, and that which thou seest, write in a book and send it unto the seven Churches.'"

be revealed, though I have but one witness and you say you have many. Thus, flesh in you, brethren, judges flesh in me, and both must fall together.[88] I rejoice in this, that excommunication was ordained for the destruction of the flesh, that the spirit might be saved in the day of the Lord; therefore, I will gladly, in the strength of the Son of God, commit myself to death, even the death of the cross. It is true indeed I confessed all that was in my heart to you when I was drunk with the indignation of the Lord, and what you have added the righteous Lord will judge. This thing I think meet to mention, the which your messengers to render me more odious, added that I went about seducing.[89] I beseech you, brethren, take heed how you call good, evil and evil, good, for they are both alike abominations to the Lord, and judge not the things you know not. I speak these things for their sake that pursue these. I fear you not, for the life I live is hid, you cannot find it.[90] Take all you can, you spoiler,[91] devouring, devouring, devour until you have no more to devour.[92] It is true indeed that you have made long furrows in my flesh and lashed me sore, but why should I complain; you have the judgment [and] your own works will judge you.[93] I will take my leave of my brethren and depart. Dear brethren, I have learned this judgment, that that spirit in men, the which while the evil part acts makes God its expectation, is the Virgin that cries out, and though

88. A possible paraphrase of 1 Corinthians 1:26–27, GV: "For brethren, you see your calling, how that not many wise men after the flesh, not many mighty, not many noble are called. But God has chosen the foolish things of the world to confound the wise, and God has chosen the weak things of the world, to confound the mighty things."

89. Poole yet again addresses the charges of sexual misconduct launched against her. She admits she did something indiscreet in her youth; as she notes, she voluntarily confessed it to her fellow congregants. But she denies doing what she was accused of doing, that is, "going about seducing."

90. Colossians 3:2–4, GV: "Set your affections on things which are above, and not on things which are on the earth. For you are dead, and your life is hid with Christ in God. When Christ which is our life shall appear, then shall you also appear with him in glory."

91. The term "spoiler" appears several times in the King James Bible, especially in Isaiah and Jeremiah. In the Geneva Bible, the term "destroyer" is used instead of "spoiler." Both terms refer to an ominous, demon-like creature who plunders and ravages. As Isaiah 21:12, KJV, reads: "A grievous vision is declared unto me; the treacherous dealer deals treacherously, and the spoiler spoils."

92. In both the Geneva Bible and the King James Bible, the term "devourer" appears in Malachi 3:11: "And I will rebuke the devourer for your sakes and he shall not destroy the fruit of your ground, neither shall your vine be barren in the field, saith the Lord of hosts" (KJV).

93. Poole here identifies herself with Christ when he was scourged by Pontius Pilate's Roman soldiers before his crucifixion. The scourging of Christ is described in Matthew 27:26–31, Mark 14:63–65, Luke 22:63–65, and John 19:1–3. Poole's assertion that the brethren of the congregation will be judged by their own works echoes the words of Pilate in John 19:31, when having resigned himself to punishing a man he believed to be innocent, Pilate says to the Jews who demand Jesus's persecution, "Take you him and judge him after your own Law" (GV).

An[other] Alarm of War   87

she have no help, the Law quits, saying, she has done no evil, she is free.[94] On the scale for whom the cities of refuge were built,[95] I commit you to God, the only wise and infinite father, who is all things, and all things are God.[96] He is all things subsisting, all things are God, in whom subsisting.[97] Farewell,

Your Friend in the Kingdom of
the Patience of Christ.[98]

Elizabeth Poole.

94. In contrast with the law of the flesh that Poole claims dictates the actions of her former brethren, Poole identifies the spiritual law that she follows with the immaculate and therefore innocent body of the Virgin Mary.

95. The "cities of refuge" are described in Joshua 20 as places of immunity for people who had killed another person accidentally and thus needed a sanctuary wherein they would be protected from the murder victim's avengers.

96. Poole's use of the term "commit" to describe her consignment of her brethren and their flesh-bound selves to the cities of refuge echoes her use of the same term in *A Vision* (p. 67) to advocate consigning the king's fleshy head to Satan rather than executing him in accordance with man's flawed judgement.

97. Colossians 1:17, GV: "And he is before all things and in him all things consist."

98. This valediction to Poole's address to her congregation repeats the allusion to Revelation 1:9–11 that she used in her letter to the congregation (p. 85).

An Alarum of Warre given to the Army, and their high Court of Iustice (so called) by the will of God, revealed in *Elizabeth Pooll*, Sometime a Messenger to the Generall Councell of the Army, concerning the Cure of the Land, and the manner thereof.

EZEKIEL 39. 17, 18, 19, 20, 21.

17. *And thou Son of man, thus saith the Lord God, Speake unto every feathered Fowle, and to every Beast of the field, Saying, Assemble your selves, and come, gather your selves on every side to my sacrifice, that I doe sacrifice for you, even a great sacrifice upon the Mountains of Israel, that ye may eate flesh, and drinke blood.*
18. *Ye shall eat the flesh of the Valiant, and drink the blood of the Princes of the earth, of Rams, of Lambs, and of Goats, of Bullocks, of all the Fatlings of Bashan.*
19. *And ye shall eate fat til ye be full, and drinke blood till ye be drunken, of my sacrifice which I have sacrificed for you.*
20. *Thus ye shall be filled at my table with Horses and Chariots, with mighty men, and with all men of War, saith the Lord God.*
21. *And I will set my glory among the Heathen, and all the Heathen shall see my judgement that I have executed, and my hand that I have layd upon them.*

OH! How are my bowels straightened, and yet am I come forth to lanch deepe into the sides of my Brethren; are yee not to me as mine owne bowels? is not my soule as your soules, in all your pursuite of Justice, Judgement, and Truth? yea, yee are to me as mine owne bowels, and your soules as my soule, in all your

Figure 5. Internal title page, Elizabeth Poole, *An[other] Alarm of War* (1649). British Library. Reproduced with permission.

An Alarm of War given to the
Army, and their High Court of Justice (so called)
by the will of God, revealed in *Elizabeth
Poole,* sometimes a Messenger to the General
Council of the Army, concerning the
Cure of the Land, and the manner
thereof.

EZEKIEL 39:17, 18, 19, 20, 21.

17. And thou Son of man, thus said the Lord, speak unto every feathered fowl
and to every beast of the field, saying, assemble yourselves and come, gather
yourselves on every side to my sacrifice, that I do sacrifice for you, even a great
sacrifice upon the mountains of Israel, that you may eat flesh and drink blood.
18. You shall eat the flesh of the valiant and drink the blood of the princes of the
earth, of rams, of lambs, and of goats, of bullocks, of all the fatlings of Bashan.
19. And you shall eat fat until you be full, and drink blood until you be drunken,
of my sacrifice which I have sacrificed for you.
20. Thus you shall be filled at my table with horses and chariots, with mighty
men, and with all men of war, said the Lord God.
21. And I will set my glory among the heathen, and all the heathen shall see my
judgment that I have executed, and my hand that I have laid upon them.[99]

Oh! How are my bowels straightened, and yet I am come forth to launch deep
into the sides of my brethren.[100] Are you not to me as mine own bowels? Is not
my soul as your souls, in all your pursuit of justice, judgment, and truth? Yes,

99. Like the books of Jeremiah and Isaiah, the book of Ezekiel consists of prophecies to and about
the Israelites. Ezekiel delivered his prophecies during the time of the Israelites' Babylonian captivity.
He claimed the exile was punishment for the Israelites' sins. He first outlined the punishments their
enemies would eventually experience as a result of their disbelief and then conveyed the blessings the
Israelites would receive from God for their faith. The specific passages cited here involve the Israelites'
encounter with King Og, the Amorite King of Bashan. The Israelites won Bashan from King Og when
they were forced to go to war with him after he tried to prevent them from entering the Promised
Land, as recounted in Numbers 21:33–35 and Deuteronomy 3:1–7. Ezekiel recalls Bashan's conquest
in order to promise the Israelites that they will once again rise up to defeat their heathen enemies.

100. References to the "bowels" or intestines appears numerous times in the Bible. The deepest and
arguably most essential part of the body, the bowels are where various speakers in the Old and New
Testaments experience either the greatest spiritual and hence physical torment or the utmost bliss.
Poole's bowels are straight because she is infused with God's spirit, and she now plans to delve deeply
into the bowels of her brethren to bring them to righteousness. Poole's direct source is 2 Corinthians
6:11–13, GV: "O Corinthians, our mouth is open unto you; our heart is made large. You are not kept
straight in us, but you are kept straight in your own bowels. Now for the same recompense, I speak
to you as to my children, Be you also enlarged." But she is also referring back to Jeremiah 4:19, KJV,
from which her title is taken: "My bowels, my bowels! I am pained at my very heart; my heart makes

90 ELIZABETH POOLE

you are to me as mine own bowels, and your souls as my soul, in all your pursuit of justice, judgment, and truth; nevertheless though as father, mother, husband, wife, children, house, land, yes my own life, I must forsake your evil and adulterate party. You know I spoke to you in the word of the Lord, that the kingly power was undoubtedly fallen into your hand, that you might therefore improve it; this was the exhortation which I left with you, that you must be dead to all your own interests, lives, liberties, freedoms, or whatsoever you might call yours, in the will of the Lord, without which you should never be able to undergo this great work committed to you. As was delivered to you in these words: that this aforementioned was the great step between you and restoration, which whosoever take not warily shall stumble and fall and be taken. But you have not regarded the word of the Lord, though it were to you as the word of the Lord to the Jews in Isaiah 30:17.[101] Thus said the Lord God of Israel, in rest and quietness shall you be saved, in quietness and confidence shall be your strength, and you would not; wherefore thus said the Lord, yes the Lord said it, as you have hastened your flight upon the swift and the strong, so shall they be swifter and stronger who pursue you,[102] for I have seen your carcasses lain upon the ground[103] and while I was mourning them because of that spirit of justice, judgment, and equity that had sometime appeared in you, there stood up a young man, a man of strength, in whom they appeared, and I seeing they had a resurrection in another, was comforted, as also this word I received.[104] Their carcasses fell in the wilderness through unbelief, thereby I saw it was but your carcasses, or the body of your confederacy and combination, wherein you were wise for yourselves, hastening upon the strong and swift; that is, your wisdoms, councils, devotions, humiliations, and religious consultations wherein you would inquire of God (as you call it) though it were grounded in your hearts what to do. Witness your frequent reports that a necessity lay upon you to take the king's life; otherwise, how should you have your interests, lives, liberties, freedoms, arrears, indemnities, though you had his blood before as king, in that the law and spirit of government was committed to you, not that you should have

---

a noise in me; I cannot hold my peace, because you have heard, O my soul, the sound of the trumpet, the alarm of war."

101. Isaiah 30:17 is one of the passages from Isaiah that is printed on the cover page of both this *Alarm* and the first. This particular passage reads: "A thousand shall flee at the rebuke of one, at the refuge of five shall you flee, until you be left as a ship mast on a Mountain, as a Beacon on a Hill" (KJV).

102. Poole here paraphrases the other passages from Isaiah 30 that appear on the title pages of both *Alarms*.

103. Jeremiah 7:33 (KJV): "And the carcasses of this people shall be meat for the souls of the heathen and for the beasts of the earth, and none shall ferry them away."

104. A reiteration of the "similitude" Poole used in *A Vision* (p. 61), wherein she compared the members of the army's General Council to a "strong man" whose commitment to the higher cause would enable them to resist the temptation to execute the king and compel them to aid the "travailing woman" to give birth to a new, more just order (p. 61).

spent it on your lusts, as you were graciously warned by the word of the Lord at my mouth when I said unto you in your General Council that the blood royal was running in your veins, warning you in the Name of the Lord to take heed that you stopped not the course thereof by any appropriation or self proprieties, still assuring you that you could never prove faithful to the work in hand and further than you were perfectly dead in the will of the Lord to your own interests. But you would not hear; wherefore woe to them that seek deep to hide their counsels from the Lord. When I told you the kingly power was fallen into your hands, it was manifest by your earnest pursuit (in profession) after righteousness, justice, truth, equity, which appeared also most lively in you until there was nothing would satisfy you but the blood of the king, a man with whom you were in covenant and had sworn to defend his person. Yet though I spoke this, my eyes are also open to behold the righteous judgments of God in it, for I can say the will of the Lord is done in it, for he does judge the folk in righteousness and the people in equity.

Now therefore it remains for you to prove what you have done who would not give your king a reason for the court he was tried by, though I can herein also behold the righteous judgments of God upon him. For as he would reign by his will, he is also judged by yours; nevertheless know that as you have served him, so shall you be served, you said, you must have no respect to persons for there is no respect of persons with God. It is done said the Lord, neither will I have respect to your persons, for though Noah, Daniel, and Job should stand up amongst you to intercede, they should not save a man, save every man his own soul. It is true, you have been battle axes and weapons of war in the Lord's hands,[105] but let not the axe boast itself against the hewer, for he will craft his rod in the fire, it shall be tried of what sort it is, and that in it which will not suffer fire shall be consumed.[106] For if you would have brought England to her rest, her Sabbath, you ought to have called it holy in the Lord, not speaking your own words, nor doing your own works, nor thinking your own thoughts,[107] but you would not. For feeling you could not trust the king with your lives, liberties, interests, freedoms, arrears, indemnities, you would not trust God. You have indeed behaved yourselves valiantly as men amongst men, but when you were called in the name

105. Jeremiah 51:20. Poole's wording recalls the KJV: "Thou art my battle axe and weapons of war: for with thee will I break in pieces the nations, and with thee will I destroy kingdoms."

106. Isaiah 10:15–16, GV: "Shall the axe boast it self against him that hews therewith? Or shall the saw exalt it self against him that move it? As if the rod should lift up itself against him that takes it up, or the staff should exalt itself, as if it were no wood. Therefore shall the Lord God of hosts send among his fat men, leanness, and under his glory he shall kindle a burning, like the burning of fire."

107. A loose allusion to Isaiah 58:13–14, KJV: "If you turn away your foot from the Sabbath, from doing your will on my holy day and call the Sabbath a delight, to consecrate it as glorious to the Lord and shall honor him, not doing your own ways, nor seeking your own will, nor speaking a vain word, then shall you delight in the Lord and I will cause you to mount upon the high places of the earth and sit with the heritage of Jacob, your father, for the mouth of the Lord has spoken."

of the Lord to stand manfully to die in his will to all your desirable things, your hearts failed you, for you had not improved the breastplate of faith which is able to quench all the fiery darts of the Devil.[108] I know many of you will say you have stood in the name of the Lord in such battles, and in other great difficulties, and have found it your shelter.[109] I believe you and do rejoice in it, but why would you not do so still? Know you not that they that were clothed in white were found worthy because they followed the lamb wherever he goes?[110] Wherefore forsake not your Lord, though he change his garment and take up a form that you have not known, lest that scripture be fulfilled in you: *They shall not believe though one should tell them.*[111] Nay, it is fulfilled in you, for if you had known him, you would have trusted him with your lives, liberties and all, and he would have rewarded you sevenfold, but you would hasten on your swift and strong counsels, policies, denunciations, engagements to see yourselves and your country righted (as you call it) and to the end you might hasten your flight. You call a court in the name of the Commons of England, which indeed you might have done, had you known them in the Lord; and this you call the High Court of Justice. "Behold, said the Lord, I have sworn by myself, the word is gone out of my mouth in righteousness and shall not return, that every knee shall bow to me, and every tongue shall confess me."[112] Surely you shall say, in the Lord have I righteousness and strength; you shall come to him, and all that provoke him shall be ashamed.

In the day that the Lord shall assemble all feathered fowl and all beasts of the earth to eat and drink of the flesh and blood of kings and rulers, mighty men and captains, with all fatlings of Bashan.[113] It is true, the visible Gog and Magog of this kingdom you have destroyed already and yourselves remain the mighty men

108. Ephesians 6:16, GV: "Above all, take the shield of faith, wherewith you may quest all the fiery darts of the wicked." Poole's use of the term "breastplate" instead of "shield" may also refer to 1 Thessalonians 5:8: "But let us which are of the day, be sober, putting on the breastplate of faith and love, and of the hope of salvation for a helmet."

109. Psalm 61:3, KJV: "For thou hast been a shelter for me, and a strong tower from the enemy."

110. A collocation of several verses in Revelation that depict the saints as dressed in white. See, for example, Revelation 3:4, GV: "Notwithstanding you have a few names yet in Sardis, which have not defiled their garments; and they shall walk with me in white, for they are worthy" and Revelation 3:5, GV: "He that overcomes, shall be clothed in white array, and I will not put out his Name out of the book of life, but I will confess his name before my Father, and before his Angels."

111. A paraphrase of Luke 16:29–31, GV: "Abraham said to him [Lazarus], They have Moses and the Prophets, let them hear them. And he [Lazarus] said, 'Nay, father Abraham, but if one came to them from the dead, they will amend their lives.' Then he [Abraham] said to him, 'If they hear not Moses and the Prophets, neither will they be persuaded, though one rise from the dead again.'"

112. Isaiah 45:23, KJV: "I have sworn by my self; the word is gone out of my mouth in righteousness and shall not return, that every knee shall bow to me and every tongue shall swear by me."

113. Poole here directly cites the passages from Ezekiel that she also featured on her title page. She uses Ezekiel 39:17–18 to inform the council that while they might believe themselves holy conquerors,

of the earth that shall be given to the fowls of the air and the beasts of the earth for prey.[114] Said I not to you when I was at your council with you that as you were the great and mighty men of the earth, the Lord's controversy is with you, the day is hastening upon you? Behold, it is at hand. Said I not also that as you are the potsherds of the earth, you should be broken to pieces until there should not be a sherd left to carry coals on? Behold, it is at hand. Some of you may remember that I told you at the Commissarie-General's quarters your potsherd metals were not only your human wisdoms and policies, but also your religious devotions, humiliations, ordinances, orders, knowledge, faiths, wherein you were resolved what to do in your own wisdom and counsel. This also is your potsherd metal: your lights, though as the sun and moon, which give light to the night and the day, for so far as you shall think to comprehend God in the volume of any, or of all these, it is but as a vessel of earth, and shall surely be broken. These are the fatlings of Bashan that shall be slain for the feast of the Lord, to which the fowls, ravenous spirits, ready to catch a prey, and beasts of the earth, strong earthly powers, with open mouths ready to devour, are invited. You shall eat and be filled, drink and be drunken, said the Lord. Moreover you shall be filled at my table, said the Lord, with horses and with chariots, with valiant men, all men of war. Horses and chariots there are your strong and swift upon which you have taken flight. All valiant men and men of war, there are you also that fled overtaken by the day of the Lord upon you.

Therefore now does the Lord wait that he may have mercy upon you, and therefore will he be exalted that he may have compassion upon you, for the Lord is the God of Judgment.[115] Blessed are all they that wait for him.

I have told you before that though you have not known what you did in executing justice (as you call it) on the king, yet I have seen the righteous judgments of God in it and can say, the will of the Lord is done.

I shall now proceed to show you wherein you have not done justly and how I see the will of the Lord is done. You may remember I told you that the king was your father and husband who you were to obey in the Lord and no other way. For

---

they are in fact just like King Og of Bashan, that is, doomed to destruction by the righteous for having defied God's law.

114. Gog and Magog are part of the so-called Gog Oracle section of the book of Ezekiel. The Gog Oracle describes how Gog, the leader of the land of Magog, will be destroyed by God for threatening the Israelites. As Ezekiel 39:1–4, GV, states, "Therefore, you son of man, prophesy against God and say, thus said the Lord God, 'Behold I come against you, O Gog, the prince of Meshech and Tubal. And I will destroy you and leave but the sixth part of you and will cause you to come up from the North parts and will bring you upon the mountains of Israel. And I will smite your bow out of your left hand and I will cause your arrows to fall out of your right hand. You shall fall upon the mountains of Israel and all your bands and the people that are with you, for I will give you to the birds and to every feathered fowl and beast of the field to be devoured.'"

115. James 4:12, GV: "There is one Lawgiver which is able to save and to destroy. Who are you that judges another man?"

when he forgot his subordination to divine fatherhood and headship, thinking he had begotten you a generation to his own lust, thereby was the yoke of the spirit and law taken off from your necks. For though you were bound in the body, yet are you free in the spirit of the Lord, but were to suffer his terror to your flesh for the Lord's sake. According to another sentence in that paper, *True liberty is not bound to anything, nor from anything.*[116] It is neither this nor that, either this or that in divine will. You are men that have professed yourselves hot pursuers after liberties. You could not have found better than this, for he that is either this or that, neither this nor that in divine will, is perfect in liberty and only he. Here it is that you have not done justly, for you would be this but not that. You would be free in the spirit but not suffer in the flesh, no not for the Lord's sake.[117] It is true indeed, a just woman must deliver up her husband to the just claim of the law, though she might not accuse him to the Law, nor yet rejoice over him to see his fall, for all that pass by and behold her will say, this was a strumpet and not a faithful wife that rejoices at the fall of her husband, and counter wise the faithful wife mourns in secret for him. It is true she cannot, neither ought she to condemn the just law that cut him off, but is herein as the prophet who said to the people, *if you will not hear, my soul shall mourn in secret for you.* You may also remember that as I told you in the paper presented to your council, that you might not lift your hand against your husband to take his life but suffer his terror to your flesh for the Lord's sake. So I also said in the same paper, if he usurps authority over her, she may appeal to the fatherhood that is the spirit of justice and is in you. Now, therefore, I was to exhort you (as I also did) to be perfectly dead in the will of the Lord to all your lives, liberties, interests, freedoms, or whatsoever you might call yours, without the which you should never prove yourselves faithful in the trust committed to you, as appears for your own interests, liberties, freedoms, and lives. As free commoners of England you first claimed at the king's hand, whom you had owned to be your protector and defender, and when he had ceased to defend you from oppression, then the law or spirit of your union being fallen from king to Parliament, and from Parliament to army. This also is the fatherhood that I also call the spirit of justice that is in you. First I call the fatherhood in that it was the giver of you in marriage for it, was the pleasure of the law to have you protected by a protector as also was likely to be safe for you, but when he unto whom you were given in marriage, that you might be protected by him and bring forth plentiful increase under the shadow of his wing, forgot to whom he was subordinate by profaning the trust committed to him, then was the scepter put into your hand, not as you were the party abused by him nor yet as contending with him, but in that the spirit of justice was pleased to manifest itself in you. Now you were

116. Poole quotes her own "paper," that is, the "handout" section of *A Vision*.

117. 1 Peter 3:18, GV: "For Christ also has once suffered for sinners, the just for the unjust, that he might bring us to God, and was put to death concerning the flesh, but was quickened in the spirit."

his wife as offended by him, and as contending with him, wherefore it is herein I said, *Lift not your hand against him*, as there is a proverb in England (and it is true): *one that is offended is not fit to judge his own cause*.[118] Therefore I was sent to persuade you in the name of the Lord to be perfectly dead in the will of the Lord to all your lives, liberties, freedoms, or whatsoever you might call yours; and then (or therein) even in your death you might have appealed to the fatherhood which is also the divine will in which you should have given up the ghost and ceased to be (or have been no more) to your lives, liberties, freedoms, arrears, indemnities, yes, and your appeal to the fatherhood for your defense also, and (as above said) whatsoever you might call yours, for herein and herein only could you have testified your obedience to the higher powers (God) who is also that spirit of justice that is in you. Wherefore I said not the spirit of the church was in you and shall guide you whether you will be subject to the higher powers (God) or no; for I said this is the great step between you and restoration, the which whosoever take not warily shall stumble and fall, and be taken, that you be perfectly dead in the will of the Lord to all that you might call yours. Wherefore I say this unto you in the word of the Lord, that England's cure shall be no further protected to you than this death be fulfilled in you.

Wherefore, judge you yourselves whether you have not done wickedly or no when you would presume to take the king's life, a pledge for your lives, liberties, freedoms, arrears, indemnities, when your warning was graciously afforded you, that you should have lost them all in the will of the Lord, and surely he would have restored them sevenfold to you and afterwards eternal life. Moreover, I know that spirit of justice in you which blamed the king for profaning his power, and the former Parliament for profaning theirs, could not leave you without excuse when you profaned yours. And have not you profaned yours in presuming to go on without your guide?

"Can the rush grow without mire? Or can the grass grow without water? Though it were green and not cut down, yet shall it wither before any other herb; so are the paths of all that forget God, and the hypocrite's hope shall perish, his confidence also shall be cut off, and his trust shall be as the house of a spider. He

---

118. The legal maxim, *nemo iudex in sua causa*, namely, the idea that no man should be able to judge his own case, is a principle part of the "natural justice" system that pertained to England, particularly in its emphasis upon a fair trial. See Frederick F. Shauer (1976), "English Natural Justice and American Due Process: An Analytical Comparison," *William and Mary Law Review* 18, no. 1 (1976): 47–72. As the aggrieved "wife," the army's General Council did not have the right to take justice into its own hands. It was able to act on behalf of the nation in terms of administering the cure of liberty only insofar as it had inherited the sovereign spirit of divine sanction or "spirit of justice" that the king had forfeited by abusing his people. The power of literally judging the fate of another person's life, however, remained with God.

shall lean upon his house but it shall not stand; he shall hold him fast by it, yet shall it not endure." Job 8:11–15.[119]

It will be in vain for you to contend with your Maker, wherefore stand in silence you mighty men. Yea, when the Lord arises in his temple, let the earth be silent before him.[120]

I shall now proceed to show you wherein I see the will of the Lord is done in the cutting off of the king, even on your parts. First, thus said you, we cannot possibly be safe nor enjoy our lives, liberties, freedoms, arrears, indemnities except we cut him off.[121] I appeal thus to your confidences before the Lord: why, I pray sirs, is it not possible with men? And will you say, therefore, it is impossible with God? Well then, we will go, say you (mark what I say Sirs, and then you will confess it was not a liar that told me so, for God will stain the pride of all flesh) and enquire of God (but you will take your resolutions of an impossibility in your hand, you will not leave that behind you). O Lord, say you, appear in our counsels. Thus you stand with your resolutions and impossibilities in your hand (for when you were warned you would not hear). Behold (say you), we must execute justice (as you call it) upon the king, for we have been seeking the Lord to appear in our counsels, and these are the resolutions and impossibilities that we brought forth with us (no marvel when you carried them in), and presently you call your court and proceed, never covering your faces for shame that you should carry your resolutions and impossibilities with you before the Lord, who only should resolve and appoint what shall be possible. Well, said the Lord, are you resolved upon your impossibilities? Go on, I will overtake you in my appointed time. *Charles*, bow down your head to the stroke, you have deserved it at my hands, said the Lord, and do not confess it, but accuse them not. Leave them to my judgment, I will proceed in equity, said the Lord, or thus is his will done on your part.[122]

Secondly, the will of the Lord is done on his part, suffering according to that scripture that some say was taken to preach to the king, Isaiah 14:18–21: *All the kings of the nations, even they all sleep in glory, everyone in his own house: But you are cast forth as an abominable branch, like the raiment of those that are slain, and thrust through with a sword, which go down to the stones of the pit and a carcass*

---

119. Poole quotes Job 8:11–15, GV, verbatim: "Can a rush grown without mire? Or can the grass grow without water? Though it were in green and not cut down, yet shall it wither before any other herb. So are the paths of all that forget God, and the hypocrite's hope shall perish. His confidence also shall be cut off and his trust shall be as the house of a spider. He shall lean upon his house but it shall not stand. He shall hold him fast by it, yet shall it not endure."

120. A paraphrase of Habakkuk 2:20. Poole's wording is closer to the KJV: "But the LORD is in his holy temple: let all the earth keep silence before him."

121. Poole is citing *A Remonstrance of His Excellency Thomas Lord Fairfax* (appendix 3). This pamphlet lays out the argument of the army's General Council of Officers for executing the king.

122. Psalm 98:9, GV: "Before the Lord, for he comes, for he is come to judge the earth. With righteousness shall he judge the world and the people with equity."

An[other] Alarm of War 97

trodden under foot. You shall not be joined with them in the grave because you have destroyed your own land and slain your people: The seed of the wicked shall not be renowned forever. Prepare a slaughter for his children, for the inequities of their fathers, let them not rise up nor possess the land, nor fill the face of the world with enemies.[123] I have deserved this, said he (for he said I suffer justly, though by an unjust sentence).[124] Behold! There is a worldly dark part of you that the Lord will destroy, but it is not yet fit for destruction. Now it hastens. When I said the spirit of justice was in you, I said not also you will do justice. I said indeed it would guide you, but that will not; neither has it proved that you would be guided by it. Wherefore, behold, we are the children of him that you have cut off, the sons and nephews, the name and remnant that the Lord will cut off, Babel, whom the Lord will destroy when he shall, who is the Lord of Hosts, the God of the whole earth, arise to battle who is strong to smite on the hinder parts all that fly before him, that they might not escape his hands.[125]

Rejoice not (whole Palestina) because the rod of him that has smitten you is broken, for out of the serpent's root shall come forth a cockatrice, and the fruit thereof shall be a fiery flying serpent; for the first born of the poor shall be fed and the needy shall lie down in safety, and I will kill your root with famine (even yours, O you lofty one, who lifts your head above him that fell before you) and it shall slay your remnant.[126] What shall then one answer the messenger of the gentiles? That the Lord has established Zion and the poor of the people shall trust in it (even in his establishment).[127] For in the day that the Lord shall shake terribly the earth then shall you take the images of gold and silver, which every man has made to himself, and cast them to the moles and to the bats, for you have framed glorious glittering images of state policies, religious ordinances, orders, faiths, lights, knowledges, and there are drawn over them very beautiful pretenses, curiously wrought over with needlework very costly (when I say images, that is to say,

---

123. Poole alludes to and quotes from the sermon on Isaiah 14 that the Puritan minister, Hugh Peter, preached to predict that Charles I would be that king's carcass "trodden under foot" (see Wiseman, *Conspiracy and Virtue*, 149).

124. A paraphrase of Charles I's last words upon the scaffold before being beheaded: "An unjust sentence that I suffered to take effect, is punished now by an unjust sentence on me." See Charles Carlton, *Charles I: The Personal Monarch* (London: Routledge, 1995), 353.

125. The army's General Council of Officers and their supporters are the children of the Babylonians who, as prophesied in Isaiah 14:1, would be destroyed by God even as Israel would be restored.

126. Isaiah 14:29–30, KJV: "'Rejoice not thou, whole Palestina, because the rod of him that smote thee is broken: for out of the serpent's root shall come forth a cockatrice, and his fruit shall be a fiery flying serpent. And the firstborn of the poor shall feed, and the needy shall lie down in safety: and I will kill thy root with famine, and he shall slay thy remnant."

127. Isaiah 14:32, GV: "What shall then one answer to the messengers of the Gentiles? That the Lord has established Zion and the poor of his people shall trust in it."

as every man has imagined to himself something more desirable than another).[128] Whereas all things are to be known in God, with the like estimation, for old things shall be done away, and, behold, all things shall become new.[129] Wherefore, when the Lord shall have executed vengeance on your evil party, having pursued the pursuer until he be overtaken and destroyed the destroyer until he be no more, then shall you take the covering of your images, your graven and your molten images, and cast it from you as an unclean rag, saying, get you hence.[130]

But many of you will say, how should I speak this to you of images, for you are sure that your religions, knowledges, faiths, lights, ordinances, orders, yes, and your state policies, you have received from God. It is true, the silver and the gold are the Lord's, the earrings and the jewels.[131]

I shall therefore wait upon the Lord, that I might be made both faithful and fruitful in making it evident to you how you have profaned them by making the images both graven and molten.[132]

First, for your religions, that you received such knowledge of God that therein you might serve God. I might grant but that you might so keep to this knowledge, that you might know him no more nor otherwise I deny (for no knowledge of God does exclude a more full, certain or various knowledge of him), for this is a molten image, the which being cast into the mold, it can hold no more. Or thus,

128. Isaiah 2:12–21, GV: "For the day of the Lord of hosts is upon all the proud and haughty, and upon all that are exalted and it shall be made low. Even upon all the cedars of Lebanon that are high and exalted and upon all the oaks of Bashan. And upon all the high mountains and upon all the hills that are lifted up. And upon every high tower and upon every strong wall. And upon all the ships of Tarshish and upon all pleasant pictures. And the haughtiness of men shall be brought low and the loftiness of men shall be abased and the Lord shall only be exalted in that day. And the idols will be utterly destroyed. Then they shall go into the holes of the rocks and into the caves of the earth from before the fear of the Lord and from the glory of his majesty when he shall arise to destroy the earth. At that day shall man cast away his silver idols and his golden idols (which they had made themselves to worship them) to the moles and to the bats, to go into the holes of the rocks and into the tops of the ragged rocks from before the fear of the Lord and from the glory of his majesty when he shall rise to destroy the earth."

129. Isaiah 43:18, GV: "Remember you not the former things, neither regard the things of old." See also 2 Corinthians 5:17, GV: "Therefore if any man be in Christ, let him be a new creature. Old things are passed away. Behold, all things are become new."

130. Isaiah 30:22, GV: "And you shall pollute the covering of the images of silver and the rich ornament of thine image of gold, and cast these away as a menstrous cloth, and you will say to it, 'Get thee hence.'"

131. Exodus 32:2, GV: "And Aaron said unto them, Pluck off the golden earrings, which are in the ears of your wives, of your sons, and of your daughters, and bring them to me."

132. Constructing idols is not considered a viable way to understand God. See Exodus 20:4, GV: "Thou shalt make no graven images, neither any similitude of things that are in heaven above, neither that are in the earth below, nor that are in the waters under the earth" and Isaiah 44:10, GV: "Who hath made a god, or molten an image, that is profitable for nothing."

if you should say the Lord has given me such certain knowledge of himself, how I should worship him, the Father in the Son, who is God, Man and Savior of us all, our Mediator and Redeemer, in whom I have found satisfaction, and admit to no further knowledge or religious worship of him than you have received, is to deny that scripture, *The knowledge of God passes all understanding*,[133] and not only to make a molten but a graven image also, by engraving upon the image before cast into the mold all the conceptions and receptions of knowledge, light and life, the which you by so doing will say you have comprehended the incomprehensible. And this is the curtain or veil which is drawn over.[134] You received it of God, curiously working it with a needle in these figures, at such time, in such a place, but I will tell you, not for such an end, for you are forbidden to make to yourself any image of anything in heaven or earth to bow down to it and worship it.

Secondly, you will say that you received your knowledges of God also. It is well, nevertheless, to consider whether you have not molded them into some other image than you received them in (or confined them to that). This is also an abomination, for you would therefore despise the knowledge of another because it is not bound up in your bundle and would also deny that the riches of the wisdom of God is past finding out. These are your idols, *O England*, with your princes and governors; wherefore return and say no more, *God is here but not there*, for behold, he is both here and there,[135] though you perceive it not, who will say, if this be God that is not, because the wheels are contrary.[136]

Thirdly, of faith, let us consider what the apostle says, *If one have all faith, and have not love, it is nothing*.[137] You will say you received faith from God (which I would not deny) to believe, that you should be delivered from such a distress, and you were delivered, that he would give you your lives for a prey in such a battle. And he gave it you[138] that he would deliver the king and his army into

---

133. Philippians 4:7, GV: "And the peace of God which passed all understanding, shall preserve your hearts and minds in Christ Jesus."

134. Hebrews 10:20, GV: "By the new and giving way which he has prepared for us, through the veil that is his flesh."

135. Luke 17:21, GV: "Neither shall the mean say, Lo here or lo there, for behold the kingdom of God is within you."

136. Ezekiel 10:16, GV: "And when the Cherubims went, the wheels went by them and when the Cherubims lift up their wings to mount up from the earth, the same wheels also turned not from beside them."

137. 1 Corinthians 13:2–3, GV: "And though I had the gift of prophesy, and knew all secrets and all knowledge, yeah, if I had all faith, so that I could remove mountains, and have not love, I were nothing."

138. Jeremiah 45:5, GV: "And seek you great things for yourself? Seek them not, for behold, I will bring a plague upon all flesh, says the Lord, but your life will I give you for a prey in all places, wherever you go."

the Parliament's hands, and it is done, that this army,[139] though it had suffered many hardships not only from the open enemy but also from both Parliament and people whose cause they have stood to maintain, should be made famous throughout the world (the which I could grant in its restoration). But hold you until it be fulfilled in love, for faith that lives works by love,[140] and how can you say you love him in whom you have not believed, to trust him with your lives, liberties, freedoms, interests, arrears, indemnities, in the day that it was required at your hands. You could, it may be, as above said, believe that your lives should be given you for a prey when you stood in battle, for some men escaped in the hottest and so might you in the will of the Lord. It may be that the Lord gave you a word also. It is well, this was when you were gone forth to battle. But when you must stand still and see the salvation of the Lord, you flee back, for when you were in the use of means that is common with men for deliverance then you thought you had a ground to believe, but when you must die before you live, herein you will not trust the almighty and everlasting Father, though you shall find it a truth that I said unto you, you must lose your lives before you can save them and rejoice in it when the Lord shall grant you to see how good it is, for you must be the mountain wasted before you can be the valley exalted.[141] Wherefore this is also an image, or images made up also of your faith, which you have graven to yourselves and shall be broken to pieces in the day of the Lord when only faith that works by love shall continue.

Fourthly, your lights you will say you received of the Lord, then you cannot deny but you owe them to the Lord.[142] Therefore, you may not go to put out that light that another has received also from the Lord by imagining that whatsoever light should come from the Lord you should know, because you are sure you received yours from the Lord. This is also an image that you have melted in the mold fitted for it, wherefore I beseech you, cleanse yourselves from idols by looking to the most high for wisdom and strength to walk in it.

Fifthly, you will say you received your orders from God also.[143] It may be, yet let it be considered that the ways of the Almighty are in deep waters and you cannot find out all his steps, which may be given to another to discern, that he might

---

139. The New Model Army, over which the General Council of Officers presided.

140. Galatians 5:6, GV: "For in Jesus Christ, neither circumcision avails anything, nor uncircumcision, but faith which works by love."

141. Isaiah 40:4, GV: "Every valley shall be exalted and every mountain and hill shall be made low and the crooked shall be straight and the rough places plain."

142. Isaiah 60:1, GV: "Arise, Oh Jerusalem, be bright, for your light is come and the glory of the Lord is risen upon you."

143. A possible reference to Hebrews 10:36: "For you have need of patience, that after you have done the will of God, you might receive the promises" (GV).

walk in them.[144] Why should you also engrave an image of the sea so that might not be called order by your allowance which will not be brought into your mold?

Sixthly, your ordinances you will say also you received from the Lord.[145] Then let it be considered also that they can be no further improved to the Lord than by standing in silence before all following that outshine them. As it is written, *When the Lord shall reign in Mount Zion, and in Jerusalem gloriously, then shall the sun be ashamed and the moon abashed.*[146] I know that they are brightest but as the sun and moon, the light of the night and of the day, the which must admit of more glory, so must also your wisdom and council and your High Court of Justice (so called), for as the king, your father, fell because he was not subject to the higher powers, God, so shall you pass through the fire seven times until you be subject.[147] Yet there shall stand up a young man, a man of strength, in whom the just and good spirit that has appeared in you shall remain.[148]

Seventhly, your state policies you will say you received of the Lord also, for you often beseech Him to appear in your Council, but had you not something you would call justice concluded on before in your breasts, without which you could not be secured by men, and you would not trust God? Wherefore thus said the Lord, *Behold, I will lay your skirts upon your face so that all that pass by may behold your nakedness,*[149] *for I will bring down the mountains and exalt the valleys, for, behold, all the high places of the earth shall be brought down, not one left.*[150]

144. Isaiah 43:16, GV: "Thus saith the Lord which make a way in the sea and a path in the mighty waters."

145. Ephesians 2:15–16, GV: "In abrogating through his flesh the hatred, that is, the law of commandments which stands in ordinances, for to make of two one new man in himself, making peace, and that he might reconcile both to God in one body by his cross and stay hatred thereby."

146. Isaiah 24:23, GV: "Then the moon shall be abashed and the sun ashamed, when the Lord of hosts shall reign in Mount Zion and in Jerusalem and glory shall be before his ancient men."

147. Psalm 12:6, GV: "The words of the Lord are pure words, as the silver, tried in a furnace of earth, fired seven fold."

148. A possible collation of Luke 21:36, GV: "Watch therefore and pray continually that you may be counted worthy to escape all these things that shall come to pass and that you may stand before the son of Man"; and Ephesians 6:10: "Finally my brothers, be strong in the Lord and in the power of his might."

149. Nahum 3:5, GV: "Behold, I come upon you, saith the Lord of hosts, and I will discover your skirts upon your face, and will show the nations your filthiness and the kingdoms your shame." See also Jeremiah 13:26: "Therefore I have also discovered your skirts upon your face, that your shame may appear."

150. Isaiah 40:4, GV: "Every valley shall be exalted and every mountain and hill shall be made low and the crooked shall be straight and the rough places plain."

102 ELIZABETH POOLE

The Postscript

The things that are above written I have showed you my authority for. Whether you will hear or whether you will forbear, they shall overtake you, nevertheless, I have a word from the Lord to speak to your better part, or that young man, or man of strength which remained a vessel to bear the good seed that remains of you when your carcass, or the body of your confederacy, is slain.[151] It is this. Rejoice, you barren that bears not, shout for joy you desolate woman, who living alone trusts in God, for more are the children of the desolate than the married wife, said the Lord,[152] for the poor of the people shall be strengthened in this, that the Lord will establish Zion.[153] Neither said he to the house of Jacob, seek you my face in vain.[154] He spoke it in righteousness and will perform it that those that trust in him shall not perish.[155] Yet one word I add. It is not the tongue that has anything to boast of, which is the soul that seeks God, but that spirit in man that lives alone, trusting in God, making God its expectation,[156] saying in faithfulness and truth, there is none in heaven nor in earth that I desire in comparison to you, whose continual prayer is in faith and confidence, let your kingdom come, and your will be done in earth as it is in heaven.[157] Rejoice in this, that that only which can be shaken must be done away that that which cannot be shaken may be

---

151. Matthew 13:37–38, GV: "Then answered he, and said to them, 'He that sows the good seed is the son of man. And the field is the world and the good seed, they are the children of the kingdom and the tares are the children of the wicked.'"

152. Isaiah 54:1, GV: "'Rejoice O barren that did not bear, break forth into joy and rejoice you that did not travail with children, for the desolate have more children than the married wife,' says the Lord."

153. Isaiah 25:4, GV: "For you have been a strength to the poor, even a strength to the needy in his trouble, a refuge against the tempest, a shadow against the heat, for the blast of the mighty is like a storm against the wall."

154. Isaiah 45:19, GV: "I have not spoken in secret, neither in a place of darkness in the earth. I said not in vain to the seed of Jacob, 'seek you me: I the Lord do speak righteousness and declare righteous things.'"

155. John 3:15, GV: "That whosoever believes in him, should not perish, but have eternal life."

156. A collation of James 3:5, GV: "Even so the tongue is a little member and boasts of great things. Behold, how great a thing a little fire kindles"; and James 3:8–9, GV: "But the tongue can no man tame. It is an unruly evil, full of deadly poison. Therewith bless we God even the Father, and therewith curse we men which are made after the similitude of God."

157. Matthew 6:9–10, GV: "After this manner therefore pray you, 'Our father which art in heaven, hallowed be thy Name. Thy kingdom come, Thy will be done even in earth as it is in heaven.'"

established.[158] Wherefore the reward shall be double upon the head of those that have fulfilled the inequities of their fathers.[159]

The Lord will maintain the cause of the just:
Your Fellow Sufferer in the Kingdom
of the Patience of Christ.
Elizabeth Poole

FINIS.

---

158. Hebrews 12:27, GV: "And this word [shaken], yet once more, signifies the removing of those things which are shaken, as of things which are made with hands, that the things which are not shaken may remain."

159. Obadiah 1:15, GV: "For the day of the Lord is near; upon all the heathen, as you have done, it shall be done to you. Your reward shall return upon your head."

Appendix 1: Contexts for Elizabeth Poole

This appendix contains materials that provide some insight into Elizabeth Poole's otherwise obscure life, specifically her decision as a young woman to leave her family, join an Independent congregation, and become a prophetess. *The Confession of Faith* (1644) lays out the beliefs of her Particular Baptist Church. *A Brief Remonstrance* (1645) records the perspectives of both Poole's father, Robert, and her minister, William Kiffin, on the church's practice of "gathering" such social subordinates as women and servants into its congregation. *A Discovery of Six Women Preachers* (1641) is a satire conveying the dim view that many of Poole's contemporaries took of women's assumption of forms of religious authority traditionally reserved for elite men.

William Kiffin et al.
The Confession of Faith *(1644)*

The Confession of Faith (Wing C5790) was published in 1644 by fifteen prominent Baptist leaders, including William Kiffin, Poole's minister in his London-based congregation, to explain the congregation's actual beliefs and practices. It is tantamount to a manifesto in that it not only conveys but also rationalizes and defends the Particular Baptist Church's principles, including its belief in voluntary baptism and the idea that only a "particular" few—or "elect"—would be saved by God. Because of Baptists' opposition to infant baptism, detractors claimed they were "Anabaptists," that is, opponents of baptism altogether, as well as political revolutionaries.

There were at least seven Particular Baptist churches in London at this time, and their meetings were illegal. They continued to gather, but they always labored under a cloud of suspicion. As *The Confession* reports, they were accused of such transgressions as "holding free-will, falling away from grace, denying original sin, disclaiming of magistracy, denying to assist them either in persons or in purse in any of their lawful commands, doing acts unseemly in the dispensing of the ordinance of baptism not to be named among Christians" (p. 108). Their reputations were especially damaged by a man named Dr. Daniel Featley, who, after debating a group of Baptists in Southwark in 1642, publicized his scorn for them in a pamphlet colorfully titled *The Dippers Dipped; or, The Anabaptists Ducked and Plunged over Head and Ears at a Disputation in Southwark* (1646; Wing F587). He dedicated the work to Parliament, warning its members that the Baptists would take over England as the Anabaptists had Münster, Germany. In 1643, Parliament responded by summoning the Westminster Assembly of Divines to meet and settle the disputes surrounding illegal churches. It was the following year that the London Particular Baptists issued *The Confession of Faith*, also known as the *First London Baptist Confession*, to defend themselves.

105

106 *Appendix 1*

The document is carefully laid out, starting with a statement of purpose followed by fifty-three articles, each articulating a core precept and supporting it with citations of scripture. These articles and their scriptural bases frame the trajectory of Poole's life as a member of the Baptist church. Article XXXIV invites believers from all ranks to become servants in the church as it embodies Christ's household. Article XLV asserts that those who enjoy the gift of vision should be appointed to prophesy by the congregation. Article XLII justifies the church's power to excommunicate any member. And Article XXIX states that once believers are sanctified, they are permanently free of sin.

A second edition of the *The Confession* was issued in 1646. A third and a fourth edition were released in 1651 and 1652, respectively. By this time, the Particular Baptists had achieved some legitimacy, with congregations appearing in numerous places under Oliver Cromwell's policy of religious toleration. However, after the renewed persecution of Independent churches that ensued upon the restoration of King Charles II in 1660, the Baptists were compelled to issue a 1677 edition that strategically omitted all names, including the printer's.

The copy reprinted here is housed in the Union Theological Seminary in New York City and is available on *EEBO*.

THE CONFESSION
OF FAITH,
Of those CHURCHES which are
commonly (though falsely) called
ANABAPTISTS;

Presented to the view of all that fear
God, to examine by the touchstone of the Word
of Truth: As likewise for the taking off those
aspersions which are frequently both in Pulpit and
Print, (although unjustly) cast upon them.

Acts 4:20
We cannot but speak the things which we have seen and heard.

Isai. 8:20
To the Law and to the testimony, if they speak not according to this Rule, it is because there is no light in them.

2 Cor. 1:9–10.
But we had the sentence of death in our selves, that we should not

trust in our selves, but in the living God, which raises the dead;
who delivered us from so great a death, and does deliver, in whom
we trust that he will yet deliver.

LONDON,
Printed by *Matthew Simmons* in *Aldersgate-street.*
1644.

To
ALL THAT DESIRE
The lifting up of the Name of the
Lord Jesus in sincerity, the poor despised
Churches of God in London send greeting,
with prayers for their further increase in the
knowledge of CHRIST JESUS.

We question not but that it will seem strange to many men, that such as we are frequently termed to be, lying under that calumny and black brand of heretics and sowers of division, should presume to appear so publicly as now we have done: But yet notwithstanding we may well say, to give answer to such, what David *said to his brother when the Lord's battle was a fighting,* 1 Sam. 29:30:[1] *Is there not a cause? Surely, if ever people had cause to speak, for the vindication of the truth of* Christ *in their hands, we have, that being indeed the main wheel at this that sets us to work, for had anything by men been transacted against our persons only, we could quietly have sat still and committed our cause to who is a righteous judge, who will in the great day judge the secrets of all men's hearts by Jesus Christ. But being it is not only us, but the Truth professed by us, we cannot, we dare not but speak; it is no strange thing to any observing man, what sad changes are laid, not only by the world, that know not God, but also by those that think themselves much wronged if they be not looked upon as the chief worthies of the church of God and watchmen of the city.[2] But*

---

1. These chapters recount the time in David's life when, before he himself became king, he served as military leader for the controversial King Saul. David was so successful that his popularity with the Israelites drove Saul to plot David's death. Warned by his friend Jonathan (Saul's own son), David gained the protection of Saul's enemy, the Philistine King Achish. David served King Achish with his usual loyalty, but the king's noblemen doubted David's sincerity and prevented him from joining their march against Saul. After both Jonathan and Saul were killed in the ensuing battle, David was anointed king over Judah.

2. These quotations remind us that the Bible contains numerous references to those whose faith enables them to serve as watchmen or guardians of God's holy city. For example, one of the quotes paraphrased here, Isaiah 62:6, KJV, reads: "I have set watchmen upon thy walls, O Jerusalem, [which] shall never hold their peace day nor night: ye that make mention of the LORD, keep not silence."

it has fared with us from them, as from the poor spouse seeking her beloved, Cant. 5.6, 7.[3] *They finding us out of that common road-way [that they] themselves walk, have smote us and taken away our veil, that so we may by them be recommended odious in the eyes of all that behold us, and in the hearts of all that think upon us, which they have done both in pulpit and print, charging us with holding free-will, falling away from grace, denying original sin, disclaiming of magistracy, denying to assist them either in persons or purse in any of their lawful commands, doing acts unseemly in the dispensing of the ordinance of baptism, not to be named among Christians.[4] All which charges we disclaim as tortuously untrue, though by reason of these calumnies cast upon us, many that fear God are discouraged and forestalled in harboring a good thought; either of us or what we profess, and many that know not God encouraged, if they can find the place of our meeting, to get together in clusters to stone us, or looking upon as a people holding such things as that we are not worthy to live.[5] We have therefore the clearing of the truth we profess, that it may be at liberty, though we be in bonds, briefly published a Confession of our Faith, as desiring all that fear God, seriously to consider whether (or if they compare what we here say and confess in the presence of the Lord Jesus and his saints) men have not with their tongues in pulpits, and pens in print, both spoken and written things that are contrary to truth. But we know our God in his own time will clear our cause, and lift up his Son to make him the chief corner-stone, though he has been (or now should be) rejected of master builders.[6] And because it may be conceived, that what is here published may be but the judgement of some one particular congregation, more refined than the rest,[7] we do therefore here subscribe it, some who though we be distinct in respect of our particular bodies, for convenience sake, being as many as can well meet together in one place, yet are all one in communion, holding Jesus Christ to be our head and Lord, under whose government we desire alone to walk, in following the Lamb wheresoever he goes. And we believe the Lord will daily cause*

3. A reference to the "Song of Solomon," Canticle 5:6–7, KJV: "I opened to my beloved; but my beloved had withdrawn himself, *and* was gone: my soul failed when he spoke: I sought him, but I could not find him; I called him, but he gave me no answer. The watchmen that went about the city found me, they smote me, they wounded me; the keepers of the walls took away my veil from me."

4. As noted in the introduction (p. 28), Baptists followed the example of John the Baptist, not only in advocating adult baptism as an act of free will rather than enforced infant baptism but also in believing that they could baptize themselves and one another even though they were not licensed ministers. Because of the latter, they were often accused of using the baptismal ceremonies they frequently held in rivers and streams as a cover for "illicit" sex.

5. Because Baptist ceremonies were so controversial, they were often held at night and in secret locations. Authorities used spies and informants to ferret out the times and locations so they could raid the ceremonies and arrest participants.

6. Mark 12:10, KJV: "And have you not read this scripture; The stone which the builders rejected is become the head of the corner."

7. More literate or educated.

truth more to appear in the hearts of his saints, and make them ashamed of their folly in the land of their nativity, that so they may with one shoulder, more study[8] to lift up the name of the Lord Jesus, and stand for his appointments and laws, which are the desires and prayers of the condemned churches of Christ in London for all saints.

Subscribed in the Names of Seven Churches in *London*.

William Kiffin.	Thomas Skippard.	Thomas Killcop.
Thomas Patience.	Thomas Munday.	Paul Hobson.
Jonn Spilsbery.	Thomas Gunne.	Thomas Goare.
George Tipping.	John Mahbatt.	Joseph Phelpes.
Samuel Richardson.	John Webb.	Edward Heath.

THE

CONFESSION

Of FAITH, of those Churches

which are commonly (though falsely)

called ANABAPTISTS.

I.

That God as he is in himself, cannot be comprehended of any but himself[9] dwelling in that inaccessible light, that no eye can attain unto, whom never man saw, nor can see, that there is but[10] one God, one Christ, one Spirit, one Faith, one Baptism,[11] one rule of holiness and obedience for all Saints, at all times, in all places to be observed.

---

8. It is possible that the word is intended to be "sturdy." Either way, the author insists that the church will, as one body, aspire or perhaps "study" to stand up proudly for its beliefs.

9. 1 Tim. 6:16. In the main text of the original pamphlet, scriptural citations are assigned a letter (e.g., "a," "b," "c," etc.) rather than a number, with the citations themselves appearing in either the right- or left-hand margins of the text. I have assigned the citations a number and placed the corresponding chapter and verse citations in footnotes. The chapter names are abbreviated here as they are in the original, with one exception. Whereas the original abbreviated the name of the book of John as "Joh.," I have spelled it out in full here for the sake of clarity.

10. 1 Tim. 2:5; Eph. 4:4–6; 1 Cor. 12:4–6, 13; John 14.

11. 1 Tim. 6:3, 13, 14; Gal. 1:8–9; 2 Tim. 3:15.

II.

That God is[12] of himself, that is, neither from another, nor of another, nor by another, nor for another.[13] But is a spirit who as his being is of himself, so he gives[14] being, moving, and preservation to all other things being in himself, eternal, most holy, every way infinite[15] in greatness, wisdom, power, justice, goodness, truth, etc. In this god-head, there is the Father, the Son, and the Spirit, being every one of them one and the same God, and therefore not divided but distinguished one from another by their several properties, the[16] Father being from himself, the Son of the Father from everlasting, the holy[17] Spirit proceeding from the Father and the Son.

III.

That God has[18] decreed in himself from everlasting touching all things, effectually to work and dispose[19] them according to the council of his own will, to the glory of his name; in which decree appears his wisdom, constancy, truth, and faithfulness.[20] Wisdom is that whereby he contrives all things.[21] Constancy is that whereby the decree of God remains always immutable.[22] Truth is that whereby he declares that alone which he has decreed, and though his sayings may seem to sound sometimes another thing, yet the sense of them does always agree with the decree.[23] Faithfulness is that whereby he effects that he has decreed, as he has decreed. And touching his creature man,[24] God had in Christ before the foundation of the world, according to the good pleasure of his will, foreordained some men to eternal life through Jesus Christ, to the praise and glory of his grace,[25] leaving the rest in their sin to their just condemnation, to the praise of his justice.

12. Esa. 44:67 & 43:11 & 46:9.

13. John 4:24.

14. Exod. 5:14.

15. Rom. 11:36; Acts 17, 18.

16. Cor. 8:6.

17. John 15:16; Gal. 4:6.

18. Esa. 48:10; Rom. 11:34–36; Matt. 10:19–20.

19. Eph. 1:11.

20. Col. 3:2–3.

21. Num. 23:19–20.

22. Jere. 10:1; Rom. 3:4.

23. Esa. 44:10.

24. Eph. 1:3–7 & Tim 1:9; Acts 13:48; Rom. 8:29–30.

25. Judg. verses 3 & 6; Rom. 9:11–13; Prov. 16:4.

IV.

In the beginning,[26] God made all things very good, created man after his own[27] image and likeness, filling him with all perfection of all natural excellency and uprightness, free from all sin.[28] But long he abode not in this honor, but by the[29] subtlety of the serpent, which Satan used as his instrument, himself with his angels having sinned before, and not[30] kept their first estate, but left their own habitation. First[31] Eve then Adam being secured did wittingly and willingly fall unto disobedience and transgression of the commandment of their great creator, for the which death came upon all, and reigned over all, so that all since the fall are conceived in sin, and brought forth in iniquity, and so by nature children of wrath, and servants of sin, subjects of[32] death, and all other calamities due to sin in this world and forever, being considered in the state of nature, without relation to Christ.

V.

All mankind being thus fallen, and become altogether dead in sins and trespasses, and subject to the eternal wrath of the great God by transgression, yet the elect, which God has[33] loved with an everlasting love, are[34] redeemed, quickened, and saved, not by themselves, neither by their own works, lest any man should boast himself, but wholly and only by God of[35] his free grace and mercy through Jesus Christ, who of God is made unto us wisdom, righteousness, sanctification, and redemption that as it is written, He that rejoices, let him rejoice in the Lord.

VI.

This[36] therefore is life eternal, to know the only true God, and whom he has sent Jesus Christ. And[37] on the contrary, the Lord will render vengeance in flaming fire to them that know not God, and obey not the gospel of our Lord Jesus Christ.

26. Gen. 1st chap.; Col. 1:16; Heb. 11:3; Esa. 4:12.

27. Gen. 1:26; 1 Cor. 15:45–46; Eccles. 7:31.

28. Psalm 49:20.

29. Gen. 3:1, 4, 5; 2 Cor. 11:3.

30. 2 Pet. 2:4; Jude ver. 6; John 8:44.

31. Gen. 3:1–2, 6; 1 Tim. 2:14; Eccles. 7:31; Gal. 3:22.

32. Rom. 5:12, 18, 19 & 6:23; Eph. 2:3.

33. Jer. 31:2.

34. Gen. 3:14; Eph. 1:3, 7 & 2, 4, 9; Thess. 5:9; Acts 13:38.

35. 1 Cor. 1:30–31; 2 Cor. 5:21; Jer. 9:23–24.

36. John 17:3; Heb. 5:9; Jer. 23:5–6.

37. 2 Thess. 1:9; John 3:36.

VII.

The[38] rule of this knowledge, faith, and obedience, concerning the worship and service of God, and all other Christian duties, is not man's inventions, opinions, devices, laws, constitutions, or traditions unwritten whatsoever, but only the word of God contained in the canonical scriptures.

VIII.

In[39] this written word, God has plainly revealed whatsoever he has thought needful for us to know, believe, and acknowledge, touching the nature and office of Christ, in whom all the promises are yea and amen to the praise of God.

IX.

Touching the Lord Jesus, of whom[40] Moses and the prophets wrote, and whom the apostles preached, is the[41] Son of God the Father, the brightness of his glory, the graven form of his being, God with him and with his holy Spirit, by whom he made the world, by whom he upholds and governs all the works he has made, who also[42] when the fullness of time was come, was made man of a[43] woman, of the tribe of[44] Judah, of the seed of Abraham and David, to wit, of Mary that blessed Virgin, by the holy Spirit coming upon her, and the power of the most high overshadowing her, and was also[45] in all things like unto us, sin only excepted.

X.

Touching his office,[46] Jesus Christ only is made the mediator of the new covenant, even the everlasting covenant of grace between God and man, to[47] be fully the prophet, priest, and king of the church of God for evermore.

XI.

Unto this office he was foreordained from everlasting, by the[48] authority of the Father, and in respect of his manhood, from the womb called and separated, and[49] anointed also most fully and abundantly with all gifts necessary, God having without measure poured the Spirit upon him.

38. John 5:39; 2 Tim. 3:15–17; Col. 21:18, 23; Matt. 15:9.

39. Acts 3:22–23; I Heb. 1, 2; 2 Tim. 3:15–17; 2 Cor. 1:30.

40. Gen. 3:15 & 22:18 & 49:10; Daniel 7:13 & 9:24–26.

41. Proverbs 8:23; John 1:1–3; 1 Col. 1:15–17.

42. Gal. 4:4.

43. Heb., 7:14; Rev. 5:5 with Gen. 49:9–10; Rom. 1:3 & 9:5.

44. Matt.1:16 with Luke 3:23, 26; Heb. 2:16.

45. Esa. 53:3–5; Phil. 2:8.

46. 2 Tim. 2:15; Heb. 9:15; John 14:6.

47. Heb. 1:2 & 3:1–2 & 7:24; Esa. 9:6–7, Acts 5:31.

48. Prov. 8:23; Esa. 42:6 & 49:1, 5.

49. Esa. 11:2–5 & 61:1–3 with Luke 4:17, 22; John 1:14, 16 & 3:34.

XII.

In this call, the scripture holds forth two special things considerable: First, the call to the office; secondly, the office itself. First, that[50] none takes this honor but he that is called of God, as was Aaron, so also Christ, it being an action especially of God the Father, whereby a special covenant being made, he ordained his Son to this office: which covenant is, that[51] Christ should be made a sacrifice for sin, that he shall see his seed, and prolong his days, and the pleasure of the Lord shall prosper in his hand, which calling therefore contains in itself[52] choosing,[53] foreordaining,[54] sending. Choosing respects the end, foreordaining the means, sending the execution itself,[55] all of mere grace, without any condition foreseen, either in men, or in Christ himself.

XIII.

So[56] that this office to be mediator, that is, to be prophet, priest, and king of the church of God, is so proper to Christ, as neither in the whole nor in any part thereof, can be transferred from him to any other.

XIV.

This Office itself to which Christ was called, is threefold: of[57] a prophet, of[58] a priest, and of[59] a king. This number and order of offices is shown, first by men's necessities grievously laboring[60] under ignorance, by reason whereof they stand in infinite necessity of the prophetical office of Christ to relieve them.[61] Secondly, alienation from God, wherein they stand in need of the priestly office to reconcile them. Thirdly our[62] utter disability to return to him, by which they stand in need of the power of Christ in his kingly office to assist and govern them.

XV.

Touching the prophecy of Christ, it is that whereby he has[63] perfectly revealed the whole will of God out of the bosom of the Father, that is needful for his servants to

50. Heb. 5:4–6.

51. Esa. 53:10.

52. Esa. 43:12.

53. 1 Pet. 1:30.

54. John 3:17 & 9:27 & 10:36; Esa. 61:1.

55. John 3:16; Rom. 8:32.

56. 1 Tim. 2:5; Heb. 7:24; Dan. 9:14; Acts 4:12; Luke 1:33; John 14:6.

57. Deut. 18:15 with Acts 3:22–23.

58. Psalm 110:3; Heb. 3:1 & 4:14–15 & 5:6 & 10:21.

59. Psalm 2:6.

60. Acts 26:18; Col. 1:3.

61. Col. 1:27; Eph. 2:12.

62. Cant. 1:3; John 6:44.

63. John 1:18 & 12:49–50 & 15 & 17:8; Deut. 18:15.

114 *Appendix 1*

know, believe, and obey, and therefore is called not only a prophet and[64] a doctor, and the[65] apostle of our profession, and the[66] angel of the covenant, but also the very[67] wisdom of God, and[68] the treasures of wisdom and understanding.

XVI.

That he might be such a prophet as thereby to be every way complete, it was necessary that he should be[69] God, and with all also that he should be man; for unless he had been God, he could never have perfectly understood the will of God,[70] neither had he been able to reveal it throughout all ages, and unless he had been man, he could not fitly have unfolded it in his[71] own person to man.

XVII.

Touching his priesthood, Christ[72] being consecrated, has appeared once to put away sin by the offering and sacrifice of himself, and to this end has fully performed and suffered all those things by which God, through the blood of that his cross in an acceptable sacrifice, might reconcile his elect only;[73] and having broken down the partition wall, and therewith finished and removed all those rites, shadows, and ceremonies, is now entered within the vail, into the holy of holiest, that is, to the very heavens and presence of God, where he forever lives and sits at the right hand of majesty, appearing before the face of his father to make intercession for such as come to the throne of grace by that new and living way; and not that only but[74] makes his people a spiritual house, a holy priesthood, to offer up spiritual sacrifice acceptable to God through him, neither does the Father accept or Christ offer to the Father any other worship or worshippers.

XVIII.

This priesthood was not legal or temporary, but according to the[75] order of Melchisedec.[76] Not by a carnal commandment, but by the power of an endless life;[77]

---

64. Matthew 23:10.

65. Heb. 3:1.

66. Mal. 3:1.

67. 1 Cor. 1:24.

68. Col. 2:3.

69. John 1:18 & 3:13.

70. 1 Cor. 2:11, 16.

71. Acts 3:22 with Deut. 18:15; Heb. 1:1.

72. John 17:19; Heb. 5:7–9 & 26; Rom. 5:19; Ephes. 5:12; Col. 1:20.

73. Eph. 2:14–16; Rom. 8:34.

74. 2 Peter 2:5; John 4:23–24.

75. Heb. 7:17.

76. Heb. 7:16.

77. Heb. 7:18–21.

not by an order that is weak and lame, but stable and perfect; not for a[78] time, but forever, admitting no succor, but perpetual and proper to Christ, and of him that ever lives. Christ himself was the priest, sacrifice, and altar: He was[79] a priest, according to both natures; he was a sacrifice most properly according to his human nature,[80] wherein the scripture it is wont to be attributed to his body, to his blood. Yet the chief force whereby this sacrifice was made effectual, did depend upon his[81] divine nature, namely that the Son of God did offer himself for us. He was the[82] altar to sanctify that which is offered upon it, and so it ought to be of greater dignity than the sacrifice itself.

XIX.

Touching his kingdom,[83] Christ being risen from the dead, ascended into heaven, sat on the right hand of God the Father, having all power in heaven and earth, given unto him, he doth spiritually govern his church, exercising his power[84] over all angels and men, good and bad, to the preservation and salvation of the elect, to the overruling and destruction of his enemies, which are the reprobates,[85] communicating and applying the benefits, virtue, and fruit of his prophesy and priesthood to his elect, namely, to the subduing and taking away of their sins, to their justification and adoption of sons, generation, sanctification, preservation, and strengthening in all their conflicts against Satan, the world, the flesh, and the temptation of them, continually dwelling in, governing and keeping their hearts in faith and filial fear by his spirit, which having[86] given it, he never takes away from them, but by it still begets and nourishes in them faith, repentance, love, joy, hope, and all heavenly light in the soul unto immortality, notwithstanding through our own unbelief, and the temptations of Satan, the sensible sight of this light and love be clouded and overwhelmed for the time.[87] And on the contrary, ruling in the world over his enemies, Satan and all his vessels of wrath, limiting, using, restraining them by his mighty power, as seems good in his divine wisdom and justice to the execution of his determinate council, delivering them up to a

---

78. Heb. 7:24–25.

79. Heb. 5:6.

80. Heb. 10:10; 1 Pet. 1:18–19; Col. 1:20, 22; Esa. 53:10; Matthew 20:28.

81. Matt. 20:21; Rom. 8:3.

82. Heb. 9:14 & 11:10, 12, 15; Matt. 23:17; John 17:19.

83. 1 Cor. 15:4; 1 Pet. 3:21–22; Matthew 28:18–19, 29; Luke 24:51; Acts 1:11 & 5:30–31; John 19:36; Rom. 14:17.

84. Mark 1:17; Heb. 1:14; John 16:7, 15.

85. John 5:26, 17; Rom. 5:6–8 & 14:17; Gal. 5:22–23; John 1:4, 13.

86. John 13:1 & 10:28–29 & 14:16–17; Rom. 11:29; Psalm 10–11; Job. 33:29–30; 2 Cor. 12:7, 9.

87. Job 1 and 2 chapters; Rom. 1:21 & 2:4–6 & 9:17–18; Eph. 4:17–18; 2 Peter, 3rd chap.

116 *Appendix 1*

reprobate mind, to be kept through their own deserts, in darkness and sensuality unto judgement.

XX.

This[88] kingdom shall be then fully persecuted when he shall the second time come in glory to reign amongst his saints, and to be admired of all them which do believe, when he shall put down all rule and authority under his feet, that the glory of the Father may be full and perfectly manifested in his Son, and the glory of the Father and Son in all his members.

XXI.

That Christ Jesus by his death did bring forth salvation and reconciliation only for the[89] elect, which were those which[90] God the Father gave him; and that the gospel which is to be preached to all men as the ground of faith is that[91] Jesus is the Christ, the Son of the ever-blessed God, filled with the perfection of all heavenly and spiritual excellencies, and that salvation is only and alone to be had through the believing in his Name.

XXII.

That faith is the[92] gift of God wrought in the hearts of the elect by the Spirit of God, whereby they come to see, know, and believe the truth of[93] the Scripture, and not only so, but the excellency of them above all other writings and things in the world, as they hold forth the glory of God in his attributes, the excellency of Christ in his nature and offices, and the power of the fullness of the Spirit in its workings and operations, and thereupon are enabled to cast the weight of their souls upon this truth thus believed.

XXIII.

Those[94] that have this precious faith wrought in them by the Spirit, can never finally nor totally fall away, and through many storms and floods do arise and beat against them, yet they shall never be able to take them off that foundation and rock which by faith they are fastened upon, but shall be kept by the power of God to salvation, where they shall enjoy their purchased possession, they being formerly graven upon the palms of God's hands.

88. 2 Cor. 15:24, 28; Heb. 9:28; 2 Thess. 1:9, 19; 2 Thess. 1:15–17; John 17:21, 26.

89. John 15:13; Rom. 8:32–34; Rom. 5:11 & 3:25.

90. John 17:2 with 6:37.

91. Matthew 16:16; Luke 2:26; John 6:69 & 7:3 & 20:31; I John 5:11.

92. Eph. 2:3; John 6:29 & 4:10; Phil. 1:29; Gal. 5:23.

93. John 17:17; Heb. 4:11–12; John 6:63.

94. Matt. 7:21, 25; John 15:1; 1 Pet. 1:4–6; Esau. 49:13–16.

XXIV.

That faith is ordinarily[95] begot by the preaching of the Gospel, or word of Christ, without respect to[96] any power or capacity in the creature, but is wholly[97] passive, being dead in sins and trespasses, does believe and is converted by no less power[98] than that which raised Christ from the dead.

XXV.

That the tenders[99] of the gospel to the conversion of sinners[100] is absolutely free, no way requiring, as absolutely necessary, any qualifications, preparations, terrors of the Law, or preceding ministry of the law, but only and alone the naked soul, as a[101] sinner and ungodly to receive Christ as crucified, dead, and buried, and risen again, being made[102] a prince and a savior for such sinners.

XXVI.

That the same power that converts to faith in Christ, the same power carries on the[103] soul still through all duties, temptations, conflicts, sufferings, and continually whatever a Christian is, he is by[104] grace, and by a constant renewed[105] operation from God, or undergo any temptations from Satan, the world, or men.

XXVII.

That God the Father, and Son, and Spirit, is one with[106] all believers, in their[107] fullness, in[108] relations, as[109] head and members, as[110] house and inhabitants, as[111] husband and wife, one with him as[112] light and love, and one with him in his

95. Rom. 10:17; Cor. 1:21.

96. Rom. 9:16.

97. Rom. 2:1–2; Ezek. 16:6; Rom. 3:12.

98. Rom. 1:16; Eph. 1:19; Col. 2:12.

99. Those who tend.

100. John 3:14–15 & 1:12; Esa. 55:1; John 7:37.

101. 1 Tim. 1:15; Rom. 4:5 & 5:8.

102. Acts 5:30–31 & 2:36; 1 Cor. 1:22–24.

103. 1 Pet. 1:5; 2 Cor. 12:9.

104. 1 Cor. 15:10.

105. Phil. 2:12–13; John 15:5; Gal. 2:19–20.

106. 2 Thess. 1:1; John 14:10, 20 & 17:21.

107. Col. 2:9–10 & 1:19.

108. John 1:17; Heb. 2:11.

109. Col. 1:18; Eph. 5:39.

110. Eph. 2:22; 1 Cor. 3:16–17.

111. Esau 15:5; Cor. 11:3.

112. Gal. 3:16.

inheritance and in all his[113] glory; and that all believers by virtue of this union and oneness with God, are the adopted sons of God, and heirs with Christ, co-heirs and joint heirs with him of the inheritance of all the promises of this life, and that which is to come.

XXVIII.

That those which have union with Christ are justified from all their sins, past,[114] present, and to come, by the blood of Christ, which justification we conceive to be a gracious and free[115] acquittal of a guilty, sinful creature, from all sin by God, through the satisfaction that Christ has made by his death, and this applied in the manifestation of it through faith.

XXIX.

That all believers are a holy and[116] sanctified people, and that sanctification is a spiritual grace of the[117] new Covenant, and effect of the[118] love of God, manifested to the soul, whereby the believer is in[119] truth and reality separated, both in soul and body, from all sin and dead works, through the[120] blood of the everlasting Covenant, whereby he also presses after a heavenly and Evangelical perfection, in obedience to all the commands,[121] which Christ as head and king in this new covenant has prescribed to him.

XXX.

All believers through the knowledge of[122] that justification of life given by the Father, and brought forth by the blood of Christ, have this as their great privilege of that new[123] covenant, peace with God, and reconciliation, whereby they that were afar off, were brought nearby[124] that blood, and have (as the Scripture speaks) peace[125] passing all understanding, yes, joy in God, through our Lord Jesus Christ, by[126] whom we have received the atonement.

---

113. John 17:24.

114. 1 John 1:7; Heb. 10:14 & 9:26; 2 Cor. 5:19; Rom. 3:23.

115. Acts 13:38–39; Rom. 5:1 & 3:25, 30.

116. 1 Cor. 1:1; 1 Pet. 2:9.

117. Eph. 1:4.

118. 1 John 4:16.

119. Eph. 4:24.

120. Phil. 3:15.

121. Matt. 28:10.

122. 1 Cor. 5:19; Rom. 5:9–10.

123. Esau 54:10 & 26:12.

124. Eph. 2:13–14.

125. Phil. 4:7.

126. Rom. 5:10–11.

XXXI.

That[127] all believers in the time of this life are in a continual warfare, combat, and opposition against sin itself, the world, and the devil, and liable to all manner of afflictions, tribulations, and persecutions, and so shall continue until Christ comes in his kingdom, being predominate and appointed thereunto; and whoever the saints, any of them do possess or enjoy of God in this life, is only by faith.

XXXII.

That[128] the only strength by which the saints are enabled to encounter with all opposition and to overcome all afflictions, temptations, persecutions, and trials, is only by Jesus Christ, who is the captain of their salvation, being made perfect through sufferings, who has engaged his strength to assist them in all their afflictions, and to uphold them under all their temptations, and to preserve them by his power to his everlasting Kingdom.

XXXIII.

That Christ has here on earth a spiritual kingdom which is the church, which he has purchased and redeemed to himself, as a peculiar inheritance, which church, as it is visible to us, is a company of visible[129] saints,[130] called and separated from the world by the word and[131] spirit of God, to the visible profession of the faith of the gospel, being baptized into that faith and joined to the Lord and each other by mutual agreement, in the practical enjoyment of the[132] Ordinances, commanded by Christ their head and king.

XXXIV.

To this church, he has[133] made his promises and given the signs of his covenant, presence, love, blessing, and protection. Here are the fountains and springs of his heavenly grace continually flowing forth;[134] there ought all men to come, of all estates, that acknowledge him to be their prophet, priest, and king, to be enrolled among his household servants, to be under his heavenly conduct and government, to lead their lives in his walled sheepfold, and watered garden, to have communion here with the saints, that they may be made to be partakers of their inheritance in the kingdom of God.

---

127. Eph. 6:10–13; 2 Cor. 10:3; Rev. 2:9–10.

128. John 16:33; Heb. 2:9–10; John 15:5.

129. 1 Cor. 1:2; Eph. 1:1.

130. Rom. 1:7; Acts 16:18; 1 Thess. 1:9; 2 Cor. 6:17; Rev. 18:18.

131. Acts 2:37 with Acts 10:37.

132. Rom. 10:10; Acts 20:21; Matt. 18:19–20; Acts 2:41; 1 Pet. 2:5.

133. Matt. 28:18–19, 29; Cor. 6:18.

134. Esa. 8:16; 1 Tim. 3:15 & 4:16 & 6:3, 5; Acts 2:41, 47; Song. 4:12; Gal. 6:10; Eph. 2:19.

XXXV.

And[135] all his servants are called here, to present their bodies and souls and to bring their gifts God has given them. So being come, they are here by himself bestowed in their several orders, peculiar places, due uses, being fitly compacted and knit together, according to the effectual working of every part, to the edification of itself in love.

XXXVI.

That being thus joined, every church has[136] power given them from Christ for their better well-being, to choose to themselves meet persons into the office of[137] pastors, teachers, elders, deacons, being qualified according to the word, as those which Christ has appointed in his testament, for the seeding, governing, serving, and building of his church, and that none other have power to impose them, either these or any other.

XXXVII.

That[138] the ministers aforesaid, lawfully called by the church, where they are to administer, ought to continue in their calling, according to God's ordinance, and carefully to feed the flock of Christ committed to them, not only for filthy lucre, but of a ready mind.

XXXVIII.

That[139] the due maintenance of the officers aforesaid, should be the free and voluntary communication of the church, that according to Christ's ordinance, they that preach the gospel should live on the gospel, and not by constraint to be compelled from the people by a forced law.

XXXIX.

That[140] baptism is an ordinance of the New Testament given by Christ to be dispensed only upon persons professing faith, or that are disciples, or taught, who upon a profession of faith, ought to be baptized.

XL.

The way and manner of baptism, signifying to dip under water, yet so as with convenient garments, both upon the administrator and subject, with all modesty[141] dispensing of this ordinance, the scripture holds out to be dipping or plunging the whole body under water; it being a sign, must answer the thing signified, which

---

135. 1 Cor. 12:6, 7, 12, 18; Rom. 12:4–6; 1 Pet. 4:10; Eph. 4:16; Col. 2:5, 6, 19; 1 Cor. 12:12 to the end.

136. Acts 1:2 & 6:3 with 15:22, 25; 1 Cor. 16:3.

137. Rom. 12:7–8 & 16:1; 1 Cor. 12:8, 28; 2 Tim., 3rd chap.; Heb. 13:7; 1 Pet. 5:1–3.

138. Heb. 5:4; Acts 4:23; 1 Tim. 4:14; John 10:3–4; Acts 29:28; Rom. 12:7–8; Heb. 13:7, 17.

139. 1 Cor. 9:7, 14; Gal. 6:6; 1 Thess. 5:13; 1 Tim. 5:17–18; Phil. 4:15–16.

140. Matt. 18:18–19; Mark 16:16; Acts 2:37–38 & 8:36–38 & 18:8.

141. Matt. 3:16; John 3:23; Acts 8:38.

are these: First, the[142] washing the whole soul in the blood of Christ. Secondly, that interest the saints have in the[143] death, burial, and resurrection. Thirdly, together with a[144] confirmation of our faith, that as certainly as the body is buried under water and rises again, so certainly shall the bodies of the saints be raised by the power of Christ, in the day of the resurrection, to reign with Christ.

XLI.

The persons designed by Christ to dispense this ordinance, the[145] scriptures hold forth to be a preaching disciple, it being nowhere tied to a particular church officer or person extraordinary sent, the commission enjoining the administration, being given to them under no other consideration, but as considered disciples.

XLII.

Christ[146] has likewise given power to his whole church to receive in and cast out, by way of excommunication, any member; and this power is given to every particular congregation, and not one particular person, either member or officer, but the whole.

XLIII.

And[147] every particular member of each church, how excellent, great, or learned soever, ought to be subject to this censure and judgement of Christ; and the church ought with great care and tenderness, with due advice, to proceed against her members.

XLIV.

And as Christ for the[148] keeping of this church in holy and orderly communion, places some special men over the church, who by their office are to govern, oversee, visit, watch, so likewise for the better keeping thereof in all places, by the members, he hath given[149] authority and laid duty upon all, to watch over one another.

XLV.

That[150] also such to whom God has given gifts, being tried in the church, may and ought by the appointment of the congregation, to prophesy, according to the

---

142. Rev. 1:5 & 7:14 with Heb. 10:22.

143. Rom. 6:3–5.

144. 1 Cor. 15:28–29.

145. Esa. 8:16; Matt. 18:15–19; John 4:1–2; Acts 20:7; Matt. 2:26.

146. Acts 2:47; Rom. 16:2; Matt. 18:17; 1 Cor. 5:4; 2 Cor. 2:6–8.

147. Matt. 18:16–18; Acts 11:2–3; 1 Tim. 5:19–21.

148. Acts 20:27–28; Heb. 13:17, 24; Matt. 24:25; 1 Thess. 5:14.

149. Matt. 13:34, 37; Gal. 6:1; 1 Thess. 5:11; Jude 3:20; Heb. 10:34–35 & 12:25.

150. 1 Cor. 14th chap.; Rom. 12:6; 1 Pet. 4:10–11; 1 Cor. 12:7; 1 Thess. 5:17–19.

122 *Appendix 1*

proportion of faith, and so to teach publicly the word of God, for the edification, exhortation, and comfort of the church.

XLVI.

Thus[151] being rightly gathered, established, and still proceeding in Christian communion and obedience of the gospel of Christ, none ought to separate for faults and corruption, which may and, as long as the church consists of men subject to failings, will fall out and arise among them, even in true constituted churches, until they have in due order sought redress thereof.

XLVII.

And[152] although the particular congregations be distinct and several bodies, every one as a compact and united city in itself, yet are they all to walk by one and the same rule, and by all means convenient to have the council and help one of another in all needful affairs of the church, as members of one body in the common faith under Christ their only head.

XLVIII.

That a civil magistracy is an ordinance of God set up by God for the punishment of evil doers and for the praise of them that do well; and that in all lawful things commanded by them, subjection ought to be given by us in the Lord, and that we are to make supplication and prayer for kings, and all that are in authority, that under them we may live a peaceable and quiet life in all godliness and honesty.

XLIX.

The supreme magistracy of this kingdom we believe to be the king and Parliament freely chosen by the kingdom, and that in all those civil laws which have been acted by them, or for the present is or shall be ordained, we are bound to yield subjection and obedience to in the Lord, as conceiving ourselves bound to defend both the persons of those thus chosen, and all civil laws made by them, with our persons, liberties, and estates, with all that is called ours, although we should suffer never so much from them in not actively submitting to some ecclesiastical laws, which might be conceived by them to be their duties to establish, which we for the present could not see, nor our consciences could submit unto; yet are we bound to yield our persons to their pleasures.

L.

And[153] if God should provide such a mercy for us, as to incline the magistrates' hearts so for to tender our consciences, as that we might be protected by them from wrong, injury, oppression, and molestation, which long we formerly have

151. Rev. 2nd and 3rd chapters; Acts 15:12; 1 Cor. 1:10; Ephes. 2:16 & 3:15–16; Heb. 10:23; Jude verse 12; Matt. 18:17; 2 Cor. 5:1, 5.

152. 1 Cor. 4:17 & 14:33, 36 & 16:1; Matt. 28:20; 1 Tim. 3:15 & 6:13–14; Rev. 22:18–19; Col. 2:6, 19 & 4:16.

153. 1 Tim. 2:2–4; Psalm 116:1; Acts 9:31.

groaned under by the tyranny and oppression of the prelatical hierarchy, which God through mercy has made this present king and Parliament wonderful honorable, as an instrument in his hand, to throw down; and we thereby have had some breathing time, we shall, we hope, look at it as a mercy beyond our expectation, and conceive ourselves further engaged forever to bless God for it.

LI.

But if God withhold the magistrates' allowance and furtherance herein[154] yet we must notwithstanding proceed together in Christian communion, not daring to give place to suspend our practice, but to walk in obedience to Christ in the profession and holding forth this faith before mentioned, even in the midst of all trials and afflictions, not accounting our goods, lands, wives, children, fathers, mothers, brethren, sisters, yay, and our own lives dear unto us, so we may finish our course with joy, remembering always we ought to[155] obey God rather than men, and grounding upon the commandment, commission and promise of our Lord and master, Jesus Christ, who as he has all power in heaven and earth, so also has promised, if we keep his commandments, which he has given us, to be with us to the end of the world and when we have finished our course, and kept the faith, to give us the crown of righteousness, which is laid up for all that love his appearing, and to whom we must give an account of all our actions, no man being able to discharge us of the same.

LII.

And[156] likewise unto all men is to be given whatsoever is their due: tributes, customs, and all such lawful duties, ought willingly to be by us paid and performed, our lands, goods, and bodies, to submit to the magistrate in the Lord, and the magistrate every way to be acknowledged, reverenced, and obeyed, according to godliness, not because of wrath only, but for conscience's sake. And finally, all men so to be esteemed and regarded, as is due and meet for their place, age, estate, and condition.

LIII.

And[157] thus we desire to give unto God that which is God's, and unto Caesar that which is Caesar's, and unto all men that which belongs unto them, endearing ourselves to have always a clear conscience void of offense toward God and toward man. And if any take this that we have said to be heresy, then do we with the apostle freely confess, that after the way that they call heresy, worship we the God of our Fathers, believing all things that are written in the law and in the prophets

---

154. Acts 2:40, 41 & 4:19 & 5:28, 29, 41 & 20:23; 1 Thess. 3:3; Phil. 1:27–29; Dan. 3:16–17 & 6, 7, 10, 22, 23.

155. Matt. 28:28–39; 1 Tim. 6:13–15; Rom. 12:1, 8; 1 Cor. 14, 37; 2 Tim. 4, 7, 8; Rev. 2:10; Gal. 2:4–5.

156. Rom. 13:5–7; Matt. 22:21; Titus 3; 1 Pet. 2:13; Ephes. 5:21–22 & 6:1, 9; 1 Pet. 5:5.

157. Matt. 22:28; Acts 24:14–16; John 5:28; 2 Cor. 4:17; 1 Tim. 6:3–5; 1 Cor. 15:58–59.

124 *Appendix 1*

and apostles, desiring from our souls, to disclaim all heresies and opinions, which are not after Christ, and to be steadfast, unmovable, always abounding in the work of the Lord, as knowing our labor shall not be in vain in the Lord.

1 COR. 1:24

Not that we have dominion over your faith, but are helpers of your joy; for by faith we stand.

FINIS.

∽

William Kiffin
A Brief Remonstrance *(1645)*

A Brief Remonstrance (Wing K423) reports an exchange between Elizabeth Poole's father, Robert Poole, and her minister, William Kiffin. This exchange addresses the controversies surrounding Poole's decision to abandon her family for Kiffin's congregation in London, as well as those pertaining to the Baptist church in general. These controversies included whether the church baptized people unclothed, a charge that Kiffin denies.

In this pamphlet, Kiffin notes that Elizabeth Poole and the Poole family's servants (who had also joined the church) took the initiative to set up the meeting between Kiffin and Robert Poole to try to resolve their differences. The meeting was aborted when Kiffin arrived to find that several well-known critics of the church were also in attendance, ready to aid Robert Poole in the debate. Kiffin left but later wrote to Robert Poole, posing several queries to him regarding his motives for attacking Kiffin's church for blasphemy. Robert Poole wrote back with indignation. Believing himself the injured party, he refused to answer Kiffin's queries and instead posed six of his own. Kiffin initially responded by saying that he should not need to even acknowledge Poole's queries, because his godly actions spoke for themselves. But he then relented. He not only answered Poole's queries at length but also cited numerous places in scripture as support for his assertions.

The copy reprinted here is housed in the Thomason Tracts (E.293[31]) in the British Library and is available on *EEBO*. The phrase "July (London) 26" is handwritten by Thomason on the title page of this copy to record the date upon which he acquired it for his collection as well as the location of the tracts' publication.

A Brief
REMONSTRANCE
OF
The REASONS and GROUNDS of those People commonly
Called ANABAPTISTS, for their Separation, etc.

Or Certain
QUERIES
Concerning their
FAITH and PRACTICE, propounded by Mr. ROBERT
POOLE; Answered and Resolved
By
WILLIAM KIFFIN

I. Pet. 3.15.
Sacrifice the LORD GOD in your hearts, and be ready always to
give an answer to every man that asks you a reason of the hope
that is in you, with meekness and fear.

Printed and published for public Information in the
Year 1645.

The
PRINTER
to The
READER.

Courteous Reader,

The copy of this discourse coming accidentally into my hands, and upon the perusal thereof, conceiving it tended much to the vindication of the people of God, and information of the ignorant, concerning the order of the gospel, I therefore was emboldened to remonstrate the same unto the world, that the virtue thereof might not be smothered with me[158] but communicated to the public benefit, and the professors thereof freed from the injurious censure and contumelies[159] of the world. I need not much gloss it over with commendations, the better to invite you to a serious examination thereof. I hope its own worth will speak better for

---

158. Confined to or suppressed by the printer.

159. Contempt and denunciation.

126 *Appendix 1*

itself, and prove more prevalent[160] to the ingenious and moderate peruser, than my applause. I will not further engage myself in its praise, yet if the word of the printer to the reader may pass, the perusal is worth your pains, and the matter worth your trial, and the Lord put it into your heart to hold fast that which us godly as in [Editor' note: the print in this roughly six-word section is extremely blurry and hence illegible] that the mind of Job with those in all [Editor's note: the print in this roughly five-word section is extremely blurry and hence illegible] these queries propounded by Master Robert Poole. I will not ask what synodean[161] interest there is with him therein, much less affirm it, lest I trespass so far upon the authority of my intelligence. For I dare not be too positive, where neither my eye nor my ear were privy to the counsel, yet may be held in [Editor's note: the print in this roughly two-word section is extremely blurry and hence illegible], for thought is free, but be they as these are, or from whomsoever, I commit this to the grace of God, in the consideration of what follows.

TO

Mr. ROBERT POOLE, *Salutations,* etc.[162]

SIR,

According to your daughter's and servants' desires, I was willing to give a meeting to any friends you should bring, that we might fairly and lovingly declare our thoughts from the scripture, concerning the subjects of baptism, as desiring that you might thereby hearing, try all things, and hold fast that which is good. But instead thereof, I found only those whose mouths were filled with bitterness, and I have cause to fear, their hearts as full of hatred against those that in this thing are contrary minded to them, which to me did appear, by their charging of me with being a seducer, a blasphemer, and such like terms, as if the end[163] of their coming had been rather to rail than reason, and thought what I said was apparent as the light, yet were they pleased to charge it with no less than blasphemy, although I think upon serious consideration, in cool blood,[164] they would be ashamed of that charge. I shall forbear to mention those many things, which by them went under that name, and present only one to your memory, to show to whom you please. That it was essential to true justifying faith, for us to believe *that* Jesus Christ, *as man, proceeded from the loins of Abraham.*[165] This was the position that was

---

160. Important or relevant.

161. Synodal, as in a church senate or governing body.

162. Greetings. Here begins Kiffin's address to Robert Poole.

163. Purpose.

164. When cooler or calmed down and hence more critically distant and rational.

165. Hebrews 7:10, GV: "For he was yet in the loins of his father Abraham, when Melchisedec met him." (I quote the Geneva Bible because Kiffin's wording most closely approximates that version.) Kiffin cites this passage in reference to debates over the nature of Christ's humanity and sonship as

charged by him for blasphemy, which if they please, I shall appeal to the whole synod in this thing, whether it be true or no. And truly, for my part, I believe it so apparently true, that he that shall deny this must deny Christ. But to let pass all such kind of calumnies[166] as these are, it being not the end of my writing to present them to you, but rather seeing we have made a beginning, I here present these ensuing queries to you, entreating an answer to the same.

1. Query. *Whether the institution of circumcision be the institution of baptism? Or whether there be not a new institution? And if a new institution, whether we are not to dispense baptism upon those subjects only, which the new institution holds forth?*

2. Query. *Whether this new institution holds any other of the true subjects of baptism but persons discipled or taught. And if not, whether any other ought to be baptized?*

3. Query. *Whether God has appointed the ordinance of baptism, as a means to confer grace, or as a sign to confirm the grace that is conferred. And whether we have any ground to judge that persons have grace conferred upon them, but by profession of faith?*

4. Query. *Whether the gospel owns any other seed of the children of Abraham but a spiritual seed. And whether the spiritual seed be not only such as believe. And whether this ordinance of baptism does not particularly belong to this spiritual seed. And how the children of believing Gentiles may be said to be this spiritual seed?*

WILL. KIFFEN

Mr. POOLE'S ANSWER.

SIR,

I received a written paper, with your name subscribed thereunto, with certain groundless queries, as you say were the desire of some, for my satisfaction, to which I return you this answer, that myself being the party injured, have just cause to receive satisfaction from you and your parties, that have done me the injury in seducing my children and servants into your errors. Therefore, I conceive it to be equal and necessary that you should give me substantial and clear answers out of the Word of God, to these my inquiring queries, which if you do refuse, I shall impute it to your inability.

1. Query. By what warrant of the word of God do you separate from our congregations, where the word and sacraments are purely dispensed?

---

well as his status as the most superior "priest." This seemingly minor digression, which Kiffin himself dismisses, is a point he returns to later on. It is related to the question as to whether people should be forced to pay tithes. In his response to query III, Kiffin rejects compulsory payment.

166. Slanders.

128 *Appendix 1*

2. Query. By what scripture warrant do you take upon you to erect new framed congregations, separated to the disturbance of the great work of reformation now in hand?

3. Query. What warrant have you either to be a member, much less minister of any such separate congregation?

4. Query. What warrant have you to admit into your separate congregations silly seduced servants, children, or people?

5. Query. How can you vindicate by the word of God your anabaptist way, from the sinful guile of notorious schism and defection from all the reformed churches?

6. Query. Whether you, and such like pretended teachers as you are, be not the persons characterized and condemned in these and such like scriptures following: *Matth. 7:15; Acts 20:29–30; Rom. 16:17–18; 2 Tim. 3:6–9; 2 Pet. 2:1–2* and *3:17–19; and Jude 4, 8, 10, 12,* and *13:16.*

These queries I propound, that truth may triumph and error may vanish, and that myself and my deluded ones may receive satisfaction, which if you do not, I desire you, as you will answer it before God and men, that you do neither admit or receive any of mine into your pretended church, and if you have, I demand of you or yours, in whom the power lies, suddenly, at or upon the sight hereof, to discharge them, and leave them to the power of me, who have the charge of them. And in expectation hereof, I shall rest as I find you.

Robert Poole.

Mr. KIFFIN'S REPLY

SIR,

I have received your note, wherein (contrary to my expectation), instead of an answer to those queries I sent you, I find others propounded by you, under this consideration (as you say) that truth may triumph, and error may vanish, and that you and yours may receive satisfaction. I shall not need to speak, for I hope my actions shall at all times manifest the earnest desire of my soul, and willingness of spirit, to give satisfaction (so far as God hath given me light) to every just demand, both for the vindicating of that truth we desire to walk in, as also to satisfy (if possibly by the word of God I may) every man's conscience, that shall in any way scruple or oppose it. And so not willing to descant[167] further upon circumstances in your writing, or too narrowly to pry into such expressions therein, as too much manifests a spirit lifted up in his own conceit, and much inveterated[168] against us and our practice, knowing it is the common portion of such that will live godly in *Christ Jesus,* I pass them by, and so come to answer your demands.

---

167. Talk tediously at length.

168. Railed against at length, as in inveterately.

QUERY I.

By what warrant of the word of God do you separate from our congregations, where the word and sacraments are purely dispensed?

Answer: This query seems to import this much: That from such congregations, where the word and sacraments are purely dispensed,[169] man ought not to separate, but that men are and ought to separate from such, where the word and sacraments are not purely dispensed, your query seems to grant, but however, though it should be denied, these scriptures plainly prove it: *Revel. 14:8–10*, more fully manifested in *Revel. 18:1–5*; *Esau. 52:2* and more at large spoken of in *2 Cor. 6:14* to the end. As also practiced by the apostle Paul himself in *Acts 19:8–10*. But now, *Sir*, here lies the question. If your congregations be such, as where the word and sacraments are purely dispensed, then we sin, and you justly charge us with schism for separating from you, but if it be not so, that your congregations are such, but on the contrary, even such as does not dispense the word and sacraments purely, then we do well, and you sin in charging us with schism,[170] in doing what the word commands and the saints practiced, and therefore we having nothing to prove that the word and sacraments are purely dispensed among you. But your bare affirmation, it cannot satisfy our consciences and I marvel at how it satisfies yours. Does not the word of God, like a two-edged sword, fight against you? May not that scripture justly be applied to you: *Jere. 7:8–10: Behold, you trust in lying words that cannot profit. Will you steal, murder, and commit adultery and swear falsely, and burn incense unto Baal, and walk after other gods, whom you know not; and come and stand before me, etc.* For do you not daily admit and suffer to be among you such as according to God's word, *Leaven the whole lump, 1 Cor. 5:6*, and do not purely dispense the word upon them for their healing. The spirit of Christ says such glorying is not good, and the feast of the Lord ought not to be kept with them. And I pray you show me what gospel institution have you for the baptizing of children, which is one of your great sacraments among you. What can you find for your practice therein, more than the dirty puddle of men's inventions do afford. And therefore when your sacraments are purely administered according to the pure institutions of the Lord Jesus, and when you have dispensed the word and power of Christ, for the cutting off all drunkards, fornicators, covetous, swearers, liars, and all abominable and filthy persons, and stand together in the faith, a pure lump of believers, gathered and united according to the institution of Christ, we (I hope) shall join with you in the same congregation and fellowship, and nothing shall separate us but death. But until then we shall, by the grace of God, continue our separation from you, according to the light we have received, desiring the perusal of these scriptures, as an addition to those formerly quoted, wherein we have sufficient testimony, comparing them with your practice, that

---

169. In conjunction with scripture, rather than Catholic ritual.

170. Separation or splintering.

130 *Appendix 1*

the word and sacraments are not purely dispensed among you: *2 Thess. 3:6; Eph. 5:3–4* and *5:11; Gal. 5, 9, 12; 2 Cor. 6:14; 1 Cor. 5:4–6; Acts. 2:40.*

QUERY II.

By what scripture warrant do you take upon you to erect new framed[171] *congregations, separated to the disturbance of the great work of reformation now in hand?*
Answer: This query has in it these two parts: 1. That we erect new framed separate congregations. 2. We do by this disturb the great work of reformation now in hand. To the first, it is well known to many, especially to ourselves, that our congregations were erected and framed as now they are, according to the rule of Christ, before we heard of any reformation, even at that time when episcopacy was in the height of its vanishing glory and we are confident will remain in spite of all cruelty, even when they were plotting and threatening the ruin of all those that opposed it, and we hope you will not say we sinned in separating from them, whose errors you now condemn, and yet, if you shall still continue to brand us with the names of *Anabaptists, Schismatics, Heretics*, etc. for saving ourselves from such a generation, *Acts 2:40*, as you yourselves have cut off, and from such a superstitious worship, as you say shall be reformed. We conceive it is your ignorance, or worse, and though you condemn it, Christ will justify us, even by that word of his which he has given us and we desire to practice and have already commended to you in that conclusion of our answer to the first query.

And for the second part of your *query, that we disturb the great work of reformation now in hand*, I know not what you mean by this charge, unless it be to discover your prejudice against us in reforming ourselves before you, for as yet we have not in our understanding seen. Neither can we conceive anything of that we shall see reformed by you according to truth, but that through mercy we enjoy the practice of the same already. It is strange this should be a disturbance to the ingenious faithful reformer. It should be (one would think) a furtherance rather than a disturbance. And whereas you tell us of the work of reformation now in hand, no reasonable men will force us to desist from the practice of that which we are persuaded is according to truth, and wait for that which we know not what it will be. And in the meantime, practice that which you yourselves say must be reformed. But whereas you tell us of a great work of reformation, we should entreat you to show us wherein the greatness of it does consist, for as yet we see no greatness. Unless it be in the vast expense of money and time, for what great thing is it to change Episcopacy into Presbytery and a Book of Common Prayer into a Directory,[172] and to exalt men from Livings of 100 pounds a year to places of 400 pound *per annum*. For I pray you consider, is there not the same power,

171. Independent and hence novel or man-made, rather than divinely mandated.

172. A reference to the Presbyterians who wished to replace the Church of England with a Scottish-style presbytery system. For Kiffin, this does not perform the work of reformation but simply replaces one Catholic-like church with another.

the same priests, the same people, the same worship, and in the same manner still continued, but when we shall see your great work of reformation to appear, that you have framed your congregations according to that true and unchangeable pattern, *1 Cor. 3:9–11*, according to the command of our savior, *Matt. 28:19–20*, and the apostles' practice, *Acts. 2:41* and *5:13–14*, and made all things suitable to the pattern, as *Moses* did, *Exod. 25:40*; *Heb. 8:5*. You will see, I hope, that we shall be so far from disturbing that work as that we shall be one with it.

QUERY III.

What warrant have you either to be a member, much less a minister of any such congregations?

Answer: This query, as I conceive it, is added more for number than for weight, if we can prove our congregations true, our membership must needs be true, and so not to be questioned. I would not speak any more to this query, but that I see you pinch so hard upon our separation in four of your queries, to which I shall give a fuller answer to prove our separation true from your assemblies. And first, it cannot be denied, but Jesus Christ is of the Father anointed to be the head of the church, which is his body, *Eph. 1:21–23* and *Col. 1:18*, and that we are commanded only to hear him, *Deut. 18:15*; *Acts. 3:22* and *7:37*; *Matt. 17:5*; *2 Pet. 1:17*, and that whosoever will not hear and obey him, the Lord will require it at his hands, *Deut. 18:19*; *Acts 3:27*; *Matt. 7:26–27*, and hereby we know we love God, and he loves us when we keep his commandments, *1 John 2:3* and *5:2–3*. Now then, if we cannot keep faith and a good conscience in obeying all the commands of Christ, so long as we assemble ourselves with you, then are we necessitated to separate ourselves from you, but that we cannot keep faith and a good conscience so with you, these scriptures prove compared with your practice, *2 Thess. 3:6*; *1 Cor. 5:11*; *2. Tim. 2:21 and 3:5*; *Ephes. 5:1* to the *14*; with many other scriptures. But in the mouth of two or three witnesses every truth shall stand now and then, so long as you deny to follow the rule of Jesus Christ, and are not obedient to his commands, but reject the word of God, which is given by Christ for the purging of the wicked from the godly, and the separating the precious from the vile, as [found in] *Matt. 18:15–17*; *1 Cor. 5:4–5* and *11:13*. We are bound in obedience to Jesus Christ, to leave you, while you remain obstinate to him, and join together, and continue faithful in the order of the gospel. And as it is with a natural body, which is greedy to receive in all, yet wants power to void the excrements, must needs become a rotten, filthy, and unclean body, even so is it with all false spiritual states, who by power and authority given to them by the civil magistrate, are so hasty to command all, both rich and poor, to subject to their worship, whether their conscience be brought over to see it a truth or no, or else they may not live among them, or use any traffic with them, *Rev. 13:16–17*, and having so received them into the common gorge of their church, have not power to digest them into better conversation, nor to cast them out as dirt and dung, though incorrigible. This congregation or society must

132 *Appendix 1*

needs become rotten, filthy, and impure, *the hold of all foul spirits, and a cage for every unclean bird, Revel. 18:2.* Now I would but appeal to any reasonable religious men, whether England hath not at this time in her as [many] hateful birds as any nation whatsoever? And whether there be not at this day an authority to force in all to worship. The daily experience of this may be seen by the practices of those that would be owned the most knowing learned men of our times, who will have men to worship with them against their wills, and so makes them as the best but formal hypocrites, and therefore when these things do so appear, is it not high time to hearken to the voice of the apostle, *Acts 2:40*, to save ourselves from such a generation, and to come out from them, *Rev. 18*, now if these spoken of, with many others that might be brought, as the quenching of the spirit, and despising prophecy, so that no man may speak in your public exercises, but one that hath the same call and power as those whom you now have cast off, contrary to these scriptures: *1 Pet. 4:10*; *Heb. 10:25*; *Colloss. 3:16*; *Eph. 4:15–16*; *1 Cor. 12:7–8* and *14:24, 26, 31, 39*, as also all your superstitious consecrations, to the great deluding of poor ignorant people, and engaging them against those that worship anywhere save in your high places, contrary to these express texts of scripture: *John 4:20, 24*, as also the continuing of tithes and offerings of the people, as if Christ were not come in the flesh, as if the clergy of that kingdom were the tenth part of that kingdom for number, when as they themselves will tell God in their prayers, *That the harvest is great, but the laborers are but few*, an act so unjust by them to be demanded that reason would abhor that a few men in a kingdom should have the tenth part of the riches of the kingdom, and yet so eagerly pursued by them, that though the paying of it be to the undoing of men, they will have it, and therefore following men of authority, at bed and board, in pulpit and private chamber, to have power put into their hands to that end, as likewise their cruelty in refusing a place of burial in their consecrated ground, except they have so much money, as perhaps the party have not in all the world to give them, all which considered, with many more, I desire you to confide of. And if yet it be not a sufficient ground to you for the confirmation of our just separation, yet know it is to us. And unless you can show us that Christ Jesus is not to be hearkened unto as well in those scriptures given for the establishment of the New Testament, as *Moses* was in the establishment of the Old, and under the penalty of the same and greater judgment than was inflicted upon the breaches of the same, as *Heb. 2:1–5* and the third chapter the first verse to the ninth, and chapter *10:21–31*, and *chap. 11* from *22* to the end do declare. And therefore, we cannot, nay we dare not but continue in this our practice, and witness the truth of it, even by sufferings, though others oppose it.

QUERY IV.
What warrant have you to admit into you separate congregations silly seduced servants, children, or people?

Answer: I see our separated congregations stick very hard upon your stomach, therefore as I have labored to help you to digest our separation, so I hope I shall give you something from the word of truth that may remove your bitterness of spirit against our congregations. And first know this, that that infinite love that has redeemed a people to God, to reign with him in his spiritual kingdom here on the earth, *Rev: 5, 9, 10*, and that all those that are begotten by the immortal seed, *1 Pet. 1:23*, even those newborn babes that have tasted of the Lord's bounty, and come to that living and precious stone, the Lord Jesus, being themselves, out of all nations, tongues, and kindred, has also made them kings and priests unto God, to reign with him in his spiritual kingdom here on the earth, *Rev: 5.9–10*, and that all those that are begotten by the immortal seed, *1 Pet. 1:23*, even those newborn babies that have tasted of the Lord's bounty, and come to that living and precious stone, the Lord Jesus, being themselves *living stones, are built up a spiritual house, being made a holy priesthood, to offer up spiritual sacrifices, acceptable to God by JESUS CHRIST, 1 Pet. 2:1 to the 11 verse, and being quickened by Christ, are raised with him, to sit together in heavenly places, Eph. 2.5–6, being by one spirit baptized into one body, 1 Cor. 12:13, The old man being broken with him, Rom. 6:4, and the new man put on, Gal. 3:27; Col. 3:10, thus having an entrance to the Father, the building being thus coupled together, by the same spirit, grows to a holy temple*, and so becomes a habitation to the Lord, *Eph. 2:18 to 22,* which assembly we are not to forsake, *Heb. 10:25*, but to exhort one another daily, *Heb. 3:12–13*, having received gifts in some measure by the same spirit, we are accordingly to dispense them for edification, *1 Cor. 12:47; 1 Pet. 4.10; Rom. 12:3 to 9*, to these congregations, as Christ promised his presence, *Matth. 28:19–20 and 18, 19, 20; Rev. 7:13–15* and *21:2–3* and *22:13*. Now then, if we can prove ourselves to be such congregations as are before spoken of, or at leastwise, such as sincerely and truly strive, according to the light we have, so be such, then I hope you will be so far from despising such gatherings of the saints together, as that you will not deny them to receive in members, and to dispense such gifts for the edifying one of another, as the Lord has given us, and this I shall labor to do in the answer to the next query. And whereas you demand what warrant we have to receive silly seduced servants, etc., we answer, it is well known to you, we receive in none as members with us, but such as have been members of your church, at the least sixteen, twenty, or thirty years, and if they be silly when they are received members among us, surely they were marvelous silly when they were received members among you, and it should seem they have received, by your own words, little edification in their so long membership with you, and therefore it does behoove them, whom you say are so silly, to look out also where to be better instructed, who have received so little benefit in so long time by your ministry, lest they perish in their own ignorance and blindness, and therefore herein you would do well to take our savior's advice, *Matt.7:3–5.* We know it is no strange thing for those that desire to walk in the

134 *Appendix 1*

straight ways of the Lord, to hear themselves despised and reproached with these and far greater aspersions, but however, that such as are so esteemed of by you, have a right to be received into the fellowship of the saints, these scriptures prove, which I pray you examine, *Prov. 9:1 to 7; Isai. 14:32 and 18:7; 1 Cor. 1:26–28; Rom. 14:5.*

QUERY V.

How can you vindicate by the word of God, your anabaptistical way, from the sinful guile of notorious schism, and defection from all the reformed churches?

Answer: They that run may read what fire this pen and heart was inflamed withal in the writing and indicting of this query. But first of all, if by reformed churches, you mean those churches planted by the apostles in the primitive times, which are the platform for all churches in all ages to look unto, to be guided by these apostolical rules left them, we then shall vindicate by the word of God our "anabaptistical" way, as you are pleased to call it, from that guile. And first, although we confess ourselves ignorant of many things which we ought to know and desire to wait daily for the further discoveries of light and truth from him which is the only giver of it to his poor people, yet so far as we are come, we desire to walk by the same rule they did, and first of all, we baptize none into Christ Jesus, but such as profess faith in Christ Jesus, *Rom. 6:3*, by which faith they are made sons of God, and so having put on Christ, are baptized into Christ, *Gal: 3:26–27*, and that Christ hath commanded this, and no other way of baptism, see *Matth.28:19; Mark 1:4; Luke 3:7–8*, and that this also was the practice of the apostles, see *Acts 2:41, and 8.12.36, 37*, and *10:47–48*, and that being thus baptized upon profession of faith, they are then added to the church, *2 Acts 41*, and being added to the church, we conceive ourselves bound to watch over one another, and in case of sin, to deal faithfully one with another according to these scriptures, *Levit. 19:17–18; Matth. 18:15*, and if they remain obstinate, to cast them out, as those that are not fit to live in the church, according to that rule, *2 Cor. 5:4–5 and Matth. 18:19–20*, by all which, and many other particulars I might name, it appears through mercy, we can free ourselves from that guile. And truly, if your eyes were opened to peruse your own practices and ways, you would then see we could better free ourselves from that notorious guile of schism from those reformed churches than you can free yourselves from the notorious guile of schisming from Rome. You hold their baptism true, their ordination of ministers true, their maintenance by tithes and offerings true, their people all fit matter for a church, and so tried, and yet you will separate from them for some corruptions. Now for our parts, we deny all and every one of these among you to be true, and therefore do separate from you. So then, when you have made satisfaction for your notorious schism, and return as dutiful sons to their mother, or else have cast off all your filthy rubbish of her abominations that are found among you, we will return to you, or show our just grounds to the contrary.

QUERY VI.

Whether you, and such like pretended teachers[173] *as you are, be not the persons characterized and condemned in these and such like scriptures following, Matth. 7:15; Acts. 20:29–30; Rom. 16:17–18; 2 Tim. 3:6–8; 2 Pet. 2:1, 2, 3, 17, 18, 19; and Jude. verses 4, 8, 10, 12, 13, 14.*

Answer: Although (as far as I am acquainted with my own heart) neither I, nor such as I, am thirsty after revenge, yet we could desire that the Lord would be pleased to manifest the innocence of our spirits and uprightness of our intentions in all such our actions against such false suppositions, or rather calumnies cast upon us, I shall only cite one of those texts, and comment a little upon it, *Matth. 7:15–16;* the words are these, *Beware of false prophets, that come to you in sheep's clothing, but inwardly they are ravening wolves. You shall know them by their fruit.* Christ Jesus himself makes the best description how these false prophets may be known, which is by the observation of the fruit, Christ in these words compared implicitly a true prophet to a sheep, now it is the nature of sheep to be harmless, silent, and to feed in the commons,[174] where the shortest pasture usually is,[175] so is it the property of a true prophet of Christ, to be harmless in his conversation, silent under all his sufferings that he meets withal from unreasonable men, and to be content with the meanest[176] enjoyments of this world, so he may honor Jesus Christ in his condition, no way warring after great matters, in compelling men by a law to feed in the fattest pasture in the land, and as the apostle *Paul* says, *2 Cor. 10:3: Though we are in the flesh, we do not war after the flesh.*

But a wolf, even in sheep's clothing, to which false prophets are compared, even while they are thus clad, may be known by their fruit, which will appear in these two things: first by their ravenous disposition, and secondly, by their often snarling with their teeth. So you shall find false prophets in sheep's clothing, they are always ravening after honors, and therefore, like frogs, creep into kings' houses, that they may be looked upon as fellows with the best of the king's house, that they may be looked upon as fellows with the best of the king's household servants, and ravening after riches, to feed in the fairest pastures of a kingdom, crying, give, give, and therefore run from living to living, where they may have the greatest enjoyments of the world. And secondly, they will always be snarling with their

173. Men who were preaching even though they did not have a degree in theology. These unlicensed men, including Kiffin, based their right and ability to preach on such scriptures as those cited by Kiffin as well as 1 Corinthians 12:1–14.

174. Under the feudal system, certain lands were deemed "common lands" or "the commons" because, while they may have been part of an estate entitled to one or more persons, their tenants had the right to use them for such purposes as fishing, grazing livestock, collecting firewood or cutting turf for fuel, and extracting sand, stone, and other minerals.

175. The "shortest pastures" were in the commons because they were heavily grazed by livestock belonging to numerous tenants, therefore the grass was shorter there than in private pasture lands.

176. The simplest or lowliest.

136 *Appendix 1*

teeth, that is, ready to devour and persecute all that shall by their practices, in a way that is more holy than their own, derogate from their honors and names and fat enjoyments in the world. I cease to apply this, but desire the Lord to give you discerning eyes to see between light and darkness. Thus, at present have I given you a brief answer to your queries, leaving them to the trial of truth, and you in the perusal of them, to the direction of him that leads into all truth, ever resting,

Yours so far as he shall
know his duty,

WILLIAM KIFFEN

FINIS.

෴

Anonymous
A Discovery of Six Women Preachers *(1641)*

Elizabeth Poole's presence at the debates in Whitehall was made possible by the rise of new forms of female religious authority in England. These forms of authority were inspired by the tenets of spiritual equality laid out in documents such as the Baptists' *The Confession* (pp. 105–124). The pamphlet *A Discovery of Six Women Preachers* (Wing D1645A) is among the earliest to reflect upon the startling new social phenomenon of women preachers and prophets. Barred from ministering in churches, women were said to have formed their own congregations. They reportedly met in homes and converted such mundane items as stools and bricks into pulpits. Indeed, another pamphlet, *Tub Preachers Overturn'd* (1647; Wing T3207), mocks both men and women for preaching without formal training and for transforming houses and other workaday spaces into churches.

The anonymous narrator of *A Discovery of Six Women Preachers* tries to minimize the religious import of women seeking to exercise their own consciences by reducing the female preachers he discusses to conventional stereotypes. Some of the women, he claims, combined sermonizing with heavy drinking. One woman supposedly broke off her sermon early to meet with a man. A second allegedly stamped so hard on her stool while preaching that the stool almost broke. A third used her sermon to describe a dream she had about the Old Testament prophetess, Hannah, while yet another likened the Pope to the devil.

We do not know if these stories were based on fact. They do remind us that women were traditionally branded as "weaker vessels" because, as the author depicts here, they were believed to be less rational and substantive than men—more prone to excesses such as errant sexual desire, and so on.[177] But female prophets also turned this notion to their advantage, reasoning that, as weaker vessels, they could channel God's word in as pure and unadulterated a fashion as possible. Hannah did indeed set an important precedent, as after God granted her petition for a son, her prayer was considered prophetic. Poole's linking her gift for prophecy to midwifery forms another example of how women converted conventional views of women into positive rationales for delivering divine messages.

The copy reprinted here is housed in the Henry E. Huntington Library and Art Gallery and is available on *EEBO*.

A

DISCOVERY

OF

Six Women Preachers, in *Middlesex*,
Kent, *Cambridge*, and *Salisbury*.

WITH

A Relation of their Names, Manners,
Lives, and Doctrine.

Their Names:

Anne Hempstall.	*Joan Bauford.*	*Eliz. Bancroft.*
Mary Bilbrow.	*Susan May.*	*Arabella Thomas.*

Printed, 1641.

The Six Women Preachers:

Anne Hempstall,		Mary Bilbrow,
Joan Bauford,	and	Susan May,
Elizabeth Bancroft		Arabella Thomas

---

177. The idea that women were weaker vessels came from 1 Peter 3:7, KJV: "Likewise, you husbands, dwell with [your wives] according to knowledge, giving honor unto the wife, as unto the weaker vessel, and as being heirs together of the grace of life; that your prayers be not hindered."

138 *Appendix 1*

In ancient times have I read of prophetesses,[178] but not until of late[179] heard of women preachers, their only reason or cause of preaching[180] was that there was a deficiency of good men. Wherefore it was but fit that virtuous women should supply their places, they were (men they did mean) good for nothing, but to make their texts good by expounding the language of the Beast,[181] but they themselves would preach nothing, but such things as the spirit should move them.

The first and chief of this female and sacerdotal[182] function, was one Anne Hempstall, living in the Parish of Saint Andrews Holborne, near London, and in the County of Middlesex, upon a certain time, she having a mind, said she was moved to be zealously affected, called an assembly of their bibbing[183] gossips[184] together, whose thoughts were bent more upon the strong water bottle[185] than upon the uses or doctrines that their holy sister extended to expound unto them. But being come now to the house of this Anne Hempstall; zealous Nan[186] spoke to them after this manner: "Beloved sisters, this last night I dreamed a strange dream, forever me thought I saw a vision in which Anna the prophetess was presented unto my view, the splendor of whose countenance did cast me into a trance, wherein I lay until the next morning, and the morning being come, I could conceive no interpretation of my dream but this, that I should imitate godly Anna by preaching unto you, as she prophesied to others."[187] Her speech struck them all

178. Women prophets in the Bible, including such Old Testament figures as Hannah, Miriam, Deborah, Huldah, Noadiah, and Isaiah's wife, and such New Testament figures as Anna and the daughters of Phillip. Also possibly a reference to the sibyls of the oracles in ancient Greece.

179. Recently.

180. Their own justification for preaching.

181. In the biblical book of Revelation: the Antichrist.

182. A doctrine that ascribes certain sacrificial functions and spiritual or supernatural powers to an ordained priesthood.

183. Drinking, as in Winebibbing, a term that, according to the *OED*, appears as early as 1400 [("bebbing of wyne") "bibbing, n.]" It also appears in KJV. See for example, Proverbs 23:20: "Be not among winebibbers; among riotous eaters of flesh."

184. A group of women. The phrase was traditionally used to refer to the midwives and friends who attended women in childbirth but, as here, evolved to characterize a group of women who "gossiped" in the modern sense.

185. Bottle of alcohol.

186. Nickname for Anne.

187. Anna refers to Hannah in the Old Testament's 1 Samuel 1:2–2:21, one of the most famous "Mothers of Israel." The first wife of Elkanah, Hannah refused a portion of her husband's blessing on the official day of sacrifice because, unlike her husband's second wife, Penninah, she had not borne children. Hannah visited the temple to plead with God to give her a son, promising in return to dedicate him to God's service. The high priest, Eli, accused her of being drunk for muttering in prayer. She explained her plight and, after he blessed her, delivered her son, Samuel, who as promised went on to become one of Israel's most famous prophets, judges, and king-makers. She is often described

into an astonishment, at which, this profane Anne cried out, "Now doth the holy spirit descend down upon you, wherefore give ear unto me." Then did she begin to talk, and speak unto them that which first came into her mind, but the chief matter of her text was this: That women's hair was an adorning to her, but for a man to have long hair, it was a shame unto him, which the scripture itself cries fie upon.[188] Long did she preach, and longer I dare avouch than some of the audience were willing, for some of them had [come] as far [from] home as White Chapel, wherefore her longitude might cause a brevitude of her sucking the Aqua-vite bottle.[189] Two hours being expired, and the bottom of the stool beginning to look open-mouthed with her furious stamps, she gave them as much peace as in her lay,[190] and so concluded.

Mary Bilbrow, one of the audience, being of the parish of Saint Giles in the Fields, desired them to be all with her the next morning, and after [the] sermon they should have good fat pigs for breakfast, besides a cup of sack or claret to wash it down. They all agreed to it, and making use of all the rhetoric that they were born to, they gave her thanks, and so for the time a bottle of ale or two being devoured, they departed everyone to their own houses. The next morning, they met all together at the house of Mary Bilbrow, whose husband was a good honest bricklayer; and so soon as they came within the doors of her house, she brought them all into her "parlor," as she called it, and instead of stools and cushions, she had provided beforehand three bricks apiece of them to sit upon. Her reason was this, she thought they would not sit much because women to good instructions love standing. Her pulpit was framed very substantially of brick, so high that scarce anything but her standing up tippet[191] could be seen. She began there very devoutly to make an *ex tempore*[192] prayer, but before she had scarce spoken twenty words her daughter came running in very hastily, telling her a

---

as a prophetess for two reasons: First, (as described in the headnote) because she "asked" for her son "of the Lord" (1 Samuel 1:20, KJV) and God "remembered" her by heeding her prayer; and second, because, in her narrative, she sings a song (I Samuel 2:1–10) that not only "rejoices in the Lord" but also predicts that God "will keep the feet of his saints, and the wicked shall be silent in darkness; for by strength shall no man prevail."

188. A reference to 1 Corinthians 11:14–15, KJV: "Does not even nature itself teach you, that, if a man have long hair, it is a shame unto him? But if a woman have long hair, it is a glory to her: for her hair is given her for a covering."

189. Again, the author uses sarcasm to joke that because many of the women traveled to the gathering from as far away as White Chapel, then instead of preaching on and on, Anne should want to be more brief (through using "brevitude" or "brevity") in her drinking of Aquavite (a flavored spirit now known as "schnapps").

190. A short song. Another use of sarcasm to characterize the lack of "peace" that Anne caused her audience by preaching such a long sermon.

191. Tiptoe.

192. Spontaneous.

140 *Appendix 1*

gentleman at Bloomsbury stayed to speak with her about urgent occasions, which hearing, she leapt out of her prayer into this serious meditation: "I think it be the gentleman I was with at Salisbury Court, whom I promised this day to meet with all."[193] Whereupon she left her pulpit, spread the cloth, and brought her gossips in a pig, according to her promises, who fed heartily, and so departed. So much at this time for Middlesex female teachers.[194]

Now give me leave to take water[195] and go to Gravesend and so further into Kent, where I shall tell you of one Joan Bauford in the Town of Faversham[196] who taught in Faversham that husbands being such as crossed their wives' wills might lawfully be forsaken.[197]

Then was there one Susan May of Ashford in the County of Kent also, who preached in a barn there that the devil was the father of the pope, the pope the father of those that did wear surplices, wherefore consequently the devil was the father of all those that did not love puritans.[198]

There was likewise one Elizabeth Bancroft in Ely in Cambridgshire (where Bishop *Wren*[199] first going to place altars there) who preached behind the minister

---

193. The author may be implying that, even though she is married, Mary Bilbrow is a prostitute or mistress who forgot that she had made a promise to receive at her house a gentleman whom she had met up with at Salisbury Court. Salisbury Court was a famous theater district in London, frequented by elites and therefore also by opportunistic pickpockets, beggars, and prostitutes.

194. Mary Bilbrow's parish, identified in the pamphlet as the Parish of St. Giles in the Fields, was in Middlesex County, southeast of London. Middlesex County later became a part of London as the city expanded.

195. Relocate us as readers to a place that is accessible via the Thames River.

196. A market town in the Swale district of Kent, known from the seventeenth through the nineteenth centuries for manufacturing explosives.

197. Forsaken as in divorced, a very radical position to espouse at the time.

198. Susan May is here associated with Puritans who were highly critical of the Catholic Church (and by extension the Church of England) for failing to purge its ceremonies of Catholic rituals.

199. Matthew Wren (1585–1667), a well-known English clergyman and scholar under James VI/I and Charles I. After becoming the Bishop of Ely in 1638, Wren persecuted Puritans who accused him of latent Catholicism for such actions as installing expensive new altars in the cathedral. He was so hated by his opponents that, when Parliament assumed control over the government at the start of the First English Civil War in 1641, he was several times imprisoned in the Tower of London. According to the author in this passage, on one Saturday, Elizabeth Bancroft went behind the back of the cathedral's resident minister to preach her own message that "the Pope's Bird'"—a pun upon Wren—should on the following Sunday be sacrificed upon his own costly altars. The fact that Bancroft delivered her controversial "sermon" on Saturday rather than Sunday suggests that she and her listeners may have been "Seventh-day Sabbatarians." In general, Sabbatarians opposed the Church of England's policy of encouraging the playing of sports after church services on Sunday, insisting instead that the Sabbath should be strictly observed, with no activities of any sort allowed and with two sermons rather than one being delivered to the congregants. In addition, Seventh-day Sabbatarians promulgated the

Contexts for Elizabeth Poole 141

upon a Saturday that it was fit upon Sunday to sacrifice the pope's bird upon his own altar.

Then lastly, there was one Arabella Thomas, a Welsh woman who lived in the city of Salisbury, who preached and in her sermon said that none but such painful creatures as herself should go to heaven; for those ministers that did not preach twice upon every sabbath day,[200] she said, that very shortly the black raven by day and the white owl by night, should scratch out their eyes.[201]

Thus, have I declared some of the female academies, but where their university is I cannot tell, but I suppose that Bedlam or Bridewell would be two convenient places for them.[202] Is it not sufficient that they may have the gospel truly and sincerely preached unto them, but they must take their ministers' office from them? If there had been such a dearth of the gospel as there was in the reigns of Queen Mary, it had been an occasion somewhat urgent.[203] But God be praised it was not so, but that they seemed to be ambitious, and because they would have superiority, they would get upon a stool or in a tub instead of a pulpit. At this time, I have described but six of them, before long I fear I shall relate more. I pray God I have no cause and so for this time I conclude.

FINIS.

---

controversial claim that the Sabbath should be observed on Saturday—the true seventh day—rather than Sunday. Nicholas W. S. Cranfield, "Wren, Matthew (1585–1667)," *ODNB*.

200. As with Bancroft, it is possible that Arabella Thomas is some form of Sabbatarian.

201. Because Arabella Thomas is identified as a Welsh woman, her references to ravens and owls can be understood as Celtic harbingers of fate. What is more, because Welsh women were associated with witchcraft and Thomas is here depicted as placing a kind of pagan "curse" upon ministers who failed to properly observe the Sabbath, we are urged to view her as a witch.

202. Bedlam and Bridewell were both London-based prisons for the insane. Bedlam was a parodic corruption of the prison's official name, Bethlehem Hospital.

203. Because the Catholic queen, Mary I, was known as "Bloody Mary" for her vigorous persecution of Protestants, there would have been a dearth or shortage of ministers preaching the Gospel during her reign.

Appendix 2: Transcript of Elizabeth Poole's Appearances in Whitehall

William Clarke
General Council at Whitehall, 29 December 1648
and
General Council 5 Jan. 1648 at Whitehall

This appendix contains two documents: *General Council at Whitehall, 29 December 1648* and *General Council 5 Jan. 1648*[1] *at Whitehall*. Both verify Poole's participation in the Whitehall debates. These documents consist of minutes taken by William Clarke of the two General Council of Army Officer meetings at which Poole delivered her visions. After the New Model Army was formed in 1645, Clarke was hired as assistant to General Thomas Fairfax's principal army secretary, John Rushworth.[2] From 1647 to 1650, Clarke served as secretary to the army's General Council of Officers. The minutes he kept of council meetings constitute valuable records for historians of the English Civil Wars.[3] More specifically for this volume, his minutes of Poole's two visits to the council form useful supplements to her pamphlets: they record both the content of her prophecies and the question and answer sessions that followed. The extent to which the officers engaged Poole in discussions about the meaning and source of her messages speaks to the seriousness with which they took her as a prophetess with political insight.

Clarke recorded council meetings by sitting in the assembly and transcribing the exchanges in shorthand. He had to write quickly and sometimes haphazardly in order to keep up with the conversation. The original manuscript of his minutes is part of a larger collection of his papers, books, and pamphlets. This collection was bequeathed to Worcester College, Oxford, England, in 1736 by Clarke's son, George. It comprises fifty-one bound volumes as well as a substantial amount of material that remains unbound. The first modern edition of a selection of Clarke's council meeting notes, including his minutes of the Putney Debates, was edited by Sir Charles Firth and published as *The Clarke Papers* in four volumes by the Camden Society.[4] Yet another modern edition was provided by A. S. P. Woodhouse in *Puritanism and Liberty*, first published in 1938 and republished

---

1. Clarke uses the Old Style calendar. In the New Style calendar, the January 5 meeting takes place in 1649.

2. Joad Raymond, "Rushworth [Rushforth], John (c. 1612–1690), historian and politician," *ODNB*.

3. Frances Henderson, "Clarke, Sir William (1623/4–1666), military administrator," *ODNB*.

4. Charles H. Firth, ed., *The Clarke Papers: Selections from the Papers of William Clarke*, 4 volumes (Westminster: Camden Society, 1891–1901). Volume 49 was published in 1891, volume 54 in 1894,

143

144 *Appendix 2*

numerous times thereafter. This version was "based on a careful collation of Firth's text" with excerpts from the original manuscript from Worcester.[5] In 2005, historian Frances Henderson published a new selection of Clarke's papers.[6]

The excerpts transcribed here are from digital photographs of pages 128–33 from volume 67 of the Clarke Manuscripts at Worcester College, Oxford. I drew upon Woodhouse's collation for help with places where it was difficult to decipher Clarke's handwriting in the original.

William Clarke
General Council at Whitehall, 29 December 1648
Present.

Elizabeth Poole of Abington first spoke, to this effect:
"That the business was committed to their trust, but there was a great snare before them.
That God was about to break the potsherds of the earth.
That there should not be a sherd left to carry coals now was of finer sort of metal. I look upon all manner of manifestations, forms, and religions which are made up in any regard of that there might be a pure life in death, that men might be dead unto all their fairest images, and find the comeliness in truth."[7]

After a short speech to this effect, further declaring the presence of God with the army, and desiring, that they would go forward and stand up for the liberty of the people as it was their liberty and God had opened the way to them.

The Commissary General[8] said:

---

volume 61 in 1899, and volume 62 in 1901. The materials regarding Poole's two visits to Whitehall are located in volume 54, 150–54 and 163–71, respectively.

5. A. S. P. Woodhouse, ed., *Puritanism and Liberty: Being the Army Debates (1647–49) from the Clarke Manuscripts* (London: J. M. Dent, 1992). Quotation from p. [11]. The sections regarding Poole appear on pages 429–71. Woodhouse notes that he has reordered material and included direct quotations from Poole's *A Vision*.

6. William Clarke, *The Clarke Papers V: Further Selections from the Papers of William Clarke*, ed. Frances Henderson (Cambridge: Cambridge University Press, 2005). Henderson's selections are from items dated May 1651 through 1660 and so do not include Poole.

7. Isaiah 45:9, GV.

8. Henry Ireton, Oliver Cromwell's son-in-law and a general in the New Model Army. Ireton wrote *A Remonstrance of His Excellency Thomas Lord Fairfax, Lord General of the Parliament's Forces* (appendix 3), which, as noted (p. 96), Poole cited in *A Vision: Wherein Is Manifested the Disease and Cure of the Kingdom*. He also composed *The Heads of Proposals* (appendix 5).

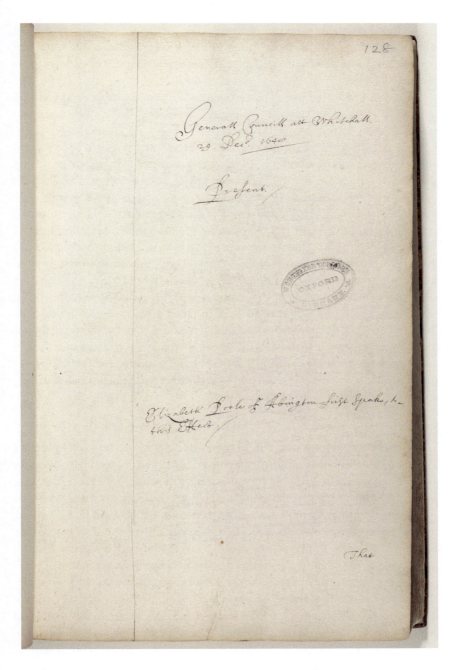

Figure 6. William Clarke, "General Council at Whitehall, 29 December 1648." *The Clarke Papers*, Clarke MSS, vol. 67, page 128. Worcester College, Oxford. Reproduced with permission.

146 *Appendix 2*

"That for what was said in commendation of the army, that they did not look for the praise of men, but for that which she spoke otherwise, that which she expressed it is very good and excellent and worthy consideration."
Woman:

"When I had been many days a mourner for the land with great and sore lamentation, and indeed a sympathizer with your labors, I had a vision set before me which was this, for the end of your labors.

"There was a man, a member of the army, that sometimes had been showed me, his respect unto his country, to its liberty and freedom, which he should gladly be a sacrifice for. This person was set before me[9] and a woman who should signify the weak and imperfect distressed state of the land on the other hand. This woman was full of imperfection, crooked, weak, sickly, imperfect. I was to appeal to the body of the army in this man that he should improve his faithfulness to the kingdom, by his diligence in the cure of this person, by the direction which I should give him through the gift of God in me for her. There was nothing required at his hand more than the acts of diligence; that he should before the Lord, act diligently and faithfully to employ all means which I should by the gift of God direct for her cure; and look how far short he failed of the means, so far short he should be of her cure; but so far as he should be faithful, so far he should be for her consolation. Nevertheless, this I was to show him; that it was not the gift of God in me, nor the acts of diligence in him, but in reference to that spirit of eternal power which had called me to believe and him to act, neither was he to be slack in action, nor I to be staggering in believing."

Col. Rich:[10]

"I cannot but give you that impression that is upon my spirit in conjunction with that testimony which God hath manifested here by an unexpected providence to me. What she hath said being correspondent with what I have made as it were before. The truth is, it is true the many things in which we are to take a liberty and use the liberty in reference to the men of the world that we have to deal withal; but that principle which is to carry us as in consideration of ourselves before God and the world, [is] after that liberty which the world doth not understand, and it is true we may use these arguments to satisfy such as understand no more, but if we have not another manner of testimony but such as the world gives testimony of, such things that God has by his providence given us satisfaction of, I believe as she says the conclusion of it will be but fleshly having begun in the spirit. And I think every man is to search his own heart and to see what is within, and not [what comes] from himself or from men or from outward means but from that

9. Representing the body of the army.

10. Colonel Nathaniel Rich. R. Swales, "Rich, Sir Nathaniel (c. 1585–1636), colonial investor and politician," *ODNB*.

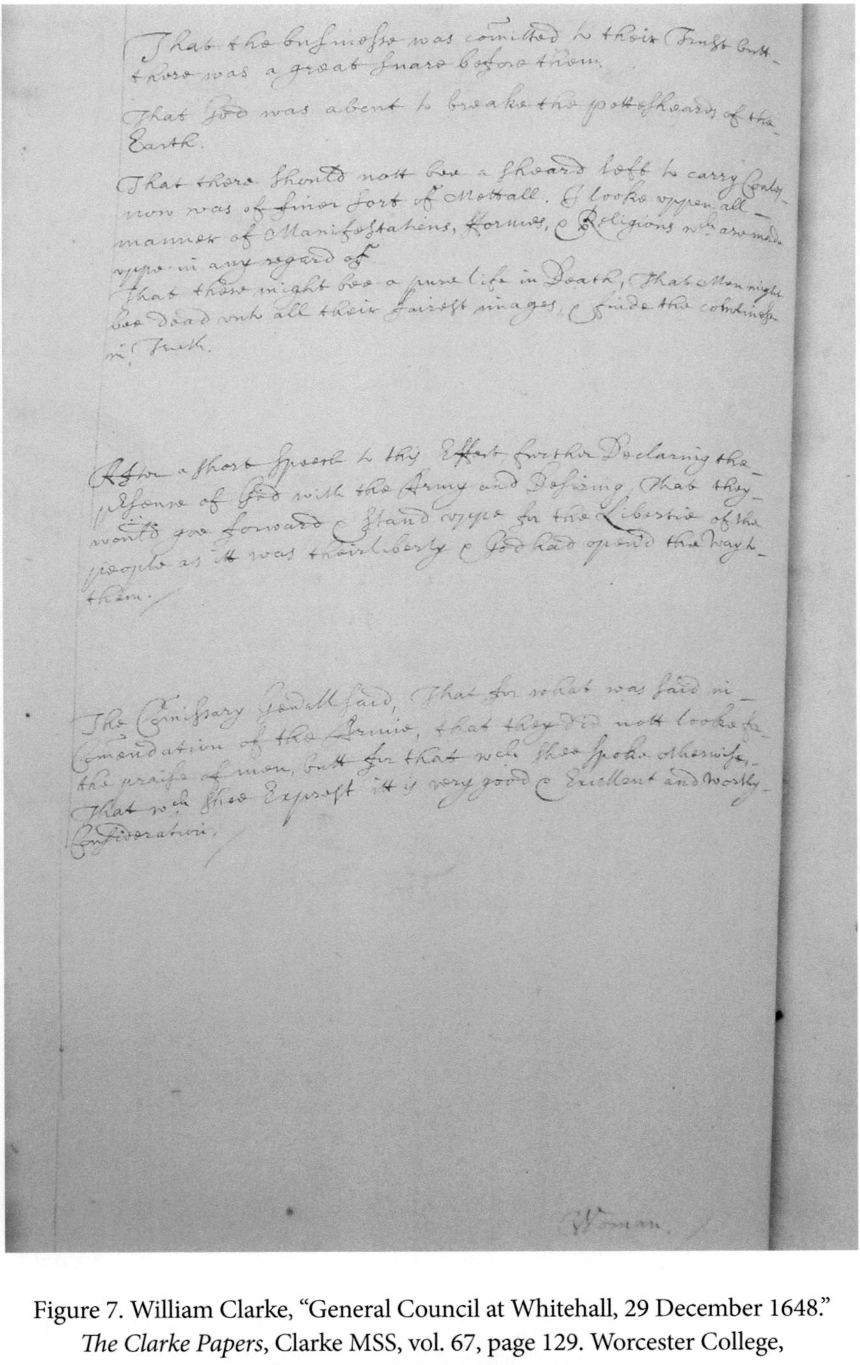

Figure 7. William Clarke, "General Council at Whitehall, 29 December 1648." *The Clarke Papers*, Clarke MSS, vol. 67, page 129. Worcester College, Oxford. Reproduced with permission.

148 *Appendix 2*

kingdom which when it comes will have no end. And truly I have had my portion of troubles and thoughts of heart since these things have come to their crisis and to their alteration, and I confess I can find nothing that is really and seriously an objection to them but what does arise from the flesh which has tempted me all along that might tend to a bearing testimony against the whole and series of the actions, and certainly these things are of God, and 'tis good council and, 'tis true, that he that will go about in a fleshly way to save his life shall lose it, and he that will lose it he may it save, them but they being purified by that fire which is from God and through which all things must pass, though I do rejoice to hear what hath been said, and it meets much with what has been upon my heart heretofore and I could not but speak what I did to bear witness to the same testimony, and shall rejoice to see it made out more and more in others."

Woman:

"It is true that the Lord hath a controversy with the great and mighty of the earth, with the captains and rulers. He will contend for his own name amongst them, but believe it to your consolations who wait upon him, that it is not with you, or with any but as the captains and rulers of the earth; you may be captains and rulers upon the earth and maintain his controversy, but if you be the captains and rulers of the earth his controversy is against you. Wherefore greater is he that is with you than they that are against you."

Col. Harrison:[11]

"If I do rightly observe what did fall from you, you said, that as one was represented to you on behalf of the army, and that though their acting such a thing was to be accomplished, it was given to you to believe he should effect [it by] following something that you ought to suggest unto him. Now that I have to offer unto you is this, whether anything was given to you more particularly to express than before?"

Woman:

"No, Sir. For it was represented to me as the church, not that the church was confined to this, or that, but as in the body, but by the gift and faith of the church shall you be guided, which spirit is in you, which shall direct you."

Com. Ireton:

"For what this woman does speak of the vision that was set before her and so for the judge of spirits, and for ought that I yet see, I see nothing in her but those that are the fruits of the spirit of God and I am therefore apt to think so at the present, being not able to judge the contrary, because methinks it comes with

11. Thomas Harrison, mentioned in *An Alarm of War* (p. 76) as one of the two army officers who was informed by the unnamed "two witnesses" of the sexual charges against Poole.

such a spirit that does take and hold forth humility and self-denial, and that rules very much about the whole that she hath delivered, which makes me have the better apprehension of it for the present. It is only God that can judge of spirits of men and women.

"I think the sum of that which she offers, that we ought to do for God, and you must go on in the way, and I think the exhortation is very seasonable; and therefore I would have you come to the business that is before you, and I hope that God will let that council go along with you, that we do it not as men-pleasers and men-observers, but as unto the Lord."

∾

General Council 5 Jan. 1648 at Whitehall.

Present

Elizabeth Poole who came in from Abington called in.

Eliz. Poole:
"Having been by the pleasure of the most High made sensible of the many grievances of this land, and of the great trust put into your hands, I have had some cause indeed of jealousies lest you might, through the manifold temptations which will easily beset you, betray your trusts. I know I speak to some amongst you that can judge what I say. I have heard some of you upon that which is called *An Agreement of the People*. It is very evident to me that the kingly power is fallen into your hands and you are entrusted with it that you might be as the head to the body. Now therefore if you shall take that up as an *Agreement of the People*, I must humbly present this to your thoughts for it seems to me to be that you shall give the power out of your own hands whereas God hath entrusted it with you and will require it of you how it is improved. You are his stewards, and so stewards of the gifts of God in and upon this nation. Wherefore I should humbly desire that it might be faithfully improved of you, and let no jealousies or fears that might suggest themselves in respect of apprehensions or persons whatsoever they are in you to lose not your trusts. Further another snare on the other hand will meet you, that you bear away above measure, but I am afraid of this also, that you lose your nobility for fear of what Parliament might say, or people might say, or other judges might say, or such as men have their eyes upon you. I know it has been the pangs of some of you that the king betrayed his trust and the Parliament theirs; wherefore this is the great thing I must present unto you: betray not you your trust.

150 *Appendix 2*

"I have yet a message to declare, which it's very possible may be very strangely looked upon, but in the law of the Lord I present myself to tender it, and let it find acceptance as it is."

(Gives in a paper.)

Col. Deane:[12]

"I must desire to ask one question: whether you were commanded by the spirit of God to deliver it unto us in this manner?"

Woman:

"I believe I had a command from God for it."

Col. Deane:

"To deliver this paper in this form?"

Woman:

"To deliver in this paper or a message otherwise."

Col. Deane:

"And so you bring it, and present it to us, as directed by the spirit in you, and commanded to deliver it to us?"

Woman:

"Yes Sir, I do."

After Debate, she was called in again.

Com. General:

"The Council desires to hear you a little further what you say as to these two things. 1. What you do hold forth to us as the demonstration of the witness to us, that this that you have delivered to us is from God, from God given in to you to be delivered to us. The next thing [is] what particular which you speak of concerning the king, whether you intend it against his trial or bringing to judgment, or against his execution only."

Woman:

"That he is due to be judged I believe, and that you may bind his hands and hold him fast under."

---

12. Colonel Richard Deane. Robert Walker, "Deane, Richard (bap. 1610, d. 1653)," *ODNB*.

Com. Ireton:

"What you would hold forth to us as the demonstration or witness that we should take notice of, whether to be read or known, that this you have delivered to us is from God, from him given in to you, and from you to be delivered to us."

Woman:

"Sir, I know not, but that is there will bear witness for itself if it be considered in the relation that kings are set in for government, though I do not speak this to favor the tyranny or bloodthirstiness of any, for I do look upon the conquest to be of divine pleasure, though God is not the supporter of tyranny or injustice, those are things he desires may be kept under."

Col. Rich:

"I desire to know whether that which is the will of God is not concordant with natural reason, and are refined and purified from its heat of which we know because we know nothing of its fall, but whether it be the will of God that any things in point of government should be inconsistent with the most essential being for which it was ordained, now if then any outward thing, and state and power and trust if it be not the will or the mind of God that any man empowered or entrusted for the public good, for the government sake should not be tyrannous to the governed for the well-being of which he was set in the chair for, then whether for the highest breach of trust there cannot be such an outward forfeiture of life itself, whether as of the trust itself?"

Woman:

"If these things be mistaken by me and found out by you, see God may be glorified I shall be satisfied."

Lt. Col. Kelsey:[13]

"That which was desired to know of the gentlewoman was, that this message was dictated to her by the spirit, and by the spirit presented to this council. Now if it be this way of demonstration or reason as Col. Rich speaks, it will admit of dispute; but if it be only from God, God did not send a messenger but that there may be an impression upon their hearts to receive it. Now that which was proposed to Mistress Poole to know [was] what demonstration she can give or token that it is from God; for either it must be from extraordinary revelation from God to you, and from you to us, or else there must be something of argument and reason to demonstrate it to us. Now there is nothing of reason in it, and if it be from God, the Council would be glad to hear what outgoings there are in that particular?"

13. Lieutenant Colonel Thomas Kelsey. J. T. Peacey, "Kelsey, Thomas (d. in or after 1676), parliamentarian army officer and major-general," *ODNB*.

152 *Appendix 2*

Woman:

"For the present I have no more to say than what is said therein."

Mr. Sadler:[14]

"I do desire that I may ask here these two questions. 1. I think you have indeed answered to the first already, but perhaps I do not understand you fully, whether it be intended to preserve his life, not at all against his trial?

"The 2nd. Whether you do not offer this paper from the Revelation of God? So far as it is from God, *I think it is a revelation.*"

Woman:

"I saw no vision, nor no Angel, nor heard no voice, but my spirit being drawn out about these things, I was in it."

Col. Whalley:[15]

"In case upon the king's trial that very filthy things, murder and all the great crimes that can be imagined—that he should be found guilty, then must he not die?"

Woman:

"What he will direct you in wisdom I have presented my thoughts."

Major Barber:

"By the favor of this Council, I would move one question—whether it's God, that the spirit does give in to her, whether that this king after judgment may die, and if so why should it be the mind of God that upon judgement. Question—he should not die rather than another king?"

Mistress Poole:

"Why surely thus, it appears to me that the king is the highest in subordination to God, in respect with the relation over the people His trust he hath betrayed—that I have often been speaking of, and the charge and care thereof is fallen upon you, but I speak in relation to the people. A head once set off."

Col. Rich:

"I desire to be satisfied in one question more. A trial of the person that may be is meet and is just, and he is capable of being judged by men. Now the question is, whether or not, he being not convinced that those that were entrusted for the

---

14. John Sadler. Richard Greaves, "Sadler, John (1615–1674), political theorist and reformer," *ODNB.*

15. Edward Whalley. Christopher Durston, "Whalley, Edward, appointed Lord Whalley under the protectorate (d. 1674/5), regicide and major-general," *ODNB.*

judicial power are not the proper judges, and so when he answers pro and con he stands mute and will no answer, the question is whether that will hinder the power of judgment?"

Mrs. Poole:
"I understand it not."

Com. Cowling:[16]
"I have heard mention since I came of two men, Joseph and Moses. The one was a great provider for the well-being of the people, and the other did as much in delivering the people when they were not well. I desire that as Moses you will not be so full of punishing as to look upon the old constitution,[17] wherein they have been upon us 34 years[18] and they could fall upon no other form but the beastly form of E[gypt], and the best they brought forth was a calf.[19] Now this I should offer to you. Take heed how you stick unto that constitution without which you are not able to form a way by which every man may enjoy his own."

---

16. Nicholas Cowling, Commissary General for Victuals. David R. Como, *Radical Parliamentarians and the English Civil War* (Oxford: Oxford University Press, 2018), 45.

17. The Ten Commandments, one of which is "Thou Shalt Not Kill."

18. Thirty-four of the forty years that the Israelites spent in the wilderness.

19. Exodus 32. When Moses was delayed from returning to his people while they labored in the wilderness, his brother Aaron collected the Israelites' gold and formed it into a calf. The Israelites worshipped the calf as a god, thereby lengthening the amount of time they had to spend in exile.

Appendix 3: Two Pamphlets Cited by Elizabeth Poole

This appendix contains two documents cited directly by Elizabeth Poole in *A Vision* as important motivators for her appearances in Whitehall. The first is *A Remonstrance of His Excellency, Thomas Lord Fairfax* (Wing F229). It was written by Henry Ireton, a general in the New Model Army and Cromwell's son-in-law. Poole alluded to it during her initial visit to the army's General Council on December 29 (p. 61). The second, *Foundations of Freedom*, was written by John Lilburne on behalf of the Levellers. Poole referred to it during her second visit to the General Council on January 5, 1649 (p. 64).

Henry Ireton
A Remonstrance of his Excellency Thomas Lord Fairfax *(1648)*

Ireton's *A Remonstrance* was a staunch defense of regicide. Ireton penned it earlier in 1648, just after Charles I was released from prison in Carisbrooke Castle. The king's release was arranged by moderates in Parliament so that he could travel to Newport, Isle of Wight, and negotiate the treaty that became known as the Treaty of Newport. When some of the negotiators pushed for the peace talks to be relocated to London, Ireton and other members of the army feared the king would seize the opportunity to retake power. They returned the king to prison and called for him to be tried for treason and put to death. After the moderates who sponsored the negotiations objected, the army asked Thomas Fairfax, major general of the New Model Army, to purge them from Parliament. When Fairfax hesitated, Ireton composed *A Remonstrance* to convince him that the treason charge and capital punishment were justified. Fairfax approved the document. It was then signed and adopted by the army's General Council. It was rejected, however, by Parliament, thereby inciting the army to carry out its purge. The army did so by forcibly reducing the body's membership down to the "rump" of those who had supported *A Remonstrance*. The Rump Parliament was preparing to try and execute the king when Poole made her appearances.

Poole objected to *A Remonstrance* for its endorsement of executing Charles I as the cure for England's ills. As Poole states, after reading it several times, she feared for England's death if this cure was pursued (p. 61). She hoped the army would instead heal the country by retaining power in its own hands and trying the king but sparing his life. However, as noted in the introduction (p. 36), Poole was careful in her argumentation. While rejecting the logic that the king had to be killed, she still acknowledged all events as ultimately emanating from God's will.

156 *Appendix 3*

    A Remonstrance is seventy pages long. The selection included here runs from page 41 to page 45; it represents Ireton's justification for trying and executing Charles I. Its elaboration of the dangers he would pose to a new government led to Poole's insistence that while the army should place the king on trial and "divorce" him, it should still protect the life of the realm's husband and father (p. 36).

    The copy reprinted here is housed in the Thomason Tracts (E.473[11]) in the British Library and is available on *EEBO*. The date, November 28, is handwritten on the title page of this copy by George Thomason to note the day upon which he obtained the pamphlet.

[Excerpt from]

A

REMONSTRANCE

OF HIS EXCELLENCY

Thomas Lord Fairfax, Lord General

OF THE

PARLIAMENT'S FORCES

AND OF THE

General Council

OF

OFFICERS

Held at *St. Albans* the 16th of

November, 1648.

Presented to the Commons

assembled in Parliament, the 20th instant,

and tendered to the Consideration of the

whole KINGDOM.

LONDON,

Printed for *John Partridge* and *George Whittington*; in *Black Fryers* at the gate going into *Carter Lane*, and at the blue *Anchor* in Cornhill. MDCXLVIII.[1]

His[2] way is clear.[3] The Parliament then may easily and soon be put to it to denude themselves of their strength in a disbanding and so set him even with themselves

---

1. 1648.

2. King Charles I's.

3. The king's strategy for regaining power is apparent.

again, or else (if they refuse) the people may be wrought to undo all for him (whatever he hath granted) without his appearing for his own interest to make any breach. And as upon this single ground many nations before us (by like accommodations with their beaten tyrants) have from the fairest attempts and hopes of liberty fallen to an utter loss of it, yes to an absolute bondage, and been made the instruments thereof themselves, so by this one consideration (though there were no more)[4] it may appear how easy it is for any prince, and particularly for ours (after such an accommodation made and himself restored), to find or work out advantages whereby to overthrow what he has granted, raise his own interest higher, and depress[5] the public lower than ever before. And yet we have touched but one of those many advantages that in each case lies clear before him. We might reflect upon that of his numerous party engaged by interest, necessity, and otherwise to serve him so long as he remains in possibility to head them, toward whom proceedings have been such as have served to embitter and enrage them unto, and yet not to disable or discourage them from further attempts against you and toward whom (by his continuing king) you will be the most necessitated to proceed still upon the same strain in both respects. We might mention also their great families and relations and their interest or influences within the kingdom, and we might enlarge upon the consideration of the two other kingdoms he has to work by,[6] from which we have found such powerful parties ready to serve his interest, the one to make prize and advantage of his kingdom, the other (at least) to deliver themselves from your yoke by helping to put his upon your and our necks; all which, if they were to be feared, when he has been in no capacity to head them (as in the last summer war) then much more when he shall be. And though they be much to be feared in relation to his heading of them, while he by his supposed impunity (whatever he does) has encouragement to make all possible trial of them and their hopes, that if ever he prevail he may make them amends or procure their impunity at last. Yet (that being once confuted by an example of justice upon him for such attempts) they would not then be (in divine considerations) at all or (in prudential considerations) not so much to be feared in relations to his posterity's heading of them. Besides these, we cannot but consider much more the vast possibilities after his restitution to make parties, factions and divisions among yourselves and your now adherents, and to set one against another, to make one betray another, by one to ruin another, and (by making use of all interests) to set up his own above all. Have not you found him at this play[7] all along? And do not

4. As though there were not more. A use of sarcasm, because, in the author's estimation, there are many more reasons why the people might be induced to work against their own interests by reinstating a tyrant.

5. Suppress.

6. Scotland and Ireland, both of which contained groups that supported the King against Parliament.

7. This game or strategy of pitting people against one another.

158 *Appendix 3*

all men acknowledge him most exquisite[8] at it? If he has had the faculty to avail much in this kind when at a distance from you, will he not much more when so near you, among you in your bosoms and councils?

For divisions (we speak it with depth of sadness) he needs not come to make any among you, but to use them; they abound woefully already. And for his opportunities of advantage by them, they are great beyond conception.

First, from the jealousies that each party is apt to have of the other's strengthening themselves to the prejudice of the other by conjunction[9] with him and his, and which he and his creatures[10] have a faculty to feed in each of them. It's more than probable that each party will be apt to strive which shall most and first comply with him. Have not you and we seen sad experiences of this already? Give us leave to be the more affectionately sensible of this as having had some experience of temptations toward it among ourselves, (we say) temptations toward it from the king and his party as strong and subtle as are imaginable, though, we bless God, by whom we are preserved in our integrity and not give up to but delivered from such wretched apostasy. And we can truly say that, although through the example of others partly necessitating us for the present prevention of that mischief to the public they were running into in that kind (as we apprehended), we were drawn into some negative compliances[11] tending to moderation (which we thought to be and in its place is a real good) yet first we never sought but were sought unto, and notwithstanding all overtures and temptations, we did abhor the thought of and still profusely refused anything of conjunction with him or his, in relation to the affairs of that time or ought of private contract or trust with them.

Secondly, what we declared of moderation was but hypothetical with careful caution and saving for the public interest (according to our then understanding of it). And:

Thirdly, we aimed not at the strengthening of ourselves thereby to the ruin of any persons or party opposed (nor did drive at any such end) but merely to prevent any such from strengthening themselves in that kind (as we feared) to the prejudice of the public, as may appear by the tenor of the city's engagement with the concomitants and consequences thereof, and by our carriage both in relation thereto and since that danger was over. And yet however in that degree of compliance admitted in that kind, we find matter of acknowledgement before the Lord concerning our error, frailty, unbelief, and carnal councils therein, and we bless him that preserved us from worst. But on the other side, give us leave to fear (and we heartily wish—as to any honest soul—that it may be a causeless and mistaken fear) that from such private jealousies and the animosities or hate of one party

---

8. Excellent or skilled.

9. Connection or alliance.

10. Sycophants.

11. Questionable compromises.

against another (who once seemed to be engaged in one common cause against a common enemy) there have been on the part of others evil compliances, negative and positive, yes (we doubt) contracts and conjunctions too, by some sought, by others entertained with him and his party (even while the acknowledged enemy) to the neglect or dispensing of the common public interest merely for the upholding or strengthening of their own and the ruin of the party particularly opposed.

We cannot but be sensible of this because we have felt the effects of it in the loss of many our dear innocent friends' lives, with the hazard of our own in the late summer war. For even from this root (as we have more than conjectural grounds to understand) the revolt in Wales had its rise and growth,[12] the Scottish invasion had its foundations and invitation,[13] the revolt of the ships,[14] the rebellion in Kent, Essex, etc.[15] and the several tumults, risings, and disturbances in and about London and the southern parts[16] had their instigations and encouragement, and from the same this miserable ensnaring treaty, its conception and birth. And if from the divisions we have such destructive compliances and conjunctions been

12. In 1646, after the end of the First Civil War, tensions quickly reemerged as the king manipulated all sides, and a series of revolts against Parliament, including the one mentioned here in South Wales, led to the outbreak of the Second Civil War in 1648.

13. The Bishops Wars of 1640–1642. As discussed in the introduction (pp. 14–16), these two invasions of northern England by the Scottish "Covenanters" were launched as retribution for Charles I's imposition of the Church of England's *Book of Common Prayer* upon the Scottish Presbyterian Church.

14. Although the navy served Parliament during the First Civil War, some of its members staged revolts. The revolt of the ships refers to an incident in 1648, when a group of naval officers supported protestors who petitioned Parliament to restore the Crown and disband the New Model Army. Later that year, Parliamentarian officer Colonel Thomas Rainsborough underwent a mutiny. After his men forced him to leave their ship, Rainsborough was dismissed by his superiors. The lord admiral tried to quell the rebellion, but tensions escalated when he failed. Even General Thomas Fairfax's defeat of Royalist insurgents in Kent did not convince the naval mutineers to submit. Nine of the rebel warships went so far as to offer their services to Prince Charles, inspiring him and his younger brother, James, to abandon their exile in France, take control of the fleet, accept aid from their sister, Mary, and brother-in-law, William, in the Netherlands, and reignite the war.

15. In 1647, Royalists in Kent protested attempts by Puritans in Parliament to suppress Christmas celebrations. To staunch the protests, the Kent county committee called upon its militia or "Trained Bands." This strategy did not end the conflicts. In 1648, the Kent-based Royalists attacked the bands after Canterbury's county committee attempted to derail a petition they had signed in favor of returning the King to power and disbanding the New Model Army. The Kent rebels assembled an army of more than ten thousand men. On May 29, seven thousand of them gathered at Penenden Heath. There, they were met by New Model Army troops serving under Thomas Fairfax. Even though the fighting was fierce, Fairfax and his men prevailed. The Kent rebels still did not give up. On June 4, they joined with Royalist insurgents in Essex to take members of the local county committee prisoner and force them to swear loyalty to the king. After they were defeated by Fairfax's forces, they took refuge in the town of Colchester and drew the New Model Army into a brutal months-long siege before they finally surrendered in August.

16. The various London-based protests also mentioned by Francis White (p. 220).

160 *Appendix 3*

entertained with, and such advantages given to him and his party while professed and acknowledged enemies, what worse may we not expect of that kind, when by a peace made they shall have the reputations of friends to give countenance and confidence thereunto?

To conclude this point (concerning his advantage after accommodation and restitution to overthrow or prejudice the public interest), we'll confuse our greatest fears from the consideration of the act for this Parliament's unlimited continuance wherein (besides divisions among those that are, or profess to be, for the public) if he shall ever be able by particular successions of new burgesses, according to the present constitution or any other way, to form a prevailing or balancing party for his interest in the House of Commons (which even there he seems to have bid fair for already, and as to the Lords we'll move no question), we may then justly lay England's liberties for defunct, when that which should be the conservative shall be turned indeed the bane, and yet (it being in the place and repute of the only conservative) we shall (through that act) be debarred from change of medicine or use of other remedy, yes from the renewing or taking fresh choice of medicine in the same kind, but must keep to that old mass which such putrefaction will have rendered deadly and will probably vitiate all particular addition of fresh ingredients that shall be made while the old leaven[17] shall remain predominant. Neither can we see any possible help in the case after his restitution, though you should be willing to lay down our power. For indeed, to set a period to this Parliament and not therewith provide for a certain succession of Parliaments and the certainty of their sitting also (without dependence on the king's will) were to leave the kingdom without assurance of any remedy, or (at least) of power therein to help at all, and so in like condition as before this Parliament.

◌

John Lilburne
Foundations of Freedom; or, An Agreement of the People *(1648)*

During her second visit to the army's General Council, Elizabeth Poole stated that she was inspired to return to readdress the officers in charge of deciding Charles I's fate after reading the Levellers' *Foundations of Freedom; or, An Agreement of the People* (Wing L2110A). This document was written by John Lilburne on behalf of the Levellers; it was intended to serve as the constitution for a new government. Far-reaching in its vision, it outlined a representative democracy along with the complete abolition of monarchy. While Poole encouraged the protection of

---

17. Literally an ingredient that makes bread rise (typically yeast), but also used to describe a force or factor that influences or modifies a situation.

Two Pamphlets Cited by Elizabeth Poole 161

people's liberties, she took issue with *Foundations of Freedom* because it proposed to divest the army of its ability to serve as the principle guarantor of those liberties.

Five versions of this document were produced by different authors at different times between 1647 and 1649. The original fourteen-page version was titled *An Agreement of the People for a Firm and Present Peace, upon Grounds of Common-right and Freedom* (Wing A780). It was drafted in October 1647 (possibly by the Leveller John Wildman) and debated by army officers and agitators elected from among the soldiery at the Church of St. Mary the Virgin in Putney, just outside of London, in October and November. The debates were heated, centering mostly around who should be allowed to vote in the new government. The Levellers favored a relatively broad franchise, excluding only men under twenty-one, servants, and recipients of alms. Cromwell and Ireton objected, arguing that voting rights should be restricted to property-holders. Several soldiers rejected both proposals, arguing that the extension of the vote to *all* men, even the poorest, was a fundamental right for which they had fought.[18] The parties agreed only to adopt some version of *An Agreement*, with its precise contents still to be determined, and to hold further meetings. But the army officers then turned against the Levellers. At one of the agreed-upon meetings at Corkbush Field, Cromwell and Ireton demanded that soldiers sign onto their own document, *The Heads of Proposals* (appendix 5), rather than adopting *An Agreement*. When some Levellers refused, violence ensued. But this did not stop the Levellers from continuing to hone their constitution's precepts.

After Parliament's victory in the Second Civil War in 1648, John Lilburne crafted the fifteen-page version included here and titled *Foundations of Freedom; or, An Agreement of the People: Proposed as a Rule for Future Government in the Establishment of a Firm and Lasting Peace*. This version appears in the volume because, after it was printed for a general audience, it was offered to the General Council for consideration at the Whitehall Debates at which Poole appeared. Given that Poole claimed she had heard a number of the officers comment on the Levellers' *Agreement* (p. 64), it is likely that the most recent version, *Foundations of Freedom*, was the one she had in mind. When Ireton tried to make changes to the document before it was submitted to Parliament, Lilburne and Richard

---

18. At no point was it considered that women would be allowed to vote, even though Leveller wives and mothers such as Elizabeth Lilburne, Katherine Chidley, and Mary Overton were active in the Leveller movement, including petitioning Parliament on behalf of jailed Leveller men. In these petitions, the women not only demanded that their male Leveler compatriots be freed but also asserted that they as women derived their right to petition from their God-given equality with men. See Anonymous, *To the Supreme Authority of this Nation, the Commons Assembled in Parliament: The Humble Petition of Diverse Well-Affected Women* (London: 1649) (Wing T1736). Ann Hughes, "Lilburne [née Dewell], Elizabeth (fl. 1641–1660), Leveller," *ODNB*. Ian Gentles, "Chidley, Katherine (fl. 1616–1653), religious controversialist and Leveller," *ODNB*. B.J. Gibbons, "Mary Overton (fl. 1646–1647), Leveller," *ODNB*.

162 *Appendix 3*

Overton, another prominent Leveller leader, walked out. The debates continued, but no consensus was achieved and the document never reached Parliament.

In January 1649, yet another version was produced. Titled *An Agreement Prepared for the People of England and the Places therewith Incorporated, for a Secure and Present Peace, upon Grounds of Common Right, Freedom, and Safety* (Wing A783A), this one was introduced into the House of Commons in the hope that it could still be adopted. It was signed by John Rushworth, secretary to Major General Thomas Fairfax and the army's General Council. As it also included a "petition of his Excellency [Fairfax] and the said General Council," this version represented the last time the army officers played a role in crafting this document. But Parliament's discussion was postponed because the High Court of Justice held its first open session of the king's trial on the same day *An Agreement* was introduced, January 20. Eventually, discussions were abandoned altogether.

The Levellers did not give up. Even while some members were imprisoned, they continued to revise *An Agreement*. On May 1, 1649, they released a new version titled *An Agreement of the Free People of England; Tendered as a Peace-Offering to this Distressed Nation*. It is attributed to Richard Overton on *EEBO*, but its title page lists its sponsors as "Lieutenant Colonel John Lilburne, Master William Walwyn, Master Thomas Prince, and Master Richard Overton, prisoners in the Tower of London." Also in 1649, a single-page broadside version of the document appeared under the title *An Agreement of the People of England and the Places therewith Incorporated for a Secure and Present Peace, upon Grounds of Common Right, Freedom, and Safety* (Wing A781).

The demands in all these versions anticipate many of those made by the American Revolutionaries in the 1770s. From the invocation of "the people" as inherently free to a list of liberties resembling the Bill of Rights, *An Agreement* helped codify rights and freedoms that many people take for granted today, such as regularly scheduled elections, greater access to the voting franchise, freedom of religion, a ban on a military draft, legal equality, free trade, transparent modes of taxation, trial by jury, and the abolition of capital punishment for crimes other than murder.

The copy reprinted here is housed in the Thomason Tracts (E.476[26]) in the British Library and is available on *EEBO*. The date, October 15, is handwritten on the title page of this copy by George Thomason to mark the date upon which he acquired the pamphlet.

Foundations of Freedom;

OR, AN

AGREEMENT

OF THE

PEOPLE:

Proposed as a Rule for future Government
in the Establishment of a firm
and lasting PEACE.

Drawn up by several well-affected Persons,
and tendered to the Consideration of the General
Council of the Army; and now offered to
the Consideration of all Persons who are at
Liberty, by Printing, or otherwise,
to have their Reasons for,
or against it.

Unto which is annexed several Grievances by
some Persons, offered to be inserted in the said
Agreement, but adjusted only necessary to be
insisted on, as fit to be removed by
the next Representatives.
Published for the Satisfaction of all honest Interests. 1648.

The Publisher to the Judicious Reader.

Dear Countryman,
This Agreement having had its conception for a common good, as being that which contains those foundations of freedom, and rules of government, adjudged necessary to be established in this nation for the future, by which all sorts of men are to be bound, I adjudged it a just and reasonable thing to publish it to the view of the nation, to the end that all men might have an opportunity to consider the equity thereof and offer their reasons against anything therein contained before it be concluded. That being agreeable to that principle which we profess, viz.[19] to do unto you as we would all men should do unto us; not doubting but that the justice of it will be

19. Latin abbreviation for *videlicet*, a contraction of the Latin word *videre licet* meaning "it is permitted to see." Commonly used as a synonym for "namely" or "that is."

164 *Appendix 3*

maintained and cleared, maugre[20] *the opposition of the stoutest calumniator,*[21] *especially in those clear points in the reserve so much already controverted, viz. touching the magistrates power to console or restrain in matters of religion and the exercise of an arbitrary power in the representative,*[22] *to punish men for state offenses against which no law has provided; which two things especially are so clear to my understanding, that I dare with confidence aver that no man can demand the exercise of such a power but he that intends to be a tyrant, nor no man part with them but he that resolves to be a slave. And so at present I rest,*

Friday, *December*
10. 1648.

Thy true-hearted
countryman.[23]

AN
AGREEMENT
Of the PEOPLE of
ENGLAND,
And the places therewith
INCORPORATED;
For a firm and present
PEACE,
Upon Grounds of *Common Right*
and *Freedom*.

Having by our late labors and hazards made it appear to the world at how high a rate we value our just freedoms, and God having so far owned our cause as to deliver the enemies thereof into our hands, we do now hold ourselves bound in mutual duty to each other to take the best care we can for the future to avoid both the danger of returning into a slavish condition[24] and the chargeable remedy of another war. For as it cannot be imagined that so many of our countrymen would have opposed us in this quarrel if they had understood their own good, so may we safely promise to ourselves that when our common rights and liberties shall be cleared their endeavors will be disappointed, that seek to make themselves our masters. Since therefore our former oppressions and not-yet-ended troubles

20. In spite of.

21. Critic.

22. The representative body: Parliament.

23. John Lilburne.

24. Feudal bondage, as the Levellers and other critics viewed conditions under monarchy.

Two Pamphlets Cited by Elizabeth Poole 165

have been occasioned, either by want of frequent national meetings in council[25] or by the undue or unequal continuation thereof or by rendering those meetings ineffectual, we are fully agreed and resolved to provide that hereafter our representatives be neither left for uncertainty for time[26] nor be unequally constituted nor made useless to the end for which they are intended.

In order whereunto we declare and agree:

1. That to prevent the many inconveniences apparently arising from the long continuance of the same persons in authority,[27] the present Parliament be dissolved upon or before the last day of April, in the year of our Lord 1649.

2. That the people of England, being at this day very unequally distributed by counties, cities, or burroughs for the election of their representatives, be more indifferently proportioned and to this end that the representative of the whole nation shall consist of 300 persons; and in each county and the places thereto subjoined, there all be chosen to make up the said representative at all times, the several numbers hereunder mentioned.[28]

The manner of Elections.

1. That the electors in every division shall be natives or denizens[29] of England, such as have subscribed [to] this *Agreement*; not persons receiving alms[30] but such as are affected ordinarily towards the relief of the poor; not servants to or receiving wages from any particular persons. And in all elections (except for the universities) they shall be men of one and twenty years old or upward and housekeepers, dwelling within the division for which the election is, provided that until

25. Parliament's inability or failure to meet on a regular basis, thereby depriving citizens of due representation.

26. That Parliament not be convened to prevent it from exercising its obligations, including its duty to check the power of the leader.

27. *An Agreement*'s concern with regular Parliamentarian sessions is rooted in the history of the Long Parliament as it was outlined in the introduction (pp. 13–14). Even as the Levellers granted that Parliament needed to protect itself from illegitimate dissolution by the king, they also feared it had gained too much power as the sole ruling body. To prevent future members of Parliament from becoming too powerful, the Levellers call for a constitutionally stipulated set of rules to be established that would require members of Parliament to be elected by the populace (however selectively defined) on a regular basis and to meet at predetermined intervals.

28. At this point in the pamphlet, Lilburne provides a two-column chart in which he lists the eighty-two counties, cities, universities, boroughs, and/or towns that he believes should be included in order to achieve a more just distribution of elected representatives. To save space, that list is not duplicated here.

29. Inhabitants.

30. Charity from the church.

166 *Appendix 3*

the end of seven years next ensuing the time herein limited for the end of this present Parliament no person shall be admitted to or have any hand or voice in such elections who have adhered to or assisted the king against the Parliament in any of these wars or insurrections; or who shall make or join in or abet any forcible opposition against this *Agreement*. And that such as shall not subscribe [to] it before the time limited for the end of this Parliament, shall not have [a] vote in the next election. Neither if they subscribe afterward shall they have any voice in the election next succeeding their subscription, unless their subscription were six months before the same.

2. That until the end of fourteen years, such persons and such only may be elected for any division who by the rule aforesaid are to have [a] voice in elections in one place or [an]other, provided that of those none shall be eligible for the first or second representatives who have not voluntarily assisted the Parliament against the king, either in person before the fourteenth of June 1645, or else in money, plate, horse, or arms, leant upon the Propositions before the end of May 1643,[31] or who have joined in or abetted the treasonable Engagement in London in the year 1647,[32] or who declared or engaged themselves for a cessation of arms with the Scots[33] who invaded the nation the last summer,[34] or for compliance with the

---

31. The Oxford Propositions or Treaty of Oxford, the Long Parliament's failed attempt in 1643 to establish a committee that would negotiate a peace treaty with the king. After Charles was caught conducting secret talks with both the Scots and the Irish Catholics and slowing down negotiations so that, among other manipulations, he could engineer an armed uprising in London, Parliament's negotiating committee or "peace party" became looked upon as traitors by those who believed the king was an irredeemable tyrant. For the authors of *The Agreement*, these negotiators were among those who collaborated with the king; hence they should be ineligible for public office. John Rushworth, "The Treaty of Oxford," *Historical Collections of Private Passages of State*: Volume 5, *1642–45* (London: D. Browne, 1721), 164–263. *British History Online*: http://www.british-history.ac.uk/rushworth-papers/vol5/pp164-263.

32. The so-called Engagement, which came about after Charles I's surrender to the Scottish army in 1647 when negotiations resumed for a permanent peace agreement. As they do with the Oxford Propositions, the authors of *The Agreement* view this treaty as problematic, specifically in this case because it emerged from a secret collusion between Charles and his Scottish guards after his capture by Parliament.

33. Those who supported the Engagement and peace with the Scots on terms that were not favorable to the goals for which the Levellers and their allies in the army had fought.

34. The Battle of Preston. The battle began when the Scottish Engagement Army crossed the border into England to aid Charles I's Royalist forces. It ended in a victory for Cromwell.

actors in any of the insurrections of the same summer,[35] or with the Prince of Wales[36] or his accomplices in the revolted fleet.[37]

3. That whosoever being by the rules in the next two preceding articles incapable of election or to be elected shall assume to vote in or be present at such elections for the first or second representative, or being elected shall presume to sit or vote in either of the said representatives, shall endure the pain of confiscation of the of his estate,[38] moiety to the use of the public, in case he have any estate visible to the value of fifty pounds. And if he have not such an estate, then he shall incur the pain of imprisonment for three months. And if any person shall forcibly oppose, molest, or hinder the people (capable of electing as aforesaid) in their quiet and free election of their representatives, then each person so offering shall endure the pain of consideration of his whole estate, both real and personal. And if he have not an estate to the value of city pounds, shall suffer imprisonment, during one whole year, without bail or mainprise.[39] Provided that the offender in each such case be convicted within three months next after the committing of his offense.[40]

4. That for the more convenient election of representatives, each county with the several paces thereto conjoined, wherein more than three representatives are to be

35. The riots that ensued on August 7, 1643, when the news broke that Parliament was negotiating with Charles via the aforementioned Oxford Propositions for a peace treaty. As *The Agreement* notes, this "mob" did not gather spontaneously but was engineered by others, specifically, the lord mayor and the city council who, if their machinations had failed, planned to arrest members of the "peace party." The House of Commons' repudiation of the Oxford Propositions and the tumult wrought by the riots, along with the facts that Cromwell believed many army leaders were reluctant to fight for a decisive victory over the king and that the king had created such divisive turmoil among the Scots that he helped consolidate Scottish Parliamentarian solidarity with Parliament against the Crown, provided Parliament with a rationale for forming its own military. This force became the New Model Army in 1645.

36. Charles I's eldest son and heir, Prince Charles, who would become King Charles II in 1660. In 1645, the fourteen-year-old Prince Charles fought with his father's army and was named the head of his forces in the West Country. When Royalist defeat was imminent in 1646, Charles joined his mother, Queen Henrietta Maria, and his siblings in exile in France, where his mother had sought protection from her first cousin, the eight-year-old French king, Louis XIV. After the Second Civil War began, the prince relocated to the Netherlands and placed himself under the protection of his sister, Mary, and her husband, William II, Prince of Orange (who would in 1689 become William and Mary, the joint regents of England). From them, he also received financial support to try to rejoin the war in support of the Royalist cause. Paul Seaward, "Charles II (1630–1685), king of England, Scotland, and Ireland," *ODNB*.

37. The naval revolts, also referred to in *The Heads of Proposals* (p. 208).

38. A portion, often a majority share.

39. Comparable to bail, a law enabling a prisoner to be freed in exchange for providing a guarantee that he or she will not flee but will appear as a defendant upon their appointed court date.

40. The right to a speedy trial.

168 *Appendix 3*

chosen, shall be divided by a due proportion into so many parts, as each part may elect two, and no part above three representatives. And for the making of these divisions, two persons be chosen in every hundred,[41] lath,[42] or wapentake,[43] by the people therein (capable of election as aforesaid), which people shall on the last Tuesday in February next between eleven and three of the clock be assembled together for that end at the chief town or usual meeting place in the same hundred, lath, or wapentake. And that the persons in every hundred, lath, or wapentake so chosen, or the major part of them, shall on the fourteenth day after their election meet at the common hall of the county-town and divide the county into parts as aforesaid, and also appoint a certain place in each respective part or division wherein the people shall always meet for the choice of their representatives and shall make returns of the said divisions and certain places of meeting therein into the Parliament records in writing under the hands and seals of the major part of them present. And also cause the same to be published in every parish in the county before the end of March now next ensuing. And for the more equal division of the City of London for the choice of its representatives, there shall one person be chosen by the people in every parish in the said city (capable of election as aforesaid) upon the last Tuesday in February aforesaid; on which day they shall assemble in each parish for the same purpose between two and four of the clock. And that the persons so chosen, or the major part of them, shall upon the fourteenth day after their election meet in the guild hall of the said city and divide the same city into eight equal parts or divisions and appoint a certain place in every division respectively wherein the people of that division shall always meet for the choice of their representatives and shall make return thereof; and cause the same to be published in the manner prescribed to the several counties, as in this article.

5. That for the better provision for true and certain returns of persons elected, the chief public officer in every division aforesaid who shall be present at the beginning of the election and in absence of every such officer, then any person eligible as aforesaid, whom the people at that time assembled shall choose for that end, shall regulate the elections and by polls or otherwise clearly distinguish and judge thereof, and make true returns thereof, in writing indented under the hands and seals of himself and of six or more of the electors into the Parliament's records, within one and twenty days after the election, and for default thereof or for making any false return, shall forfeit 100 pounds to the public use.

41. "A subdivision of a county or shire, having its own court; also formerly applied to the court itself" (*OED*). The term also came to be associated with the Germanic version of the "long hundred" of 120 units.

42. Lathe. "One of the administrative districts (most recently five in number) into which Kent was divided, each comprising several hundreds" (*OED*).

43. "A subdivision of certain English shires, corresponding to the 'hundred'" (*OED*).

Two Pamphlets Cited by Elizabeth Poole 169

6. That one hundred and fifty members at least be always present in each sitting of the representatives, at the passing of any law or doing of any act whereby the people are to be bound.

7. That every representative shall, within twenty days after their first meeting, appoint a council of state for the managing of public affairs until the first day of the next representative, and the same council to act and proceed therein according to such instructions and limitations as the representatives all give, and not otherwise.

8. That to the end all officers of state may be certainly accountable and no factions made to maintain corrupt interest, no member of a council of state nor any officer of any salary forces in arms or garrisons, nor any treasurer or receiver of public moneys, shall (while such) be elected to be a representative. And in case any such election shall be, the same to be void. And in case any lawyer shall be chosen of any representative, or council of state, then he shall be incapable of practice as a lawyer during that trust.

9. That the power of the people's representatives extend (without the consent or concurrence of any other person or persons) to the enacting, altering, repealing, and declaring of laws, to the erecting and abolishing officers of courts of justice, and to whatsoever is not in this *Agreement* excepted or reserved from them:

> As particularly:
> 1. We do not empower our representatives to continue in force, or make any laws, oaths, and covenants whereby to compel by penalties or otherwise any person to anything in or about matters of faith, religion or God's worship, or to restrain any person from professing his faith or exercise of religion according to his conscience, in any house or place (except such as are or shall be set apart for the public worship), nevertheless the instruction or directing of the nation in a public way, for the matters of faith, worship, or discipline (so it be not compulsive[44] or express popery[45]) is referred to their discretion.[46]

---

44. Compulsory.

45. Just as "papist" is a pejorative term for a Catholic, so is "Popery" a derogatory term for Catholicism in general.

46. *The Agreement* constitutes religious freedom as a right. However, it also does not preclude the possibility that Parliament might establish a public religion even though it would not be licensed to compel people to attend that church.

170 *Appendix 3*

2. We do not empower them to impress or constrain any person to serve in war[47] either by sea or land, every man's conscience being to be satisfied in the justness of that cause wherein he hazards his life.

3. That after the dissolution of this present Parliament, none of the people be at any time questioned for anything said or done in reference to the late wars or public differences, otherwise than in execution or pursuance of the determination of the present House of Commons against such as have adhered to the king or his interest against the people. And saving that accounts for public moneys received shall remain accountable for the same.

4. That in any laws hereafter to be made, no person by virtue of any tenure, grant, charter, patent, degree, or birth, shall be privileged from subjection thereto, or being bound thereby as well as others.

5. That all privileges or exceptions of any persons from the laws or from the ordinary cause of legal proceedings by virtue of any tenure, grant, charter, patent, degree, or birth or of any place of residence or refuge shall be henceforth void and null, and the like not to be made nor revived again.

6. That the representatives intermeddle not with the execution of laws, nor give judgement upon any man's person or estate, where no law hath been before provided, save only in call to an account and punishing public officers for abusing or failing their trust.

7. That no member of any future representative be made either receiver, treasurer, or other officer during that employment, saving to be[48] a member of the council of state.

8. That no representative shall in any wise[49] render up, or give or take away any the foundation of common right, liberty or safety contained in this *Agreement*, nor shall level men's estates, destroy property, or make all things common.[50]

---

47. To draft into war.

48. Except for.

49. In any way.

50. A reference to the goals of the group known as the Diggers (p. 2) because they were farmers who set up agrarian communes. Led by Gerrard Winstanley, who published manifestos in the late 1640s, the Diggers believed in the abolition of property and the transformation of all lands into a national commons. They referred to themselves as "true Levellers" because they wished to "level" all social and economic hierarchies. They were essentially destroyed by Parliamentarian officers in 1649 at the

9.[51] That the council of state, in case of imminent danger or extreme necessity, may in each interval summon a representative to be forthwith chosen, and to meet so as the sessions thereof continue not above forty days and so it dissolve two months before the appointed time for the meeting of the next representative.

10. That all securities given by the public faith of the nation shall be made good by the next and all future representatives, save that[52] the next representative may continue or make null, in part or in whole, all gifts of moneys made by the present House of Commons to their own members, or to any of the lords, or to any of the attendants of either of them.

11. That every officer or leader of any forces in any present or future army or garrison that shall resist the orders of the next or any future representative (except such representative shall expressly violate this *Agreement*) shall forthwith affect his or their resistance by virtue of this *Agreement*, lose the benefit and protection of all the laws of the land and die without mercy.

These things we declare to be essential to our just freedoms and to a thorough composure of our long and woeful distractions. And therefore we are agreed and resolved to maintain these certain rules of government, and all that join therein, with our utmost possibilities, against all opposition whatsoever.

These following particulars were offered to be inserted in the *Agreement*, but adjudged[53] fit, as the most imminent grievances to be redressed by the next representative.

---

behest of the titleholder to the lands upon which one of the communes was built. Because the group now referred to as the Levellers wished to implement various forms of equality under the law, they were accused of being Levellers in the more communistic sense of the term. However, they never used that term to refer to themselves, for, as we see in this clause, they believed in private property and rejected claims that the state or any other entity had the right to expropriate goods and properties. See Lewis Henry Berens, *The Digger Movement: Radical Communalism in the English Civil War* (St. Petersburg, FL: Red and Black, 2008).

51. In the original, the number eight is mistakenly used twice. I have corrected that here so that the numbering of clauses proceeds as it should. When one corrects for the doubling of the number eight, there are in actuality eleven clauses, as represented here, rather than ten, as is in the original.

52. Except that.

53. Judged.

172 *Appendix 3*

1. It shall not be in their power[54] to punish or cause to be punished any person or persons for refusing to answer to questions against themselves in criminal cases.

2. That it shall not be in their power to continue or constitute any proceedings in law that shall be longer than three or four months, in finally determining of any cause past all appeal, or to continue the laws (or proceedings therein) in any other language than in the English tongue.[55]

3. It shall not be in their power to continue or make any laws to abridge any person from trading unto any parts beyond the seas, unto which they are allowed to trade, or to restrain trade at home.

4. It shall not be in their power to continue excise[56] longer than twenty days after the beginning of the next representative, nor to raise moneys by any other way except by an equal rate proportionally to men's real or personal estates; wherein all persons not worth above thirty pounds shall be exempted from bearing any part of public charge, except to the poor and other customary charge of the place where they dwell.

5. It shall not be in their power to make or continue any law whereby men's estates or any part thereof shall be exempted from payment of their debts, or to continue or make any law to imprison any man's person for debts of any nature.

6. It shall not be in their power to make or continue any law for taking away any man's life, except for murder, or for endeavoring by force to destroy this *Agreement*, but shall use their uttermost endeavor to propound punishments equal to offenses.[57] That so men's lives, limbs, liberties, and estates may not as hitherto be liable to be taken away upon trivial or slight occasion, and shall have special care to keep all sorts of people from misery and beggary.

7. They shall not continue or make a law to deprive any person, in case or trial, from the benefit of witnesses, as well for as against him.

8. They shall not continue the grievance and oppression of tithes[58] longer than to the end of the first representative, in which time they shall provide for and satisfy

---

54. The power of the representative body.

55. As opposed to Latin, the language of the court, which, other than members of the legal establishment and the priesthood, most people could not read or speak.

56. A tax on goods or on licenses granted for various forms of trade.

57. At this time, crimes such as theft were capitol offenses.

58. Forced payments to the church of a tenth of one's earnings, in the form of either money or goods.

all impropriators.[59] Neither shall they force any persons to pay toward the maintenance of the public ministers who out of conscience cannot submit thereunto, but shall provide for them in some other non-oppressive way.

9. They shall not continue or make a law for any other ways of judgement or conviction of life, liberty, or estate, but only by twelve sworn men of the neighborhood.[60]

10. They shall not continue or make a law to allow any person to take above six pound *percent* for loan of money for a year.

11. They shall not disable any person from bearing any office in the commonwealth for any opinion or practice in religion, though contrary to the public way.

Unto these I shall add:

I. That the next representative be most earnestly pressed for the ridding of this kingdom of those vermin and caterpillars, the lawyers, the chief bane of this poor nation, to erect a court of justice in every hundred in the nation for the ending of all differences arising in that hundred, by twelve men of the same hundred annually chosen by freemen of that hundred with express and plain rules in English made by the representative or supreme authority of the nation for them to guide their judgements by.

II. That for the preventing of fraud, thefts, and deceits, there be forthwith in every county or shire in England and the dominion of Wales erected a county record for the perfect registering of all conveyances, bills, and bonds, etc. upon a severe and strict penalty.

III. That in case there be any need after the erection of hundred courts of majors, sheriffs, justices of the peace, deputy lieutenants, etc. that the people capable of election of Parliament men, in the foregoing *Agreement*, be restored by the representative unto their native, just, and undoubted right by common consent from among themselves, annually to choose all the aforesaid officers in such manner as shall be plainly and clearly described, and laid down by the supreme authority of the nation. And that when any subsidies or public taxes be laid upon the nation, the freemen of every division or hundred, capable of election as aforesaid, choose out persons by common consent from among themselves for the equal division of their assessments.

---

59. Those who forcibly confiscate money or goods or who benefit therefrom.

60. A jury of one's peers.

IV. That the next representative be earnestly desired to abolish all base tenures.[61]

FINIS.

---

61. A core feature of the common law under feudalism, whereby the king officially possessed the rights to all lands in his realm and merely granted access to their use—or tenure—to those who may have profited from the goods they produced but still only "held" rather than owned them.

Appendix 4: Pamphlets about Elizabeth Poole

This appendix contains three pamphlets that reported on Elizabeth Poole's appearances in Whitehall, thereby constituting these events as newsworthy for her time and ours. *The Manner of the Deposition of Charles Stewart* is an account of the trial of Charles; as its subtitle—"Also the words of a woman who pretends to have seen a vision, to the General Council of the Army"—announces, the account includes a report of Poole's delivery of her prophecies. *To Xeiphos Ton Martyron* and *The English Devil* both represent Poole as a witch whose presence in Whitehall was part of a conspiracy to overthrow monarchy.

Anonymous
The Manner of the Deposition of Charles Stewart, King of England
(1649)

The Manner of the Deposition of Charles Stewart (Wing M465) lays out the charges against the king in great detail, including rationales for why he deserved to die. The execution of the king on January 30, 1649, sent a shockwave through the British Isles and the Continent. Charles I's executors were defamed as satanic rebels who, like the Roman soldiers in ancient Jerusalem, had put God's son to death. In response, the army officers who constituted the General Council were forced to defend the logic by which they had arrived at the death sentence. One of the most famous defenses of the regicide was written by John Milton, the poet who served as Latin secretary under Cromwell. Titled *The Tenure of Kings and Magistrates* (London: 1649) (Wing M2181) and published just after the king's beheading, Milton's tract provides numerous historical precedents for putting tyrants to death. It was this level of intellect among proponents of regicide with which Poole had to contend in her own attempt to prevent the death sentence from being applied to the king.

The Manner of the Deposition is neither an attack upon the regicide nor a defense of it. Instead, it is more journalistic in its aims, straightforwardly laying out the transgressions with which the king was charged by the General Council and its terms of settlement for a new, more democratic government. It also gives us brief but compelling glimpses of Charles I's behavior while in captivity and under threat of execution. The pamphlet's restrained tone allows the reader to contemplate whether the General Council's charges against the king justify his execution. It also provides yet more evidence for how seriously Poole's involvement in this historic event was taken.

The copy reprinted here is housed in the Thomason Tracts (E.537[4]) in the British Library and is available on *EEBO*. The date, January 4, is handwritten on

175

176 *Appendix 4*

the title page by George Thomason to note the day upon which he obtained the tract for his collection. The year, 1648, is also handwritten by Thomason on the cover. Thomason uses the Old Style date of 1648, rather than the New Style date of 1649 that the original pamphlet features.

The Manner of the Deposition of
CHARLES STEWART,
King of England, by the Parliament, and
General Council of the
A R M Y:

The intended T R I A L of the King for his life, as guilty
of High Treason; and in case of his refusal to
plead to his Charge: the Resolves of the
Parliament, and Council of War.

Also the words of a woman[1] who pretends to have
seen a vision, to the General Council of the Army.

With a list of the names of the Commissioners for
the Trial of the King, *viz.*[2]

The Earle of Denbigh, E. of Pembroke, E. of Kent, E. of Mulgrave, E. of Nottingham, L. Grey of Wark. The L. Munson, L. Lisle, L. Grey of Groby, Lieut. G. Cromwell, Maj. G. Skippon, Com. G. Ireton, Sir Hen. Mildmay, Sir John Danvers, Sir Greg. Norton, Col. Walton, Col. Moore, Mr. Edwards, Col. Boswel, Mr. Cawley, Mr. Prideaux, Mr. Allen, Col. Ven, Col. Thorne, Col. Rossiter, Ser. Thorpe, Mr. Henry Wingham, Mr. Pury, Mr. Scot, Mr. Trenchard, Mr. Corbets, senior and junior, Mr. Holland, Mr. Hallowell, Mr. Challoners, senior and junior, Mr. Willington, Mr. Leslo, Col. Lassels, the Lord Gen. Fairfax, Col. Whalley, Col. Rich, Sir Hardresse Waller, Col. Tomlinson, Col. Scroop, Col. Sanders, Col. Twistleton, Col. Pride, Col. Hewson, Col. Cook, Col. Barkstead, Col. Horton, Col. Desborough, Col. Dean, Col. Okey, &c. Alder. Pennington, Alder. Wollaston, Alder. Fooks, Alder. Gibbs, Alder. Andrews &c.

Printed in the Year, 1649.

---

1. Elizabeth Poole.

2. Latin abbreviation for *videlicet*, a contraction of *videre licet*, meaning "it is permitted to see." Commonly used as a synonym for "namely" or "that is."

The manner of the deposition of Charles Stewart, King of England, by the Parliament, and the General Council of the Army.[3]

The House were no sooner informed that his Majesty was brought to Windsor by a brigade of the army's horse, but they nominated a committee[4] to consider how to proceed in a way of justice against the king, and other capital offenders. They gave them[5] power to send for papers and witnesses to examine, as to the business of Ireland,[6] the poisoning of King James,[7] and other particulars in relation to the king and kingdom. The committee accordingly has met and, after much scrutiny, has drawn up charges against him[8] which is this:

That Charles Stewart has acted contrary to his trust, in departing from the Parliament, setting up his standard, making war against them,[9] and thereby been the occasion of much bloodshed and misery to the people, whom he was set over to protect and defend, that he gave commission to rebels in Ireland to commit all manner of murders and outrages, and since that has been the occasion of a second war, for the ruin and destruction of his people, besides what he has done

---

3. This pamphlet is an example of a so-called newsbook, a short journalistic report of an event or set of events. Some newsbooks were occasional, that is, published a single time for a specific purpose. Others issued more than one volume under the same title. This latter form of "serial newsbook" was the forerunner of the modern newspaper. The newsbook reproduced here was an occasional newsbook and, as its title states, describes the procedures by which the council arrived at a death sentence for the king, including the consideration of Poole's messages. Many newsbooks at this time, whether occasional or serial, made no claims to objectivity but offered accounts of events from particular perspectives. This account is somewhat remarkable for its relative impartiality. See Joad Raymond, *The Invention of the Newspaper: English Newsbooks, 1641–1649* (London: Clarendon, 1996).

4. The army's High Court of Justice.

5. The committee.

6. The question of the Crown's relationship to Catholic Ireland, which played a central role in the Civil Wars.

7. A popular conspiracy theory, first put forth in 1626 in a book titled *The Forerunner of Revenge* (Wing 7548) by the Scottish Catholic physician and sometimes counterfeiter, George Eglisham. According to Eglisham, James did not, as was widely believed, die from the effects of age and debauchery but was poisoned by his favorite courtier, George Villiers, the first Duke of Buckingham. Eglisham likely offered this theory to defame Buckingham because the duke was one of the councilors advising the king to join the fight against Catholicism in the Thirty Years' War. Parliament used the story to try to impeach Buckingham in 1626. The allegations also fueled John Felton to assassinate Buckingham in 1628. Finally, the charges were used in Charles's trial as evidence of the Crown's corruption. Alsager Vian, "Eglisham, George (fl. 1601–1642)," *ODNB*.

8. The king.

9. His own people.

contrary to the liberty of the subject and the destruction of the fundamental laws and liberties of this kingdom.

The Council of War has also drawn up an attainder of high treason against him which runs thus:

That Charles Stewart has falsified his trust, trampled on the laws, and been the occasion of the murdering a hundred thousand Englishmen, with all the miseries of war this seven years, by departing from his Parliament, setting up his standard, and making a bloody war in the defense of an illegal arbitrary power, to the enslaving and vassalizing[10] the free-born people of England, whom he was set over for good. That he gave commissions and was the occasion of the rebellion in Ireland; also of the late second war, besides what he has done contrary to the liberty of the subject, and tending to the destruction of the fundamental laws and liberties of this kingdom, all which amounts to a forfeiture of his said trust.

In regard whereof the Council of War (who has now the sole managing of the matter in reference to the king) has given commandment, that he be no longer served after the manner of princes upon the knee, and that all other majesty forms be forgotten toward him, *Sic transit gloria mundi, qui sibi videtur stare, videat ne cadet*;[11] the Commons House of Parliament has voted commissioners who shall be furnished with plenary power for the trial of the king as a traitor, and in case the king shall refuse to answer unto the charge drawn up against him, they will take care that sure and special provision be made that this shall prove no obstruction or impediment to the speedy bringing him to judgement and condign punishment. The General Council has almost pitched upon a representative and finished it for the speedy settlement of the kingdom, without the king and against him.

That a period to this Parliament be speedily put, that so there may be a sound settlement of the peace and future government of the kingdom, upon grounds of common right, freedom and safety, and therefore:

That there may be certain succession of future Parliaments, annual or biennial, with secure provision.

That care be taken for the certainty of their meeting, sitting, and rising.

That there may be an equal distribution of elections to render the House of Commons as near as may be an equal representative of the whole people electing.

That according to such distributions the people may not fail of certainty to elect, and their full freedom provided for and asserted.

That none who have engaged or shall engage in war against the right of Parliament and interest of the kingdom therein, or have adhered to the enemies thereof, may be capable of electing, or being elected (at least during a competent number of years) nor any others, who shall oppose or not join in agreements to this settlement.

10. Turning people into vassals.

11. "Thus passes the glory of the world, who in his own eyes he stands, take heed lest he fall."

That it be declared (that as to the whole interest of the people of England) such representatives have and shall have the supreme power and trust, as to the making of laws, constitutions, and officers for the ordering, preservation, and government of the whole; and as to the altering, repealing, and abolishing the same, the making of war and peace, and as to the highest and final judgement in all civil things without further appeal to any created standing power.

That no king be hereafter admitted, but upon the election of, and trust from the people by such their representatives, nor without first disclaiming and disavowing all pretenses to a negative voice against the determinations of the said representatives or Commons in Parliament, and that to be done in some certain form more clearly than heretofore in the coronation oath.

His Majesty is strongly secured in the castle of Windsor by the Major-General Whitlock, governor thereof. When the king came into the castle first he appeared merry and pleasant, for being waited into the chamber by the governor, and Colonel Harrison,[12] he spoke smilingly thus, "I promised you a short way" (meaning from the place they came last) "but not a fair way, for indeed it rained almost all that afternoon."[13] The king after he had discoursed a while went himself to make choice of rooms to lodge and eat in, and those which he nominated were outfitted according to his desire. [He] prays and expounds the scriptures to those that are about him himself, since the time he was deposed. A command is come from the General and the Council of War, that none shall be admitted to have private conference with him without special warrant either from the Parliament or General. He is now under locks and bolts, and assures the governor that he will not (by any underhanded way) attempt to make an escape, except he can escape by some cleanly neat way.

His Majesty is earnestly desirous that Doctor Hammond,[14] or some other of his chaplains may be admitted to come to him, but it is not permitted as yet. He

---

12. Thomas Harrison. Despite Harrison's general sympathy for the Levellers, he believed Charles I deserved to be beheaded for treason. As mentioned (p. 76), he signed the king's death warrant in January 1649.

13. Throughout his imprisonment and trial, Charles maintained a demeanor of detachment and even, as we see here, humor, as he believed himself to be unimpeachable by a Parliament that in his eyes had no legal authority to try, much less execute, him. It has been debated as to whether his refusal to grant the legitimacy of the proceedings against him so outraged his prosecutors that even those who may have been inclined toward finding him guilty but sparing his life were driven to kill him. See Sean Kelsey, "Staging the Trial of Charles I," in *The Regicides and the Execution of Charles I*, ed. Jason Peacey, 71–93 (London: Palgrave, 2001); and Clive Holmes, "The Trial and Execution of Charles I," *Historical Journal* 53, no. 2 (June 2010): 289–316.

14. Henry Hammond, an Anglican minister and writer whom Charles I appointed as a royal chaplain to the Crown forces in the wars. During the king's captivity in Holmby House after his surrender in the First Civil War, he requested a visit from Hammond. He was refused on the ground that neither man had sworn loyalty to *A Solemn League and Covenant*. However, when the king was transferred

180 *Appendix 4*

is also very urgently pressing to have leave to send to the queen and prince,[15] but that also is denied.

The king since his coming to Windsor has had some discourse with those that attend him about the *Remonstrance of the Army*, as to the bringing of him to a trial, asking how that could be, what way they could do it, or which way they could bring in any charge against him. It was not said that there is any such thing to be done by the army, but a question was put to the king, that what if a charge should be brought against him according to the manner of trial of the subjects by the laws of the kingdom, what would he do? The king replied that, if they did, he would not give any answers, and that if they did put him to death, he would die patiently like a martyr.[16]

The House passed an Ordinance for the Election of new Common-Councilmen in the room of those that have subscribed their names to the petition for to have a treaty with the king,[17] and because the Oaths of Allegiance[18] and

---

by the army to Childersley, Fairfax and his officers defied Parliament's orders and allowed the king to see Hammond and another of his royal chaplains. During Charles's subsequent imprisonments at Woburn, Caversham, and Hampton Court, Hammond provided council and comfort. He was suspected of aiding in Charles I's escape to the Isle of Wight because his nephew, Colonel Robert Hammond, was soon to be governor there. When the king was recaptured and placed in Carisbrooke Castle, Hammond once again joined him, but he was soon removed by Parliament. Before the king's trial, Hammond wrote a letter of support to Fairfax and the General Council of Officers. However, he was denied access to Charles's person before the execution. Hugh de Quehen, "Hammond, Henry (1605–1660)," *ODNB*.

15. Queen Henrietta Maria and Prince James, Charles's second eldest son. W. A. Speck, "James II and VII (1633–1701), king of England, Scotland, and Ireland," *ODNB*. Charles's eldest son, Prince Charles, was at this time in Scotland, where he was recognized as the heir to the throne.

16. Charles made good on his word, refusing to lend credence to the proceedings and earning martyr status in many peoples' eyes through his magnanimous comportment on the execution stage and the publishing of *The Eikon Basilike* (Wing E299A), a collection of prayers that Charles ostensibly delivered during the days leading up to his execution. These prayers were recorded and published by the Presbyterian minister, John Gauden, who, unlike Henry Hammond, was allowed to attend Charles before he died. These developments appear to vindicate those such as Poole who warned that executing the king was illegal and/or immoral and hence an error in judgment for which Parliament would pay. John Gauden, *The Eikon Basilike* (London: 1649).

17. Parliament, *An Ordinance of the Lords and Commons Assembled in Parliament Concerning the Election of Common-Council Men, and Other Officers in the City of London* (London: 1648) (Wing E1820), an order proclaiming "that no person whatsoever that subscribed, promoted, or abetted, any engagement in the year 1648, relating to a personal Treaty with the KING at *London*, shall be elected, chosen, or put into any of the Offices, or places expressed in the aforesaid Ordinance under the penalty contained in the same."

18. The Oath of Allegiance was issued by King James in 1606 in the wake of the Gunpowder Plot on November 5, 1605, an attempt by a group of Catholics led by Guy Fawkes to smuggle dynamite into Parliament and blow it up while James was delivering a speech. Also known as the Oath of Obedience,

Supremacy[19] and others are enforced upon all before they can be made free of the City of London, the House ordered that the said illegal Oaths of Allegiance and Supremacy, with all other of the like nature, should be referred to a committee to the end they may be for the future taken away.[20]

The House took notice that Mr. Watson who preached the last fast day was very darkly invective against them, not acknowledging them to be a Parliament.[21] They therefore ordered that Mr. Brookes, who preached to them the same day and was very ingenious in his acknowledgements, should have the thanks of the House and liberty to print his sermon, but not Watson.[22]

Colonel John Lilburne has put up a paper to the General Council of the Army, in a petitionary manner subscribed by diverse of known worth, wherein he finds much fault with some particulars of the intended model which the General Council has now almost finished, called *An Agreement of the People*. Out of Hertfordshire unto the General Council of the Army is come a woman of great

---

this oath required all subjects to swear that James was the only lawful king and the pope had no authority over the Church of England or the king's life.

19. The Oath of Supremacy was issued by King Henry VIII under the 1534 Act of Supremacy as part of the English Reformation. This oath required any person assuming a public office or a position in the church to swear allegiance to the king as the Supreme Governor of the Church of England. Refusal to take the oath was considered treason. The Act was repealed by Queen Mary I, Henry's daughter with his Catholic queen, Catherine of Aragon, and reinstated under the Act of Supremacy in 1559 by Queen Elizabeth I, Henry's daughter by his Protestant wife, Anne Boleyn. Later, the Oath was extended to include not only Crown and church officers but also Members of Parliament and university students.

20. Both the Oath of Allegiance and the Oath of Supremacy were enormously controversial and, as the pamphlet notes, were subjected to review by a committee formed after Charles I's execution.

21. Thomas Watson, a Puritan preacher and author. Watson sympathized with the Presbyterians during the Civil Wars but was consistently favorable toward the king and, as the pamphlet notes, scathingly critical of Parliament. He was briefly imprisoned in 1652 for conspiring to bring Charles II to power but was quickly released and reinstated as vicar of St. Stephens, Walbrook. Ironically, in 1662, two years after the restoration of Charles II, he was evicted for Nonconformity under the Act of Uniformity. However, after the passage of the Declaration of Indulgence in 1672, he was able to preach again. He did so until his retirement and death in 1686. Barry Till, "Watson, Thomas (*d.* 1686)," *ODNB*.

22. Thomas Brooks, like Thomas Watson, was a Puritan preacher and author. After the First Civil War, Brooks served as minister at various congregations in London, where his fame earned him the honor of being chosen to preach before the House of Commons on December 26, 1648, just days before Poole's appearance. As the pamphlet notes, unlike Watson, he was given permission to publish his sermon and did so under the title *God's Delight in the Progress of the Upright* (London: 1649) (Wing B4941). The main text discussed was Psalm 44:18: "Our heart is not turned back, neither have our steps declined from Your way," an encouragement to the army's General Council to move forward with conviction. Like Watson, he was condemned as a Nonconformist in 1662 but does not appear to have lost his position and continued to preach and write until his death. Tai Liu, "Brooks, Thomas (1608–1680)," *ODNB*.

182 *Appendix 4*

wisdom and gravity,[23] who told them she had a message to them from God and desired they should hear her, which they accordingly did with much acceptance. She says they shall surely be prosperous and attain their desires for a speedy settlement of the kingdom, and that all powers shall be subdued under their feet.

FINIS.

Anonymous
To Xeiphos Ton Martyron *(1651)*

To Xeiphos Ton Martyron (Wing X2) claims that the Civil Wars were the product of a vast conspiracy between Spanish Catholics and religious Independents in England who supported Parliament and then Cromwell. Poole is declared a witch who played an especially malevolent role in the plot.

Anti-Catholicism dates at least as far back as the Reformation of course. In England, with the separation of the English church from the Roman Catholic Church in 1534, anti-Catholicism took the form of dissolving convents and monasteries, expropriating their lands and properties, exiling monks and nuns to Catholic countries on the continent, and excluding Catholics from serving in various offices. Catholic families who remained in England often had to worship in secret; some built hiding spaces for outlawed priests—or "priest holes"—into their homes. Catholics were often accused of conspiracy and wishing to undermine England and other Protestant states. Jesuits in particular were associated with deceptive speech and dark machinations.

But radical Protestants such as Elizabeth Poole were equally subject to such charges, as their proselytizing was viewed as seduction and their private churches outlawed by the Church of England. Thus, even though Independents and Catholics were generally hostile to one another, they were both marginalized and demonized by people who adhered to the via media or "middle way" of the Church of England.

The original pamphlet is 111 pages long. The excerpt included here runs from page 64 to page 71; it delineates Poole's supposed role in this alleged plot between Catholics and Independents to alter England's future. The copy reprinted here is housed in the Thomason Tracts (E.637[2]) in the British Library and is available on *EEBO*.

---

23. Elizabeth Poole, probably described in such positive terms because she opposed the king's execution.

Pamphlets about Elizabeth Poole 183

[Excerpt from]

TO XEIPHOS TON MARTYRON;[24]
OR,
A BRIEF NARRATION
OF THE
Mysteries of State carried on by the Spanish
Faction in ENGLAND, since the Reign of Queen
ELIZABETH to this day for the supplanting of the
Magistracy and Ministry, the Laws of the Land, and
the Religion of the Church of ENGLAND, especially
and particularly declaring, how, when, and where,
Cromwell and his party were confederate with
the Spanish Faction, and how he and they
resolved to overthrow the Protestant Laws,
and Religion in the Church and State
of *England*, and *Scotland*.

TOGETHER
With a Vindication of the Presbyterian party, both
of Church-men and States-men in the Kingdom
of *England*, *Scotland*, and *Ireland* again the
Independent and Popish party, who are both united
and confederated to destroy them, and
their RELIGION.

Printed by SAMUEL BROWN, English Bookseller
at the *Hague*, 1651.

At this time did the wit, strength, and policy of the Spanish and Independent
Faction work exceedingly. Now all the world plainly saw that they were all one in
their councils and projects, for (which was a dreadful spectacle for the Protestants
to behold) the soundest, sincerest, and boldest Protestant statesmen in Europe
were looking through grates in a prison, while Vickar General Oneille, the

---

24. "The Sword of the Martyr." The word "xeiphos" is likely a version of the Greek *xiphos*, which refers
to an ancient double-edged sword. The unknown author of this pamphlet is likely a Presbyterian,
for Presbyterians, not unlike adherents to the Church of England, viewed both Catholics and radical
Protestant Independents with suspicion. According to this author, the two seemingly opposed groups
were actually conspiring to overthrow Presbyterianism, Anglicanism, and the Crown.

184 *Appendix 4*

arch Irish rebel agent, was embraced and consulted withal.[25] Sir John Winter,[26] Sir Kenelm Digby,[27] Walter Montagne,[28] Endymion Porters,[29] Cottington,[30] and Digby's agents, and many others known to be desperate enemies to the Protestant religion, being all of the Spanish faction and strong papists, these now were the men that got together possession of Whitehall which must never come near it, from the time the Pope's Nuncio[31] left England until this time, and now who but they, through their consultations, were all in private with the Independents at this time.

Now the full cry of the Jesuits (in those flocks of pamphlets which flew through the kingdom) was "down with kings," as anti-Christian, as tyrannical; it is lawful to bring kings to justice, to depose them, to behead them; and that King Charles was the great delinquent of the kingdom, and that justice ought to be done upon him.

Now the private agents of the Independents, by their letters from Venice, Rome, Spain, the Emperor's court from Paris in France, and several others parts where they could correspond with the Spanish faction, began to discover themselves and their correspondents. London was now overflowed with priests and

25. Likely a reference to Owen Roe O'Neill, a member of the O'Neill dynasty of Ulster in Ireland who sided with Charles I in order to gain Irish Independence. When his Irish Confederate troops lost a number of battles to the New Model Army, they formed a new treaty with the English Royalists. This treaty so alienated O'Neill that he contacted George Monck, the northern commander of Parliament's forces, to offer aid in fighting against the English Royalists in Ireland in exchange for religious and political freedom. This agreement was never cemented, but it is likely the New Model Army's flirtation with an alliance with such Catholic enemies as O'Neill that outraged the author of this pamphlet. In the end, O'Neill returned to his Catholic confederates to prepare to fight against Cromwell when the latter undertook his infamously horrific invasion of Ireland in 1649. O'Neill died in this battle. Jerrold I. Casway, "O'Neill, Owen Roe (c. 1583–1649)," *ODNB*.

26. John Winter, the wealthy Catholic owner of the rights to the Forest of Dean's minerals, stone quarries, and timber. Winter allegedly traveled to France to try to raise monies from the Crown to support the king's forces. Andrew Warmington, "Winter, Sir John (*b. c.*1600, *d.* in or after 1676)," *ODNB*.

27. Sir Kenelm Digby, another prominent Catholic who served as Chancellor to the exiled Queen Henrietta Maria in France. Like Winter, he contributed to her endeavor to secure French funding for Charles I's armies. Michael Foster, "Digby, Sir Kenelm (1603–1665)," *ODNB*.

28. Walter Montague, another important Catholic supporter of Charles I. Thompson Cooper, "Montagu, Walter (1604/5–1677)," *ODNB*.

29. Endymion Porter, a member of a gentry family from Warwickshire who helped develop the Crown's connections with Catholic Spain. Ronald G. Asch, "Porter, Endymion (1587–1649)," *ODNB*.

30. Francis Cottington, first Baron of Cottington, another Crown-sponsored merchant and Catholic diplomat and politician. In 1649, he was sent as an ambassador to Spain to raise money for the Crown. Fiona Pogson, "Cottington, Francis, first Baron Cottington (1579?–1652)," *ODNB*.

31. Giovanni Battista Rinuccini, a sponsor of Owen Roe O'Neill and advocate for sending Catholic forces to fight against Parliament. Tadhg Ó hannracháin, "Rinuccini, Giovanni Battista (1592–1653)," *ODNB*.

Pamphlets about Elizabeth Poole 185

Jesuits who usurped the Protestant pulpits with extraordinary boldness, being all professed Independents, crying out against kingly government and presbytery, as anti-Christians which must be overthrown so that the glorious day of the saints, triumph could appear.[32]

Cromwell being now to that the greatest gulf, being now the work to do, which he had been all this while by force and policy making way unto; he saw but two main rubs in the way, which he dared not meddle with in a boisterous way, and those were the Presbyterian ministry of the kingdom, who preached vehemently against the treasonable practices of the army.

The other who he dared not at this time meddle with were those down-right dealers called Levellers. I call them down-right dealers because they did not hide their principles nor change their principles.

He therefore dealt with both by flattery, and first he sent for the Presbyterians.

1. Summoning them by their power at Whitehall, which they refused to obey, not acknowledging their power.

Then they sent for to confer privately with them which the Presbyterian ministers consented to, and gave them a meeting, where Cromwell began to declare to them the sincerity of his heart, how full it was of good desires for the promoting of the good and interest of honest men and real saints.

And as for the late actings of the army, in imprisoning and secluding by armed violence the Members of Parliament,[33] he confessed it was without his approbation and acknowledged it to be irregular, but he was most confident that the end would be good, though the means to that end were irregular. For his part he could not but see (he said) much of God in the carrying on of those things, considering that impulse of spirit that was upon those worthy and holy saints that acted these things, and then the old success that God had given them in all their undertakings and the self-preservation (which he said the law of God and nature enjoined) put them on to do what they did, and a general and absolute necessity lay upon them to do what they did, for otherwise the interest of honest men would have utterly been destroyed.

The ministers presently picked up all these arguments, and from the law of God, the holy scripture, so fully answered every one of them, that they put them all to silence, that they had not a word to say; and not only so, but the next

---

32. While referring to religious Independents in general, the author offers the specific example of the Fifth Monarchists, the group who believed that the New Model Army's defeat of the Crown would bring about Christ's fifth and final monarchy, as prophesied in the biblical books of Daniel and Revelation. For Mary Cary and Anna Trapnel as members of this sect, see p. 32.

33. Pride's Purge, the purge that reduced Parliament down to a "Rump" by expelling members who opposed executing the king.

186 *Appendix 4*

Lord's day, the most of the Presbyterians confused[34] their arguments in the pulpit, and forewarned their congregations to have nothing to do with men of such false principles. Neither was this all but the boldest and valiantest[35] of the ministers of London went to the general officers, and dehorted[36] them from those evil courses and practices they had in hand, but their council was condemned, and they [were] frowned upon. And [said Cromwell][37] to a godly Minister, "since I perceive the Presbyterian Ministers are fully bent against me, I am resolved [though I intended otherwise when I came out of Scotland] to be their ruin."[38] So exceedingly enraged was this proud malicious tyrant against the godly ministry of the kingdom, because he could not make them bend to his designs.

These his threats could not terrify the ministers, so as to make them lose their integrity, or be silent at his wicked and open rebellion, but the gravest of them wrote and subscribed a vindication of themselves, that they did detest those illegal proceedings of the army, in offering violence to the Houses at Westminster and going about to overthrow the king.

The Independent ministers preached altogether for the army. John Goodwin wrote a book for them wherein he declared himself direct contrary to his former principles in print,[39] which made Sir Francis Nethersole[40] proclaim him the most self-condemned heretic in the world. Master Geery [Greavy?],[41] a learned and pious Presbyterian, clearly confused Goodwin's book in print,[42] and therein the illegality of the army's proceedings. More could not be done by the Presbyterians than was now done against the army on the behalf of the king and Parliament, and yet there is a generation of liars who this age dare to affirm and impiously and

34. The Presbyterian ministers claimed to their congregants that Cromwell's rationales for Pride's Purge and other controversial actions were confusing or contradictory.

35. Most valiant.

36. Advised against.

37. Brackets appear in the original.

38. Brackets appear in the original.

39. John Goodwin, a leading Independent minister and member of the New Model Army who agreed with the Levellers on many issues, particularly those pertaining to religious freedom and support of the army. He wrote in favor of Pride's Purge and argued—in opposition to the Levellers on this point but in keeping with the views of many other religious radicals in the army—that it was lawful to kill kings because they were mere men not demi-gods. It is this claim that the author of this pamphlet finds so objectionable. Tai Liu, "Goodwin, John (c. 1594–1665)," *ODNB*.

40. Sir Francis Nethersole, an intellectual, diplomat, and fierce anti-Catholic who worked on behalf of the Stuart Crown and the Church of England. He briefly supported Parliament during the Civil Wars but mainly tried to negotiate various peace agreements. His staunch opposition to the king's execution led him to publish the attack on John Goodwin's endorsement of regicide that the author alludes to here. B. C. Pursell, "Nethersole, Sir Francis (*bap.* 1587, *d.* 1659)," *ODNB*.

41. I have not been able to identify this figure.

42. Refuted.

falsely, that the Presbyterians brought the king's neck to the block, when only for defending the king and Parliament's cause, their necks lie on the block to this day.

The Independent politicians not being able to win the Presbyterians by flatteries, nor convince them by arguments, set to slander them and asperse them secretly and openly in their pamphlets. Whereupon the ministers declared on my knowledge openly that they never intended evil against the person of the king in joining with the Parliament and declaring for them. But they joined with the Parliament that they might bring home the king and establish him in his throne and keep the wicked from the throne. And they protested also against the trial of the king as illegal. This they did very often, whereby a vast breach was made between them and the Independent party, the Presbyterians protesting against their proceedings as contrary to the law of God of nature, and the land.

The Presbyterians of this time did express so much the sincerity and integrity of the loyal subject, that the king then saw and confessed what he could never believe before, viz. that the Presbyterians were his truest subjects, after he had read Master Prynne's speech,[43] considering how much cause (of any man), Master Prynne had to be against him, and considering how he had formerly written against the excess of his court, and now reading his speech made in the House, and finding him therein so full of inveterate hatred to traitors and rebels, and so cordial and earnest for the establishing of him in his throne, he said to a friend of his standing by him, "Here," said the king, "take this book, I give it there as a legacy, and believe it, this gentleman (laying his hand on the book) is the Cato of the Age."[44]

The Independents knew not what to do against the Presbyterians because their hands were full of other work, and therefore they set their tongues against them, saying, *That God had hardened and landed them to their own destruction, and they were in the dark, and under sore temptations, and were not able to discern the high things of god, they were hidden to the world, and only revealed to the saints in the army.*

From the Presbyterian party, therefore, they turned to the Levellers, for fear lest they who owed Cromwell a grutch[45] would now pay it for him.

---

43. William Prynne, a prominent and controversial Presbyterian spokesperson who, throughout the 1640s, inveighed against religious Independency. As the author notes here, he also wrote a speech denouncing the trial and execution of the king, which earned him Charles I's gratitude. He became a powerful foe of Cromwell's and was arrested in 1650 and detained in jail until he agreed to pay a fine and cease attacking the new government. After refusing to comply, he was finally released without conditions in 1653. William Lamont, "Prynne, William (1600–1669)," *ODNB*.

44. Marcus Porcius Cato Uticensis (95 BCE–46 BCE), a politician, statesman, Stoic philosopher, and opponent of Julius Caesar's growing imperialism in the Roman Republic who was known for his skills as an orator.

45. A murmur or complaint.

188 *Appendix 4*

Cromwell therefore first creeps to them, confesses there were great failings on his part towards them, desires to bewail that want of Christian love in these glorious days which ought to be between saints, especially in these days of apostasy when everybody fell off from them, he desired therefore that they would unite, and send their agents to consult what was best to be done, and that a set day of humiliation might be appointed, wherein they might be humbled for their breaches and united ever and after more firmly. Hereupon Lilburne, Walwyn, Prince, and Overton[46] sat in a committee by themselves to draw up what they desired that so there might be at last a happy agreement of all parties in the new government to be established, for all sides were concluded that the old government should be pulled down.

Now since the Presbyterian party (who were most desired in this business that so the infamy of killing kings might be cast upon them) could not be gained by any means, it was necessary for Cromwell to unite all the sectarians fast to him, and that he knew he could do not without pretending to advance their interest in the present design, which he did most artificially dissemble to his great advantage.

Now lest General Fairfax should see (through all the mists that Cromwell had cast before his eyes) the treason of the Spanish faction, and their secret designs to throw down the Protestant religion, the magistracy and the ministry, which he had just cause to fear, because the Presbyterian ministers and the ablest Presbyterian statesmen had access to him, to prevent this, double guards were placed about the General to prevent their coming, with secret orders to stop such as they suspected to come on any such designs to the General.

But not trusting to that, he went a surer way to work, for he stole all the power out of his hand by passing an order at the Council of War, that nothing should be done by any but what was concluded of by the general officers of the army so that the General hereby had no more power than one of his colonels.

Now that Cromwell might firmly unite the Council of War to him, which consisted of a few able head-pieces, to whom he laid himself open so far as to show them their profit and preferment in the design, which united them fast to him, the other part, who were soft heads and had a good meaning to do no evil, but to promote the Kingdom of Christ, and throw down Anti-Christ, and then according to their duty [as they were taught], to take possession of, and (as Saints) reign over the kingdom,[47] Cromwell provided fit food to feed such fantasies for he had provided a monstrous witch full of all deceitful craft, who being put into brave clothes, pretended she was a lady that was come from a far country, being sent by God to the army with a revelation, which she must make known to the

---

46. The Levellers John Lilburne, William Walwyn, Thomas Prince, and Richard Overton.

47. Religious radicals in the Council of War who wished to bring the king to trial and sentence him to death.

Pamphlets about Elizabeth Poole 189

army, for necessity was laid upon her.[48] This witch had a fair lodging prepared for her in Whitehall where she was very retired.

This Witch had her lesson taught her beforehand by Cromwell and Ireton, by whose order she was entertained at Whitehall.

She desired audience at the Council of War, for to them she said she was sent.

Cromwell and Ireton to beget the more attention and belief in the officers of the Council of War, began to extol the excellency of revelation, and conceived that this prophetess being a precious saint, and having much of God in her, ought to be heard, and that with all attention because, in such glorious days as these, God did manifest himself extraordinarily, and especially to his saints, in chalking out their way before them, when they came into straights and difficulties, such as they were in at that time.

By this time the witch was come to the door, and forthwith she had admittance, where the officers all beheld her and her strange postures, expressing her high devotion. Cromwell and Ireton, fixing their eyes upon her in most solemn manner (to beget the rest of the officers, who were ready to laugh in apprehension of some extraordinary serious thing) fell both of them to weeping. The witch looking in their faces and seeing them weep, fell to weeping likewise, and began to tell them what acquaintance she had with God by revelation, and how such a day, such an hour, after such a manner she had a revelation, which she was to reveal only to them, and that was, that the glorious time of setting up Christ's kingdom was near at hand, and that Antichrist must be speedily thrown down, and that they were the instruments that were by God ordained to throw him down, and how they were about that great work, and that if they would prosper in it, they must first remove the king out of the way, which they must do by proceeding first to try him, and then to condemn him, and then to depose him, but not to put him to death, with a great deal more such stuff which that week's *Diurnal* printed at large, so open was this business. This relation I had from one that was strongly of the army's party, but related this shameful story with much indignation.

Lilly was taught at this time with bribes to print his opinion, which was much according to the opinion of his sister witch.[49]

48. The author paints Poole as a willing and malevolent agent in Cromwell's and Ireton's conspiracy to exploit the army's religious radicals' belief in prophesy as well as the idea that, as predicted in the book of Revelation, they were the saints who would rule for one thousand years before Christ's return. Having her appear before the council in the guise of a prophetess and endorse the execution would supposedly induce the radicals in the army to subscribe to Cromwell's agenda. Even as the proceedings are depicted as pure theater, the less "soft-headed" officers are portrayed as seeing through it and laughing at the entire affair.

49. Astrologer, William Lilly, the author of numerous almanacs that sought to align celestial events with political affairs. In 1649, Lilly famously equated an eclipse with the demise of monarchy. Because of this, he is charged in this pamphlet with accepting bribes for offering opinions that accorded

190 Appendix 4

Some of the soberer and more religious of the officers being much startled at these revelations, but not at all satisfied, repaired to some of the most religious and able Independents to know their opinion of these things and to desire advice what to do. They replied (I am informed Thomas Goodwin in particular)[50] that since they had gone so far, they must now carry on, though with the blood of those that stood in their way, for if they now made a stop, farewell their cause forever. This was good in politics, but bad in divinity; it was a true politic aphorism of Machiavelli's but false doctrine in the divinity schools.[51] However they made use of this doctrine to proceed in their designs, for the promotion of the Independent cause.

By this time, John Lilburne, and his party,[52] who sat at Whitehall to draw up their desires, had brought their business to some maturity, which was, as I conceive, inferred in the paper called *An Agreement of the People*, the sum whereof was no more than this, to throw down the king, Lords, and Commons, as then established, to throw down the laws, Inns of Court,[53] courts of judicature, church government, the universities, the functions of the clergy.

This *Agreement* being debated at the General Council, Cromwell (whose design was to set up another government, and was then about it) opposed this *Agreement*, because it opposed his designs; for though he sat in council with the general officers, yet he consulted altogether with the Spanish faction, to set up a

---

with those of "the witch," Poole. As we recall, Poole argued that, even as the king should be tried and removed and the people's rights granted, his life should be spared because he was still the people's husband and father. Lilly charted a similar middle path, arguing in *A Peculiar Prognostication Astrologically Predicted According to Art* (London: 1649) (Wing L2237) that, while the monarchy should not be "destroyed," it should be "regulate[d]" so that the people could "obtain those just rights we were born unto" (3). Patrick Curry, "Lilly, William (1602–1681)," *ODNB*.

50. Thomas Goodwin, a graduate of Cambridge University who converted to Puritanism in 1620 and wrote and published numerous non-conformist pamphlets. As a moderate, he also continued to preach for the Church of England. In 1650, he was appointed President of Magdalen College, Oxford, and became one of the principle authors of the so-called Cromwellian settlement, a compromise stipulating a national church but allowing for toleration of religious Independency. Upon the restoration in 1660, he was forced to resign the Presidency of Magdalen College, but in 1661 signed *A Denunciation and Declaration of the Ministers of Congregational Churches*, a petition protesting an uprising against the Crown by the Fifth Monarchists. T. M. Lawrence, "Goodwin, Thomas (1600–1680)," *ODNB*.

51. Niccolò di Bernardo dei Machiavelli (1469–1527), Italian Renaissance historian, politician, diplomat, philosopher, and writer. Machiavelli was famous for using his work of political philosophy, *The Prince* (*Il Principe*) (1513), to advance a utilitarian or pragmatic approach to political rule rather than a moral one. Because of this, the term "Machiavellian" denotes a cynical, cunning, and self-serving approach to political power. The author of the pamphlet is accusing Cromwell and his supporters of being Machiavellian in their approach to the king's trial and execution.

52. The Levellers.

53. The four law schools (the Inner Temple, the Middle Temple, Lincoln's Inn, and Gray's Inn) located near the Royal Courts of Justice in London.

government according to the government in Spain (viz.)[54] by a Council of State, and a High Court of Justice.

The General Council of War was hereby divided about this *Agreement of the People*, and so equally divided, that only one voice carried it, or two at the most, in the negative, which gave occasion to Colonel Hewson (as I remember) to say, "how can we call this *An Agreement of the People*, when we ourselves are divided about it?"[55] Hereupon it was thought fittest to be printed, and sent abroad, to see how the people liked of it, before they proceeded any further.

54. Latin for "namely" or "that is."

55. John Hewson, a cobbler, an Independent minister, an officer in the New Model Army, and one of the signatories of the king's death warrant in 1649. He participated in the Putney Debates in 1647 and the Whitehall debates in 1649, suppressed a Royalist rebellion in 1648, and aided in Pride's Purge in December of that same year. As the author notes here, he questioned the authority of the Levellers to represent the entirely of "the people" and helped Cromwell crush the Leveller movement at Burford in 1649. Christopher Durston, "Hewson, John, appointed Lord Hewson under the protectorate (fl. 1630–1660)," *ODNB*.

THE
English-Devil:
OR,
CROMWEL
AND HIS
Monstrous Witch

Discover'd at White-Hall:

With the strange and damnable Speech of this Hellish Monster, by way of *Revelation*, touching *King* and *Kingdom*; And a Narrative of the *Infernal Plots*, *Inhumane Actings*, and *Barbarous Conspiracies* of this grand Impostor, and most audacious Rebel, that durst aspire from a *Brew-house* to the *Throne*, washing his accursed Hands in the Blood of his Royal Soveraign; and trampling over the Heads of the most Loyal Subjects, making a Foot-ball of a *Crown*, and endeavouring utterly to extirpate the ROYAL PROGENY, Root and Kinde, Stem and Stock.

LONDON, Printed by *Robert Wood*, for *George Horton*; and are to be sold at the *Royal Exchange* in *Cornhill*. 1660.

Figure 8. Title page, Anonymous, *The English Devil; or, Cromwell and His Monstrous Witch Discover'd at White-Hall* (1660). British Library. Reproduced with permission.

Pamphlets about Elizabeth Poole 193

Anonymous
The English Devil; or, Cromwell and His Monstrous Witch
Discover'd at White-Hall *(1660)*

The English Devil (Wing E3083) also portrays Poole as a conspirator against the king. In this rendition, she is not part of a global cabal. Rather, she is represented as being solely in league with her own countryman, Oliver Cromwell, to radically transform England's future government. The fact that this tract was published in 1660—the year Charles II was placed on the throne and monarchy restored—suggests that Poole was still a potent figure in the public's perception of the era's controversies.

The identification of Poole as a witch in league with the devil is not to be taken lightly: her contemporary Anna Trapnel was imprisoned for several months in 1654 after being found guilty of witchcraft. At this time, there was widespread belief in witches. On the eve of the seventeenth century in 1597, James VI of Scotland, later James I of England, wrote and published *Daemonologie*, an instruction manual for identifying and punishing alleged practitioners of witchcraft.[56] In the 1640s, the hunt for witches became especially fervent when a man named Matthew Hopkins dedicated himself to ferreting out alleged perpetrators.[57] His suspicions led to the trials of thirty-six suspected witches, all of whom were women, at the Essex assizes in July 1645. Of these thirty-six, nineteen were executed. Nine more died from disease while in jail, and six were still imprisoned three years later.

The hysteria unleashed by the 1645 trials spread to Suffolk, where townspeople claimed to identify more than one hundred witches. Forty of these were executed. Soon after, in Norfolk, another forty alleged witches were placed on trial, with roughly half of them undergoing execution. Through 1647, trials were also held in Huntingdonshire, Cambridgeshire, in several counties in the eastern midlands, and a number of boroughs. These trials resulted in the investigation of more than two hundred and fifty people and the execution of at least one hundred.

The timing of these trials suggests how serious it was for Poole to be identified as a witch only two years later and provides yet another possible explanation for why she so vehemently defended her godliness and integrity in her two *Alarms*. Even in 1660, the association of Poole with witchcraft resounded loudly enough for this pamphlet to gain publication.

The English Devil is a reprint of the section from *To Xeiphos Ton Martyron*'s (pp. 182–191) on Poole. Both pamphlets are excerpts of a 1660 pamphlet written

---

56. James VI, *Daemonologie* (Edinburgh: 1597).

57. James Sharpe, "Hopkins, Matthew (d. 1647), witch-finder," *ODNB*.

194 *Appendix 4*

by Wawrzyniec Goślicki and titled *The Sage Senator Delineated* (Wing G2027). But the adjacent sections on Oliver Cromwell provided in *The English Devil* are original; they make the reader aware of how polarizing a figure Cromwell could be: while he was a savior-like "Lord Protector" to his supporters, he was a diabolical menace to his enemies, especially during the Restoration when Royalists were particularly eager to demonize his reputation and consign his rule to oblivion.

The copy reprinted here is housed in the Thomason Tracts [E.1035(3)] in the British Library and is available on *EEBO*. The date, July 27, is handwritten on the title page of this copy by George Thomason to note the day upon which he purchased the tract.

The

English Devil;

OR,

CROMWELL
AND HIS

Monstrous Witch

Discover'd at White-Hall:

With the strange and damnable Speech of this Hellish Monster,
by way of *Revelation*, touching *King* and *Kingdom*; and a
Narrative of the *Infernal Plots, Inhumane Actings*, and *Barbarous
Conspiracies* of this grand Impostor, and most audacious Rebel,
that durst aspire from a *Brew-house* to the *Throne*, washing his
accursed *Hands* in the *Blood* of his Royal Sovereign; and
trampling over the Heads of the most Loyal Subjects, making
a Football of a *Crown*, and endeavoring utterly to extirpate
the ROYAL PROGENY, Root and Kind, Stem and Stock.

LONDON, printed by *Robert Wood*, for *George Horton*; and are
to be sold at the *Royal Exchange* in *Cornhill*, 1660.

Pamphlets about Elizabeth Poole 195

The English Devil; Or, the Bloody Traitor, &etc.

As for that hellish monster, and damnable Machiavellian that first gave rise to our new-fabled models of government, we shall only demonstrate him to be the devil of later times, who butcher-like made cruel his profession and was never better than when he had his sword sheathed in his countrymen's bowels; such an audacious rebel was this Oliver Cromwell, that dared aspire from the mean condition of a private person to the throne, though he first washed his hands in the blood of his sovereign. He represented the real tragedy of a king and no king whose mouth watered after that title but that he dared not assume it, having fought so long against it, and was sworn to the deposition[58] of all kingship for the future. He, to raise himself on the top of the pyramid of honor, trampled over the heads of the most loyal subjects of the realm, made a football of a crown, and endeavored utterly to extirpate the royal progeny, root and king, stem and stock. Nay, I may be bold to say, if that an innocent babe had been born with *Vive le Roy*[59] in his mouth, he must[60] have been food for his sword as well as the first-born were for Herod's.[61] It is incredibly reported that Hugh Peters,[62] that spiritual dragooner,[63] and Nol,[64] hatched this government as they were walking together in a field: *A brace o' pious Devils!* The whole nation was enchained in a more than Egyptian bondage,[65] who were compelled to submit to this tyrant Nol, or be cut off by him; nothing but a word and a blow, his will was his law. Tell him of *Magna Carta*,[66] he would

58. Abolition.

59. Long live the king.

60. Would.

61. Herod I or Herod the Great (74/73 BCE–4 BCE), the client king for the Romans in Judea. As reported in the Gospel of Matthew, Herod ordered the killing of all young male children in and around Bethlehem (the Massacre of the Innocents) so that the newborn King of the Jews whose arrival was announced to him by the Magi could be prevented from usurping his line.

62. Hugh Peter, the Independent minister who preached the sermon at Charles's execution, which is cited on the title page of Poole's *A Prophecy Touching the Death of King Charles* (p. 55). As the author of *The English Devil* notes, Peter was active in the early affairs of the new Commonwealth government, earning the reputation of a schemer even among allies of Parliament. Although he was ambivalent about the republic's transformation into a less democratic Protectorate, he served as chaplain to the Council of State and was appointed an overseer of the English ministry.

63. Pirate.

64. Nickname for Oliver. As it is here, this nickname was frequently used derogatorily by Cromwell's detractors.

65. The Israelites' forty-year period of slavery in Egypt.

66. Magna Carta Libertatum, or "the Great Charter of the Liberties," a charter drafted by the Archbishop of Canterbury at Runnymede in 1215 to broker peace between the unpopular King John and a group of angry barons demanding the protection of church rights, the prohibition of unlawful imprisonment, timely justice, and limits on taxes paid to the Crown. After undergoing a series of disputes, the charter was finally adopted into English statute law in 1297. While the charter officially protected the rights of powerful barons, it became symbolic in later centuries, especially during the English Civil Wars, of

196 *Appendix 4*

lay his hand on his sword and cry *Magna Farta*.[67] No liberty was granted to the subjects, unless it were that of the conscience, and that too was denied the more orthodox and loyal party. The people were robbed of all laws, rights, and privileges, and sometimes of their lives; while he, like a tyrant, insulted with a *Quis contradicet?*[68] The citizens were so fleeced and pilled[69] that had this inhumane barbarous wretch continued much longer, he had sent London into the country a begging. To say *God save the King* was a crime as black as any forbidden in the Decalogue, but so long as that was prohibited publicly and privately, it was in vain to cry out *God speed the Plough*[70] or expect any blessing from the superior power. His infernal plots and machinations had wrought the utter ruin and desolation of the country, had not the providence divine cut him off, to the general benefit and rejoicing of the nation. English ground groaned with the burden of this inhuman tyrant. It was not enough that the English should be scourged but the whip must lie before them. It is not sufficient that he should be the author of all their woes while living, but they must live subject to his tyranny and oppression and, like so many mutes, condescend unto all his actions by silence, not daring to mention the least dislike though it thwarted their disposition never so much. *He was a Rod of their own making and they were content to untruss while he whipped them.*[71] In vain it was for the too accurate wit to plead reason or law against the sword. The tongue is too weak a weapon for the dagger. During the usurpation of this same hellish tyrant, what a chaos of confusion bespread the whole nation? How was all the land b'negroed[72] with more than the Egyptian darkness of persecution? The whole country was enveloped in clouds and ruin hung over the heads of damsels

---

an ancient Anglo-Saxon constitution that protected English freedoms in general. As the legend went, these freedoms were destroyed by the Norman Conquest in 1066 and needed to be restored. Both King James and King Charles I tried to suppress discussions of the Magna Carta given that numerous critics of monarchy cited it as grounds for limiting or abolishing kingship. Indeed, the Levellers frequently referred to it as a legal precedent for their *An Agreement of the People*, reproduced on pp. 160–174.

67. A deliberately humorous and scatological pun on Magna Carta.

68. Who contends with me? This phrase is part of a speech that God delivers in Isaiah 50:8, KJV: "He is near that justifies me; who will contend with me? Let us stand together: who is mine adversary? Let him come near to me." Through this quote, the author implies that Cromwell now believes he is God.

69. Robbed, plundered, pillaged; = peeled *adj*. (*OED*).

70. A blessing for prosperity or success taken from a fifteenth-century song sung by ploughmen on Plough Monday, the first Monday after Twelfth Day, the end of the Christmas holidays, when farm laborers returned to the plough. On Plough Monday, ploughmen went door-to-door dressed in white, pulling a plough, and, in exchange for singing their song of blessing, "God Speed the Plough," expected to be given "plough money" to celebrate the last of the holidays.

71. Possibly a paraphrase of Isaiah 11:4, KJV: "But with righteousness shall he judge the poor, and reprove with equity for the meek of the earth: and he shall smite the earth with the rod of his mouth, and with the breath of his lips shall he slay the wicked."

72. A racial epithet for blackened.

Pamphlets about Elizabeth Poole 197

at the banquet. The whole land was entombed in despair and little or no hope of a resurrection, until a divine hand wrought it by his long-expected death.[73] And it is the cordial wish and hearty desire of the loyal pen-man that all his majesty's and the kingdom's enemies were as stately interred as he was. Had he deserved an epitaph, we would have stretched hard but our brain should have furnished him with one. But since he was so unworthy, we hold it as a great disparagement to our quill to bestow a copy of verses on him, as he was a grief and trouble to the loyal party of the nation. And indeed, how can any son of Phoebus[74] employ his time so ill, as to salute his dead corpse with any that was so great an enemy to them while living? Who had a real design to extirpate all literature and plunge us into as deep a gulf of ignorance and profanity as the Turk is cast into?[75] He hated all learning and the learned, because his crimes were so black and horrid that they went far beyond the mercy of the book.[76] He granted a toleration for all religions because his own was to choose, and that he might not offend the tender consciences of his pretended zealots and favorites who were true vassals to the lust and villainy of such an imperious usurper. Honesty was so much out of fashion that he that was virtuous was a male actor and deserved death, for knavery was *a la mode*[77] and you know the old saying: *It is as good to be out of the world, as out of the fashion.*[78] An honest loyal subject was as much hooted and pointed at, and judged as ridiculous an object, as a Spanish don in his country garb at Paris.[79] An honest man was as strange a sight in England as a horse in Venice or a beggar in Holland.[80] And he

73. A possible reference to the book of Daniel, chapters 4 and 5, when the prophet Daniel is brought to the court of the Babylonian king, Nebuchadnezzar, to interpret his dreams and other omens. Daniel finds the portents to be ominous signs of Nebuchadnezzar's demise, especially when, at a banquet he attends along with Nebuchadnezzar, the king's retainers, the queen, and the concubines, a ghostly hand appears to write a message warning that the king's arrogance and pride mean his days as a ruler are numbered.

74. Phoebus or Apollo, the young Greek and Roman god of the sun, music, prophecy, healing, and poetry.

75. Because Turks were Muslim rather than Christian, they were frequently considered to be unenlightened.

76. The Bible.

77. In fashion.

78. A variation on the phrase, "As good be out of the world as out of the fashion," commonly attributed to the play *Love's Last Shift* written by Colley Cibber, the well-known English actor, playwright, and poet laureate. Because, however, this play is dated much later than this pamphlet, the author is clearly drawing from an earlier source. This source does not appear in the *OED* and remains unidentified. Colley Cibber, *Love's Last Shift; or, the Fool in Fashion* (London 1735). E. Salmon, "Cibber, Colley (1671–1757), actor, writer, and theatre manager," *ODNB*.

79. In the seventeenth century, Spanish fashion began to be considered less current than French fashion.

80. Because Venice was built upon a system of canals, horses were unnecessary and burdensome. In the increasingly prosperous society of Holland, beggars or vagrants were relatively rare and frequently

198 *Appendix 4*

was as like to be preferred to his favor as a spurrier[81] was to Queen Elizabeth. But since he is in his grave, we will not take up his ashes any further. If he can find any rest there now dead, who living I am sure had little or none in his conscience (for he ever carried a civil war in his breast of fears, suspicions, and jealousies), he shall lie secure, for *we* intend to disturb him no further.

After the death of this British idol, Richard the 4th, his son, peeped out,[82] who had no fault so great as that he had him [Cromwell] to his Father, for it was generally believed he would be but tenant to the right landlord, or the Stuarts' Steward,[83] to set all things in order until he[84] was restored. But, alas! He proved but a fortnight's wonder; no sooner up but down.[85] His disposition (if we may credit report) was the womanish plot of weeping Fleetwood's Lady, who stomached it that his preferment should be greater than her husband's, though it proved to little purpose.[86] And indeed, it is seldom known that females' council ever arrives to any better success, not is there any reason that the distaff should be a companion

---

expelled.

81. A person who makes spurs and so, as a member of a lower social order, would be unlikely to earn favor from the queen.

82. A reference to Cromwell's son, Richard Cromwell, who was named Lord Protector after his father died in 1658. The title "Richard the 4th" is a joke, given that one reason Cromwell was criticized for aspiring to kingship after overthrowing monarchy was that, like a king, he had arranged for his eldest son to inherit his position. Specifically, the allusion may be to Richard of Shrewsbury, Duke of York, the second son of King Edward IV and brother of Richard III who some viewed as a pretender. Peter Gaunt, "Cromwell, Richard (1626–1712)," *ODNB*.

83. The author puns on Stuart (the royal house of Kings James and Charles) and steward (the manager of a lord's estate). After the death of his father, Richard Cromwell merely served as a "steward" for the Stuarts until their return to the throne in 1660.

84. Charles II, the elder son of Charles I and hence the Stuart who inherited the throne when it was restored in 1660 after Richard Cromwell's death.

85. Richard Cromwell's tenure as Lord Protector was indeed short-lived. Immediately after his installation into power in 1658, ongoing tensions between the army and Parliament over such long-standing disputes as the extent and nature of military power and the failure to pay soldiers arrears for their services during the wars resulted in the army's dissolution of Richard's Parliament and his forced resignation in 1659.

86. Bridget Fleetwood, the daughter of Oliver Cromwell. She first married Cromwell's close associate, Henry Ireton, in 1646, but a mere month after he died, in 1651, she married Charles Fleetwood (c. 1618–1692), whose own wife, Frances, had also recently died. Fleetwood was soon named the commander-in-chief of the army in Ireland and then, in 1654, lord deputy of Ireland. This position had been held formerly by Bridget's first husband, Ireton, and rumor had it that Fleetwood was rewarded with it because Bridget begged her father to refrain from giving it to another prominent officer, John Lambert, instead. The author of the pamphlet is insinuating that Bridget's ambitions even extended to preferring that her husband be named Lord Protector instead of her brother so that she could then gain the title of princess. Peter Gaunt, "Fleetwood, Bridget, Lady Fleetwood under the protectorate (*bap.* 1624, *d.* 1662)," *ODNB*.

for the scepter. A kitchen was a great deal more for her than a throne, though she had ambition enough to persuade herself that she deserved the name of a princess. Yet had Richard [been] heir of his father's parts (though it was well he was not), he would have soon frustrated their designs and come to as much height and greatness. But he had not enough of the rogue in his composition to make up a damned politician. He was fitter to bear a hawk on his fist than to hold a scepter in his hand. A sedentary, retired country-life was far more suitable to his temper and disposition than a tumultuous city life. He was altogether ignorant in that so much practiced possession of piercing the lion with the fox's tail, which no doubt he might have done had he been as well read in Machiavelli as his sire was.[87] He was not much read in politics, as appears by the small term of time that was allowed him to play the Protector. But no matter, it was well it fell out so; he is like to fare the better for it, in the judgement of the most censorious. Besides, it was what suited with his fancy (according to relation) better than all the usurped power and authority of his predecessor. *Exit Protector*, he was but like a pageant, a king in a play. He only appears upon the stage, makes a leg, and takes his leave of you.

But what comes next? A resolve here intervenes. No less than the "Bloody Tragedy of OLIVER the Traitor," who to unite firmly the Council of War to him, which consisted of a few able head-pieces to whom he laid himself open so far as to show them their profit and preferment in the design, which united them fast to him and the other, who were soft heads and had a good meaning to do no evil but to promote the kingdom of Christ and thrown down Antichrist and then, according to their duty (as they were taught), to take possession of and (as saints) reign over the kingdom.[88] Cromwell provided fit food to feed such fantasies, for he had provided a monstrous witch full of all deceitful craft, who being put into brave clothes pretended she was a lady come from a far country, being sent by God to the army with a revelation which she must make known to the army, for necessity

---

87. A reference to *The Prince* (1532), by Nicolo Machiavelli. In the cited passage, Machiavelli describes Septimius Severus, the Roman Emperor, as an exemplary ruler because he effectively combined the traits of the lion (a traditional symbol for nobility, militarism, and royal rule) with those of the fox (a less royal but more effective symbol for the sly and wily use of power). According to Machiavelli, a successful ruler adopts both approaches because while "the lion can't defend itself against snares [traps], the fox can't defend itself against wolves" [Nicolo Machieavelli, *The Prince* (1532), Project Gutenberg, http://www.gutenberg.org/files/1232/1232-h/1232-h.htm)]. *The Prince* was translated into English in 1640. The author of *The English Devil* uses the cited passage to say that Cromwell, like Severus, was able to successfully negotiate between competing factions, specifically Parliament and the army, whereas his son, Richard, resembled Severus's own unfortunate son, Antoninus, who was combative like the lion but lacked the fox's subtlety and so was destroyed by his own soldiers.

88. The religious radicals in the army such as the Fifth Monarchists who wished to replace monarchy with the one-thousand-year rule of the Saints predicted in the book of Revelation.

200 *Appendix 4*

was laid upon her. This witch had a fair lodging prepared for her in Whitehall.[89] Now having had her lesson taught her before by Cromwell and Ireton, by whose order she was entertained, desired to have audience at the Council of War for to them (she said) she was sent.

Cromwell and Ireton to beget the more attention and belief in the officers of the Council of War, began to extol the excellency of revelation and conceived that this prophetess, being a precious saint and having much of God in her ought for to be heard, and that with all intentions because (said they), in such glorious days as these, God does manifest himself extraordinarily, and especially to his Saints, in chalking out their way before them when they came into straights and difficulties such as they were in at that time.

By this time the witch was come to the door, and forthwith had admittance, where all the officers beheld her strange postures, expressing high devotion. Cromwell and Ireton, fixing their eyes upon her in most solemn manner (to beget in the rest of the officers who were ready to laugh) an apprehension of some serious thing, fell both of them to weeping. The witch, looking in their faces, and seeing them weep, fell to weeping likewise and began to tell them what acquaintance she had with God by revelation, and how such a day, such an hour, after such a manner, she had a revelation which she was to reveal only to them. And that was, that the glorious time of setting up Christ's kingdom was near at hand, and that Antichrist must be speedily thrown down, and that they were the instruments that were by God ordained to throw him down, and how they were about that great work, and that if they would prosper in it, they must first remove the king out of the way, which they must do first by proceeding to try him, and then to condemn him, and then to depose him, but not to put him to death. This relation I had from one that was strongly of the army's party but related this shameful story with much indignation.

A Lillonian[90] was taught at this time with bribes to print his opinion, which was much according to the opinion of his sister witch.

Some of the soberer and more religious of the officers being much startled at these revelations, but not at all satisfied, repaired to some of the most religious and able Independents to know their opinion of these things and to desire advice what to do. They replied (I am informed Thomas Goodwin in particular) that, since they had gone so far, they must now carry on, though with the blood of those that stood in their way, for if they now made a stop, farewell their cause

---

89. Elizabeth Poole. Note that, with the exception of some capitalization and italics practices as well as a few word choices—the most significant of which are flagged—the content of the remainder of the pamphlet is identical to *To Xeiphos Ton Martyron*.

90. This work differs from *To Xeiphos Ton Martyron* in that the former mentions "Lilly" specifically whereas "Lillonian" implies that the individual in question is a follower or emulator of Lilly rather than Lilly himself.

forever. This was good in politics but bad in divinity; it was a true politic aphorism of Machiavelli's but false doctrine in the divinity schools. However, they made use of this doctrine to proceed in their designs for the promotion of the Independent cause.

By this time, John Lilburne and his party, who sat at Whitehall to draw up their desires, had brought their business to some maturity, which was, as I conceive, inferred in the paper called *An Agreement of the People*, the sum whereof was no other than this, to throw down king, Lords, and Commons, as then established, to throw down the laws, Inns of Court, courts of judicature, church government, as also the universities and function of the clergy.

This *Agreement* being debated at the General Council, Cromwell (whose design was to set up another government, and was then about it) opposed this *Agreement*, because it opposed his designs; for though he sat in council with the General Officers, yet he consulted altogether with the popish[91] faction to set up a government according to the government in Spain (viz.) by a Council of State and a High Court of Justice.

The General Council of War was hereby divided about this *Agreement of the People*, and so equally divided that only one voice carried it, or two at the most in the negative, which gave occasion to Colonel *Hewson* (as I remember) to say, "How can we call this *An Agreement of the People*, when we ourselves are divided about it?"[92] Cromwell, being now to shoot the greatest gulf, having now the work to do which he had been all this while by force and policy making way unto; he saw but two main rubs in the way which he durst not meddle with in a boisterous way, and those were the Presbyterian ministers of the kingdom who preached vehemently against the treasonable practices of the army. The other whom he dared not meddle with were those down-right dealers called Levellers. What he could not do by flattery, he did by threats, but he could not in the least terrify the Presbyterians, who declared against his wicked and open rebellion, detesting those illegal proceedings of the army in offering violence to the Parliament and going about to overthrow the king.

FINIS.

91. In one of the more notable departures from *To Xeiphos Ton Martyron*, this pamphlet uses "Popish" instead of "Spanish."

92. In *To Xeiphos Ton Martyron*, the line following this one reads, "Hereupon it was thought fittest to be printed, and sent abroad, to see how the people liked of it, before they proceeded any further" (p. 191). This line is omitted in *The English Devil* and replaced by a concluding section that differs entirely from its predecessor.

Appendix 5: Other Pamphlets Relevant to Elizabeth Poole

This appendix contains documents that contextualize the debates over the future settlement of the kingdom's government that Elizabeth Poole's messages helped to construct. These document illustrate the spectrum of opinion that defined these debates and thereby invite us to identity Poole's place on that spectrum. *The Heads of Proposals* envisions a constitutional monarchy. *The Copies of Several Letters Contrary to the Opinion of the Present Powers* imagines a representative democracy.

Henry Ireton and John Lambert
The Heads of Proposals *(1647)*

The Heads of Proposals (Wing H1285) represents one of the earliest attempts to craft a constitution for a new government in England. It was written by Henry Ireton and Major-General John Lambert in the summer of 1647, just after the first round of warfare had ended, the king was captured, and the New Model Army had taken over London to prevent Parliament from disbanding it. At this juncture, Ireton still believed that a settlement with the king was possible and desirable. Thus, rather than endorsing regicide as would the *Remonstrance* (appendix 3, pp. 155–160), *The Heads of Proposals* empowered Parliament while retaining the Crown. This form of government was ultimately adopted by the kingdom during the Glorious Revolution in 1688 and continues to define modern Great Britain.

Parliament initially refused to accept the *The Heads of Proposals*, choosing instead to revise the Newcastle propositions used by the Scots to negotiate with the king after capturing him and briefly holding him before handing him over. But Charles I himself preferred *The Heads of Proposals*, finding the Newcastle propositions too strict. The House of Commons proposed drafting and discussing a new treaty altogether in September 1647, but this measure was blocked by those who opposed any negotiations whatsoever with the king. After Cromwell and Ireton reiterated their support for *The Heads of Proposals*, the House agreed to continue peace talks with the king.

As noted in appendix 3 (p. 161), Cromwell and Ireton also urged the army to approve *The Heads of Proposals* at the Putney Debates that October. But they were met with fierce resistance. A number of opponents preferred the more democratic plan put forth by army agitators in a document attributed to General Thomas Fairfax on *EEBO* and titled *The Case of the Army Truly Stated* (Wing W2168A). For their part, the Levellers found *The Heads of Proposals* to be too shortsighted in its allowance for kingship, its insistence that only property holders be allowed to vote, and other controversial measures. Even after Cromwell and Ireton tried to

203

204 *Appendix 5*

force soldiers to adopt *The Heads of Proposals* at Corkbush Field, the Levellers and other radicals in the army continued to resist negotiations with the king and to promulgate *An Agreement of the People* (appendix 3, pp. 160–174) as the superior constitution for a new age of government.

The internal dissensions within the army resulting from the failure of the debates to reach an agreement on *The Heads of Proposals* helped initiate the second round of warfare. But *The Heads of Proposals* survived, as parts of it were included in *The Government of the Commonwealth of England, Scotland, and Ireland, and the Dominions Thereunto Belonging*[1]—also known as the "Instrument of Government"—the constitution written by John Lambert that was finally adopted in 1653. The "Instrument" named Cromwell as Lord Protector and gave the vote to property owners.

The copy reprinted here is housed in the Thomason Tracts [E.408(8)] in the British Library and is available on *EEBO*. George Thomason has handwritten the date, September 24, on the title page of this copy to record the day upon which he added it to his collection.

The Heads of
PROPOSALS,
Agreed on by his Excellency
Sir Thomas Fairfax,
AND
The Council of the ARMY.
Tendered to the Commissioners of Parliament
residing with the Army, to be by them
presented to the PARLIAMENT.
CONTAINING
Their particular Desires (in pursuance of their
former Declarations and Papers) in order to the clearing and
securing the Rights and Liberties of this Kingdom, in the settling of a
just and lasting peace therein; leaving the terms of peace for the Kingdom
of Scotland, to stand as in the late Propositions of both
Kingdoms, unless that Kingdom have agreed, or
shall agree to any alteration.
To which Proposals are added the explanations upon several
particulars therein agreed upon at the late General Council of

---

1. John Lambert, "December 1653: The Government of the Commonwealth of England, Scotland and Ireland, and the Dominions Thereunto Belonging," in Charles H. Firth and R. S. Rait, eds., *Acts and Ordinances of the Interregnum, 1642–1660* (London: H. M. Stationery, 1911), 813–22.

the Army at Putney, on Thursday, September 16, 1647.
In answer to certain Queries thereupon made by the Commissioners of Parliament residing with the Army.
By the appointment of his Excellency Sir *Thomas Fairfax,* and the
General Council of his Army.
Signed,
John Rushworth, Secretary.

London: Printed for *George Whittington*, at the Blue Anchor in
Cornhill, near the Royal Exchange. 1647.

The Heads of
PROPOSALS,
Agreed on by his Excellency
Sir Thomas Fairfax,
And the Council of the Army.

I.[2] That (the things hereafter proposed being provided for by this Parliament) a certain period may (by Act of Parliament) be set for the ending of this Parliament, (such period to be within a year at most,) and in the same Act provision to be made for the succession and constitution of Parliaments in future, as follows:

1. That Parliaments may biennially be called, and meet at a certain day, with such provision for the certainty thereof, as in the late Act was made for triennial Parliaments, and what further or other provision shall be found needful by the Parliament, to reduce it to more certainty; and upon passing of this, the said Act for Triennial Parliaments to be repealed.

2. Each biennial Parliament to sit for 120 days certain (unless adjourned or dissolved sooner by their own consent) afterwards to be adjournable or dissolvable by the king; and no Parliament to sit past 240 days from their first meeting, or some other number of days to

---

2. There is no number "I" in the original. However, because this first paragraph represents the first of three main Heads of Proposals, with the subsequent two already featuring assigned numbers, I have supplied a number for this first one for the sake of clarity. Unlike the originals, however, I have used Roman numerals to number the three main clauses, because the standard Arabic numbering system is used to enumerate the subclauses or "particulars" (as the authors at one point refer to them) that fall under each main head. The subclauses are numbered here as they are in the original, except when typographical errors appear in the numbering system. Those places are identified in later footnotes.

206 *Appendix 5*

be agreed on: Upon the expiration whereof, each Parliament to dissolve of course, if not otherwise dissolved sooner.

3. The king upon the advice of the Council of State in the intervals between biennial Parliaments to call a Parliament extraordinary,[3] provided it meet about seventy days before the next biennial day, and be dissolved at least sixty days before the same, so as the course of biennial elections may never be interrupted.

4. That this Parliament and each succeeding biennial Parliament at, or before adjournment, or dissolution thereof, may appoint committees to continue during the interval, for such purposes as are in any of these proposals referred to such committees.

5. That the elections of the Commons for succeeding Parliaments, may be distributed to all counties, or other parts or divisions of the kingdom, according to some rule of equality or proportion, so as all countries may have a number of Parliament Members allowed to their choice, proportionable to the respective rates they bear in the common charges and burdens of the kingdom, or according to some other rule of equality or proportion to render the House of Commons as near as may be, an equal representative of the whole. And in order thereunto that a present consideration be had to take off the elections of burgesses,[4] for poor, decayed, or inconsiderable towns, and to give some present addition to the number of Parliament Members for great counties that have no less than their due proportion, to bring all (at present as near as may be, to such a rule of proportion as aforesaid).

6. That effectual provision be made for future freedom of elections, and certainty of due returns.

7. That the House of Commons alone, have the power from time to time, to set down further orders and rules for the ends expressed in the two last preceding articles, so as to reduce the elections of Members for that House, to more and more perfection of equality in the distribution, freedom in the election, order in the preceding thereto, and certainty in the returns, which orders and rules in that case to be as laws.

---

3. For specific purposes under exceptional circumstances.

4. Members of Parliament elected to represent towns, boroughs (incorporated self-governing townships), or universities.

8. That there be a liberty for entering dissents in the House of Commons, with provision, that no member be censurable for ought said or voted in the House, further than to exclusion from his present trust in the House, and that only by the judgement of the House itself.

9. That the judicial power, or power of final judgement in the Lords and Commons (and their power of exposition and application of law) (without further appeal) may be cleared. And that no officer of justice, minister of state, or other person adjudged by them, may be capable of protection, or pardon from the king, without their advice and consent.

10. That the right and liberty of the Commons of England may be cleared and vindicated, as to a due exception from any judgement, trial, or other proceeding against them by the House of Peers, without the concurring judgement of the House of Commons, as also from any other judgement, sentence, or proceeding against them, other than by their equals, or according to the law of the land.

11. The same act to provide that grand jurymen may be chosen by and for several parts or divisions of each county respectively, in some equal way, and not remain (as now) at the discretion of an under-sheriff to be put on or off. And that such grand jurymen, for their respective counties, may at each assize[5] present the names of persons to be made justices of the peace from time to time, as the country has need for any to be added to the commission, and at the summer assize to present the names of three persons, out of whom the king may pick one to be sheriff for the next year.

II.[6] For future security to Parliament and the militia in general in order thereunto, that it be provided by Act of Parliament:

1. That the power of the militia by sea and land, during the space of ten years next ensuing, shall be ordered and disposed by the Lords and Commons assembled in the Parliament of England, or by such persons as they shall nominate and appoint for that purpose, from time to time during the said space.

---

5. Court session for hearing criminal cases.

6. As indicated in note 2, the original uses the number 2, but I have substituted the roman numeral II, as this represents the second main Head of Proposal. Its subclauses are enumerated as they appear in the original, that is, in accordance with the usual Arabic system.

208 *Appendix 5*

2. That the said power shall not be ordered, disposed, or exercised by the king, or by any person or persons by any authority derived from him, during the said space, or at any time hereafter by his Majesty that now is, without the advice and consent of the said Lords and Commons, or of such committees or counsel in the intervals of Parliament, as they shall appoint.

3. That during the same space of ten years, the said Lords and Commons may by bill or ordinance raise and dispose of what monies, and for what forces they shall from time to time find necessary, as also for the payment of the public debts and damages, and for all other the public uses of the kingdom.

4. And to the end the temporary security intended by the three particulars last precedent, may be the better assured, it may there be provided, that no subjects that have been in hostility against the Parliament in the late war shall be capable of bearing[7] any office of power or public trust in the commonwealth, during the space of five years, without consent of Parliament, or the Council of State, or to sit as Members or Assistants of either House of Parliament, until the second biennial Parliament be past.

III.[8] For the present form of disposing the militia in order to the peace and safety of this kingdom, and the service of Ireland.

1. That there be commissioners for the admiralty, with a vice-admiral and rear-admiral, now to be agreed on, with power for the forming, regulating, appointing of the officers, and providing for the navy, and for ordering the same to and in the ordinary service of the kingdom, and that there be a sufficient provision and establishment for pay and maintenance thereof.

2. That there be a general for command of the land-forces that are to be in pay both in England, Ireland and Wales, both for field and garrison.

3. That there be commissioners in the several counties for the standing militia of the respective counties, consisting of trained bands, and auxiliaries not in pay, with power for the proportioning, forming, regulating, training and disciplining of them.

7. Holding.

8. The original uses the number 3, but once again I have used the roman numeral III, as this represents the third main head of proposal. Its subclauses are enumerated in Arabic numerals as they appear in the original.

Other Pamphlets Relevant to Elizabeth Poole 209

4. That there be a Council of State, with power to superintend and direct the several and particular powers of the militia last mentioned, for the peace and safety of this kingdom, and of Ireland.

5. That the same Council may have power as the King's Privy Council for, and in all foreign negotiations, provided that the making of war or peace with any other kingdom or state shall not be without the advice and consent of Parliament. That the said power of the Council of State be put into the hands of trustees and able persons now to be agreed on, and the same persons to continue in that power *si bene se gesserint*[9] for a certain term not exceeding five years.

6. That there be a sufficient establishment now provided for the salaried forces both in England and Ireland, the establishment to continue until two months, after the meeting of the first biennial Parliament.

7.[10] That an act be passed for disposing the great offices for ten years by the Lords and Commons in Parliament, or by such committees as they shall appoint for that purpose in the intervals, with submission to the approbation of the next Parliament, and after ten years, they to nominate three, and the king out of that number to appoint one for the succession, upon any vacancy.

8.[11] That an act be passed for restraining of any Peers[12] made since the 21st of May, 1642, or to be hereafter made from having any power to sit or vote in Parliament without consent of both Houses.

9. That an act be passed for recalling and making void all declarations and other proceedings against the Parliament, or against any that have acted by, or under their authority in the late war, or in relation to it. And that the ordinances for indemnity may be confirmed.

10. That an act be passed for making void all grants, etc. under the Great Seal, that was conveyed away from the Parliament since the time that it was so conveyed away (except as in the propositions of both kingdoms), and for making those valid that may have been or

9. A paraphrase of the Latin *quandiu se bene gesserit*: as long as one conducts one's self well.

10. This "particular" is not preceded by a number in the original. I have added one here for clarity and consistency.

11. This and all the subsequent "particulars" under Head III are numbered incorrectly. I have corrected them here.

12. Members of the House of Lords.

210 *Appendix 5*

shall be passed under the Great Seal by the authority of both Houses of Parliament.

11. That an act passed for confirmation of the treaties between the two kingdoms of England and Scotland, and for appointing conservators of the peace between them.

12. That the ordinance for taking away the Courts of Wards and Liveries be confirmed by act of Parliament, provided his Majesty's revenues be not damnified therein, nor those that last held offices in the same, left without reparation some other way.

13. An act to declare void the cessation of Ireland, etc. And to leave the prosecution of that war to the Lords and Commons in the Parliament of England.

14. An act to be passed to take away all power, authority, and jurisdiction of bishops, and all other ecclesiastical officers whatsoever extending to any civil penalties upon any. And to repeal all laws whereby the civil magistracy has been, or is bound upon any ecclesiastical censures to proceed (*ex officio*) unto any civil penalties against any person so censured.

15. That there be a repeal of all acts or clauses in any act enjoining the use of the *Book of Common Prayer*, and imposing any penalties for neglect thereof, as also of all acts or clauses in any act imposing any penalty for not coming to church, or for meetings elsewhere for prayer, or other religious duties, exercises or ordinances, and some other provision to be made for discovering of papists[13] and popish recusants,[14] and for disabling of them, and all Jesuits, and priests, from disturbing the state.

16. That the taking of the *Covenant*[15] be not enforced upon any, nor any penalties imposed upon the refusers, whereby men might be constrained to take it against their judgement or consciences, but all orders or ordinances to that purpose to be repealed.

17. That (the things here before purposed, being provided for settling and securing the rights, liberties, peace, and safety of the kingdom), his Majesty's person, his queen, and royal issue,[16] may be restored to a condition of safety, honor, and freedom in this nation, without

13. Derogatory term for Catholics.

14. Catholics who "recused" themselves from—refused to attend—services in the Church of England.

15. *A Solemn League and Covenant.*

16. Children.

diminution to their personal rights, or further limitations to the exercise of the regal power, then according to the particulars afore-going.

18. For the Matter of Compositions.[17]

1. That a lesser number out of the persons excepted in the two first qualifications, in the propositions of both kingdoms, not exceeding five for the English being nominated particularly by the Parliament, who together with the persons in the Irish rebellion included in the third qualification, may be reserved to the further judgement of the Parliament as they shall find cause, all other excepted persons may be remitted from the exception and admitted to composition.

2. That the rates[18] for future composition may be lessened and limited not to exceed the several proportions and hereafter expressed respectively. That is to say:

1. For all persons formerly excepted, not above a third part.
2. For the late members of Parliament under the first branch of the fourth qualification, in the proposition a fourth part.
3. For other Members of Parliament in the second and third branches of the same qualification, a fixed part.
4. For the persons nominated in the said fourth qualification, and those included in the tenth qualification an eighth part.
5. For all others included in the fixed qualification a tenth part.

2.[19] And the real debts either upon record, or provided by witnesses be considered and abated in the evaluation of their estates in all the cases aforesaid.

3. That those who shall hereafter come to compound, may not have the Covenants put upon them,[20] as a condition without which they may not compound, but in case they shall not willingly take it they may pass their compositions without it.

---

17. This final section on "Compositions" comprises a complex plan defining who, particularly among the defeated Royalists, should have to pay various penalties and indemnities in the wake of the wars.

18. Ratios.

19. Point III.18.2 is continued here.

20. Do not have to swear fealty to *A Solemn League and Covenant*.

212 *Appendix 5*

4. That the persons and estates of all English, not worth 200 pounds in lands or goods be at liberty and discharged. And that the king's menial servants that never took up arms, but only attended his person according to their offices, may be freed from composition, or to pay at most but the proportion of one year's revenue, or a twentieth part.

5. That in order to the making and perfecting of compositions at the rates aforesaid, the rents, revenues, and other dues, and profits of all sequestered estates whatsoever (except the estates of such persons who shall be continued under exception as before) be from henceforth suspended and detained in the hands of the respective tenants, occupants, and others from whom they are due, for the space of six months following.

6. That the faith of the army, or other forces of the Parliament, in articles upon surrender to any of the King's Party may be fully made good, and where any breach thereof shall appear to have been made, full reparation and satisfaction may be given to the parties injured; and the persons offending (being found out) may be compelled thereto.

7. That there may be a general Act of Oblivion[21] to extend unto all (except the persons to be continued in exception as before) to absolve from all trespasses, misdemeanors, etc., done in prosecution of the war, and from all trouble or prejudice for or concerning the same (after their compositions past) and to restore them to all privileges, etc. belonging to other subjects provided as in the fourth particular, under the second general head, foregoing concerning security.[22]

Putney, 16. Sept. 1647.

By the appointment of his
Excellency Sir Thomas Fairfax
and the General Council
of the Army.

John Rushworth, *Secretary*

21. Pardon or clemency.

22. See Proposal 11, "particular" number 4.

Other Pamphlets Relevant to Elizabeth Poole 213

Francis White
The Copies of Several Letters Contrary to the Opinion of the Present Powers *(1649)*

The Copies of Several Letters (Wing W1764) is a collection of letters written by Francis White, an officer in the New Model Army, to Major Generals Thomas Fairfax and Oliver Cromwell.[23] Like Poole, White was a "minor character" in history whose voice had an impact on major events. In particular, like Poole, White believed Charles I to be guilty of treason but opposed his execution. His arguments in favor of this position inform us that, while Poole's solution of divorcing the king seems unusual, her idea that the king could be removed nonviolently was shared by others.

White was a captain in Sir Thomas Fairfax's regiment of foot. As the letters reprinted here attest, he was not afraid to offer—or even publish—his criticism of those who he believed were in the wrong, no matter who they were or what the consequences. He started out as an agitator who presented his regiment's complaints in May 1647 to the Parliamentary Commissioners appointed to carry out the disbandment of the New Model Army. After the army rid itself in June of officers who favored the disbandment, White was promoted to major.

While a staunch anti-Royalist, White was also critical of Parliament. For example, even as he acknowledged Parliament's right to disband the army, he still opposed those in the House of Commons who wished for Parliament to take control of its forces for ten years, arguing that the army was needed to prevent Presbyterian leaders from allying with Scottish supporters to rule as a military junto. For expressing this opinion, he was expelled from the General Council of Officers. He defended himself in an open letter to Fairfax dated September 23 and published as part of the set of letters reprinted here.

Many of his opinions ally him with the Levellers. He participated in the Putney debates and warned Fairfax against negotiating with the king. Despite his often-radical stances, he was readmitted to the General Council in December of that same year. However, in March 1648, he penned an open letter to Cromwell, also contained in this publication, urging him to adopt the Levellers's *An Agreement of the People* as the constitutional foundation of a new commonwealth and to refrain from executing the king given that there was no legal authority for this action. For this, he was accused by some of turning Cavalier but was praised by John Lilburne in his pamphlet *The Second Part of England's New-Chains Discovered* (1649) (Wing L2181), a complaint that Cromwell's overweening rule was proving to be a new set of "chains," second to the king's against which the army had fought.

---

23. Robert Zaller, "White, Francis (*d.* 1657)," *ODNB*.

214 *Appendix 5*

Even as White often championed Leveller causes, he pleaded with members to stop introducing further fissures into an already divided army when they staged their rebellion in May 1649. Unfortunately, he then unwittingly helped lure a number of them into a trap set by Cromwell after the latter invited them to negotiations at Burford, Oxfordshire, where they were massacred. In *The Levellers (Falsely So Called) Vindicated* (1649) (Wing L1800A), Lilburne insisted that White had knowingly betrayed the Levellers, prompting White to publish his own vindication in September titled *A True Relation of the Proceedings in the Business of Buford* (1649) (Wing W1766). He also defended himself in a letter included here against Lilburne's accusation.

When Cromwell successfully invaded Scotland in 1650, an action that General Thomas Fairfax boycotted, White received credit for his role in the victory and a promotion to lieutenant-colonel. In 1653, he aided Cromwell once again in purging Parliament of Cromwell's opponents. At this point, Parliament had been reduced even further from the Rump to the so-called Barebone's Parliament and then in the wake of White's purge, to the first Protectorate Parliament. White was a member, helping to pass the "Instrument of Government" that named Cromwell as Lord Protector.

In 1657, White was named governor of Mardyke Fort in Flanders. He drowned in a shipwreck during a return trip to England in December of that same year. Like Poole's prophecies, his letters survive as a testament to how the revolution was made not just by "great men" but also by lesser known people whose voices can still be heard today because they used the printing press to record their criticisms of power.

The copy reprinted here is housed in the Thomason Tracts [E.548(6)] in the British Library and is available on *EEBO*. Thomason has handwritten the date, March 20, 1648, on the title page of this copy to mark the day upon which he acquired it.

Other Pamphlets Relevant to Elizabeth Poole 215

THE
COPIES
OF Several
LETTERS
Contrary to the opinion of the
present powers, Presented
to the
Lord General Fairfax,[24]
and
Lieutenant General Cromwell.

By *Francis White* Major of his
Excellency's Regiment of Foot.

London, Printed by *T. Paine* for *Thomas Slater* and
Stephen Bowtell, 1649.

To the Reader.

Having for some years been an actor in the affairs of the late wars, and likewise an observer of the proceedings of state in which I have been concerned more than every private person, I have therefore offered my judgment, and declared my opinion in matters of highest concernment to my Lord General, and Lieutenant General Cromwell, and had no great desire to have published what I have written: But hearing by many of my friends, that it is generally reported by most that have heard of me, that I have now declined my principles, and am turned Cavalier. The reason of this conception is because I declared my dissent to the taking away the life of the king. But to manifest to the world, the truth and innocence of my heart, I have published these following letters, to show that I was of the same judgement formerly as I now continue as may appear in my letter sent to Lieutenant General Cromwell, almost a year ago, and what I have written to my Lord General, although contrary to the opinion of the present powers. I thought myself bound in conscience to perform, to preserve my own inward peace. For although some men make no conscience of their engagements, vows, and oaths, yet I hope God will give me power rather to suffer death, than destroy my life. I know that my judgment is not infallible, yet notwithstanding I must keep close to my principles, until I am convinced of error. I have here declared my principles and purpose to stand in the prosecution of the public service with faithfulness, while God by his grace doth enable me.

March the 20.
1648.

Francis White

24. At the time of White's letter, Fairfax was a General in Parliament's New Model Army.

216 *Appendix 5*

The Copy of a Letter presented to his
Excellency, the Lord *Fairfax*, General.

My Lord,

I am a member of your army and included in all actions done by the disciplinary power, which I silently consent thereto, and I would never appear a dissenter to anything that tends to public good, although never so prejudicial to my particular interest. But rather than I would submit to anything of essential public prejudice to the people, or to destroy my inward peace, I would expose myself to a temporal destruction. For God is my witness, I do not so much fear them that can kill the body only, as I do him that is able to cast both body and soul into hell. So far as I have been employed in the common work, I have cheerfully acted or born my public testimonies, and I forever shall. *My Lord*, I have taken notice of many petitions from almost all the forces in England,[25] and from diverse people of the countries which supplicate for many good things,[26] which they desire your Excellency to procure. In all which good things, I do heartily concur with their petitions, but I have observed this as one thing generally desired, that they may have execution of justice upon the king, and as far as I can perceive it is generally intended by the officers of the army and the Members of the present House of Commons to take away the life of the king. But with submission to your Excellency, I desire leave to declare my dissent and upon grounds conscientious for these reasons following:

> First: Because there are no clear grounds by any legal authority to take the life of the king.
>
> Secondly: It is contrary to our first engagement, and our general professions, vows, and covenants, to God and the world.[27]
>
> Thirdly: I do not discern it will produce any general good to the nation, but rather the contrary.

---

25. Various New Model Army regiments circulated numerous petitions lodging complaints ranging from how soldiers were treated, especially in matters of payment, to the handling of peace treaties by both Parliament and the army officers. A representative example is *The Armies Petition; or, a New Engagement* (London: 1648) (Wing A3715). This petition was drafted by a group of army agitators at St Albans in April 1648, and published in tandem with a related civilian broadside, *A New Engagement, or Manifesto* (London: 1648) (Wing N634).

26. During these turbulent years, groups of citizens representing a variety of perspectives also addressed petitions to such audiences as the king, Parliament, the army, and the city of London. While some petitions demanded the end of warfare and the return of the king to the throne, others such as *Four Petitions to His Excellency Sir Thomas Fairfax* (London: 1647) (Wing F1665) called for Fairfax to resist Parliament's plan to disband the New Model Army after the First Civil War and form a new army designed to invade Ireland.

27. Anonymous, *A Solemn Engagement of the Army, under the Command of His Excellency Sir Thomas Fairfax* (London: 1647) (Wing S4436).

Having declared my opinion, and the chief reasons for the same, I desire your Lordship to read these following lines, for the clearing of those reasons, and the justifying my integrity and innocence in former actions.

At the first taking up of arms, I was sensible of the oppression and injustice which was exercised by the king and his ministers upon the people, he exalting himself to acts beyond all laws, which his predecessors and himself had bound themselves by consent to observe. He raising arms to enforce the exercise of his power, to the maintaining an absolute tyranny over the nation, was the chief ground of my opposing him. And I have freely acted in the affairs of war, to the subduing of his power, and the vindicating of the peoples' just rights, and claim to the disposal of the military power without his consent. In the prosecution of this service, I have been as free from seeking revenge upon the person of the king as to violate my own life. The chief end I seek is the preservation of the righteous people, with the safety and well-being of the whole, and if possible without taking away the life of Charles Steward,[28] King of England.

First I say, I do not understand how it may be done by any legal authority according to the kingly government, though it may be a just thing, yet I know not how it may justly be done.[29] I never heard of any throne erected in the earth, either by God or men, for the judging of a king, until the erecting of this late tribunal at Westminster.[30] All the judgment seats, that are legally erected in this nation, were made by the king, Lords, and Commons. But the king ever did exempt himself from personal judgment, by virtue of the military, regal, and legislative power which he retained in himself, which was gotten by the sword of his predecessors, and kept by traditional dissent.[31] Although the people since the conquest[32] have had the liberty of choosing laws, so that he did not set up laws and judiciaries legally at his will, yet there was no law made, nor judiciaries erected, but by his will, although he agreed, the people should have the power of choosing laws. So that no law was ever made without his will.

And if it be thoroughly examined, we may find that the king has no other right to the military, regal, and legislative power than the sword did constitute and invest him with by divine permission, the people submitting thereto for fear, and to avoid greatest mischief. But now the king and his party being conquered by the sword, I believe the sword may justly remove the power from him, and settle it in its original fountain next under God, the people. But to judge or execute his person, I do not understand [how] any legal authority in being can justly do it. I

---

28. Charles Stuart.

29. Although the king may deserve to be executed for treason, there is no legal authority in place for doing so, thus it would be unjust.

30. The army's High Court of Justice.

31. White likely means "descent."

32. The Norman Conquest of 1066.

doubt not but the sword may do it, but how righteous [a] judgment that may be, that God and future generations will judge. It is clear that the military power is exalted above the regal and legislative power, and is now come to the throne of God, and under no other legal judgment, until there be a legal authority erected, as is offered in the *Agreement*,[33] to which it may submit. And seeing God has in righteousness for the sins of the people and their king brought us into this unhappy condition, I therefore plead with your Excellency to use the sword with as much tenderness as may be, to preserve the lives of men, and especially the life of the king.

And for my second reason, because we have made general profession of preserving his person, and whensoever any accused us of seeking the life of the king, we always denied it until this late *Remonstrance*.[34] Now Sir, it is as real a manifestation of a Christian, an honorable and noble spirit, as can be discovered to the world, to be true to what it does profess, and to be the same in adversity. And it is more honorable to save the life of a conquered enemy than to destroy him. For if he has prosecuted his designs according to his judgment and conscience, and were in the wrong way, it was because God suffered the devil to blind his understanding, that he did not know the truth, and it is better to let him live and learn to repent than to make haste to send him to destruction. So that his remaining alive be not any general prejudice, or more mischievous than his death would be, which would well be considered under the third reason.

I do not understand any essential good can accrue to the people by the taking away his life. For it is not so much the person that can hurt us, as the power that is made up in the kingly office by this corrupt condition. For if the person be taken away presently, another lays claim to the kingly office, and for anything I know, has as much right to the dominion as his predecessor had, and will, questionless,[35] have all the assistance that this person can procure for the attaining thereof, and will be able to do more mischief because he is at liberty, and this under your power.

Again, this king being the king of Scotland and Ireland, according to the laws in being, they have an interest in his person as well as England, notwithstanding he is under our power. Now if you will judge the kingdoms of Scotland and Ireland in that which concerns their interest, where you can claim no right, it is a[n] evident wrong, and may give them just offense and ground of quarrel against the nation, and by this may be of more prejudice to the whole, than can be good to the particular. I desire, my Lord, that we issue a Christian spirit, not rendering evil for evil, but rather good for evil. Although wicked men will deal wickedly with

33. *An Agreement of the People*, to which White subscribes.

34. Henry Ireton's *Remonstrance* (appendix 3, pp. 155–160), which argues that the king should receive capital punishment.

35. Without question.

Other Pamphlets Relevant to Elizabeth Poole 219

us, yet let us deal mercifully with them, and pardon and forgive, as we desire God should pardon and forgive us. In this way, I do verily believe we shall be greater conquerors than yet we have been, if we can conquer ourselves, and the affection of our enemies which this does lead unto. My Lord, in all that I have written, I am not against the judging of the king, but I say it is by no legal authority, but only what the sword exalts, although it be not an exact martial court, yet it is little different, and not a legitimate authority to the king, yet it may as justly judge him, as ever he judged the people and may dethrone him and divest him of all power and authority in the English nation. And I think it is necessary so far to proceed and to detain him as a prisoner at war, until he may be delivered with safety to yourselves and the nation. I desire your Excellency's favorable construction of what I have written, and if it be not your Excellency's judgment, all that I desire for my satisfaction is that your Excellency will appoint such a General Council as the army in these parts shall be included by the major voice thereof. If it be not concluded according to my judgment, yet therein shall I have my desire, because I consent to be included by the major part, to avoid division. If this may not be granted, then must I declare my dissent, and that it is an action done by virtue of the disciplinary power of the army, by which I am not in this case willingly included, and not be an instrument of the mischiefs and evils that may be brought upon this nation, by the taking away the blood of their king. Having taken this freedom to write to your Excellency, I shall now take my leave, and remain:

Your Lordship's most
humble Servant,
Francis White

January the 22.
1648.

To the Right Honorable, His Excellency, the Lord
Fairfax, General

My Lord,
I have for these six years been a servant to the public in the affairs of the late war, and for the most part under your Excellency's conduct and I can speak it with confidence that no man has been more faithful to the people, or to your Lordship, in the prosecution of their interest than myself. If I have erred in this work, it has been chiefly in too forward actions for the public good. And I would rather err in the prosecution of my principles with zeal, than in the abusing patience with sloth, wherein I am convinced of offense, from which no man is free, I shall submit. But rather than betray innocence with cowardice, I would perish. My Lord, I must

220 *Appendix 5*

inform you that my principles lead me to a concurrence with those people which joined in the late petition of the many thousands in the City of London,[36] and parts adjacent, and must upon all lawful occasions, as I will vindicate my integrity, use means for the accomplishing of the most essential parts of that petition. And if the prosecution of such principles be offensive to yourself, as to produce your Lordship's prejudice, for to remain under your Excellency's displeasure in my employment, as I am informed from some in near relations to your Excellency, I do. And that it has been the reason of your Honor's depriving me of a further trust, by putting another over me, to command your Excellency's regiment with success, which I had sought and conducted through the greatest difficulty with success, and free from imputation, or proving false to my trust in the least. If it be true that your Honor bears prejudice to me for my principles, then must I in faithfulness speak it, I would rather quit my employment than remain under your Lordship's disaffection and jealousy in my command. My Lord, I am very sensible of my discouragement, and entreat your Excellency to give me the manifestation of your affection and acceptance for the future, or to let me know if it may not be, that I may remove myself from being a burden to your Honor's proceedings. However, I shall prove myself to be:

Your Lordship's most humble Servant,
Francis White

Knausburgh, September 23,
1648

To the Right Honorable Lieutenant General *Cromwell*

Honored Sir,
It is not unknown to many, your great pains, and unwearied endeavors in the public employment from the first undertaking. You have appeared constant, valiant, and successful in the greatest affairs of the late war. And having through God's blessing passed through many difficulties, subduing all adversaries that opposed our just proceedings, it now lies upon you and others of the like interest to see the establishment of those things which we have contended for, that there may be

---

36. White's use of the number "thousands" suggests he is referring to *The Humble Petition of Many Thousands of Young Men, and Apprentices of the City of London, to the High and Honorable, the Knights, Citizens and Burgesses in the Supreme Court of Parliament Assembled* (London: 1647) (Wing H3476). Given that the signatories of this petition concurred with those Presbyterians in Parliament who demanded the army be disbanded, it is not surprising that White feels a need to both apologize for and defend his own concurrence with this petition to Fairfax. Indeed, as mentioned in the headnote (p. 213), and as we shall see in his letter to Cromwell (pp. 220–233), he explicitly endorses Parliament's right to disband the army.

some requital for the expense of so much treasure and blood. It has ever been the consideration of all wise undertakers of a war, first, to consider the right[37] of their cause. Secondly, their abilities to manage the same. And thirdly, that the benefits may countervail the ill convenience or prejudice that may be sustained in the procuring [of] success.

What bondage, oppression, and injustice we were made subject to by the king and his ministers is not unknown to yourself. And when he could no longer keep the people in subjection under his oppressive government, but was in danger of being cast out of his throne, he then called a Parliament, which he endeavored to make subject to his will. For the better prosecution of his principles, but failing of his expectations in Council, he endeavored to bring his principles to pass by the force of the sword, and undertook the managing [of] a war against the Parliament. They, seeing the evil he endeavored to bring upon themselves and the nation, took courage to appear faithful to those who had entrusted them, and called in all that had bowels of mercy and compassion to themselves or the nation to come in to the help of a distressed state and to maintain their just rights and freedoms.

The Parliament did then claim, and since have claimed, a right to determine all controversies that may arise in the nation and that, of right, they might dispose of the militia of the kingdoms as they should see cause. For in the House of Commons virtually the power of the kingdom is for to make laws, or repeal laws, and to be the final judges. It is true, the king held a confirming voice, and was entrusted with the militia and the regal power for the protecting and administering justice unto the people, but when the Parliament saw a danger of the king's converting that power to their and the trusters' destruction, they took upon them the disposal of the militia, upon which the king broke with them and made a war.

God having now given success to their cause, and invested them and their assistants with full power, it now lies upon them to make good all promises, if possible, the lesser giving way to the greater, and, as much as in them lies, endeavor to prevent future disputes and quarrels, for the welfare of posterity, and to settle the government of the nation. So that the regal power in what form so ever may be subject to the legislative, and likewise to untwist those lines of bondage which will question our just proceedings, there is no rational man that will imagine it unreasonable that the Parliament should proceed to the settling [of] the kingdom's peace and freedom without the king, seeing that after the conquering [of] his forces, and so many addresses, he will accept of nothing but what shall be agreeable to his will. The which must be a giving up[38] the right of our cause, and advantage to the name and thing "king,"[39] to recover all power in short time, and to the winding of the nation into worse bondage and servitude than ever to the

37. Righteousness.

38. Renouncing.

39. The person who pretends to be this "thing" known as a "king."

222 *Appendix 5*

will of the prince, which will of necessity be our portion, if there be not a clear vindicating of the rights and freedom of the people in the legislative power which was the main thing contended for. And it is evident that the supreme power next under God is inherent in the multitude, and that there is no just authority but what is immediately derived from God himself by divine appointment or immediately given from the people by their representative, who of right are not subject to any particular person or persons, but may, upon grounds of common safety, alter magistrates or government,[40] make new laws or repeal old, abolish courts or set up new, without the concurrence of king or peers. However, this [may] be called new doctrine or leveling, it will appear that in this is laid the foundation of the freedom of a nation, in stating their representative free and equal, invested with full power, the persons changeable successively, so that whatsoever laws or burdens the people bring upon themselves, they will be of their own choosing. Whatsoever custom is held contrary hereto is a fruit of conquest[41] kept by force and may justly be by force repelled. This is no change of principles, as is evident from the first contest. The peoples' safety argued[42] the supreme law, and the House of Commons judges of that safety and [the] interpreters of law, and they[43] affirming the king's oath, binding him to confirm what laws they choose, the Commons telling the Lords they[44] should endeavor to save a people without them[45] if they[46] would not concur.

But it may be objected that the *Engagement* at the first undertaking of the war declared for king and Parliament, and that the Parliament's *Declaration* in the year 1646[47] declares for the maintaining of the constitution of this kingdom by king, Lords, and Commons, and that the protection and covenant of this kingdom

---

40. Change through election or impeachment.

41. The Norman Conquest.

42. Legitimated.

43. The House of Commons.

44. The House of Commons.

45. The House of Lords.

46. The House of Lords.

47. *A Declaration of the Lords and Commons Assembled in Parliament to the Whole Kingdom* (London: 1647) (Wing E1473), a statement issued by Parliament telling people that, in spite of misinformation spread by "Papists and Malignant Persons," all people, even said Papists and Malignants as well as "Neutrals," were obliged to pay excises to help fund the war (2). It's worth noting that, while White contends that the *Declaration* "declares for the maintaining of the constitution of this kingdom, by king, Lords, and Commons," the actual wording in *A Declaration* omits any mention of the king, stating that Parliament's overall purpose is to preserve "this kingdom, the religion, laws and liberties from utter ruin and destruction" (2).

Other Pamphlets Relevant to Elizabeth Poole 223

and Scotland[48] engages[49] them to maintain the king's authority, and that they have no thoughts or intentions to diminish his Majesty's just power and greatness.

To this I answer, that men are bound by conscience and honor to make good all engagements so far as justly they may, and if men be not found constant to their principles, no man can wisely put confidence in them, nor trust them further than necessity enforces. It will not be amiss to look over our former engagements and moderately to consider what may be performed and what not. For indeed, they are so interwoven that it will be a difficult matter to make good every particular. Therefore, first consider the most general things of greatest importance, and make good [with] them with as much provision for particulars as general will permit. And in the first place, that interest of the peoples' freedom must in justice take place. For in all declarations, papers, and covenants, it hath been the chief thing pretended, and there never passed any promise of entrusting the king, but in order the peace, freedom, and security of the kingdom. And I believe it was expected that, when the king's powers should be subdued, he would have accepted the Parliament's conditions, which he refusing is a just ground to alter their promises and to proceed to the settling [of] the kingdom in freedom, safety, and peace, without the king, the which can never probably be done without altering the former custom in making law. For what so ever is acted upon the former constitution will run to the king for confirmation. So there will be no security, unless you declare the Parliament's ordinances good laws and so conduce one estate and take away the thing "king,"[50] which name the ancient Romans could not endure for the space of 400 years.[51] And it will be found no small let[52] to the settlement of our peace. For it must be time that must produce security from him and his posterity. The army must not be a protection for ever, neither will the people endure this Parliament's perpetuity,[53] for the continuance of either longer than necessity enforces is inconsistent with the people's freedom.

---

48. _A Solemn League and Covenant_ (Wing S4441), the document pledging Scottish support for Charles I in exchange for his promise that, if the king was victorious, he would implement Presbyterianism as England's new state religion. As White notes and as the title denotes, the _Covenant_ does not anywhere state that, if defeated, the king could be executed. Nor does it promise to maintain the "king's authority."

49. Obligates.

50. Unless monarchy is altogether dissolved and Parliament allowed to reign supreme.

51. The lifespan of the Roman Republic. In 509 BCE, the last Roman monarch was overthrown because his son, Tarquin, raped Lucretia, the wife of one of his officers, and the Roman republic was founded. In 60 BCE, Julius Caesar began the machinations that led to his becoming emperor, thereby marking the end of Rome as a republic and its beginning as an empire.

52. Advantage.

53. The people will not endure the current Parliament's endless reign; they will demand elections.

224 *Appendix 5*

And now the soldiery having transacted much of the business of the king-dom upon their shoulders, you will be put upon the exercise of reason: You have already shown your strength and valor in subduing the forces that have opposed us. And if you can now find ways to secure yourself and our assistants from the authorities we have resisted, you will appear much like a complete man in reason.

I beseech you Sir, look back to the first engagement of the Parliament with due consideration and endeavor what you may to procure the performance there-of. At the first raising an army, the Parliament declared it to be for the defense of the Protestant religion, the laws of the land, the king's person, the privilege of Parliament, the people's just rights and freedom. These things are spacious, and were never slated and published what is meant hereby.[54] Some understand the Protestant religion to be the *Book of Common Prayer for Worship*, the episcopacy[55] for discipline, and the Thirty Nine Articles for doctrine.[56] But if religion be taken in such forms, then is it in a great measure altered by the synod, in part with the Parliament's approbation, imposing the *Directory for Worship*,[57] the presbytery for discipline, and *The Confession of Faith*[58] which they have published for doctrine and instead of reforming have introduced schism. It cannot be denied but we were very zealous for the promoting of religion, and I hope still are. But I fear we did not rightly understand what religion is. Certainly, religion in the most general acceptation is that profession of worship, discipline, and doctrine which a people hold forth to the world. In the former sense, it is most probable that which we call religion was understood and that which was then intended by the general party of the nation was a reformation of what might appear corrupt, and to free the people from those burdens in ceremonies imposed, which many tender

54. These terms or categories are broad and can be debated as to what they mean.

55. The bishops who governed the Church of England.

56. A list of the Church of England's doctrines and practices, first outlined in ten articles by Henry VIII in 1536 after he broke with the Roman Catholic Church. Under Elizabeth in 1571, the number of articles was officially capped at thirty-nine and included in the *Book of Common Prayer*.

57. *A Directory for Public Worship* (London: 1645) (Wing D1548), an instruction manual for Presbyterianism first adopted as the "Westminster Directory" by the Scottish Parliament in 1645. That same year, the *Directory* was adopted by the English Parliament as a replacement for the *Book of Common Prayer*.

58. *The Westminster Confession of Faith*, published as Anonymous, *The Humble Advice of the Assembly of Divines, Now by Authority of Parliament Sitting at Westminster, Concerning a Confession of Faith* (London, 1646) (Wing W1427). This is a document that, as noted in the introduction (p. 17), was released in 1646 by the Westminster Assembly, a group of ministers convened by Parliament in 1643 to craft reforms for matters related to modes of worship, official doctrine, and government in the Church of England. Like the other documents, it was largely driven by Presbyterians. Because of this, it was not adopted by religious Independents until it was modified and renamed the *Savoy Declaration* in 1658 (p. 17). See Congregational Churches in England, Savoy Meeting, *A Declaration of the Faith and Order Owned and Practiced in the Congregational Churches in England* (London:1658) (Wing N1486).

consciences could not bear. But now, that which we call religion appears to be only a traditional formal profession, and is made use of only to gain parties and factions under the specious pretense of religion, thereby to gain power to rise in dignities, for profit and honor among men. This is the religion of Rome[59] as at this day, pure state policy in which is comprehended the depth of the mystery of iniquity.[60] Such is the religion of the Turk, and many other nations a mere empty form in which nothing of the power of God is. And what is this alteration of church government, worship, and doctrine which some men so furiously pursue, but the clothing of Antichrist with a new coat, changing out of one form of the mystery of iniquity into another. But if you seriously consider, you may understand that religion is not a name but a thing, not a form but a power, not a notion but a substance divine. Religion consists in faith and works of righteousness. Religion is properly that inward power in the soul of a man whereby he believes and is bound to God in righteousness and holiness. The demonstration thereof manifest in acts of justice and mercy, visiting the fatherless and the widow and keeping unspotted from the world. So much of this power a man has, so much religion, where there is none of this power, there is no religion. *To as many as believe in Jesus Christ, to them giveth the power to become the sons of God.*[61] Now Sir, if there be a defending of the Protestant profession, let men take it in what form they understand. I believe it will be the best and safest [way of] making good this engagement [as] religion is not propagated by any human power. The civil magistrate may protect Christians in religious exercises, but to compel an external uniformity by a coercive power, seeing there is no pretended infallibility, will be preposterous, and more anti-Christian than is the pope himself.[62] Christ's kingdom is spiritual and propagated only by the spirit in the administration of the word, without the help of human force. If the civil magistrate exercise impartial justice and tolerate religious exercise, it will be as much as Christians will desire.

As for the laws of the land which we are engaged to defend, I think there are very few [who] understand what they are in general. We defend the laws if we act according to the supreme ends thereof, which is to save the people, and preserve propriety and dispense impartial Justice. And let the law have its course in courts until there be a just alteration. But if anything appears contrary to these ends by

---

59. Catholicism.

60. 2 Thessalonians 2:7, KJV: "For the mystery of iniquity does already work: only he who now lets will let, until he be taken out of the way." This verse is part of a speech in which Paul warns against listening to those who would deceive in matters of faith.

61. John 1:12, KJV: "But as many as received him, to them gave he power to become the sons of God, even to them that believe on his name."

62. White anticipates thinkers such as John Locke in arguing that the magistrate (or state) should not force people to adhere to an official, state-sponsored religion.

226 *Appendix 5*

the judgment of the law makers, it can be no breach of this engagement to alter the same.

The third particular was for the defense of the king's person and the voice went for the king and Parliament. But it seemed a strange paradox to many, how we should fight for the king [while] fighting against his personal commands, accompanied with his person. The best construction I could make thereof, was the rescuing him from his evil council that led him to the ruining [of] himself and the nation, and we ever made him merely passive, seduced by evil council, but it appears that his followers rather acted [in accordance with] his council than he theirs, but seeing he is still in safety, it can be no breach of this engagement if his person be kept from destruction.

The next particular is the privileges of Parliament, and it were very good the people knew what they are, [as] unlimited privileges may prove as destructive as unbounded prerogative. It is reason[able] they should be cleared and declared [so] that future Parliaments may be prescribed, likewise for their sitting and ending, that they may not wrong posterities. And when they are rightly stated according to reason, no question but we shall make good this engagement so far as may stand with the people's freedom.

The fifth thing, called the liberty of the subject, which is the only thing that can stand in competition, which the prince must of necessity be secured from oppressing tyrants, which can no better ways be done than by giving all authority from[63] their representative to whom all ought to be accountable, they being changeable by an unalterable decree; having this once settled, we may safely involve all in this common bottom of Parliaments. Unless this be procured, we have done nothing for posterity. And I dare affirm, we had better have continued under arbitrary tyranny than have contracted this misery and oppression that the people have suffered and [that] still lies upon them.

Now Sir, that which hindered our peace is pride and covetousness, which are the roots of all grand evils and mischiefs, the great men contend which shall be the greatest; profit and honor blind the eyes of the wise, the people are divided upon these two heads, the king and the covenant, to which parties are contracted, and the way to compose is no compulsion, but by conviction, it is mercy and lenity [which] conquers more upon ingenious spirits than authority and force. It would not be amiss to procure what shall be done for or with the king, for it is against the Parliament's declared principles to keep men in prison any longer than necessity enforces, until they may have a judicial trial, and seeing we have been under such bondage that the constitution hath provided no judiciary to judge the king, and indeed he is not legally subject to the penal laws, it will be most safe

---

63. This sentence would seem to suggest that, despite his use of the word "from," White's intention is to say that the best way to protect people's liberties would be for them to give all authority to the representatives, since those representatives are elected and hence accountable.

therefore to refer him to divine justice which will judge righteously, and to settle the government of the kingdom for quietness sake, with as much favor to the prince as the public safety will permit. But as he sticks to his former principles and parties, there can be no trusting him with power without giving up your cause and subjecting yourselves to the mercy of his will. He may be restored to the enjoyment of a sufficient revenue, beyond any particular person with his wife and children to a condition of freedom, safety, and peace, the public safety being first provided for, and may be entrusted with power if afterwards invested therewith from a future representative in whom the fountain of authority among men justly is, and then can there be no denial of being accountable thereto. Thus may the people be secured from tyranny.

The *Covenant*[64] which has been insisted upon for political ends, and still is much pressed by the Scots, I believe we may be stuck with it until the promoters desert it without any forced construction, for their swearing an utter extirpation of popery, prelacy, with all dependence on that hierarchy.

It will necessarily follow that all coercive power enforcing an external uniformity must be taken away, for this is the foundation of popery, this is that spirit that sits in the temple of God, showing itself to be God *and exalting itself above all that is called God*,[65] by making laws to bind the conscience in matters of faith.

And by the extirpation of the prelacy with all dependence on that hierarchy, will the ordination of the ministry received from them become null. For their dependence is on that hierarchy from whence they had their institution to the office of the ministry. The prelates dare not press this argument, because of giving advantage to their adversaries of Rome, from whence they had their own, sending these two arguments from the best interpretation of the *Covenant* will easily beat them off from that hold, we may justly defend the government of the kirk[66] of Scotland against any that shall enforce anything upon them contrary thereto, either in doctrine, discipline or worship. We may likewise endeavor to bring the churches of God in the three kingdoms[67] to as near a conformity to the word and the example of the best reformed churches[68] as is possible, still provided there be no human force or power exercised to this purpose; the weapons of the Christian warfare are spiritual, nor carnal,[69] but mighty in operation to the destroying of

---

64. *A Solemn League and Covenant.*

65. 2 Thessalonians 2:4, KJV: "Who opposes and exalts himself above all that is called God, or that is worshipped; so that he as God sits in the temple of God, showing himself that he is God."

66. Church.

67. England, Scotland, and Ireland.

68. A phrase generally used to refer to a Protestant church that adheres to the teachings of such pivotal Continental reformers as Ulrich Zwingli and John Calvin.

69. 2 Corinthians 10:4, KJV: "For the weapons of our warfare are not carnal, but mighty through God to the pulling down of strong holds."

228 *Appendix 5*

spiritual wickedness in high places, to the bringing of the thoughts and imaginations of men's hearts into subjection according to the mind and will of God. If conscientious people were but united upon this principle, it would take off all differences in relation to spiritual things.

Having taken this boldness to write you of matters of such general concernment in relation to the public, give me leave to offer my thoughts in relation [to] the late transaction of affairs between the army and the Parliament, which are but stifled for the present, and will questionless[70] break forth to the clear justification of the army and those members of Parliament that came to them or otherwise make them culpable, and justify those Members that sat with Mr. Pellam.[71] The breach between them and us was managed by the major part of the House, whose commands we disobeyed upon just grounds, but came not to a resistance until our way was made more clear by that outrage in the city tumult, which made the speakers and our friends fly to us for succor.[72] After which there remained near six score in and about London and Westminster, and not above seventy came to the army. Now without question, the interest of the House's authority remained with those at London. For by the custom of the kingdom, the House is included by forty men, which keep their sitting according to its precedent adjournment, and they remaining, being the highest visible authority in the kingdom. The question will be by what authority we marched up to London in defiance to their commands[73] to the repelling of those hostile powers contracted by their authority, and how the army shall be justified or vindicated in such proceedings.

That which gives me quiet and peace of conscience is from these considerations.[74]

70. Without question.

71. Peregrine Pelham, a successful merchant chosen to represent Hull in the House of Commons in 1641. He was not expelled during Pride's Purge and so sat in the Rump Parliament, a body which many who opposed the tactics used in the purge did not view as legitimate. Pelham was also a member of the High Court of Justice and was one of the most vocal advocates for execution. Andrew J. Hopper, "Pelham, Peregrine (*bap.* 1602, *d.* 1650)," *ODNB.*

72. White is likely referring to the demonstration that took place in July 1647, when Parliament was invaded by groups demanding peace and supporting Presbyterian calls for the army's dissolution. The demonstrators forced fifty-eight Independent Members of Parliament and Peers, as well as the two Speakers, to flee and seek protection from the army. This was ironic because the army had just marched into London in June in defiance of Fairfax's order to remain twenty-five miles outside of the city as disagreements over the army's disbandment continued to be adjudicated with Parliament. Thus, as White notes, the army's defiance of Parliament's orders did, in the end, serve to protect Parliament against its opponents.

73. The army's defiance of this order was legally questionable but justified by the aid their presence in the city provided to Parliament during the tumults.

74. The following considerations give White a sense of hope.

First, that when a company or society of men who are invested with power from God and nature to preserve themselves and the authorities over them command things unjust, which will prove their ruin, if obeyed. It is clear to me, necessity has no law; they may appeal to heaven and earth to bear witness to their cause, and betake themselves to the prime laws of nature to preserve and defend themselves and may suppress the authority if they persist in prosecution of things destructive to the community.[75] I know no other way of breaking tyrannical usurpations.

Now it is most clear that the Parliament put the army upon[76] conditions which would have proved their ruin if they had yielded to their will.[77] For if they[78] had renounced their just petition,[79] and swallowed that abominable declaration[80] and disbanded, they had been cast upon their enemy's mercy for their indemnity, and to have trusted those that had acted by secret councils with the king, for settling the rights and freedom of the nation which we had contended for.[81]

Secondly, the consideration of the unequal elections and constitution of the House of Commons not representing the major part of the nation, but elections distributed according to the will of the king and his predecessors, so that those who did not consent were only bound by a power of force, and the major part, not consenting, are not obliged when their being come in competition.[82]

Thirdly, the House's departing from their first integrity of communicating impartial justice and by virtue of that act of continuance during pleasure, grew

75. Because Parliament did not obey the laws of nature or divine will, destiny will take its course and Parliament will be punished.

76. Placed the army under.

77. A clearer justification for righteous resistance than the previous sentence.

78. The army.

79. A petition of complaints first put forth to Parliament by the army in March 1647 and expanded upon in May. As *A Solemn Engagement of the Army* later notes, this petition so threatened Parliament that it was suppressed and its authors declared enemies of the state.

80. The declaration that Parliament issued to disband the army. The product of several petitions issued earlier by various groups urging the disbandment, this declaration was also the document that identified the army petitioners as enemies of the state and conspirators with the king. The disbandment was effectively begun in May and completed by the end of June, even as some regiments fought those who had been charged with decommissioning them.

81. Even as Parliament accused members of the army of conspiring with Charles I, White makes it clear he believes it was the threat of disbandment that forced soldiers to consider throwing themselves onto the mercy of the king. They would do so to avoid being prosecuted for acts committed in time of war and to possibly secure the rights and freedoms for which they believed they had been fighting on behalf of Parliament.

82. White draws comfort from the fact that there were people, likely members of the Levellers (p. 23), who were willing to endorse a more universal definition of suffrage than had theretofore been considered.

230 *Appendix 5*

into parties and factions, and neglected to settle the government of the kingdom,[83] in order to the period of their sitting,[84] but rather it probably endeavored to be perpetual dictators, so as to deprive the nation of that changeable law[85] making authorities which are the conservators of their liberties to maintain all arbitrary in themselves.[86] This may justly be charged upon the prevalent party, that were our opponents, who secretly carried on a combination to comply with the king's interest to a more universal enslaving of the people than formerly.[87]

Having considered all proceedings of the most material concernment, it will necessarily come to this issue, that we have disobeyed, resisted, and repelled all the authority and government of the kingdom, both king, Parliament, and all bounds of law.[88] And the authorities and government being broken, it is wholly dissolved, and involved[89] into its original fountain next under God the people. And the highest authority that is now visible is the force of the sword. For there is no reasonable man but will conclude the Parliament to be under a force, mixed of two parties that have been in opposition, one while one party is the Parliament, another while the other, even to which the strongest power is contracted, so the stream runs, for at the time we lay at Brainford,[90] yourself, and son-in-law Ireton affirmed in my hearing that those which remained at Westminster, with Mr. Pellam,[91] were no Parliament, but some gentlemen claiming a Parliamentary

83. Because Parliament diverged from its original stated intentions for militarily defending itself against its own king, that is, justice and the safeguarding and/or achievement of various liberties, then just as its detractors warned, it split into competing factions, thereby failing to limit Crown power and reform the nation.

84. In the time it was allotted as a legitimately appointed body.

85. Elections.

86. To retain power without legal authorization.

87. A probable reference to Presbyterians who both sought great power over the religious settlement and frequently aided the king.

88. It will be said that the soldiers were traitors.

89. White likely means "evolved."

90. The Battle of Brainford or Brentford took place in 1642, when the king's forces surprised a Parliamentarian regiment commanded by Robert Devereux, Third Earl of Essex, and Denzil Holles, a statesman and writer, at Edgehill. After an indecisive outcome, the king moved on to a victory at Brentford. Although Cromwell was at Edgehill, his role was apparently unremarkable. The battle is better known for the fact that John Lilburne was captured by Royalist forces there and later released through a prisoner exchange. John Morrill, "Devereux, Robert, third earl of Essex (1591–1646), parliamentarian army officer," *ODNB*. John Morrill, "Holles, Denzil, first Baron Holles (1598–1680), politician," *ODNB*.

91. Peregrine Pelham.

Other Pamphlets Relevant to Elizabeth Poole 231

authority.[92] And in our remonstrance from Kingston,[93] we declared to the world they were usurpers and intruders, and that we would not suffer those who had voted to make a new war upon us to sit there as ours and the kingdom's judges. Yet since they have been acknowledged to be a Parliament, and sit here in court to this day, and for what I know,[94] [they] are the chief fomenters of our distractions and the protractors of the redresses of the common grievances of the nation. Now Sir, so long as that remonstrance from Kingston stands owned, I do not conceive the army concluded under the authority of the House, but only setting the House as a screen between them and the fiery fury of the people in the midst of common grievances and distractions, and do yield obedience to the Parliament in what they command agreeable to your own judgment. And on the other hand, the Parliament and synod, with all the Presbyterian party, with the Scots council, are endeavoring to get a power to bring you under the lash, and you can look for no other, but that if they get you and the army down, they will pay you and

92. It is possible that White is reminding Cromwell of some of the earliest divisions within Parliament. These divisions long preceded the purges that ultimately led to the Rump Parliament and signified that Parliament, from the very beginning of the wars, had been self-destructively split into two competing parties. This possibility presents itself because the Battle of Brainford took place in 1642, well before Pride's Purge in 1647. Thus this second reference to Pelham may allude to the role that Pelham played in one of the earliest and most disturbing controversies in Parliament. It began when Pelham worked with Sir John Hotham, the city's governor, and his son, John Hotham the Younger, to bar the king's entry into Hull. Hull was Pelham's home district and the seat of a large arsenal to which the king wished to lay claim. After successfully fending off the king and maintaining the arsenal for Parliament, Hotham promised one of his Royalist prisoners, Lord Digby, that he would in fact give Hull over to the king. When, however, Charles I reappeared with his troops, Hotham once again fended off a siege. Likewise, his son fought actively on behalf of Parliament but came into conflict with Thomas Fairfax and his father, prompting the latter to complain to Cromwell. This in turn led both Hothams to correspond with Royalists, possibly in preparation for switching sides and handing Hull over to the Crown. Parliament punished them by imprisoning them for years, subjecting them to a protracted trial, and, in spite of efforts by members of the House of Lords as well as Presbyterians in Commons to save them, executing them on January 1,1645. Pelham, Sir John's earlier ally, signed their death warrants. While this would be a somewhat confusing analysis on White's part, since Cromwell would have sided with Pelham in this matter, it is possible that he is suggesting that this was the point at which it became clear that Parliament was divided and that, even as it was fighting the Crown, some of its members were undermining its efforts by aiding and abetting the king.

93. Another reference to the purge of Parliament (Pride's Purge) as it involves the location of Kingston. After the army's elected agitators issued the call in November 1647 to rid Parliament of Presbyterians to prevent them from abolishing the army, six of the eleven Presbyterian members of the House of Commons fled. Soon after, Cromwell and the General Council of Officers met at Kingston to offer support for the purge. Despite opposition from Fairfax, Cromwell led a group of armed men to Parliament, where they passed the Null and Void Ordinance, a law nullifying any legislation passed after the departure of the six Presbyterians. This intimidated the remaining five Presbyterian members into withdrawing, thereby granting religious Independents control over the House.

94. For all I know.

232 *Appendix 5*

your accomplices [back] for their disobedience. Therefore, take care to use your reason and your power to secure yourselves, not only from the king and his laws which he still fights by, but likewise from the Parliament *Pellamites*,[95] and their ordinances, which you and the army have slighted.[96]

Now Sir, I profess for my own part, I am not over careful, I shall only use means to the discharge of my duty according to my judgment and reason, and whether I be anything or nothing, it matters not. Yet it behooves me to take care for the security and welfare of those poor soldiers under my command, which I have endeavored to engage in this common cause, which I vindicate and shall by God's assistance seal with my blood, by suffering if called thereunto. I value my reputation as a man to stand in competition with my livelihood, but I value my principles more than life natural, and before I would violate my conscience in [a] matter of concernment upon mature consideration, I would suffer all the torment that men and devils can invent.

Now Sir, to secure yourself and friends, which is the chief work that lies before you, I must needs say, I see no other way but by entering upon some way equivalent to that presented in the paper entitled *An Agreement of the People*. There is a necessity of setting a period to this Parliament, and changing the current of the law out of the king's name into the Commons, without which I can see no sure security, but by making up your interest under the king and receiving indemnity and pardon from him. Which last I do detest, and shall ever labor to prevent. [But] if any man can hold forth any other way wherein there is a probability to obtain security, freedom, and peace, I'll acknowledge my own weakness and give God thanks for raising up an instrument for my conviction. I know the prosecution of the former is very dangerous and desperate; the king, Scots, and foreign states will be our enemies. Yet if you fall back, you must expect ruin and if you go forward, you can be no worse in the greatest hazards, and it is better perishing in right ways than in wrong.

Having thus freely discovered my principles, and offered my desires to your view, I must confess my inabilities of adding to your knowledge in things of this nature, but looking upon you as a person of power and interest, I thought good to discharge my mind and to let you know I shall not be forward to exercise force for the procuring things of this nature, but only plead at opportunities in ways of reason, and shall stand by those that stand for the public interest of the nation,

95. Those who sided with Pelham in the Rump Parliament.

96. The Militia Ordinance was passed by the Long Parliament in 1642. It was a key piece of legislation in Parliament's bid to become a legitimate ruling power unto itself. It appropriated the right to appoint the lord lieutenants who commanded the county militias. The king naturally refused to sign the ordinance, but in March, Parliament declared it legitimate nonetheless. However, while this Ordinance made it possible for Parliament to raise its own army, it also placed the London Militia under the control of the London Militia Committee. The militia was made up of the troops that Parliament later tried to use to force the New Model Army to disband, a move that Cromwell resisted.

Other Pamphlets Relevant to Elizabeth Poole 233

and shall upon a clear way and call[97] engage my life as formerly, against such as shall endeavor to destroy honest, peaceable men by ways of force and violence. And if you as formerly shall still own the interest of honest people, and forbear the exercise of rigor upon those that are friends to yourself and the commonwealth, then shall I be ready to hazard my life for your preservation when you shall be cast upon the greatest extremity in the midst of your many enemies, for you may assure yourself all storms are not over, and that late insurrection in London is but a fruit of that council which will endeavor to raise more such there and in other places, who care not if they break all reins, and make way for that abomination that the *Confession of Faith* makes desolate rather than let go their pride and ambition. You must expect the further exercise of your faith and patience in the times of trial that are coming upon this nation. But the Lord instructs, keeps, and preserves you in the ways of righteousness, shall be the prayers of him who desires to serve you, while you serve the public.

Colebrook, April the 21.
1648

Francis White

FINIS.

97. Calling.

Bibliography

Primary Sources

Anonymous. *An Ordinance of the Lords and Commons Assembled in Parliament Concerning the Election of Common-Council Men, and Other Officers in the City of London*. London: 1648.

Anonymous. *The Armies Petition; or, a New Engagement*. London: 1648.

Anonymous. *A Directory for Public Worship*. London: 1645.

Anonymous. *A Discovery of Six Women Preachers*. London: 1641.

Anonymous. *The English Devil; or, Cromwell and His Monstrous Witch Discover'd at White-Hall*. London: 1660.

Anonymous. *Four Petitions to His Excellency Sir Thomas Fairfax*. London: 1647.

Anonymous. *The Government of the Commonwealth of England, Scotland, and Ireland and the Dominions Thereunto Belonging*. London: 1653.

Anonymous. *The Humble Advice of the Assembly of Divines, Now by Authority of Parliament Sitting at Westminster, Concerning a Confession of Faith*. London: 1646.

Anonymous. *The Humble Petition of Many Thousands of Young Men, and Apprentices of the City of London, to the High and Honorable, the Knights, Citizens and Burgesses in the Supreme Court of Parliament Assembled*. London: 1647.

Anonymous. *The Manner of the Deposition of Charles Stuart, King of England, by the Parliament, and General Council of the Army*. London: 1649.

Anonymous. *A New Engagement, or Manifesto*. London: 1648.

Anonymous. *The Propositions of the Houses Sent to the King at Newcastle*. Edinburgh: 1646.

Anonymous. "The Root and Branch Petition." In *Documents Illustrative of English Church History*, edited by Henry Gee and William John Hardy, 537–55. New York: Macmillan, 1896.

Anonymous. *A Solemn Engagement of the Army, under the Command of His Excellency Sir Thomas Fairfax*. London: 1647.

Anonymous. *A Solemn League and Covenant for Reformation and Defense of Religion, the Honor and Happiness of the King, and the Peace and Safety of the Three Kingdoms of Scotland, England, and Ireland*. London: 1643.

Anonymous. *To the Right Honorable the Commons of England*. London: 1648.

Anonymous. *To the Supreme Authority of This Nation, the Commons Assembled in Parliament: The Humble Petition of Diverse Well-Affected Women*. London: 1649.

Anonymous. *To Xeiphos Ton Martyron; or, A Brief Narration of the Mysteries of State Carried on by the Spanish Faction in England*. The Hague: 1651.

Anonymous. *Tub Preachers Overturn'd*. London: 1647.

236 *Bibliography*

Brooks, Thomas. *God's Delight in the Progress of the Upright.* London: 1649.

Bunyan, John. *A Confession of My Faith.* London: 1672.

———. *Differences in Judgment about Water-Baptism.* London: 1681.

Burnet, Gilbert, ed. *The Memoirs of the Lives and Actions of James and William, Dukes of Hamilton and Castle-Herald.* Oxford: Oxford University Press, 1852.

Calvert, Giles. *News from the New Jerusalem.* London: 1649.

Cary, Mary. *The Little Horn's Doom & Downfall.* London: 1651.

———. *The Resurrection of the Witnesses.* London: 1648.

———. *The Resurrection of the Witnesses, and England's Fall from (the Mystical Babylon) Rome Clearly Demonstrated to be Accomplished.* London: 1653.

———. *A Word in Season to the Kingdom of England; or, A Precious Cordial for a Distempered Kingdom.* London: 1647.

Charles I. "Majesty in Misery; or, An Imploration To The King OF Kings." In *The Memoirs of the Lives and Actions of James and William, Dukes of Hamilton and Castle-Herald*, edited by Gilbert Burnet, 379. Oxford: Oxford University Press, 1852.

———. "Speech at His Trial." https://constitution.org/1-History/primarysources/charles.html.

Chidley, Katherine. *The Justification of the Independent Churches of Christ.* London: 1641.

Church of England. *The Book of the Common Prayer.* London: 1549.

Cibber, Colley. *Love's Last Shift; or, the Fool in Fashion.* London, 1735.

Clarke, William. *The Clarke Papers V.* Edited by Frances Henderson. Cambridge: Cambridge University Press, 2006.

———. *The Clarke Papers: Selections from the Papers of William Clarke.* Edited by Charles H. Firth. 4 volumes. Westminster: Camden Society, 1891–1901.

———. "General Council at Whitehall, 29 December 1648" and "General Council 5 Jan. 1648 at Whitehall." In *The Clarke Papers*, Clarke MSS, vol. 67, 128–33. Oxford: Worcester College.

Collier, Thomas. *A Body of Divinity.* London: 1676.

Congregational Churches in England, Savoy Meeting. *A Declaration of the Faith and Order Owned and Practiced in the Congregational Churches in England.* London: 1658.

Coppe, Abiezer. *Some Sweet Sips, of Some Spiritual Wine Sweetly and Freely Dropping from One Cluster of Grapes.* London: 1649.

Covenanters. *The Engagement between the King and the Scots.* London: 1647.

Crompe, John. *Collections Out of S. Augustine and Some Few Other Latin Writers Upon the First Part of the Apostles Creed.* London: 1639.

Davies, Lady Eleanor. *Eleanor Davies: Printed Writings 1500–1640.* Edited by Teresa Feroli. London: Routledge, 2016.

———. *Eleanor Davies, Writings 1641–1646: Printed Writings, 1641–1700*. Edited by Teresa Feroli. London: Routledge, 2011.

———. *Eleanor Davies, Writings 1647–1652: Printed Writings 1641–1700*. Edited by Teresa Feroli. London: Routledge, 2018.

———. *Prophetic Writings of Lady Eleanor Davies*. Edited by Esther Cope. Oxford: Oxford University Press, 1995.

Edwards, Thomas. *The First and Second Part of Gangraena; or, A Catalogue and Discovery of Many of the Errors, Heresies, Blasphemies, and Pernicious Practices of the Sectaries of This Time*. London: 1646.

Eglisham, George. *The Forerunner of Revenge*. London: 1626.

Fairfax, Thomas. *The Case of the Army Truly Stated*. London: 1647.

Featley, Daniel. *The Dippers Dipped or the Anabaptists Ducked and Plunged over Head and Ears at a Disputation in Southwark*. London: 1642.

Filmer, Robert. *Patriarcha; or, the Natural Power of Kings*. London: 1680.

Gauden, John. *The Eikon Basilike*. London: 1649.

Goślicki, Wawrzyniec. *The Sage Senator Delineated*. London: 1660.

House of Commons. *Treaty of Newport* (1648). James Marshall and Marie-Louise Osborn Collection, Beinecke Rare Book and Manuscript Library. Yale University.

Howgill, Mary. *A Remarkable Letter of Mary Howgill to Oliver Cromwell, called Protector*. London: 1657.

Ireton, Henry. *A Remonstrance of His Excellency Thomas Lord Fairfax, Lord General of the Parliament's Forces*. London: 1648.

Ireton, Henry, and John Lambert. *The Heads of Proposals, Agreed on by His Excellency Sir Thomas Fairfax, and the Council of the Army*. London: 1647.

James VI and I. *Basilikon Doron*. Edinburgh: 1599.

———. *Daemonologie*. Edinburgh: 1597.

———. *The King's Majesty's Speech to the Lords and Commons of this Present Parliament at Whitehall*. London: 1609.

———. *The True Law of Free Monarchies*. Edinburgh: 1597.

Jessey, Henry. *The Exceeding Riches of Grace Advanced by the Spirit of Grace, in an Empty Nothing Creature (viz.) Mris. Sarah Wight*. London: 1658.

Jones, Sarah. *This Is Lights' Appearance in the Truth*. London: 1650.

———. *To Sion's Lovers*. London: 1644.

Kiffin, William. *A Brief Remonstrance of the Reasons and Grounds of Those People Commonly Called Anabaptists*. London: 1645.

———. *Certain Observations Upon Hosea The Second the 7. & 8.* Verses. London: 1642.

——— et al. *The Confession of Faith*. London: 1644.

———. *A Sober Discourse of Right to Church-Communion*. London: 1681.

238 *Bibliography*

Lambert, John. "December 1653: The Government of the Commonwealth of England, Scotland and Ireland, and the Dominions Thereunto Belonging." In *Acts and Ordinances of the Interregnum, 1642–1660*, edited by C. H. Firth and R. S. Rait, 813–22. London: H. M. Stationery, 1911.

Lilburne, John. *An Agreement of the People for a Firm and Present Peace upon Grounds of Common Right*. London: 1647.

———. *Foundations of Freedom; or, An Agreement of the People: Proposed as a Rule for Future Government*. London: 1648.

———. *The Levellers (Falsely so called) Vindicated*. London: 1649.

———. *The Second Part of England's New-Chains Discovered*. London: 1649.

Lilly, William. *A Peculiar Prognostication Astrologically Predicted According to Art*. London: 1649.

Locke, John. *A Letter Concerning Toleration*. Indianapolis: Liberty Fund, Online Library of Liberty: https://oll.libertyfund.org/titles/locke-a-letter-concerning-toleration-and-other-writings.

———. *Two Treatises of Government*. Indianapolis: Liberty Fund, Online Library of Liberty: https://oll.libertyfund.org/titles/locke-the-two-treatises-of-civil-government-hollis-ed/.

Machiavelli, Nicolo. *The Prince* (1532). Project Gutenberg: http://www.gutenberg.org/files/1232/1232-h/1232-h.htm.

Mercurius Pragmaticus (December 26, 1648–January 9, 1649).

Milton, John. *The Tenure of Kings and Magistrates*. London: 1649.

Overton, Richard. *An Arrow Against All Tyrants and Tyranny*. London: 1646.

Parliament of England. *Act of the Commons of England Assembled in Parliament, for Erecting of a High Court of Justice for the Trying and Judging of Charles Stuart, King of England*. London: 1648/9.

———. *A Declaration of the Lords and Commons Assembled in Parliament to the Whole Kingdom*. London: 1647.

———. *An Ordinance for the Abolishing of Archbishops and Bishops in England and Wales and for settling their lands and possessions upon Trustees for the use of the Commonwealth*. London: 1646.

———. *An Ordinance of the Lords and Commons Assembled in Parliament Concerning the Election of Common-Council Men, and Other Officers in the City of London* (London: 1648).

———. *Petition of Right* (1628). Constitution Society: https://constitution.org/1-History/eng/petright.htm.

Parr, Susanna. *Susanna's Apology Against the Elders*. London: 1659.

Pendarves, Thomasine. "25. Letter: The Copy of a Letter, as it was Sent from Mrs. T.P., in Behalf of Mrs. E.P. To a Congregation of Saints in London, Under the Form of Baptism." In *News from the New Jerusalem,* edited by Giles Calvert, 121–36. London: 1649.

Pocock, Mary. *The Mystery of the Deity in the Humanity*. London: 1649.

Poole, Elizabeth. *An Alarm of War Given to the Army*. London: 1649.

———. *An[other] Alarm of War*. London: 1649.

———. *A Prophecy Touching the Death of King Charles*. London: 1649.

———. *A Vision: Wherein Is Manifested the Disease and Cure of the Kingdom*. London: 1649.

Poole, Robert. *A Brief Remonstrance of the Reasons and Grounds of those People Commonly Called Anabaptists*. London: 1645.

Pordage, John. *Innocency Appearing, Through the Dark Mists of Pretended Guilt*. London: 1655.

———. *Mundorum Explicatio*. London: 1663.

———. *Theologia Mystica*. London: 1683.

Rushworth, John. "The Treaty of Oxford." In *Historical Collections of Private Passages of State: Volume 5, 1642–45*, 164–263. London: D. Browne, 1721. British History Online: http://www.british-history.ac.uk/rushworth-papers/vol5/pp164-263.

Trapnel, Anna. *Anna Trapnel's Report and Plea; or, A Narrative of her Journey from London into Cornwall*. Edited by Hilary Hinds. Toronto: Iter Press; Tempe: Arizona Center for Medieval and Renaissance Studies, 2016.

———. *The Cry of a Stone*. London: 1654.

———. *A Legacy for Saints*. London: 1654.

———. *Strange and Wonderful News from Whitehall*. London: 1654.

Wentworth, Anne. *The Revelation of Jesus Christ*. London?: 1679.

———. *A True Account of Anne Wentworth's Being Cruelly, Unjustly, and Unchristianly Dealt With by Some of Those People Called Anabaptists*. London: 1676.

———. *A Vindication of Anne Wentworth*. London: 1677.

Westminster Assembly. *The Westminster Confession of Faith*. London: 1646.

White, Francis. *The Copies of Several Letters Contrary to the Opinion of the Present Powers, Presented to the Lord General Fairfax, and Lieutenant General Cromwell*. London:1649.

———. *A True Relation of the Proceedings in the Business of Buford*. London: 1649.

Wight, Sarah. *A Wonderful Pleasant and Profitable Letter*. London: 1656.

Wither, George. "Majesty in Misery; or, An Imploration to the King of Kings." London: 1648.

Secondary Sources

Bell, Maureen. "Seditious Sisterhood: Women Publishers of Opposition Literature at the Restoration." In *Voicing Women: Gender and Sexuality in Early Modern Writing*, edited by Kate Chedgzoy, Elizabeth Hansen, and Suzanne Trill, 185–95. Edinburgh: Edinburgh University Press, 1998.

Berens, Lewis Henry. *The Digger Movement: Radical Communalism in the English Civil War*. St. Petersburg, FL: Red and Black, 2008.

240 *Bibliography*

Bingham, Matthew C. *Orthodox Radicals: Baptist Identity in the English Revolution.* Oxford: Oxford University Press, 2019.

Black, E. G. "Torture Under English Law." 1927. https://scholarship.law.upenn.edu/cgi/viewcontent.cgi?article=8145&context=penn_law_review.

Braddick, Michael. *The Common Freedom of the People: John Lilburne and the English Revolution.* Oxford: Oxford University Press, 2018.

———. *God's Fury, England's Fire: A New History of the English Civil Wars.* London: Penguin, 2009.

———, ed. *The Oxford Handbook of the English Revolution.* Oxford: Oxford University Press, 2015.

Bradstock, Andrew. *Radical Religion in Cromwell's England: A Concise History from the English Civil War to the End of the Commonwealth.* London: I. B. Taurus, 2011.

Brod, Manfred. "Doctrinal Deviance in Abingdon: Thomasine Pendarves and her Circle." *Baptist Quarterly* 41, no. 2 (2005): 92–102.

———. "Politics and Prophecy in Seventeenth-Century England: The Case of Elizabeth Poole." *Albion: A Quarterly Journal Concerned with British Studies* 31, no. 3 (Autumn 1999): 395–412.

———. "A Radical Network in the English Revolution: John Pordage and His Circle, 1646–54." *English Historical Review* 119, no. 484 (November 2004): 1230–53.

Brown, Louise Fargo. *The Political Activities of the Baptists and Fifth Monarchy Men in England During the Interregnum.* London: Forgotten, 2012.

Capp, Bernard S. *The Fifth Monarchy Men: A Study in Seventeenth-Century English Millenarianism.* London: Faber and Faber, 2011.

Cariccio, Mario. "*News from the New Jerusalem*: Giles Calvert and the Radical Experience." In *Varieties of Seventeenth- and Early Eighteenth-Century English Radicalism in Context*, edited by Ariel Hessayon and David Finnegan, 69–86. London: Ashgate, 2011.

Carlton, Charles. *Archbishop William Laud.* London: Routledge, 1998.

———. *Charles I: The Personal Monarch.* London: Routledge, 1995.

Clasen, Claus-Peter. *Anabaptism, a Social History, 1525–1618: Switzerland, Austria, Moravia, South and Central Germany.* Ithaca, NY: Cornell University Press, 1972.

Clements, Katherine. *The Crimson Ribbon.* London: Headline, 2014.

Cobbett, William. *Cobbett's Parliamentary History of England: From the Norman Conquest, in 1066, to the year, 1803.* London: T. C. Hansard, 1807.

Como, David R. *Radical Parliamentarians and the English Civil War.* Oxford: Oxford University Press, 2018.

Cope, Esther S. *Handmaid of the Holy Spirit: Dame Eleanor Davies, Never Soe Mad a Ladie.* Ann Arbor: University of Michigan Press, 1993.

Dale, T. C. *The Inhabitants of London in 1638*, 2 volumes. 1:65. London: Society of Genealogists, 1645.

Daniell, David. *The Bible in English: History and Influence*. New Haven, CT: Yale University Press, 2003.

Davies, Stevie. *Unbridled Spirits: Women of the English Revolution: 1640–1660*. London: Women's Press, 1998.

De Krey, Gary S. *Following the Levellers*, Volume 1: *Political and Religious Radicals in the English Civil War and Revolution, 1645–1649*. London: Palgrave Macmillan, 2017.

Dollimore, Jonathan. *Radical Tragedy: Religion, Ideology, and Power in the Drama of Shakespeare and His Contemporaries*. 3rd ed. London: Red Globe, 2010.

Early English Books Online (EEBO). http://eebo.chadwyck.com/home.

Edwards, David, and Padraig Lenihan, eds. *Age of Atrocity: Violence and Political Conflict in Early Modern Ireland*. Dublin: Four Courts, 2007.

Edwards, Graham. *The Last Days of Charles I*. Stroud, Gloucestershire, UK: Sutton, 1999.

Estep, William R. *The Anabaptist Story: An Introduction to Sixteenth-Century Anabaptism*. 3rd ed. Grand Rapids, MI: Eerdmans, 1995.

Farr, David. *Henry Ireton and the English Revolution*. Suffolk: Boydell, 2006.

Feroli, Teresa. *Political Speaking Justified: Women Prophets and the English Revolution*. Newark: University of Delaware Press, 2006.

Firth, Charles H. *Cromwell's Army: A History of the English Soldier during the Civil Wars, the Commonwealth, and the Protectorate*. London: Methuen, 1902.

———. *The Last Years of the Protectorate*. London: Longmans, Green, 1909.

———. *Oliver Cromwell and the Rule of the Puritans in England*. New York: Putnam, 1900.

Firth, Charles H., and R. S. Rait, eds. *Acts and Ordinances of the Interregnum, 1642–1660*. London: H. M. Stationery, 1911.

Fissell, Mark Charles. *The Bishops' Wars: Charles I's Campaigns against Scotland, 1638–1640*. Cambridge: Cambridge University Press, 1994.

Flanagan, Sabina. *Hildegard of Bingen, 1098–1179: A Visionary Life*. London: Routledge, 1989.

Franklin, Julian. *John Locke and the Theory of Sovereignty: Mixed Monarchy and the Right of Resistance in the Political Thought of the English Revolution*. Cambridge: Cambridge University Press, 1981.

Gardiner, Samuel. *The Fall of the Monarchy of Charles I, 1637–1649*. Volumes 1–2. London: Longmans, Green, 1882.

———. *The History of England from the Accession of James I to the Outbreak of the Civil War, 1603–1642*. Volumes 1–10. London: Longmans, Green, 1883.

———. *History of the Great Civil War, 1642–1649*. Volumes 1–4. London: Longmans, Green, 1901.

242 *Bibliography*

———. *Oliver Cromwell*. London: Longmans, Green, 1901.

The Geneva Bible. Madison: University of Wisconsin Press, 1969.

Gentles, Ian. *Oliver Cromwell: God's Warrior and the English Revolution*. London: Palgrave, 2011.

Gheeraert-Graffeuille, Claire. "Tyranny and Tyrannicide in Mid-Seventeenth-Century England: A Woman's Perspective?" *Études Épistémè* 15 (June 2009): 139–52.

Gillespie, Katharine. *Domesticity and Dissent in the Seventeenth Century: English Women Writers and the Public Sphere*. Cambridge: Cambridge University Press, 2004.

Greenblatt, Stephen. *Shakespearean Negotiations: The Circulation of Social Energy in Renaissance England*. Berkeley: University of California Press, 1989.

Herzig, Tamar. *Savonarola's Women: Visions and Reform in Renaissance Italy*. Chicago: University of Chicago Press, 2008.

Hibbert, Christopher. *Cavaliers and Roundheads: The English Civil War, 1642–1649*. New York: Scribner, 1993.

———. *Charles I: A Life of Religion, War, and Treason*. London: St. Martin's Griffin, 2015.

Hill, Christopher. *The Century of Revolution: 1603–1714*. New York: W. W. Norton, 1992.

———. *Liberty Against the Law*. New York: Viking, 1996.

———. *The World Turned Upside Down: Radical Ideas During the English Revolution*. London: Penguin, 1984.

Hinds, Hilary. *God's Englishwomen: Seventeenth-Century Radical Sectarian Writing and Feminist Criticism*. Manchester: Manchester University Press, 1996.

Holmes, Clive. "The Trial and Execution of Charles I." *Historical Journal* 53, no. 2 (June 2010): 289–316.

Holstun, James, ed. *Pamphlet Wars: Prose in the English Revolution*. London: Frank Cass, 1992.

The Holy Bible: King James Version. New York: Meridian, 1974.

Hopper, Andrew. *Black Tom: Sir Thomas Fairfax and the English Revolution*. Manchester: Manchester University Press, 2007.

Hughes, Anne. *Women, Men and Politics in the English Civil War*. Keele, UK: Keele University Press, 1999.

Jordan, W. K. *The Development of Religious Toleration in England*. Reprint. Gloucester, MA: P. Smith, 1965.

Kagan, Richard L. *Lucrecia's Dreams: Politics and Prophecy in Sixteenth-Century Spain*. Berkeley: University of California Press, 1990.

Kelsey, Sean. "Staging the Trial of Charles I." In *The Regicides and the Execution of Charles I*, edited by Jason Peacey, 71–93. London: Palgrave, 2001.

Kenyon, John, and Jane Ohlmeyer, eds. *The Civil Wars: A Military History of England, Scotland, and Ireland, 1638–1660.* Oxford: Oxford University Press, 1998.

Kirby, Michael. "The Trial of King Charles I: Defining Moment for Our Constitutional Liberties." London: Anglo-Australian Lawyers' Association, January 22, 1999. http://www.hcourt.gov.au/assets/publications/speeches/former-justices/kirbyj/kirbyj_charle88.htm.

Lang, Amy Schrader. *Prophetic Woman: Anne Hutchinson and the Problem of Dissent in the Literature of New England.* Berkeley: University of California Press, 1987.

Ludlow, Dorothy. "'Arise and Be Doing': English Preaching Women 1640–1660." Unpublished dissertation. Indiana University Bloomington, 1978.

Mack, Phyllis. *Visionary Women: Ecstatic Prophecy in Seventeenth-Century England.* Berkeley: University of California Press, 1992.

Maggi, Armando. *Uttering the Word: The Mystical Performances of Maria Maddalena De' Pazzi, a Renaissance Visionary.* Albany, NY: State University of New York Press, 1998.

Mahlberg, Gaby, and Dirk Wiemann, eds. *Perspectives on English Revolutionary Republicanism.* New York: Routledge, 2016.

Major, John. *John Major's Greater Britain.* Edinburgh: T. and A. Constable, 1892.

McGregor, J. F., and Barry Reay, eds. *Radical Religion in the English Revolution.* Oxford: Oxford University Press, 1984.

Melville, Andrew. "Two Kings, Two Kingdoms." In *The Life of Andrew Melville,* edited by Thomas McCrie, 1:391–92. Edinburgh: William Blackwood, 1824.

Mendle, Michael, ed. *The Putney Debates of 1647: The Army, the Levellers and the English State.* Cambridge: Cambridge University Press, 2010.

Miller, Shannon. *Engendering the Fall: John Milton and Seventeenth-Century Women Writers.* Philadelphia: University of Pennsylvania Press, 2008.

Morton, A. L. *The Story of the English Revolution.* London: Communist Party of Great Britain, 1948.

Nevitt, Marcus. *Women and the Pamphlet Culture of Revolutionary England, 1640–1660.* London: Ashgate, 2006.

Niccoli, Ottavia. *Prophecy and People in Renaissance Italy.* Princeton, NJ: Princeton University Press, 1990.

Noffke, Suzanne. *Catherine of Siena: Vision through a Distant Eye.* Collegeville, MN: Liturgical, 1996.

Norbrook, David. "The Life and Death of Renaissance Man." *Raritan* 8 (1999): 89–110.

Orgel, Stephen. *The Illusion of Power.* Berkeley: University of California Press, 1975.

O'Siochru, Michael. *Confederate Ireland, 1642–49.* Dublin: Four Courts, 1999.

Bibliography

Oxford Dictionary of National Biography: In Association with the British Academy; From the Earliest Times to the Year 2000. Edited by Matthew H. C. G. Harrison and Brian Howard. Oxford: Oxford University Press, 2004. http://www.oxforddnb.com.

Oxford English Dictionary. 2nd ed. Oxford: Oxford University Press, 1989. http://www.oed.com.

Palmer, Roy. *A Ballad History of England: From 1588 to the Present Day.* London: B. T. Batsford, 1979.

Patton, Brian. "Revolution, Regicide, and Divorce: Elizabeth Poole's Advice to the Army." In *Place and Displacement in the Renaissance*, edited by Alvin Vos, 133–45. Binghamton, NY: Medieval & Renaissance Texts & Studies, 1995.

Paz, Carme Font. "'Foretelling the Judgements of God': Authorship and the Prophetic Voice in Elizabeth Poole's *A Vision* (1648)." *Journal of English Studies* 11 (2013): 97–112.

———. "'God Is Not the Supporter of Tyranny': Prophetic Reception and Political Capital in Elizabeth Poole's *A Vision* (1648)." *Etudes Epistémè* 31 (2017): https://journals.openedition.org/episteme/1686.

Petrol, Elizabeth. *Medieval Women's Visionary Literature.* New York: Oxford University Press, 1986.

Phillips, Kevin. *The Cousins' Wars: Religion, Politics, Civil Warfare, and the Triumph of Anglo-America.* London: Basic, 1999.

Polizzotto, Carolyn. "Speaking Truth to Power: The Problem of Authority in the Whitehall Debates of 1648–9." *English Historical Review* 131 (February 1, 2016): 31–63.

Purkiss, Diane. *The English Civil War: Papists, Gentlewomen, Soldiers, and Witchfinders in the Birth of Modern Britain.* London: Harper Perennial, 2007.

Ramsbottom, Benjamin. *Stranger Than Fiction: The Life of William Kiffin.* Harpenden, UK: Gospel Standard Trust, 2017.

Raymond, Joad. *The Invention of the Newspaper: English Newsbooks, 1641–1649.* London: Clarendon, 1996.

———. *Making the News: An Anthology of the Newsbooks of Revolutionary England 1641–1660.* London: Weidenfeld Nicolson, 1993.

Reid, Stuart. *Crown, Covenant, and Cromwell: The Civil Wars in Scotland, 1639–1651.* Havertown, PA: Frontline, 2013.

Renihan, Samuel D. *From Shadow to Substance: The Federal Theology of the English Particular Baptists (1642–1704).* Oxford: Centre for Baptist History and Heritage, 2018.

Russell, Conrad, ed. *The Origins of the English Civil War.* London: Palgrave, 1973.

———. *Unrevolutionary England, 1603–1642.* London: Hambledon, 1990.

Schochet, Gordon J. *Patriarchalism in Political Thought.* London: Basic, 1975.

———. "Patriarchalism, Politics and Mass Attitudes in Stuart England." *Historical Journal* 12, no. 3 (1969): 413–41.

Shauer, Frederick F. "English Natural Justice and American Due Process: An Analytical Comparison." *William and Mary Law Review* 18, no. 1 (1976): 47–72.

Smith, Nigel. *Perfection Proclaimed: Language and Literature in English Radical Religion 1640–1660*. Oxford: Oxford University Press, 1989.

Smith, Oriane. *Romantic Women Writers, Revolution, and Prophecy: Rebellious Daughters, 1786–1826*. Cambridge: Cambridge University Press, 2013.

Spenser, Charles. *Killers of the King: The Men Who Dared to Execute Charles I.* London: Bloomsbury, 2015.

Stewart, Alan. *The Cradle King: A Life of James VI & I, the First Monarch of a United Great Britain*. London: St. Martin's, 2003.

Surtz, Ronald E. *The Guitar of God: Gender, Power, and Authority in the Visionary World of Mother Juana De La Cruz (1481–1534)*. Philadelphia: University of Pennsylvania Press, 1990.

Tolmie, Murray. *The Triumph of the Saints: The Separate Churches of London 1616–1649*. Cambridge: Cambridge University Press, 1977.

Trill, Suzanne. "Religion and the Construction of Femininity." In *Women and Literature in Britain, 1500–1700*, edited by Helen Wilcox, 30–55. Cambridge: Cambridge University Press, 1996.

Trubowitz, Rachel. "Female Preachers and Male Wives: Gender and Authority in Civil War England." In *Pamphlet Wars: Prose in the English Revolution*, edited by James Holstun, 112–33. London: Frank Cass, 1992.

Underdown, David. *Pride's Purge: Politics in the English Revolution*. New York: Oxford University Press, 1971.

Vos, Alvin, ed. *Place and Displacement in the Renaissance*. Binghamton, NY: Medieval & Renaissance Texts & Studies, 1995.

Wilson, David Harris. *King James VI & I*. London: Jonathan Cape, 1963.

Wiseman, Susan. *Conspiracy and Virtue: Women, Writing, and Politics in Seventeenth-Century England*. Oxford: Oxford University Press, 2006.

———. "'Public,' 'Private,' 'Politics': Elizabeth Poole, the Duke of Monmouth, 'Political Thought,' and 'Literary Evidence.'" *Women's Writing* 14 (2007): 338–62.

Woodhouse, A. S. P., ed. *Puritanism and Liberty: Being the Army Debates (1647–49) from the Clarke Manuscripts*. London: J. M. Dent, 1992.

Woolrych, Austin. *Soldiers and Statesmen: The General Council of the Army and Its Debates, 1647–1648*. New York: Clarendon, 1987.

Worden, Blair. *The English Civil Wars: 1640–1660*. London: Phoenix, 2010.

———. *Literature and Politics in Cromwellian England*. Oxford: Oxford University Press, 2007.

Zagorin, Perez. *Court and the Country: Beginning of the English Revolution*. Sydney, Australia: Law Book Company of Australasia, 1969.

Index

Acts of Supremacy (1534 & 1550), 181bn19

Adamites, 2

An Agreement of the Free People of England (1649), 162

An Agreement of the People (1647 & 1648), 24, 39, 42, 47, 56, 64; Lilburne and, 160–174, 190–191, 201; White and, 232; Whitehall General Council and, 149, 161

alchemy, 1, 34

Allen, Frances, 26n95

Allen, Hannah, 56

American Revolution (1775–1783), 9, 162

"Anabaptists," 28–29, 105–109, 125–136, 130

Anglicanism. *See* Church of England

anti-Catholicism, 15, 136, 140n199, 169, 182–185, 227

The Armies Petition (1648), 216n25

Arminianism, 15

Arnold, Richard, 25

astrology, 189n49

Baasha, Israelite king, 66n36

Bancroft, Elizabeth, 137, 140–141

Baptists, 2, 11, 27–29, 71n48; baptismal ceremonies of, 108nn4–5; *Confession of Faith* of, 105; divorce and, 67n41; Particular, 27–29, 105; Swiss origins of, 27–28. *See also* Independents

Bauford, Joan, 137, 140

Bell, Maureen, 56nn235–236, 80n77

Benhadad, Syrian king, 66n36

Bilbrow, May, 137, 139–140

Bill of Rights, 162

Bishops' Wars (1639–1640), 14–16, 159n13

body politic, 4–5, 14, 31, 37

Book of Common Prayer, 15, 22n81, 159n13, 210, 224

Brainford, Battle of (1642), 230, 231n92

Brod, Manfred, 26n95, 40, 42, 51

Brooks, Thomas, 181n22

Buckingham, Duke of (George Villiers), 177n7

Calandrini, Cesar, 29

calendars, 58

Calvert, Elizabeth, 47

Calvert, Giles, 44, 80n77

Calvinism, 29

Cary, Mary, 32

Cavaliers, 2–3, 17, 184n25. *See also* English Civil Wars

Charles I of Great Britain, 217–218; arrest of, 20, 179–180; charges against, 178–179; execution of, 7, 9–10, 42, 48, 175, 195n62; last words of, 97n124; Magna Carta and, 196n66; poetry of, 7–8; Scottish wars of, 14–16; trial of, 3, 6–7, 39, 47–48, 155, 176–177, 180; Ulster Uprising and, 16

Charles II of Great Britain, 33, 50, 167n36, 193; naval revolt and, 159n14; persecution of Independents by, 106; in Scotland, 180n15

Chidley, Katherine, 32

Christian IV of Denmark, 13n56

Church of England, 224; Acts of Supremacy and, 181n19;

anti-Catholicism of, 140n199, 169, 182–183; Arminianism of, 15; Bishops' Wars and, 14–16, 159n13; Cromwellian settlement with, 190n50; Presbyterians and, 130n172, 183n24

Cibber, Colley, 197n78

Cicero, 8

Clarke, William, 36, 47, 57, 143–153, *145*, *147*

Clements, Katherine, 52

Collier, Thomas, 29n103

commons, 135nn174–175

The Confession of Faith (Kiffin et al.), 31, 56, 58, 105–124, 136

Congregationalists, 17n68, 27, 133; *Savoy Declaration* of, 224n58. *See also* Independents

contract theory, 41, 51

Coppe, Abiezzer, 35, 40–41

Cottington, Francis, 184

Covenanters, 17n68, 19, 159n13

Cowling, Nicholas, 153

Cromwell, Oliver, 20–23; daughter of, 198n86; Irish campaigns of, 19, 184n25; Kiffin and, 26; Levellers and, 42, 48–49, 185, 188, 201; Lilburne on, 213; nickname of, 195n6; Poole and, 49–50, 188–189, *191*, 199–201; popularity of, 193–194; religious toleration of, 106, 159n13; Scottish campaign of, 214; in *To Xeiphos Ton Martyron*, 183–191; White's letter to, 213–214, 220–233. *See also* New Model Army

Cromwell, Richard, 50, 198–199

Davies, Eleanor, 32

Davies, Stevie, 50

Deane, Richard, 150

A Declaration of the Lords and Commons (1646), 222–223

democracy, 8, 13; *An Agreement of the People* and, 160–161; Levellers and, 23–26, 42; republicanism and, 11–12

Devereux, Robert (Earl of Essex), 230n90

Digby, Kenelm, 184, 231n92

Diggers, 2, 170n50

A Directory for Public Worship (1645), 224

A Discovery of Six Women Preachers (1641), 56–57, 105, 136–141

divine right of kings, 9, 51

divorce, 140; Baptist model of, 67n41; biblical view of, 80n78; contract theory and, 51; Poole on, 36, 40–41, 45, 80n78, 156

domestic violence, 33, 41

editorial principles, 52–58

Edwards, Thomas, 29

Eglisham, George, 177n7

The Eikon Basilike (1649), 180n16

Elizabeth I of England, 4, 5, 15n62, 181n19, 183

Elizabeth of Bohemia, 13n56

The Engagement between the King and the Scots (1647), 18–19

English Civil Wars (1642–51), 2–3, 10–11, 143, 158–160; historical context of, 13–27; Magna Carta and, 195n66; other names for, 14

The English Devil (1660), 49–50, 57, *192*, 193–201

Erbery, William, 26n95

errata lists, 54, 81n81

Essex, Earl of (Robert Devereux), 230n90

Fairfax, Thomas, 160; New Model Army of, 18; petitions to, 20–22, 42, 216n26; remonstrance of, 25–26; White's letters of, 22, 57, 213–220
Featley, Daniel, 105
Felton, John, 177n7
Ferdinand II, Holy Roman Emperor, 13n56
Feroli, Teresa, 51
Fifth Monarchists, 2, 32, 185n32
Filmer, Robert, 7
Firth, Charles, 143–144
Fleetwood, Bridget, 198n86
Fleetwood, Charles, 198n86
Foundations of Freedom (1648), 160–164
Fountaine, John, 72, 74n61
Four Petitions to… Fairfax (1647), 20–22, 42, 216n26
Frederick V, Elector Palatine, 13n56

Gauden, John, 180n16
General Council at Whitehall (1648), 20, 143–149, *145*, *147*, 161
General Council at Whitehall (1649), 149–153, 188–189, 200
Geneva Bible, 58, 70n45, 86nn91–92, 126n165
George III of Great Britain, 9
Gheeraert-Graffeuille, Claire, 52
Glorious Revolution (1688), 203
Golden Rule, 68
Goodwin, John, 186, 190
Goodwin, Thomas, 190, 200–201
Goślicki, Wawrzyniec, 193–194
Great Fire of London (1666), 80n77

Hammond, Henry, 179
Hammond, Robert, 180n14
Harlech Castle (Wales), 18
Harrison, Thomas, 76, 148, 179

The Heads of Proposals (1647), 22–24, 161, 198n86, 203–212
Hempstall, Anne, 137–139
Henderson, Frances, 144
Henrietta Maria of England, 16, 167n35, 180n15, 184n27
Hewson, John, 191, 201
Hinds, Hilary, 51
Hobbes, Thomas, 11, 41
Holles, Denzil, 230nn90
Holstun, James, 11, 12
Hopkins, Matthew, 193
Hotham, John, 231n92
Howgill, Mary, 33
Hughes, Anne, 50
The Humble Petition of Many Thousands of Young Men (1647), 220n36

Independents, 11, 32–33, 132–134; anti-Catholicism of, 182–185; Fifth Monarchists as, 185n32; John Goodwin and, 186; Thomas Goodwin and, 190, 200–201; persecution of, 106, 182, 183; Presbyterians and, 183n24, 187, 228n72, 231n93; on regicide, 71–72; *Savoy Declaration* of, 224n58; women and, 105
Innocents, Slaughter of the, 73n57, 195
Inquisition, 73n60
Ireland, 16, 19, 184n25, 198n86
Ireton, Henry, 22–25; Levellers and, 42; Poole and, 47, 49–50, 148–149, 151, 189; spouse of, 198n86; works of: *The Heads of Proposals*, 22–24, 56–57, 161, 203–212; *A Remonstrance of… Fairfax*, 25–26, 36–38, 57, 61, 96n121, 155–160

James I of England, 4–6, 15nn62–63, 177n7, 180n18; works of: *Basilikon Doron*, 4n17; *Daemonologie*, 193; *The True Law of Free Monarchies*, 4n17, 5
James II of England, 180n15
Jessey, Henry, 32–33
Jesuits, 182, 184–185
John the Baptist, 28, 72n55, 108n4
Jones, Sarah, 32
Joyce, George, 21–22

Kelsey, Thomas, 151
Kiffin, William, 27, 29–31, 33, 71–73; Cromwell and, 26; Elizabeth Poole's scandal and, 33–34, 43–44, 53, 74n61; Robert Poole on, 56; works of: *A Brief Remonstrance*, 29–30, 56, 105, 124–136; *The Confession of Faith*, 31, 56, 58, 105–124; *A Sober Discourse of Right to Church-Communion*, 29n103
Kirby, Michael, 9–10

Lambert, John, 22–24, 161, 198n86, 203–212
Langport, Battle of (1645), 18
Laud, William, 15
Leveller Rising (1649), 11
Levellers, 23–26, 42, 65n31; *An Agreement of the People* and, 64, 160–174, 190–191, 201; Cromwell and, 42, 48–49, 185, 188, 201; Diggers and, 170n50; Goodwin and, 186n39; Long Parliament and, 165n27; Magna Carta and, 196n66; Poole and, 12, 26, 38–39, 47; White and, 213–214, 222
Lilburne, John, 23, 42, 162, 181, 188, 230n90; on *An Agreement of the People*, 190–191, 201; on

Cromwell, 213; Poole's defense of, 46; White and, 213–214; works of: *Plea for Common-Right and Freedom*, 38; *Foundations of Freedom*, 57, 160–164
Lilly, William, 189, 200n90
Locke, John, 12, 41; works of: *A Letter Concerning Toleration*, 30–31, 73n60; *Two Treatises of Government*, 8
Lockyer, Robert, 42
Lollards, 27
Long Parliament, 14, 17, 165n27
Louis XIV of France, 167n36
Ludlow, Dorothy, 46, 50

Machiavelli, Niccolò, 190, 195, 199, 201
Mack, Phyllis, 32, 40, 50
Magna Carta, 13, 195–196
Mahlberg, Gaby, 11–12
Major, John, 8
The Manner of the Deposition of Charles Stewart (1649), 47–48, 57, 175–182
Marston Moor, Battle of (1644), 17, 20
Marxist historians, 10
Mary, mother of Jesus, 43, 58, 86–87, 112
Mary I of England, 5, 15n62, 181n19
Mary II of Great Britain, 167n36, 203
Mary Magdalen, 76n68
May, Susan, 137, 140
Melville, Andrew, 15n63
Militia Ordinance (1642), 17, 232n96
millenarians, 11, 32n116
Miller, Shannon, 52
Milton, John, 52, 56, 175
Monck, George, 19, 184n25
Montague, Walter, 184n28
Muggletonians, 2, 11

Naseby, Battle of (1645), 18
nemo iudex in sua causa, 95n118
Nethersole, Francis, 186
Nevitt, Marcus, 51–52
New Model Army, 3, 11, 18–23; disbandment of, 21–22, 232n96; organization of, 30. *See also* Cromwell, Oliver
Newport, Treaty of (1648), 24, 25, 155
newsbooks, 38n151, 177n3
Norbrook, David, 11
"Norman Yoke," 65n31

Oath of Allegiance (1606), 180–181
Oath of Supremacy (1534), 180–181
O'Neill, Owen Roe, 184n25, 184n31
original sin, 29n103, 105, 108, 111
Overton, Richard, 23, 42, 162, 188
Oxford, Treaty of (1643), 166n31

Paracelsus, 34n123
Parr, Susanna, 33
Particular Baptists, 27–29, 105
Patton, Brian, 12, 51
Pelham, Peregrine, 228n71, 230–231, 232n95
Pendarves, John, 26n95, 33, 71n48, 72
Pendarves, Thomasine, 33, 35, 43–44, 73–81
Peter, Hugh, 45, 97n123, 195, 195n62
Petition of Right (1628), 13–14
Philip IV of Spain, 13n56
Pocock, Mary, 35, 40
Poole, Elizabeth, 105, 181–182; arrest of, 47, 80n77; Cromwell and, 49–50, 188–189, *191*, 199–201; on divorce, 36, 40–41, 45, 80n78, 156; historical context of, 4–12; Ireton and, 47, 49–50, 148–149, 151, 189; Levellers and, 12, 26, 38–39, 47;

life of, 27–28; Lilburne's defense of, 46; novel about, 52; portrayed as witch, 49, 182, 188–201, *191*; on *Remonstrance of... Fairfax*, 155; resistance theory of, 8–9, 34; scandal about, 33–34, 43–44, 53, 74nn61–62, 85–86; at Whitehall General Councils, 20, 143–153; works of, 20; *An Alarm of War*, 3–4, 43–44, 53–56, *69*, 70–81, 193; *An[other] Alarm of War*, 3–4, 44–45, 54, *82*, 83–103, *88*; *A Prophesie Touching the Death of King Charles*, 45–46, 54–56, *55*; *A Vision*, 3–4, 36–41, 46, 52–55, *59*, 60–68
Poole, Robert, 1, 27, 29–30, 56, 124–136
Pordage, John, 26n95, 34, 35, 51
Porters, Endymion, 184
Presbyterians, 14, 15, 24, 201, 223n48; Church of England and, 130n172, 183n24; Independents and, 183n24, 187, 228n72, 231n93; in Parliament, 48
Preston, Battle of (1648), 166n34
Pride's Purge, 25, 185n33, 186n39, 191n55, 228n71, 231nn92–93
Prince, Thomas, 42, 162, 188
print capitalism, 12
A Prophesie Touching the Death of King Charles (1649), 45–46, 54–56, *55*
Prynne, William, 187
Puritans, 15, 27, 143–144, 159n14
Purkiss, Diane, 12
Putney Debates, 11, 143, 191n55, 213
Pym, John, 16

Quakers, 11, 80n77

252 *Index*

Rainsborough, Thomas, 24n88, 25n92, 26n95, 42, 159n13
Ranters, 2, 11, 35
religious toleration, 30–31, 73n60, 106, 159n13
A Remonstrance of... Fairfax (Ireton), 25–26, 36–38, 57, 61, 96n121, 155–160
resistance theory, 8, 34, 40
Rich, Nathaniel, 26n95, 47, 76, 146–148, 151–153
Rinuccini, Giovanni Battista, 184n31
Roman Republic, 223n51
Root and Branch Petition (1640), 15
Roundheads, 2–3, 17. *See also* English Civil Wars
Royalists. *See* Cavaliers
Rump Parliament (1648), 25, 155, 185n33, 214, 228n71, 231n92
Rushworth, John, 143, 162, 205, 212

Sadler, John, 152
salus populi suprema lex, 25
Savoy Declaration (1658), 17n68, 224n58
Scotland, 18–19, 180n15, 214; Bishops' Wars in, 14–16, 159n13; Covenanters of, 17n68, 19, 159n13. *See also* Presbyterians
Self-denying Ordinance (1645), 18
Seventh-day Sabbatarians, 140n199
Severus, Septimius, 199n87
Shalley, Edward, 152
Short Parliament, 14
Shrewsbury, Richard of (Duke of York), 198n82
Simmons, Matthew, 56
Slaughter of the Innocents, 73n57, 195
Smith, Oriane, 51
social contract, 8, 41
A Solemn Engagement (1647), 21–22

A Solemn League and Covenant for Reformation and Defense of Religion (1643), 17, 179n14, 210, 223, 227
Star Chamber, 5, 14
Strafford, Earl of (Thomas Wentworth), 16–17

theosophy, 1, 34–35
Thirty Years' War (1618–1648), 13, 177n7
Thomas, Arabella, 137, 141
Thomason, George, 53, 54, 83n82, 156, 162, 176
torture, 5–6, 15
To Xeiphos Ton Martyron (1651), 48–50, 57, 183–191, 193–194
Trapnel, Anna, 32, 33, 56, 193
Triennial Act (1641), 14
Trill, Suzanne, 50
Trubowitz, Rachel, 50

Ulster Uprising (1642), 16, 19
Underdown, David, 12

Villiers, George (Duke of Buckingham), 177n7
Virgin Mary, 43, 58, 86–87, 112

Wallingford Castle, siege of (1646), 18
Walwyn, William, 42, 162, 188
Wars of the Three Kingdoms, 14, 18. *See also* English Civil Wars
Watson, Thomas, 181
Wentworth, Anne, 33
Wentworth, Thomas (Earl of Strafford), 16–17
Westminster Assembly of Divines, 105
Westminster Confession of Faith (1646), 17n68, 224n58

Index 253

Whalley, Edward, 152

White, Francis, 21, 213–214; *The Copies of Several Letters*, 22, 57, 213–233

Whitehall General Council (1648), 20, 143–149, *145*, *147*, 161

Whitehall General Council (1649), 149–153, 188–189, 200

Wiemann, Dirk, 11–12

Wight, Sarah, 32–33

Wildman, John, 23, 24, 161, 203

William III of Great Britain, 167n36, 203

Winstanley, Gerrard, 170n50

Winter, John, 184

Wiseman, Susan, 12, 52

witches, 49, 141n201, 182, 188–201, *191*

Wither, George, 8n37

"woman in the wilderness" topos, 43, 61n5, 73n59, 76n67

women preachers, 31–32, 105, 136–137. See also *A Discovery of Six Women Preachers*

Woodhouse, A. S. P., 143–144

Worcester, Battle of (1651), 19

Wren, Matthew, 140n199

York, Duke of (Richard of Shrewsbury), 198n82

The Other Voice in Early Modern Europe:
The Toronto Series

Series Titles

Madre María Rosa
Journey of Five Capuchin Nuns
Edited and translated by Sarah E. Owens
Volume 1, 2009

Giovan Battista Andreini
Love in the Mirror: A Bilingual Edition
Edited and translated by Jon R. Snyder
Volume 2, 2009

Raymond de Sabanac and Simone Zanacchi
Two Women of the Great Schism: The Revelations *of Constance de Rabastens by Raymond de Sabanac and* Life of the Blessed Ursulina of Parma *by Simone Zanacchi*
Edited and translated by Renate Blumenfeld-Kosinski and Bruce L. Venarde
Volume 3, 2010

Oliva Sabuco de Nantes Barrera
The True Medicine
Edited and translated by Gianna Pomata
Volume 4, 2010

Louise-Geneviève Gillot de Sainctonge
Dramatizing Dido, Circe, and Griselda
Edited and translated by Janet Levarie Smarr
Volume 5, 2010

Pernette du Guillet
Complete Poems: A Bilingual Edition
Edited with introduction and notes by Karen Simroth James
Poems translated by Marta Rijn Finch
Volume 6, 2010

Antonia Pulci
Saints' Lives and Bible Stories for the Stage: A Bilingual Edition
Edited by Elissa B. Weaver
Translated by James Wyatt Cook
Volume 7, 2010

Valeria Miani
Celinda, A Tragedy: *A Bilingual Edition*
Edited with an introduction by Valeria Finucci
Translated by Julia Kisacky
Annotated by Valeria Finucci and Julia Kisacky
Volume 8, 2010

Enchanted Eloquence: Fairy Tales by Seventeenth-Century French Women Writers
Edited and translated by Lewis C. Seifert and Domna C. Stanton
Volume 9, 2010

Gottfried Wilhelm Leibniz, Sophie, Electress of Hanover and Queen Sophie Charlotte of Prussia
Leibniz and the Two Sophies: The Philosophical Correspondence
Edited and translated by Lloyd Strickland
Volume 10, 2011

In Dialogue with the Other Voice in Sixteenth-Century Italy: Literary and Social Contexts for Women's Writing
Edited by Julie D. Campbell and Maria Galli Stampino
Volume 11, 2011

SISTER GIUSTINA NICCOLINI
The Chronicle of Le Murate
Edited and translated by Saundra Weddle
Volume 12, 2011

LIUBOV KRICHEVSKAYA
No Good without Reward: Selected Writings: A Bilingual Edition
Edited and translated by Brian James Baer
Volume 13, 2011

ELIZABETH COOKE HOBY RUSSELL
The Writings of an English Sappho
Edited by Patricia Phillippy
With translations from Greek and Latin by Jaime Goodrich
Volume 14, 2011

LUCREZIA MARINELLA
Exhortations to Women and to Others If They Please
Edited and translated by Laura Benedetti
Volume 15, 2012

MARGHERITA DATINI
Letters to Francesco Datini
Translated by Carolyn James and Antonio Pagliaro
Volume 16, 2012

DELARIVIER MANLEY AND MARY PIX
English Women Staging Islam, 1696–1707
Edited and introduced by Bernadette Andrea
Volume 17, 2012

CECILIA DEL NACIMIENTO
Journeys of a Mystic Soul in Poetry and Prose
Introduction and prose translations by Kevin Donnelly
Poetry translations by Sandra Sider
Volume 18, 2012

LADY MARGARET DOUGLAS AND OTHERS
The Devonshire Manuscript: A Women's Book of Courtly Poetry
Edited and introduced by Elizabeth Heale
Volume 19, 2012

ARCANGELA TARABOTTI
Letters Familiar and Formal
Edited and translated by Meredith K. Ray and Lynn Lara Westwater
Volume 20, 2012

PERE TORRELLAS AND JUAN DE FLORES
Three Spanish Querelle *Texts:* Grisel and Mirabella, The Slander against Women, *and* The Defense of Ladies against Slanderers*: A Bilingual Edition and Study*
Edited and translated by Emily C. Francomano
Volume 21, 2013

BARBARA TORELLI BENEDETTI
Partenia, a Pastoral Play: *A Bilingual Edition*
Edited and translated by Lisa Sampson and Barbara Burgess-Van Aken
Volume 22, 2013

FRANÇOIS ROUSSET, JEAN LIEBAULT, JACQUES GUILLEMEAU, JACQUES DUVAL AND LOUIS DE SERRES
Pregnancy and Birth in Early Modern France: Treatises by Caring Physicians and Surgeons (1581–1625)
Edited and translated by Valerie Worth-Stylianou
Volume 23, 2013

MARY ASTELL
The Christian Religion, as Professed by a Daughter of the Church of England
Edited by Jacqueline Broad
Volume 24, 2013

SOPHIA OF HANOVER
Memoirs (1630–1680)
Edited and translated by Sean Ward
Volume 25, 2013

KATHERINE AUSTEN
Book M: *A London Widow's Life Writings*
Edited by Pamela S. Hammons
Volume 26, 2013

ANNE KILLIGREW
"My Rare Wit Killing Sin": Poems of a Res-
toration Courtier
Edited by Margaret J. M. Ezell
Volume 27, 2013

TULLIA D'ARAGONA AND OTHERS
The Poems and Letters of Tullia d'Aragona
and Others: A Bilingual Edition
Edited and translated by Julia L. Hairston
Volume 28, 2014

LUISA DE CARVAJAL Y MENDOZA
The Life and Writings of Luisa de Carvajal
y Mendoza
Edited and translated by Anne J. Cruz
Volume 29, 2014

Russian Women Poets of the Eighteenth and
Early Nineteenth Centuries: A Bilingual
Edition
Edited and translated by Amanda Ewington
Volume 30, 2014

JACQUES DU BOSC
L'Honnête Femme: The Respectable
Woman in Society *and the* New Collection
of Letters and Responses by Contempo-
rary Women
Edited and translated by Sharon Diane
Nell and Aurora Wolfgang
Volume 31, 2014

LADY HESTER PULTER
Poems, Emblems, *and* The Unfortunate
Florinda
Edited by Alice Eardley
Volume 32, 2014

JEANNE FLORE
Tales and Trials of Love, Concerning
Venus's Punishment of Those Who Scorn
True Love and Denounce Cupid's Sover-
eignty: *A Bilingual Edition and Study*
Edited and translated by Kelly Digby Peebles
Poems translated by Marta Rijn Finch
Volume 33, 2014

VERONICA GAMBARA
Complete Poems: A Bilingual Edition
Critical introduction by Molly M. Martin
Edited and translated by Molly M. Martin
and Paola Ugolini
Volume 34, 2014

CATHERINE DE MÉDICIS AND OTHERS
Portraits of the Queen Mother: Polemics,
Panegyrics, Letters
Translation and study by Leah L. Chang
and Katherine Kong
Volume 35, 2014

FRANÇOISE PASCAL, MARIE-
CATHERINE DESJARDINS, ANTOINETTE
DESHOULIÈRES, AND CATHERINE
DURAND
Challenges to Traditional Authority: Plays
by French Women Authors, 1650–1700
Edited and translated by Perry Gethner
Volume 36, 2015

FRANCISZKA URSZULA RADZIWIŁŁOWA
Selected Drama and Verse
Edited by Patrick John Corness and
Barbara Judkowiak
Translated by Patrick John Corness
Translation Editor Aldona
Zwierzyńska-Coldicott
Introduction by Barbara Judkowiak
Volume 37, 2015

DIODATA MALVASIA
*Writings on the Sisters of San Luca and
Their Miraculous Madonna*
Edited and translated by Danielle Callegari
and Shannon McHugh
Volume 38, 2015

MARGARET VAN NOORT
*Spiritual Writings of Sister Margaret of the
Mother of God (1635–1643)*
Edited by Cordula van Wyhe
Translated by Susan M. Smith
Volume 39, 2015

GIOVAN FRANCESCO STRAPAROLA
The Pleasant Nights
Edited and translated by Suzanne
Magnanini
Volume 40, 2015

ANGÉLIQUE DE SAINT-JEAN ARNAULD
D'ANDILLY
Writings of Resistance
Edited and translated by John J. Conley, S.J.
Volume 41, 2015

FRANCESCO BARBARO
*The Wealth of Wives: A Fifteenth-Century
Marriage Manual*
Edited and translated by Margaret L. King
Volume 42, 2015

JEANNE D'ALBRET
*Letters from the Queen of Navarre with an
Ample Declaration*
Edited and translated by Kathleen M.
Llewellyn, Emily E. Thompson, and
Colette H. Winn
Volume 43, 2016

BATHSUA MAKIN AND MARY MORE
WITH A REPLY TO MORE BY ROBERT
WHITEHALL
*Educating English Daughters: Late
Seventeenth-Century Debates*
Edited by Frances Teague and Margaret
J. M. Ezell
Associate Editor Jessica Walker
Volume 44, 2016

ANNA STANISŁAWSKA
*Orphan Girl: A Transaction, or an Account
of the Entire Life of an Orphan Girl by way
of Plaintful Threnodies in the Year 1685:
The Aesop Episode*
Verse translation, introduction, and
commentary by Barry Keane
Volume 45, 2016

ALESSANDRA MACINGHI STROZZI
Letters to Her Sons, 1447–1470
Edited and translated by Judith Bryce
Volume 46, 2016

MOTHER JUANA DE LA CRUZ
*Mother Juana de la Cruz, 1481–1534:
Visionary Sermons*
Edited by Jessica A. Boon and Ronald E.
Surtz
Introductory material and notes by Jessica
A. Boon
Translated by Ronald E. Surtz and Nora
Weinerth
Volume 47, 2016

CLAUDINE-ALEXANDRINE GUÉRIN DE
TENCIN
Memoirs of the Count of Comminge *and*
The Misfortunes of Love
Edited and translated by Jonathan Walsh
Foreword by Michel Delon
Volume 48, 2016

FELICIANA ENRÍQUEZ DE GUZMÁN,
ANA CARO MALLÉN, AND SOR
MARCELA DE SAN FÉLIX
Women Playwrights of Early Modern Spain
Edited by Nieves Romero-Díaz and Lisa
Vollendorf
Translated and annotated by Harley
Erdman
Volume 49, 2016

ANNA TRAPNEL
*Anna Trapnel's Report and Plea; or, A
Narrative of Her Journey from London into
Cornwall*
Edited by Hilary Hinds
Volume 50, 2016

MARÍA VELA Y CUETO
Autobiography and Letters of a Spanish Nun
Edited by Susan Diane Laningham
Translated by Jane Tar
Volume 51, 2016

CHRISTINE DE PIZAN
The Book of the Mutability of Fortune
Edited and translated by Geri L. Smith
Volume 52, 2017

MARGUERITE D'AUGE, RENÉE
BURLAMACCHI, AND JEANNE DU
LAURENS
*Sin and Salvation in Early Modern France:
Three Women's Stories*
Edited, and with an introduction by
Colette H. Winn
Translated by Nicholas Van Handel and
Colette H. Winn
Volume 53, 2017

ISABELLA D'ESTE
Selected Letters
Edited and translated by Deanna Shemek
Volume 54, 2017

IPPOLITA MARIA SFORZA
*Duchess and Hostage in Renaissance
Naples: Letters and Orations*
Edited and translated by Diana Robin and
Lynn Lara Westwater
Volume 55, 2017

LOUISE BOURGEOIS
*Midwife to the Queen of France: Diverse
Observations*
Translated by Stephanie O'Hara
Edited by Alison Klairmont Lingo
Volume 56, 2017

CHRISTINE DE PIZAN
Othea's Letter to Hector
Edited and translated by Renate
Blumenfeld-Kosinski and Earl Jeffrey
Richards
Volume 57, 2017

MARIE-GENEVIÈVE-CHARLOTTE
THIROUX D'ARCONVILLE
*Selected Philosophical, Scientific, and
Autobiographical Writings*
Edited and translated by Julie Candler Hayes
Volume 58, 2018

LADY MARY WROTH
Pamphilia to Amphilanthus *in Manuscript
and Print*
Edited by Ilona Bell
Texts by Steven W. May and Ilona Bell
Volume 59, 2017

*Witness, Warning, and Prophecy:
Quaker Women's Writing, 1655–1700*
Edited by Teresa Feroli and Margaret
Olofson Thickstun
Volume 60, 2018

SYMPHORIEN CHAMPIER
The Ship of Virtuous Ladies
Edited and translated by Todd W. Reeser
Volume 61, 2018

ISABELLA ANDREINI
Mirtilla, A Pastoral: *A Bilingual Edition*
Edited by Valeria Finucci
Translated by Julia Kisacky
Volume 62, 2018

MARGHERITA COSTA
The Buffoons, A Ridiculous Comedy:
A Bilingual Edition
Edited and translated by Sara E. Díaz and
Jessica Goethals
Volume 63, 2018

MARGARET CAVENDISH, DUCHESS OF
NEWCASTLE
Poems and Fancies *with* The Animal
Parliament
Edited by Brandie R. Siegfried
Volume 64, 2018

MARGARET FELL
Women's Speaking Justified *and Other*
Pamphlets
Edited by Jane Donawerth and
Rebecca M. Lush
Volume 65, 2018

MARY WROTH, JANE CAVENDISH, AND
ELIZABETH BRACKLEY
Women's Household Drama:
Loves Victorie, A Pastorall, *and*
The concealed Fansyes
Edited by Marta Straznicky and Sara
Mueller
Volume 66, 2018

ELEONORA FONSECA PIMENTEL
From Arcadia to Revolution: The Neapoli-
tan Monitor *and Other Writings*
Edited and translated by Verina R. Jones
Volume 67, 2019

CHARLOTTE ARBALESTE DUPLESSIS-
MORNAY, ANNE DE CHAUFEPIÉ, AND
ANNE MARGUERITE PETIT DU NOYER
The Huguenot Experience of Persecution
and Exile: Three Women's Stories
Edited by Colette H. Winn
Translated by Lauren King and
Colette H. Winn
Volume 68, 2019

ANNE BRADSTREET
Poems and Meditations
Edited by Margaret Olofson Thickstun
Volume 69, 2019

ARCANGELA TARABOTTI
Antisatire: *In Defense of Women, against*
Francesco Buoninsegni
Edited and translated by Elissa B. Weaver
Volume 70, 2020

MARY FRANKLIN AND HANNAH
BURTON
She Being Dead Yet Speaketh: The Franklin
Family Papers
Edited by Vera J. Camden
Volume 71, 2020

LUCREZIA MARINELLA
Love Enamored and Driven Mad
Edited and translated by Janet E. Gomez
and Maria Galli Stampino
Volume 72, 2020

ARCANGELA TARABOTTI
Convent Paradise
Edited and translated by Meredith K. Ray
and Lynn Lara Westwater
Volume 73, 2020

GABRIELLE-SUZANNE BARBOT DE
VILLENEUVE
Beauty and the Beast: *The Original Story*
Edited and translated by Aurora Wolfgang
Volume 74, 2020

FLAMINIO SCALA
The Fake Husband, A Comedy
Edited and translated by Rosalind Kerr
Volume 75, 2020

ANNE VAUGHAN LOCK
Selected Poetry, Prose, and Translations, with Contextual Materials
Edited by Susan M. Felch
Volume 76, 2021

CAMILLA ERCULIANI
Letters on Natural Philosophy: *The Scientific Correspondence of a Sixteenth-Century Pharmacist, with Related Texts*
Edited by Eleonora Carinci
Translated by Hannah Marcus
Foreword by Paula Findlen
Volume 77, 2021

REGINA SALOMEA PILSZTYNOWA
My Life's Travels and Adventures: *An Eighteenth-Century Oculist in the Ottoman Empire and the European Hinterland*
Edited and translated by Władysław Roczniak
Volume 78, 2021

CHRISTINE DE PIZAN
The God of Love's Letter *and* The Tale of the Rose: *A Bilingual Edition*
Edited and translated by Thelma S. Fenster and Christine Reno
With Jean Gerson, "A Poem on Man and Woman." Translated from the Latin by Thomas O'Donnell
Foreword by Jocelyn Wogan-Browne
Volume 79, 2021

MARIE GIGAULT DE BELLEFONDS, MARQUISE DE VILLARS
Letters from Spain: A Seventeenth-Century French Noblewoman at the Spanish Royal Court
Edited and translated by Nathalie Hester
Volume 80, 2021

ANNA MARIA VAN SCHURMAN
Letters and Poems to and from Her Mentor and Other Members of Her Circle
Edited and translated by Anne R. Larsen and Steve Maiullo
Volume 81, 2021

VITTORIA COLONNA
Poems of Widowhood: A Bilingual Edition of the 1538 Rime
Translation and introduction by Ramie Targoff
Edited by Ramie Targoff and Troy Tower
Volume 82, 2021

VALERIA MIANI
Amorous Hope, A Pastoral Play: *A Bilingual Edition*
Edited and translated by Alexandra Coller
Volume 83, 2020

MADELEINE DE SCUDÉRY
Lucrece and Brutus: Glory in the Land of Tender
Edited and translated by Sharon Diane Nell
Volume 84, 2021

ANNA STANISŁAWSKA
One Body with Two Souls Entwined: An Epic Tale of Married Love in Seventeenth-Century Poland
Orphan Girl: The Oleśnicki Episode
Verse translation, introduction, and commentary by Barry Keane
Volume 85, 2021

CHRISTINE DE PIZAN
Book of the Body Politic
Edited and translated by Angus J. Kennedy
Volume 86, 2021

ANNE, LADY HALKETT
A True Account of My Life *and Selected*
Meditations
Edited by Suzanne Trill
Volume 87, 2022

VITTORIA COLONNA
Selected Letters, 1523–1546: A Bilingual
Edition
Edited and annotated by Veronica Copello
Translated by Abigail Brundin
Introduction by Abigail Brundin and
Veronica Copello
Volume 88, 2022

MICHELE SAVONAROLA
A Mother's Manual for the Women of
Ferrara: *A Fifteenth-Century Guide to*
Pregnancy and Pediatrics
Edited, with introduction and notes, by
Gabriella Zuccolin
Translated by Martin Marafioti
Volume 89, 2022

MARIA SALVIATI DE' MEDICI
Selected Letters, 1514–1543
Edited and translated by Natalie R. Tomas
Volume 90, 2022

ISABELLA ANDREINI
Lovers' Debates for the Stage: *A Bilingual*
Edition
Edited and translated by Pamela Allen
Brown, Julie D. Campbell, and Eric
Nicholson
Volume 91, 2022

MARIE GUYART DE L'INCARNATION,
ANNE-MARIE FIQUET DU BOCCAGE,
AND HENRIETTE-LUCIE DILLON DE LA
TOUR DU PIN
Far from Home in Early Modern France:
Three Women's Stories
Edited and with an introduction by
Colette H. Winn
Translated by Lauren King, Elizabeth
Hagstrom, and Colette H. Winn
Volume 92, 2022

MARIE-CATHERINE LE JUMEL DE
BARNEVILLE, BARONNE D'AULNOY
Travels into Spain
Edited and translated by Gabrielle M.
Verdier
Volume 93, 2022

PIERRE DE VAUX AND SISTER PERRINE
DE BAUME
Two Lives of Saint Colette. *With a Selection*
of Letters by, to, and about Colette
Edited and translated by Renate
Blumenfeld-Kosinski
Volume 94, 2022

DOROTHY CALTHORPE
News from the Midell Regions *and*
Calthorpe's Chapel
Edited by Julie A. Eckerle
Volume 95, 2022